Twin Cities by TROLLEY

Twin Cities by TROLLEY

The Streetcar Era in Minneapolis and St. Paul

John W. Diers and Aaron Isaacs

University of Minnesota Press

Minneapolis • London

The University of Minnesota Press gratefully acknowledges assistance provided for the publication of this book by the John K. and Elsie Lampert Fesler Fund.

Frontispiece: The transaction of paying a fare to the conductor inside the rear door of a streetcar happened a million times each day across the Twin Cities. Photograph courtesy of the Minnesota Historical Society.

Illustrations in the book appear courtesy of the Minnesota Streetcar Museum unless otherwise credited. See www.trolleyride.org for more information.

Book design by Daniel Leary and Ann Sudmeier.

New maps were created by Jason Podany and provided courtesy of Metro Transit.

Published by the University of Minnesota Press
111 Third Avenue South, Suite 290
Minneapolis, MN 55401-2520
http://www.upress.umn.edu

Library of Congress Cataloging-in-Publication Data

Diers, John W.
    Twin Cities by trolley : the streetcar era in Minneapolis and St. Paul /
John W. Diers and Aaron Isaacs.
        p.   cm.
    Includes bibliographical references and index.
    ISBN-13: 978-0-8166-4358-5 (hc : alk. paper)
    1. Street-railroads—Minnesota—Minneapolis Metropolitan Area—
History.   2. Street-railroads—Minnesota—Saint Paul Metropolitan Area—
History.   I. Isaacs, Aaron, 1949–   II. Title.
    TF725.M6D54 2007
    388.4'609776579—dc22
                                                        2006026050

Printed in Canada on acid-free paper

The University of Minnesota is an equal-opportunity educator and employer.

15 14 13 12 11 10 09 08 07   10 9 8 7 6 5 4 3 2 1

To the employees of the Twin City Rapid Transit Company,

who gave Minneapolis and St. Paul

the finest street railway system in America

Contents

Preface

Built at the Twin City Rapid Transit's Snelling Shops in 1908, streetcar 1300 was one of the last to carry passengers before the 1954 conversion of the transit system to buses. It was one of only two standard wood streetcars to survive completely intact and now operates between Lake Harriet and Lake Calhoun on a one-mile remnant of the Como–Harriet line, the last to operate in the Twin Cities. The Minnesota Streetcar Museum preserves and operates 1300 and other historic Minnesota streetcars, keeping alive the memory of Twin City Rapid Transit. Photograph by Michael Buck.

Fifteen years ago we started wondering aloud, during walks around Lake Harriet in Minneapolis, whether future generations would remember, or even care about, the streetcars and electric interurbans that fascinated the two of us when we were growing up in the late 1940s and early 1950s. Those were times of great change, and our generation was the last to have any personal memory of these wonderful conveyances—now long vanished.

Our grandparents, parents, and other relatives made sure that we sampled them. For one of us that meant weekend rides on every streetcar line in Minneapolis and St. Paul before the streetcars vanished in 1954. For the other it meant trips on the great Illinois Terminal electric railway, plus streetcar rides in other cities before those systems disappeared. Much later we helped restore the Como–Harriet Streetcar line now operated by the Minnesota Streetcar Museum, and we were among its early volunteers at Lake Harriet. We share a lifelong enthusiasm for history and electric railways along with two overlapping careers in public transit, which, taken together, total more than sixty years—most of them at the Twin Cities

Metropolitan Transit Commission, now Metro Transit.

This combination of friendship, interests, and careers brought some truly wonderful experiences, including the opportunity to work with and learn from Twin City Rapid Transit employees who witnessed the transition from streetcar to bus and from private to public ownership. This book is for them, but it is also for the generations that have come along since the streetcar departed the streets of Minneapolis and St. Paul.

Recognition must be given to the streetcar fans, many now gone, who preserved and donated to the Minnesota Streetcar Museum the photographs and documents used and cited in this book. Prominent among them are Eugene Corbey, James Foster, Joe Hutchinson, Edwin Nelson, William J. Olsen, Russell Olson, Arthur Rusterholz, and Robert Schumacher. George Isaacs, father of one of the authors and a founder of the Minnesota Streetcar Museum, gathered the work of numerous photographers from across the country who had visited the Twin Cities during the 1940s and 1950s. The book would have never been possible were it not for their efforts. Their photographs are now a part of the museum's archive, which is a principal resource for this book.

We thank the Minnesota Historical Society, the Ramsey County Historical Society, and the Minneapolis Public Library for letting us tap into their photograph collections.

We especially want to thank Russell Olson, the premier Twin Cities streetcar historian and author of *Electric Railways of Minnesota,* for reviewing our manuscript and correcting the errors that crept into it. His research during the past half century provides the foundation of our book, and he was very generous in allowing us to use illustrations and maps from his earlier work.

A special thank-you goes to Jason Podany, who spent many hours of his own time creating the system and individual line maps for the book, and to Brian Lamb, general manager of Metro Transit, who gave permission for the creation of the maps (now part of the Metropolitan Council's regional map database) and for Jason to use Metro's mapping software.

Todd Orjala, Daniel Leary, and Katie Houlihan at the University of Minnesota Press are owed much for their patience, assistance, and advice.

We also want to thank Mary Byers for her good work in editing the final manuscript and Wendy Holdman of Prism Publishing Center for her help in putting all the pieces together.

Larry Millett and Don Hofsommer offered many helpful suggestions.

Finally, we thank our wives, Marcia Diers and Mona Isaacs. They encouraged and supported our work, provided counsel and direction, and listened patiently during our moments of frustration.

Glossary of Streetcar Terms

backup control: With a handful of exceptions, all TCRT cars were single ended, with full controls only at the front end. Nonetheless, short backup moves were required to negotiate wyes at the ends of the lines and for switching at the carhouses. To make these moves safely, simple backup controls were installed on the rear platform, consisting only of on and off switches and an air brake lever.

bell signals: Gong-type bells mounted on the front and rear platform ceilings were connected by a leather pull cord. The motorman and conductor communicated with one another by way of bell signals, such as two to go forward and three to back up.

block signal: An automatic electric signal used to prevent collisions on sections of line having only a single track.

brake application, apply the air: The streetcars had air brakes, which were applied by opening a valve that released compressed air into the brake pipe, forcing the brake shoes to press against the steel wheel treads, thus slowing the car.

button cars, one man–two man cars: Terms for a standard streetcar rebuilt for one-man operation with air-operated folding doors. Dashboard-mounted switches, or "buttons," controlled the doors.

conductor, conductorette: On a two-man car, the conductor was responsible for collecting fares and signaling the car to start up again. The term *conductorette* was the rather awkward attempt to feminize the job title when women were hired during World War II.

controller: The motorman used the controller to regulate the amount and polarity of electricity to the car's motors, thereby determining the car's speed and direction.

deadman: A spring-loaded air brake valve that served as a safety device to stop the car if the motorman was incapacitated. When released, the springs automatically applied the brakes.

extra: An unscheduled streetcar trip. Extras ran for ball games, parades, and other events.

extra board: Motormen and conductors not assigned to a regular run. The extra board was assigned to fill in for regular crew members who were absent. Originally the extra board was unpaid unless receiving an assignment.

fare box, fare box readings: Passengers dropped their fare in the fare box. A crank on the side caused the coins and tokens to trip mechanical counters. The crew member would copy the numbers, or "take the farebox reading," and enter them on his trip sheet.

fare register: On long suburban routes with multiple fare zones, a mechanical fare register was used to record the different fares. It was located in the rear of the car, on a pole above the rear fare box.

fender: A steel mesh basket on the car front designed to scoop up a pedestrian who would otherwise have been run over by the car and killed or seriously injured; often mistakenly called a "cowcatcher."

field shunt: A connection across the field coil(s) of a streetcar's electric motor(s) that is switched in or out (on–off) by the motorman's speed controller. When the shunt is connected, the motor is capable of a much higher speed. TCRT motormen referred to the field shunt as "automatic ninth." It acted much like overdrive on an automobile and boosted the streetcar's top speed by about ten miles per hour.

flangeways: Streetcar wheels stay on the track because of flanges, the wider part of the wheel that grips the inside of the rail. Because the rails were surrounded by pavement, special grooves, or flangeways, provided a place for the flange to travel.

frog, trolley frog: The frog guides the wheel flanges through track switches where the rails divide, which requires creating a flangeway across another rail. Trolley frogs perform the similar function of guiding the double-flanged trolley wheel through switches where the trolley wire divides.

gate car: All TCRT standard cars were originally built as gate cars. All passengers boarded and alighted through wire gates at the rear of the car. During the 1930s, many were rebuilt as one man–two man, or "button," cars, with air-operated folding doors.

gate side, pole side: The gate side is the right side of the car, where the gates are. The pole side is the left side or street side. Trolley wire support poles were once in the center of the street.

gauntlet track: An unusual track arrangement in which two parallel tracks are superimposed on one another to squeeze across a single track bridge. The gauntlet was cheaper to maintain than two switches with their moving parts.

headway: The time interval between streetcars. A five-minute headway means that a car arrives every five minutes.

layover, layover point: Layover is the time between trips at the end of the line. It is taken at the layover point.

lightweight: A lighter-weight streetcar built in the 1920s to reduce electric power consumption.

line breaker: A safety device in a power feed that opens or breaks the circuit when it detects excessive current draw—as would be the case if there were an electrical short circuit.

lineups: The infrequent late-night "owl" cars all met in downtown to ensure that passengers made their connections. The lineups lasted about five minutes.

loop car: A car destined only for downtown, then referred to as "the Loop." This term came into common use in the 1890s, when most streetcar lines terminated (turned around) in the downtowns.

money changers: Multi-barreled coin changers worn by the conductor or mounted on the dash by the motorman. Exact change was not required in those days.

motorman, motorette: The crew member responsible for running the streetcar, either alone or with a conductor. As with conductorette, "motorette" was the title applied to women hired for this job during World War II.

notch 8, the "company notch": The controller position that provides the maximum speed with the least amount of power.

owl car: Streetcars that ran all night long, usually once an hour.

PCC: Short for Presidents Conference Committee, the PCC was the streetcar industry's joint effort to design a fast, modern, comfortable car that could compete with the automobile. PCC cars were first developed in 1935, but TCRT did not buy its 141 until after the war.

plug in: Motormen and conductors reported to work by placing a wood plug next to their name on the plug board.

power loss: In some spots on the system, electric voltage was reduced and cars ran slower because of the distance to the nearest substation or because of the number of cars on the line simultaneously.

pull out, pull in: Leaving or entering the streetcar station, or running not in service between the station and the route.

regular run: Work assigned to the same crew every day.

resistance heating: Electric heat, like a toaster or space heater, installed in some of the cars to replace coal-fired heaters.

retriever: The spring-loaded reel that gathered in the trolley pole rope and pulled down, or "retrieved," the trolley pole if it de-wired, to prevent it from tearing down the wire.

safety zone, safety island: Boarding areas in the middle of the street where passengers could wait for the streetcar.

shortline, turn back: An intermediate point on the line where some streetcars ended their trips.

skip-stopping: When two cars ran together, they would each stop at alternate stops, thereby expediting the trip for both.

special work: Complex track arrangements where lines crossed or diverged.

standing load: A passenger load exceeding the car's seated capacity.

starter: A supervisor located at certain important intersections to keep cars on time and reschedule as necessary to meet demand or operating conditions.

station, station clerk: *Station* was the TCRT term for carbarn or garage. The station clerk handled a wide variety of clerical chores, including assigning crews and streetcars.

switch rod, switch rod hole: A steel pole with a flattened tip used to pry track switches into position. A long rod could be lowered through the switch rod hole next to the motorman's left foot to do the job from inside the car.

terminal: The end of the line.

time points: Major intersections along the line with a scheduled departure time.

transfer table: A rolling platform on rails used to move streetcars undergoing repairs between the Snelling Shop buildings.

tripper: A short rush hour streetcar run.

trolley pole, trolley wheel: The trolley pole reached from the car roof to the overhead wire to access electricity. The trolley wheel at the end of the pole rolled along the wire.

turn on the air, pump up the air: Activate the air compressor, which powered the brakes, doors, whistle, foot gong, and windshield wiper.

work car: Any of various nonrevenue trolleys that plowed snow, hauled materials, or performed other maintenance tasks.

wye: A triangle of track used to turn cars at the end of the line. Wying a car required one backward and two forward moves to complete the maneuver.

Twin Cities
BY TROLLEY

Introduction

T*win Cities by Trolley* is the story of the streetcar and the Twin City Rapid Transit Company (TCRT) and how they shaped the Twin Cities and touched the lives of three generations of Twin Citians. It is a detailed account of a 523-mile transportation system that was built and operated without public subsidy, a system that stretched from Lake Minnetonka to the St. Croix River and carried more than 200 million passengers a year. It is about nostalgia, but it is also about the electric motor and the internal combustion engine, two competing nineteenth-century inventions that went on to battle for the urban travel market in Minneapolis and St. Paul and in every city in twentieth-century America.

That competition began with Frank Sprague, an engineering graduate of West Point and an associate of Thomas Edison. In 1888, Sprague successfully used an electric motor to propel a horsecar in Richmond, Virginia, at the same time that other inventors were perfecting the internal combustion engine and using it to propel buggies and wagons.

By 1909, just a little more than twenty years after Sprague's demonstration, electricity seemed to have gained the upper hand. There were thousands of streetcars in service in towns and cities across America. In Minnesota, there were streetcars in East Grand Forks, Moorhead, Mankato, Duluth, Winona, and St. Cloud. In a few years, more lines would appear in Wahpeton-Breckenridge and Hibbing.

The electric motor had completely triumphed over animal or cable power as a means of urban locomotion. In cities the streetcar reigned supreme, while out in the country the streetcar's twin brother, the electric interurban, ended the social and economic isolation of rural communities and farms by linking them with larger urban centers.

Elsewhere, electricity replaced steam engines on elevated railways and allowed New York City to build its first subway. Railroads began using electric locomotives to eliminate the smoke and soot produced by steam engines. Trains could access urban areas through tunnels under major thoroughfares and rivers, enabling the construction of transportation monuments such as Grand Central Terminal and Penn Station in New York City.

For centuries, the distance one could cover

A railroad laid in the middle of the street, an idea sure to horrify the modern traffic engineer. Now imagine five hundred miles of it, such as this intersection of Central Avenue and 7th Street in northeast Minneapolis. Anchored in granite, the Twin City streetcar tracks were built to last. Photograph by Norton & Peel; courtesy of the Minnesota Historical Society.

In a scene repeated countless times across the Twin Cities, passengers board a streetcar headed for downtown (also called the Loop, as the destination sign says). This is 44th Street and France Avenue in Edina.

Under the watchful eye of the school patrol, children cross Chicago Avenue at 22nd Street. Photograph courtesy of the Minnesota Historical Society.

on foot or on horseback limited a city's reach, but the urban electric railway shrank both time and distance. More than anything else, it was responsible for the growth and development of the modern city.

The streetcar and the interurban were the "dot-coms" of the Gilded Age. Power companies saw streetcar and interurban railways as ready markets for electric power and either acquired or constructed them. Entrepreneurs formed street railway companies and sought out investors. *Traction* came into common use as a synonym for electric railways. Traction moguls like

Charles Tyson Yerkes, who built and controlled the Chicago streetcar system, and Henry Villard, builder of the Northern Pacific Railway and the Milwaukee Electric Railway and Light Company, now Wisconsin Energy Corporation, Samuel Insull, and others made enormous fortunes as the trolley craze swept America.

By 1891, the trolley had nearly replaced all of the horsecars in both Minneapolis and St. Paul, and in that same year the separate Minneapolis and St. Paul systems merged, creating the Twin City Rapid Transit Company. From then until 1970, if you rode a streetcar or, later, a bus anywhere in Minneapolis or St. Paul, you probably did so as a passenger of TCRT.

At its peak in the 1920s, the company operated more than 900 streetcars, owned 523 miles of track, and was carrying in excess of 200 million passengers each year. Its assets over the years included an amusement park at White Bear Lake and a fleet of boats, a grand hotel, and yet another amusement park on Lake Minnetonka. The output of its steam and hydro-

electric power plant near St. Anthony Falls in Minneapolis, and the network of electrical substations and high-tension lines that powered its streetcars, provided enough energy to meet the needs of an entire city. Its shop facilities at Snelling and University Avenues were one of the largest in the United States. Except for its first electric cars and 141 "PCC" cars purchased after World War II, TCRT built all of the streetcars that ran in Minneapolis and St. Paul in its own shops, as well as hundreds more for Chicago, Duluth, and other smaller cities. It was one of the largest employers in the Twin Cities, with some 3,500 people operating and maintaining its cars.

Twin City Rapid Transit was an extraordinary company. Its board of directors and management were scions of the community and included names like Pillsbury, Washburn, and Goodrich. Its first president, Thomas Lowry, a real estate promoter, developed many of the neighborhoods in Minneapolis, St. Paul, and the surrounding communities and then served

them with his streetcars—profiting handsomely from both enterprises.

TCRT's monopoly over local transportation assured its prosperity through the 1910s and into the 1920s. Track extensions and service expansions into developing neighborhoods occurred throughout the 1920s and early 1930s, even though overall ridership was in slow decline. (The last four blocks of new track in the system were laid in 1947.) That downturn began with the peak year of 1920, when the company carried 238 million passengers. The prosperity of the 1920s brought more automobiles, more paved roads, and more competition for streetcars and interurban railways. Smaller city systems and the interurbans were the first to see their business dwindle as people bought automobiles and then demanded that municipal and state governments construct paved highways to accommodate them.

Street railways were granted franchises by municipal governments that gave them the right to lay their tracks in city streets, but with those

During the streetcar era everyone went downtown, where more than half the jobs and most of the shopping were located. This is 7th and Minnesota Streets in downtown St. Paul in 1946. Photograph courtesy of the Minnesota Historical Society.

rights came various responsibilities, among them snow removal and paving. Large transit systems, like TCRT, could shoulder these burdens and continue to make money, but smaller, less prosperous systems faced the ironic predicament of paying to pave streets for the automobiles that would eventually put them out of business. They either converted to buses or abandoned operations altogether. In 1914, streetcars provided 100 percent of all public transportation in U.S. cities with transit systems. By 1937, only 4 percent were streetcar only, as most systems converted exclusively to buses or a combination of streetcars and buses. In Minnesota and neighboring Wisconsin, virtually all of the smaller streetcar systems had either gone out of business or switched to buses by 1939.

Passengers boarded in the middle of the street, regardless of snow, cold, or traffic. To protect their safety, it was illegal to pass a streetcar on the right. Photograph from the Minneapolis Star and Tribune News Negative Collection; courtesy of the Minnesota Historical Society.

A motorman in 1938. The traditional pillbox hat was replaced by a flat bus driver–style hat around 1940. Long ties also partially replaced bow ties. He is wearing a coin changer, which means he is working without a conductor. By his left elbow, from top to bottom, are the whistle cord, transfer boxes, and air brake handle. Photograph from the Minneapolis Star and Tribune News Negative Collection; courtesy of the Minnesota Historical Society.

Even a well-managed system like TCRT could not stand up to the Great Depression. People who did not have jobs did not take the streetcar to work, nor did they have any money for shopping trips downtown, an evening movie, or a weekend streetcar ride to picnic at Lake Minnetonka. Those with jobs and cars continued to drive. By 1932, annual ridership was down to 113 million passengers, a 48 percent drop from 1920. TCRT responded by cutting back or abandoning unprofitable services, such as the colorful suburban lines to Lake Minnetonka and Stillwater, which disappeared in 1932.

World War II brought tire and gas rationing, forcing drivers to reacquaint themselves with streetcars and returning prosperity to the system. It also brought matériel and per-

The open rear platform is fondly remembered by many as a mostly male retreat for smokers and small boys. Roberts Shoes, seen here in the background, is still in business at Lake Street and Chicago Avenue in south Minneapolis.

sonnel shortages that stretched the company's resources. Every available streetcar was put in service, and TCRT hired women as conductors and motormen (calling them "conductorettes" and "motorettes"). Women also took over jobs in the shops, repairing and cleaning the cars and tending the coal stoves that kept them warm in the winter.

During and immediately following World War II, the streetcar was often the easiest way to get around the Twin Cities. Whether you were going to work, shopping, school, or even to Grandma's house, you could always walk to the corner streetcar stop and wait for the next car to come along. Chances were it would not be a long wait. Most lines ran every ten minutes, except late at night or in the wee hours of the morning. Still others had cars every three minutes. On University Avenue at peak hours, there were more than sixty cars in service on the St. Paul–Minneapolis line between the two cities. Stand anywhere along University Avenue and there was a steady parade of streetcars just a

A conductor purchases a buddy poppy. Photograph by the *Minneapolis Star Tribune;* courtesy of the Minnesota Historical Society.

A St. Paul Winter Carnival parade passes in front of the State Capitol in 1939. The streetcars are unscheduled extras, waiting to transport the crowd home. Photograph from the Minneapolis Star and Tribune News Negative Collection; courtesy of the Minnesota Historical Society.

block or two apart, and most of them were standing room only. No one ever bothered to look at a schedule because waiting for the streetcar was like waiting for an elevator.

Riding the streetcars was fun. They were spacious and had huge windows that opened in summer to admit breezes. A single streetcar could comfortably accommodate a seated load of fifty people and another sixty standees.

They had a unique mechanical personality and repertoire of sounds, from the roar of the gears and the electric motors as they accelerated away from a stop, to the steady *ka plunk ka plunk* of the compressor as it recharged the air brakes. Downtown, at rush hour, the groan of hundreds of traction motors echoed off buildings as long lines of cars hammered their way through track switches. You could smell them, too: a pleasant blend of hot brake shoes, gear oil, and ozone.

Then riders started to slip away. Although streetcars were very well maintained and ran on time, they could not match the convenience and flexibility of the automobile.

By the early 1950s, streetcars did not go where people wanted to go. The first-ring suburbs were booming with new development, but most streetcar lines, with a couple of exceptions, ended abruptly at the city limits of Minneapolis–St. Paul. To go farther you had to transfer to a shuttle bus or ride one of the new suburban bus lines that offered an express trip from downtown to the suburbs. Or you could simply jump in the family car.

Suburbanization also meant that fewer people were going downtown as more of the economic base shifted away from the core cities. Line extensions considered by company officials immediately after World War II were out of the question by the early 1950s. A few heavy lines continued to prosper, but their track and power infrastructures were wearing out. The cars were getting tired, too. One hundred and forty-one new streamlined cars were put into use after the war, but the rest were thirty to forty years old. They were in good repair but increasingly expensive to maintain.

More automobiles meant more congestion, especially downtown. Major downtown streets became one way, which would require expensive track relocations if rail operations were to continue. State highway engineers were busy planning a huge metro freeway system that would make it even more difficult for any form of mass transit to compete with the automobile. Declining ridership meant declining revenues, and with expenses rising, because of the post-

war inflation, there was no way that TCRT as a private company could finance improvements out of revenues or borrow money through capital bonding.

Public support withered, too. An investor group led by New York financier and speculator Charles Green emerged in 1949 demanding a stronger bottom line, improved earnings, and dividends. The conservative incumbent management resisted, wanting instead to retain earnings, pay off debt, and reinvest in the system. President D. J. Strouse had been with the company since 1903, starting as a bookkeeper. Other directors and department heads had similar tenure and experience. They had worked hard to weather the Depression and the war years and maintained a strong personal commitment to the company, its employees, and streetcar technology. But this intransigence, sincere as it was, ignored the powerful, inevitable changes overtaking the transit business.

An ugly proxy battle in November 1949 routed the Strouse management, and Charles Green became president of TCRT. Five years of rancor followed. The new group sought to

A cold and windy February day at 6th Street and Marquette Avenue in downtown Minneapolis, where the Glenwood–4th Ave. S. line crossed the Nicollet–2nd St. N.E. line. Photograph from the Minneapolis Star and Tribune News Negative Collection; courtesy of the Minnesota Historical Society.

restructure operations by reducing personnel costs and disposing of obsolete plant and rolling stock. It further sought to bring service into line with declining demand and increase revenues by raising fares. It also wanted to convert the system to buses.

These changes came to a head before the Minnesota Railroad and Warehouse Commission, which undertook an investigation. The press, ever sensitive to controversy, picked up on the issues and spread them across the pages of the Minneapolis and St. Paul newspapers. Unfriendly politicians took out rhetorical clubs to beat on the company. The public complained about poor service. How, it was asked, could there be support or sympathy for a monopolistic business that made its employees work long hours, paid them low wages, and was rumored to have underworld connections?

Brash threats from company officials to shut down and sell off the St. Paul operation because it was not making money did not help matters. Economies were needed, but the actions taken proved so ill timed and ham-handed that they drove away whatever public support remained for the beleaguered system. People were fond of streetcars but not of the streetcar company. With fewer and fewer riders the company had no one to turn to. It had no friends and was running out of money. It had to do something.

Another management coup in March 1951 ousted Charles Green and installed Fred Ossanna, then corporate counsel, as chairman and later president. Ossanna was a prominent local attorney and a former candidate for mayor of Minneapolis. He was a much smoother figure than Green and extinguished many of the PR fires that Green started. Ossanna had many friends and former clients in the business community.

A few of them were rather unsavory and eventually joined him in the federal penitentiary, but in 1951 Ossanna remained the respected transit executive as he and other company officials opened talks with General Motors for the purchase of new buses. GM responded with favorable terms, and three years later, on June 19, 1954, the remaining streetcars pulled into the car barns for the last time. There were fond reminiscences and editorials in the press and a local railfan group chartered two cars for one last ride over the system, but the era of the trolley was at an end.

There are two popular theories about the disappearance of streetcars and rail transit. One holds that the automobile, oil, and tire trusts conspired to put the streetcar out of business. But there was no conspiracy, just millions of consumers who bought all the cars the auto companies could make and sell. Unscrupulous people did conspire to plunder the assets of the Twin City Rapid Transit Company, profiting personally from real estate and scrap metal sales, but they were convicted and served prison terms. Those responsible were opportunists grabbing dishonestly at easy money.

The other theory asserts that the automobile is inherently a superior technology and that its triumph over the streetcar, as well as the demise of the privately owned transit companies, are free market outcomes. This view is only partially accurate. The automobile and the culture around it may be the ultimate expression of a democratic, mobile society, but its ascendancy had enormous assistance from public policy decisions that put billions of tax dollars into road and highway improvements. All of this took place at the expense of private companies such as TCRT that paid taxes and had to survive on revenues earned from passenger fares.

As early as 1921, all governments spent $1.4 billion on roads while private systems struggled to make money and were often thwarted by regulatory bodies that would not let them raise fares to offset increasing costs. By the early 1920s, a third of the streetcar and interurban companies were bankrupt. This situation worsened between the world wars as low fares and declining ridership, along with the Great Depression, made it impossible for systems to attract capital to modernize equipment and improve service to compete with the automobile. In 1940, public spending on highways reached $2.7 billion. In 1950, while TCRT struggled to stay afloat, public spending for roads was at $4.6 billion, with virtually nothing allotted for transit. By 1960, with the coming of the interstate highway system, allocations for roads reached $11.5 billion. The thinking of transportation experts held that rail could never hope to compete with the automobile, and buses could more efficiently serve what little business remained. Planners and policy makers gave the nod to sprawling development that ate up land, requiring more highway capacity and creating even more congestion, which in turn caused a clamor for even more highway construction. It was widely believed that more capacity was the answer and that metropolitan areas could build their way out of the problem. All the while, highways constructed in the 1950s and 1960s started wearing out, putting further pressure on government transportation budgets. Other bills were coming due. The energy crisis of the early 1970s was a hint of future shortages and higher prices. Air quality became a serious problem.

Fifty years after the streetcar disappeared from Minneapolis and St. Paul, the internal combustion engine and the automobile continue to shape the future of the Twin Cities and most metropolitan areas. But the exclusive reliance on them and the long-term sustainability of that reliance are being questioned even as the Twin Cities welcome their first light-rail line and the streetcar returns in a new form.

An everyday streetcar scene: a blind man with guide dog sits behind the motorman, who has, against the rules, lowered the shade behind him. The shade was meant to eliminate windshield glare at night, but some motormen used it to discourage interaction with passengers. Photograph courtesy of the Minnesota Historical Society.

From Horsepower to Electric Power

The Early Years

1

An Evolving Technology

On Christmas Eve, 1889, groups of people huddled at street corners and in doorways all along 3rd Street in Minneapolis. It was 4:00 p.m. and the long shadows of winter had banished the sun far to the south. At 3rd Street and 2nd Avenue South, flakes of wind-blown snow dusted the Lake Superior sandstone and New Hampshire granite of Louis Menage's Guaranty Loan Building, Minneapolis's first skyscraper and the tallest building west of Chicago. But this group was not there to pay homage to Menage's pile of stone, which they had watched rise for almost a year. They shivered and waited for something less monumental but no less important for the future of the Twin Cities.

Looking north up 3rd Street someone in the crowd remarked at a spark of light. A distant hum came closer. There were more sparks and the roar of metal meeting metal. Harnesses rustled in the cold as a drayman cursed and pulled up his team, stopping short as the first electric streetcar in Minneapolis crossed his path and

rumbled through the intersection. Farther down 3rd Street another crowd cheered as the car turned the corner at 4th Avenue and headed south for its appointment with open country and the end of the line at 34th Street.

The streetcar's Twin Cities debut came fourteen years after the first horsecar rolled down Washington Avenue and some forty years after the area around Minneapolis—originally part of the Ft. Snelling Military Reservation—was opened to settlement. A year later, the 1890 census declared the western frontier closed. That same census found 298,000 people living in Minneapolis and St. Paul, and with more people arriving and the area growing, there was a need for public transportation. But what form would it take? Just a few years before, there had been only one answer to that question, the horse, but now there were other options.

Early cities existed for protection or for commerce, often both. Ancient and medieval cities occupied defensible sites on high ground or were otherwise guarded by natural barriers. Large bodies of water offered both protection and the opportunity for commerce. Walls kept out enemies even as they pressed people close

Concerts at Lake Harriet, a Minneapolis tradition, began when Minneapolis Street Railway built the first pavilion there in 1888. This is the second pavilion, opened in 1891. Photograph by F. E. Haynes; courtesy of the Minnesota Historical Society.

together. Draft animals and feet furnished all the transportation needed to move goods or people about. It was the emergence of manufacturing and industrial activity, particularly its concentration near sources of waterpower, that drew more people into cities, pushing settlements well beyond their ancient walls. Cities became more economically self-sustaining even as they grew larger and more spread out and took on expanded roles as centers of government, education, and the arts.

By the late eighteenth century, European cities had grown so large that some form of urban transportation was needed. Paris responded first, in 1819, with a system of horse-drawn stagecoaches operating on its major streets. London followed. In the United States, a line opened in New York City along Broadway in 1827.

These coaches were small, cramped, and uncomfortable. John Stephenson, an American carriage builder, introduced a newer, larger design in New York City in the late 1820s. Termed omnibuses, they proved popular. More of them appeared in Philadelphia and Boston.

A few years later the idea of putting a railway in the streets was tried in New York City. John Mason, a banker, incorporated the New York and Harlem Street Railway in 1831, the first street railway in America. Its cars came from the same shops of John Stephenson, whose company later switched completely from omnibuses to horsecars, becoming one of the largest car builders of the nineteenth century. New Orleans followed New York, opening its first street railway in 1835.

Horsecars offered no amenities, but they did give a smoother ride than the omnibuses that lumbered and bounced along the mostly unpaved, rutted streets. Built entirely of wood, the car body sat on a set of cast iron flanged wheels. The wheels rolled on iron straps fastened atop wooden timbers called stringers, which were then supported by wooden ties embedded in the dirt. The small, enclosed cabins, typically ten to fifteen feet long, had windows that could be opened for ventilation in hot weather, but in the winter, there was very little heat. Some had a small coal or wood stove. For the most part people just bundled up and huddled together to keep out the chill. Straw on the floors offered scant warmth for cold feet. At night a kerosene lamp provided a feeble flickering light. The driver had the worst of it. He stood out on an open platform at the front of the car and was expected to collect fares and handle the horse that pulled the car down the street. These "bobtails," as they were called, typified the horsecar era, although many companies bought larger cars to handle increased business. The bigger cars required a second employee, a conductor, to collect fares and assist passengers. Even so, companies tried to get by with a single employee to hold down expenses.

The U.S. population reached 3.5 million in 1850. Several cities were well over 100,000, and, as they grew, street railways followed. Boston's first street railway opened in 1856; Philadelphia's began operation in 1858. Ridership kept increasing despite the primitive accommodations and the cars' reputations as hangouts for drunks and cutpurses. Proper Victorian ladies tried to avoid using the cars. Regardless, by 1881 there were 415 street railways in the United States and a total of 18,000 cars and 3,000 miles of track.

The only problem was the horse. By the 1880s, there were more than 100,000 in street

railway service. They were the only means of propulsion and an enormous, ongoing expense requiring food, shelter, and innumerable farriers, blacksmiths, harness makers, and veterinarians. Their manure was an endless disposal problem not to mention a safety and health hazard, especially if it was left to ripen in the streets. A horse-drawn streetcar had a top speed of five to six miles per hour. At that speed the horse had to be replaced every four to five hours lest it exhaust itself and drop dead—and some of them did.

Diseases were ever present. An outbreak of equine influenza in 1872, the Great Epizootic, infected and killed or severely disabled almost every horse in the eastern half of the United States. Those that survived were terribly weakened and unfit for work. So awful was the epidemic that gangs of men were hired or released from jail to drag wagons and street railway cars through the streets.

Another form of propulsion had to be found. A proven technology, the steam engine, already existed. It had energized the Industrial Revolution and was already moving people and freight across the continent on the transcontinental railway, but adapting steam to an urban setting presented a serious challenge. The steam engine was noisy and dirty, and it terrified horses, but there were some marginally

The Monroe Street and 8th (now Chicago) Avenue horsecar line stretched about six miles from end to end, so each one-way trip took more than an hour. The physical endurance of the horses had its limits, so teams were replaced during the day, as is happening in this photograph. Judging from the shadows, this is the 8th Avenue barn, just north of Franklin Avenue. Photograph courtesy of the Minnesota Historical Society.

Cable cars were installed on St. Paul's Selby Avenue because of this hill, which was too steep for either horses or electric cars relying on adhesion. The 16 percent grade (one foot of rise for every sixteen feet traveled) was reduced to 7 percent by the completion of the Selby Tunnel. The Amherst Wilder mansion on the left is long gone, but the retaining wall next to it remains in place today. Photographs courtesy of the Minnesota Historical Society.

successful efforts at taming it for street railway service by shrouding the entire locomotive in a cab, or box, making it look much like a horsecar. The engine pulled a train of cars behind it. The first application was in San Francisco in 1860, and other cities followed, although San Francisco returned to horsepower after using steam for just a few years. Presumably the noise, soot, and a few runaway teams put it to rest.

The steam engine eventually went to work on the elevated railways (Els) in New York City and Chicago only to be replaced by electricity once it became practical in the 1890s. In the Twin Cities the Minneapolis, Lyndale & Minnetonka Railway and the North St. Paul Railroad, forerunners of TCRT, used steam, but here, too, it succumbed to electric traction.

Other alternatives were attempted. Inventors tried mixing various chemicals, creating compressible gases that could be stored under pressure in cylinders. When released the gases drove a piston, which transferred its power to driving wheels much like a steam locomotive. One such contraption, the soda motor, was tried in the Twin Cities and failed like all the rest.

The cable car emerged in 1873 as the

first really practical alternative to the horse. Its inventor, a San Franciscan named Andrew Hallidie, owned a company that manufactured wire rope (a cable made up of many strands of individual wires). California mining companies bought Hallidie's rope for use in aerial tramways that carried gold ore to smelters from mines high in the Sierras. Hallidie reasoned that the same principle could be used to move people by laying a continuous cable in a slot, or trough, between the two running rails in the street. The cable could then be connected to a large drum, or spindle, turned by a steam engine located at a central power plant. As the drum turned, it pulled the cable. Passengers rode in cars attached to the cable by a device called a grip, which extended down from the car, grasping the cable as it moved along through the slot. By applying or releasing the grip on the cable, a grip man could start or stop the car. A hand brake was also available to halt the car or secure it on steep grades.

Hallidie's invention succeeded, and the cable car quickly attracted national attention. Soon other cities were building systems, including one in St. Paul. The largest system, next to San Francisco's, was Chicago's, with eighty-two miles of line, 710 cars, and an investment of nearly $25 million. In 1894, there were 662 miles of cable railway and some 5,000 cable cars representing approximately twenty-eight cities with cable railway systems. Roughly 400 million passengers a year rode the cars.

Cable car systems were costly to build, and ongoing maintenance expenses were equally burdensome. Cables had to be inspected and replaced regularly. There were also serious operational problems. A cable break or a failure at the power plant could bring a single line or even the entire system to a halt. Chicago's system suffered wintertime buildups of compacted ice and snow in the cable slots. The only remedy was to use a portable steam boiler to thaw the ice. The cable railway was an important step, but electricity would replace it, just as rapidly as the cable was replacing the horse.

A long line of nineteenth-century scientists and inventors grappled with electrical energy and tried to make it do useful work. In 1821, the British scientist Michael Faraday demonstrated that electricity could create mechanical motion. An American, Thomas Davenport, invented a small rotary engine powered by a primitive storage battery in 1835. Davenport's motor was taken several steps further by a succession of inventors who used it to power a variety of experimental devices, none of them commercially practical.

It was not until 1838 that a Scotsman named Robert Davidson built an electric locomotive powered by storage batteries. A few years later an American, Moses Farmer, constructed an electric locomotive that was powerful enough to pull a car carrying two people on a small circular track. However, battery power continued to limit the usefulness and practicality of these efforts until the 1860s and 1870s, when the first mechanical dynamos, or generators, were perfected. Then, in 1879, the German engineer Ernst Werner von Siemens appeared at the Berlin Industrial Exhibition with an electrically powered locomotive and train that drew power from a third rail fed by a dynamo. Two years later he built a small electric street railway in Lichterfelde near Berlin, the first commercially practical electric railway in the world.

Siemens's success inspired others, including Thomas Edison and another American, Stephen Field, both of whom experimented

These maps span the period from 1872 to 1891 and show the Minneapolis and St. Paul horsecar lines, the Minneapolis, Lyndale & Minnetonka steam-powered Motor Line, the Selby Avenue and East 7th Street cable lines, and attendant facilities. The year of construction appears next to each track segment and facility. If a segment or facility was abandoned during this period, that year appears in parentheses. Segments and facilities with no abandonment year were converted to electric streetcars during 1890–91.

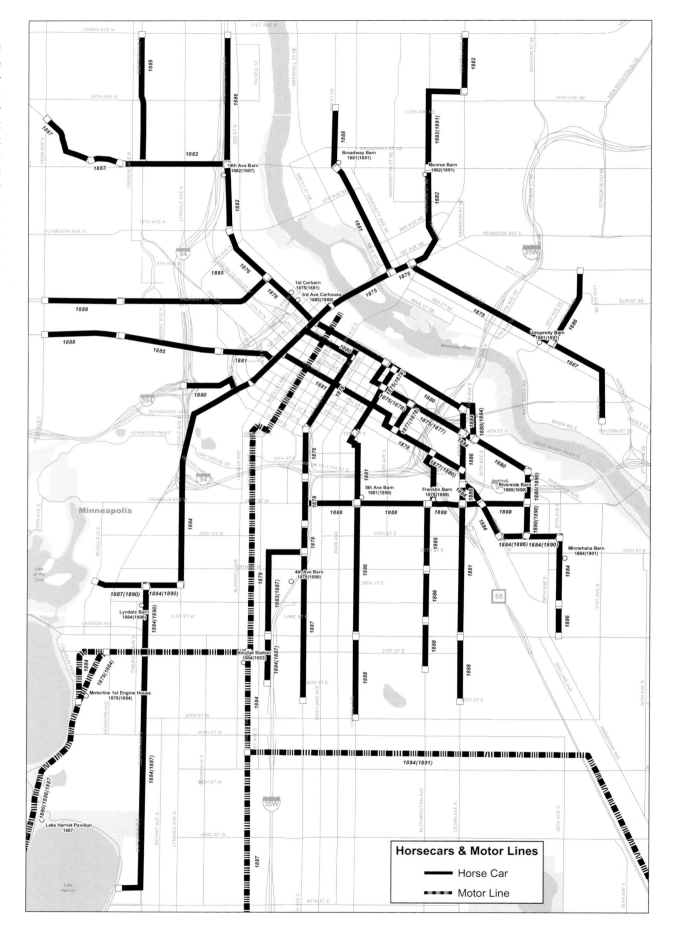

Horsecars & Motor Lines

— Horse Car

▮▮▮ Motor Line

From Horsepower to Electric Power

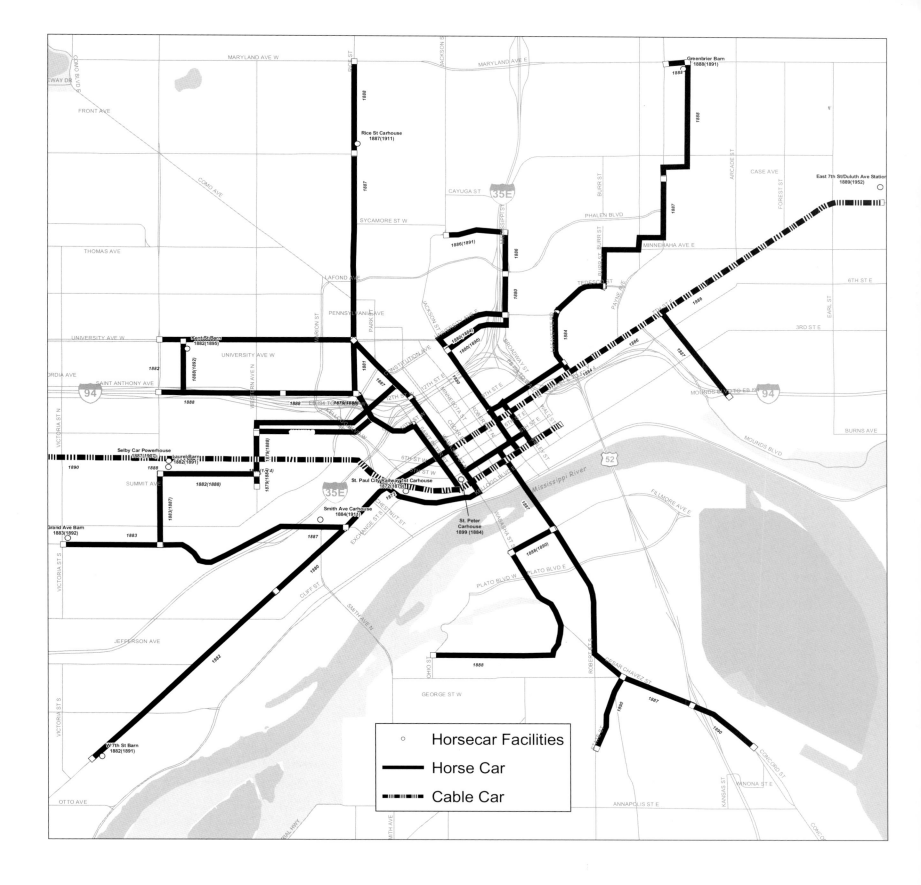

MARYLAND AVE W
RICE ST
JACKSON ST
MARYLAND AVE E
Greenbrier Barn
1888(1891)
1888
FRONT AVE
EWAY DR
OWO BLVD
1888
1888
Rice St Carhouse
1887(1911)
CAYUGA ST
35E
CASE AVE
East 7th St/Duluth Ave Station
1889(1952)
1887
ARCADE ST
FOREST ST
THOMAS AVE
SYCAMORE ST W
PHALEN BLVD
BURR ST
6TH ST E
1886(1891)
1887
MINNEHAHA AVE E
LAFOND AVE
1886
BURR ST
BURR ST
TEDESCO ST
PAYNE AVE
3RD ST E
MARION ST
PENNSYLVANIA AVE
PARK ST
1880
EARL ST
UNIVERSITY AVE W
1886
1886
1884
1887
Kent St Barn
1882(1895)
BROADWAY ST
1880(1884)
1880(1890)
MOUNDS BLVD TO EB I-94
94
1882
1888(1892)
UNIVERSITY AVE W
1881
1884
BURNS AVE
ORDIA AVE
SAINT ANTHONY AVE
WESTERN AVE N
1887
7TH ST E
MOUNDS BLVD
94
1888
1888
EB I-94 TO 1879(1888)
12TH ST
MINNESOTA ST
1886
Selby Car Powerhouse
1887(1907)
Laurel Barn
1882(1891)
1879/1888
1882(1888)
6TH ST W
52
1890
1888
1886(1884)
1879(1888)
St. Paul City Railway 1st Carhouse
1872(1879)
Mississippi River
SUMMIT AVE
1882(1888)
Smith Ave Carhouse
1884(1911)
CHESTNUT ST
St. Peter
Carhouse
1899 (1884)
1887
FILLMORE AVE E
1883(1887)
EXCHANGE ST S
Grand Ave Barn
1883(1892)
1883
1887
WABASHA ST S
KELLOGG BLVD
35E
VICTORIA ST S
CLIFF ST
1880
1888(1890)
PLATO BLVD W
PLATO BLVD E
SMITH AVE N
JEFFERSON AVE
OHIO S
1888
ROBERT ST S
GEORGE ST W
CESAR CHAVEZ ST
1890
1887
1882
FILLMORE
1890
CONCORD ST
VICTORIA ST S
W 7th St Barn
1882(1891)
KANSAS ST
WINONA ST E
OTTO AVE
ANNAPOLIS ST E

Horsecar Facilities
Horse Car
Cable Car

with electrically powered railways. The three subsequently applied for patents at about the same time. Edison later joined Field in the Electric Railway Company of the United States, building a small electric locomotive that was demonstrated at the 1883 Exposition of Railway Appliances at Chicago.

Three other men contributed to the progress of the electric railway during the 1880s: Leo Daft, John King, and Charles Van Depoele. Each attempted electrification of horsecar systems in various cities. Van Depoele installed his version in Minneapolis for the Minneapolis, Lyndale & Minnetonka Railway, replacing steam power on 1st Avenue South (Marquette Avenue) between Washington Avenue and 6th Street. None of their efforts were completely successful.

Two problems dogged electric propulsion, one being current collection. The Edison and Siemens designs picked up power from an exposed third rail, still used today in subways and elevated railways but ill suited, if not deadly, in urban streets.

Daft and Van Depoele used overhead wires, but their current collector, a wheeled contraption called a troller that rolled along two overhead wires and was connected to the car by flexible cable, proved extremely unreliable. All too often it fell off the overhead wire, sometimes tearing down the entire overhead installation.

A far more serious problem was the mounting of the electric motor on the car and the method used to transmit power to its wheels. Earlier systems used belts or chains that were driven directly by the electric motor, which was mounted inside the car or on the front platform. Chains and belts broke or slipped, making it difficult to reliably control the car. The problem

of current collection was solved by adoption of the single trolley pole and underrunning trolley wheel. Van Depoele experimented with this arrangement on some of his later installations. It was left to Frank Sprague, however, to solve the motor mounting problem and eventually build and operate the first successful streetcar system in the United States.

Sprague was born in 1857 and entered the U.S. Naval Academy in 1874. Trained as an engineer, he served in the navy until 1883, resigning to work as an assistant to Thomas Edison. While in the navy, Sprague pursued his interests in electricity. On a visit to London he observed that city's steam-powered subway, and his thoughts turned to applying electric power to public transportation. At the time he sketched out some preliminary ideas for the trolley pole and an underrunning wheel to collect power from a single overhead wire, an approach that resulted in a patent dispute with Charles Van Depoele.

Sprague spent only a year with Edison and then left to establish his own company. In 1885, he designed a way to mount an electric motor on the truck (or wheel assembly) of a railcar such that the motor could drive the axle directly through gears and bearings, thus eliminating belts and chains. This invention proved the last step in perfecting the electric streetcar. In 1887, Sprague was given a contract to electrify the horsecar system in Richmond, Virginia. It was so successful that by 1889, the Sprague motor system and overhead trolley were in use in 154 street railway systems in the United States, including the Minneapolis Street Railway Company.

Sprague's innovations made him a wealthy man. He went on to develop the high-speed electric elevator and a system that allowed a single operator to control all the electric motors in a multiple-car train, thereby making both the skyscraper and the subway a reality.

How Streetcars Work

More than a century separates Sprague's electric streetcar of 1888 and the high-speed, electrically powered trains and light-rail cars of the twenty-first century. Nineteenth-century engineers and inventors might have been surprised by the sophistication of today's technology, but they would easily grasp its principles, because the fundamentals of electric traction are the same.

In early streetcar power plants, steam from a coal-fired boiler spun electric dynamos that fed direct current power directly to the overhead trolley wire. As systems expanded geographically, and the number of streetcars in service increased, more and/or larger power plants were needed. Electric power also had to be transmitted over greater distances. Because direct current power can only travel short distances before the resistance of the conducting wire or cable dissipates its energy, alternating current power came into use. Hydropower, where it was available, augmented coal, as did natural gas. Street railway systems often turned to commercial power. Many were even owned by power companies.

Larger generating plants and a geographically dispersed streetcar system demanded a network of transmission lines to transmit high-voltage alternating current to substations. Transformers at the substations dropped the voltage to a lower value. The power output of

these transformers was connected to a motor generator (called a rotary converter), which then generated direct current at 600 volts. This direct current went to the overhead trolley wires over a network of feeder lines, which were carried along in underground conduits or attached to the same poles that supported the overhead trolley suspension system. Every 500 to 1,000 feet the feeders were connected to the trolley wire.

A wheel or a graphite shoe, mounted at the tip of the trolley pole and attached to the roof of the car, contacted the trolley wire as the car moved along. It picked up the 600-volt current, which then flowed to a controller operated by

In the early 1890s, a crew poses with its Kenwood car at the terminal at 21st Street and Penn Avenue. This is typical of the first generation of electric cars: they were little more than overgrown horsecars with motors. The four-wheel truck gave a bouncy, lurching ride that limited top speed. Narrow with lengthwise seating inside, they were neither comfortable nor capacious, and would be replaced within a decade by much more substantial double-truck home-designed cars.

the motorman. The controller was a vertically mounted drum with electrical contactors and a handle on top that could be rotated through various settings, or "notches." A notch on the controller switched in, or out, a combination of resistors connected in series, or parallel, that regulated the amount of electric power fed to the motors and, therefore, the speed of the car.

The circuit that began at the power plant continued on through the distribution system—rotary converter, trolley wire, controller, car motors—and was completed by the car wheels contacting the running rails, which were bonded together and connected to a common ground at the power plant.

The first streetcars used hand brakes. As they grew larger and heavier, air brakes came into use. An electric compressor furnished compressed air for the braking system and accessory controls that opened and closed doors, and operated warning devices such as gongs, bells, and whistles. Cars were lighted by electricity and, in later years, heated electrically, although coal stoves and hot air, or hot water, heat were common.

The earliest electric cars were often just horsecar bodies modified to accommodate one motor mounted on a double-axle, single truck. As time passed cars became larger and heavier, requiring two trucks and four motors, one on each axle and two axles per truck.

Horsecar tracks were built as cheaply as possible. The gauge (distance between the rails) usually was 3 or 3½ feet. Horsecars were much lighter than the electric cars and did not need heavy rails or a reinforced roadbed. Iron rails, fastened to rough-cut, untreated ties were common. There was no rock or gravel ballast to support the ties, just dirt, a construction method

conducive to rapid deterioration. Ties rotted in the muddy streets; eventually the entire track structure disintegrated.

As cable and electric cars came into use and cities began paving streets, heavier, more durable track construction became common. By the turn of the century, following electrification, track was generally constructed to the standard railway gauge of 4 feet 8½ inches. Heavy steel rails were used, spiked or otherwise securely fastened to hardwood ties that rested on several inches of rock or stone ballast. Cement or asphalt was poured between the rails, or the space was filled with sand and cobblestone or granite pavers were set in place atop the sand and then grouted with cement.

With heavier track construction came more expense, more so when cities demanded that the streetcar companies take responsibility for paving that portion of the street occupied by their tracks plus two feet on either side of the outermost rails. As an example, TCRT estimated that its cost for double track ran to $60,000 per mile (in 1900 dollars).

The most complicated and expensive track work was at intersections where lines crossed or diverged. Here again, early construction was cheap and simple but not very durable. Later installations (termed special work) used prefabricated switches and crossing frogs made of special alloy steels. Switches set in the street had a movable point in the rail flangeway that, depending upon its position, forced the streetcar wheels (mounted in a swiveled truck assembly) to go straight, turn left, or turn right.

Most track switches were thrown by hand. The motorman dropped a switch rod through a slot in the floor of the car, engaging the movable point in the street. At busy intersections there

Besides presenting the recently built (and now long gone) Metropolitan Building, this is the only known photograph that shows the Minneapolis conversion from narrow gauge (3 feet 6 inches between the rails) to standard gauge (4 feet 8½ inches) that took place during 1890–91. Note that each track temporarily has three rails, permitting both horsecars and electric cars to share the track during the transition period. Photograph by Norton & Peel; courtesy of the Minnesota Historical Society.

were electric switches that could be activated remotely by the motorman.

Electric Streetcars Reach the Twin Cities

Thomas Lowry was just twenty-four years old when he arrived in Minneapolis in 1867. The electric streetcar had not been invented, and Lowry, recently admitted to the bar, was intent on establishing a law practice and seeking his fortune in what was then a frontier town of some eight thousand people. He could scarcely have imagined that he would bring the electric streetcar to the Twin Cities and forty years later preside over one of the finest street railway properties in America.

Lowry was born in Logan County, Illinois, in 1843. His mother and father farmed near the village of Pleasant View about fifty miles west of Springfield. Growing up, Lowry was a regular

attendee at the Methodist church and the nearby school, which were both held in log cabins.
He went on to enroll at Lombard College but
became ill, possibly from tuberculosis, and was
forced to withdraw after two years. To recover
his strength he traveled through the western
states, briefly visiting Minneapolis. Returning
to Illinois and his father's farm, he decided that
he wanted to become a lawyer and moved on
to Rushville, where he read law under Judge
John C. Bagby.

It is not known what caused Lowry to de-
cide on the legal profession except for one remarkable coincidence. His father, Sam, needed
a lawyer and turned to an up-and-coming young
man from Springfield named Abraham Lincoln.
Young Tom accompanied his father on trips to
Lincoln's Springfield office and became a great
admirer, attending the Lincoln–Douglas sena-
torial debates at Galesburg in 1858.

Lowry in many ways resembled Lincoln.
He was a lean and angular six feet two inches
tall, affected an easy manner, and possessed
a great sense of humor. People were drawn
to Lowry by his personality and his gifts as a
storyteller. It is not surprising that he made
friends in Minneapolis. Like him, many would
become influential in the future direction of
the city. One of them was Dorilus Morrison,
the first mayor of Minneapolis. Another was
Dr. Calvin Gibson Goodrich, a prominent physi-
cian and local property owner. Prior to moving
to Minneapolis, Goodrich purchased a 148-acre
farm for $5,180 on what would later become
Lowry Hill. Lowry went on to marry Goodrich's
daughter, Beatrice, as well as become lifelong
friends with Goodrich's son, Calvin. Calvin subsequently joined Lowry in the management of
the Minneapolis Street Railway Company and

Thomas Lowry, founder of
the Twin City Rapid Transit
Company and its president until
1909. Photograph courtesy of
the Minnesota Historical Society.

succeeded him as president of the Twin City
Rapid Transit Company on Lowry's death.

But in 1867, Lowry had no intention of
going into the street railway business. He would
spend the next eight years buying and selling
real estate and adding influential clients to his
law practice. His first real estate transaction occurred shortly after his arrival in Minneapolis,
when he purchased a lot in the vicinity of what
is today Seven Corners. Then, a few months
later he bought 168 acres near Medicine Lake.
Between 1868 and 1875, Lowry, in partnership
with other investors, acquired, subdivided, and
sold large tracts of prime property. These parcels, among others, included the Lowry Addition, some 6⅔ acres south of Franklin between
Park and Portland Avenues, and the Groveland
Addition, encompassing 220 acres bounded by

today's Interstate 394, Franklin, Lyndale, and Fremont Avenues. In 1873, he formed a business partnership with Dorilus Morrison, who owned the Minneapolis Harvester Works, located near Hiawatha Avenue and Lake Street. That partnership became the South Side Addition, a subdivision that took in 150 acres between Lake and 26th Streets and Minnehaha and 31st Avenues.

One of Lowry's many law clients during those years was Colonel William S. King, whose Lyndale Farms encompassed approximately 1,400 acres adjoining Lakes Calhoun and Harriet. King arrived in Minneapolis from upstate New York in 1858. He was a fervent supporter of abolitionist causes and founded a newspaper, the *State Atlas,* which became a leading voice for the then new Republican Party. In later years, Colonel King helped establish the Minneapolis park system, donating his farmstead at 38th Street and Dupont Avenue South, along with other choice properties, to the city of Minneapolis. But in the early 1870s, the colonel was in deep financial trouble. His properties were all heavily mortgaged, including the farm, which was then outside the city limits.

The colonel's fortune hinged on developing his holdings; hence his interest in and involvement with the Minneapolis Street Railway Company, organized on July 1, 1873. Besides Colonel King, its officers were all familiar names in Minneapolis's early history: Morrison, W. D. Washburn, R. J. Mendenhall, W. P. Westfall, J. C. Oswald, Paris Gibson, W. W. Eastman, R. B. Langdon, and W. W. McNair. One objective of the railway was to provide access to Colonel King's property and the farm. This effort was at least the second attempt at establishing public transportation in Minneapolis. The first,

in 1867, was the Minneapolis Horse Rail Road Company, which, as far as can be determined, never came into operation.

Unfortunately, the Minneapolis Street Railway fell victim to the financial panic of 1873 and was unable to raise cash for construction. By 1875, things were much worse. Creditors had filed liens against most of Colonel King's property, and he was forced to turn to Philo Remington for financial assistance. Remington was an old friend from upstate New York and owner of the Remington Arms Company. As King's attorney, Thomas Lowry met with Remington's representatives to negotiate a financing agreement. During these negotiations Lowry was either invited, or chose, to involve himself in the Minneapolis Street Railway.

The Minneapolis City Council gave the company an exclusive charter in 1875 calling for the construction of two lines. The first was to be from Washington and 4th Avenue North along Washington to Hennepin, then via Hennepin and Central Avenues to 4th Street Southeast and along 4th to 14th Avenue Southeast. This line was to be completed within four months of the granting of the charter. The second line was to run from Plymouth Avenue and Washington via Washington to 12th Avenue South, then on to Franklin Avenue. This line was to be in operation within one year.

Both lines were built to the standards of that era and were not unlike early lines elsewhere. The running rails were five-by-six-inch wooden stringers (beams) about sixteen feet long, on top of which bent iron plates were spiked. The two rails were then fastened (spiked or bolted) to wooden ties resting on the ground. Dirt filled the space between the running rails, which were brought even with the surface of

A Minneapolis horsecar plods down a dirt street on the Monroe–6th Street–8th Ave. line. Photograph courtesy of the Minnesota Historical Society.

Service was provided every fifteen minutes between 5 a.m. and 11 p.m. The average speed was around five miles per hour, not surprising given the limits of the rolling stock, horsepower, and primitive track. Passengers all too often had to alight in the muddy streets and help the driver put the car back on the track or get off and assist the horse by pushing the car up an abrupt grade. Complaints must have been frequent but were just as likely ignored. There were no refunds or apologies, just basic transportation.

Expenses routinely exceeded revenues, and the directors of the company regularly had to dig into their own pockets or borrow money to keep the system afloat.

Minneapolis was still on the frontier. Only a few years had gone by since ox carts were rolling through St. Anthony on their way to the Red River Valley. The early St. Paul, Minneapolis & Manitoba (the future Great Northern) and the Northern Pacific railways built westward, but neither penetrated beyond the Dakotas. In 1876, Bismarck was as far as General Custer could travel by rail to keep his appointment at the Little Bighorn.

People and settlement followed the railroads, and, as more people moved west, Minneapolis and St. Paul became important gateway cities. It came as no surprise to the owners and directors of the Minneapolis Street Railway, particularly Tom Lowry, that the company would have an important effect on real estate development and property values. Build a horsecar line, sell lots and homes, and people and money would follow.

The years between 1875 and 1889 brought incredible growth. From the initial 2.1 miles of line in 1875, the system expanded to 66

the street. The track gauge was narrow, 3½ feet between the rails.

The company met both deadlines. The first line went in service on September 2, 1875. Two cars were used, and the receipts for the first day of operation totaled $21.50, a good sum of money in 1875.

The rolling stock consisted of six horsecars acquired from the John Stephenson Company of New York. Each car weighed about 1,000 pounds, was ten to fifteen feet long, and could seat up to fourteen passengers. Boarding passengers dropped their nickel fare in a box at the front of the car next to the driver, who stood out on an open platform completely exposed to all kinds of weather. Drivers worked twelve to sixteen hours a day, except for a dinner break. They washed their cars every day and tended to the needs of the horses. Wages were thirty-five dollars per month.

miles by 1889, just prior to the conversion to electric power. Much of this development and growth can be attributed to Lowry's shrewd diligence. He continued to devote time to his growing real estate business but became more and more involved in the affairs of the street railway, acquiring a controlling interest and becoming its president in 1877. His friend and brother-in-law, Calvin Goodrich, became vice president and general manager the following year. By 1889 Lowry was the major stockholder in MSR, besides serving as president of the Minneapolis, St. Paul & Sault Ste. Marie Railway, the Soo Line.

St. Paul Street Railway

Lowry's influence eventually reached across the Mississippi River to St. Paul, where a small network of horsecar lines had been built a few years before those in Minneapolis. St. Paul was several years older and had developed earlier because of its location at the head of navigation on the Mississippi River and its proximity to Ft. Snelling and nearby Mendota.

The legislature chartered the St. Paul & St. Anthony Railroad in 1853. It remained dormant until 1872, when it took on a new name, the St. Paul City Railway. The city of St. Paul granted a franchise in January 1872, and the first line commenced service in July 1872, three years before the first line opened in Minneapolis.

The incorporators of the St. Paul City Railway were J. W. Bass, J. C. Burbank, H. L. Carver, William Dawson, Warren H. Dean, Girard Hewitt, W. R. Marshall, Lafayette Shaw, and Horace Thompson. Soon after the first line began service, Dean and Marshall bought out the other shareholders and took sole control of the property. Marshall in turn acquired all of Dean's stock. Lafayette Shaw and W. R. McComb leased the property in 1874, but McComb backed out the following year and turned his shares over to Shaw. These changes were symptomatic of the company's shaky finances.

By 1877, the railway had completed 3.75 miles of track, owned two horsecar barns, fifteen horsecars, thirty-four horses, six mules, two snowplows, and three sleighs. That same year it defaulted on interest charges on the mortgage bonds and was sold at a sheriff's sale to Thomas Cochran Jr., trustee for the mortgage holders, a group of eastern investors. The company was then reincorporated by the bondholders and placed under the management of J. R. Walsh of St. Paul, who served as treasurer and general manager until the eastern interests sold out to a local group in 1882.

The company at this juncture was in better shape both physically and financially, and its new owners, responding to the same growth and prosperity then affecting Minneapolis, proceeded to reinvigorate the property. New lines were constructed, and there were extensions to the existing system. However, these improvements came at such great expense and were supported by such low revenues that the investors became alarmed and sought out Thomas Lowry to buy them out and take over operations. In 1883, Lowry, Calvin Goodrich, Lowry's brother-in-law, and Dorilus Morrison became the major stockholders. By 1886, they had secured operational control of the company through a financing arrangement with Lee Higginson and Company of Boston.

Calvin Goodrich, Thomas Lowry's brother-in-law and business partner, and president of Twin City Rapid Transit Company from 1909 to 1915. Photograph courtesy of the Minnesota Historical Society.

The Nicollet Avenue and Como–Harriet lines began as the narrow gauge, steam-powered Minneapolis, Lyndale & Minnetonka, better known as the Motor Line. Its lines to Lake Harriet and Minnehaha Park met at this junction at 31st Street and Nicollet Avenue, next to the company's roundhouse. The steam "motor," shown here pulling a single coach, was a conventional locomotive disguised inside the facade of a passenger car; the theory behind this deception was that it would be less likely to frighten horses. Since 1886, this site has hosted a streetcar factory, two different carhouses, and a Metro Transit bus garage.

The "Motor Line"

One year later another property came under Lowry's control. This was the Minneapolis, Lyndale & Minnetonka Railway, more popularly known as the "Motor Line," a name derived from the small, enclosed steam engines (termed motors) that pulled its trains. Incorporated as the Lyndale Railway Company in 1878, the Motor Line opened for business in May 1879 as the Minnespolis, Lyndale & Lake Calhoun Railway. Starting at Bridge Square, now the intersection of 1st Street and Hennepin Avenue, the line continued south along Marquette Avenue to 13th Street, to Nicollet Avenue, to 31st Street. Near the intersection of 31st and Hennepin, it entered private right of way on a long, gentle curve to the southwest that extended to 34th Street adjoining Lake Calhoun. The company had earlier negotiated an agreement with the Minneapolis Street Railway to operate trains within the city limits (then 26th Street).

The Motor Line was built to promote development by providing reliable transportation from the fringes of the city to the downtown. Investors saw it as a way to open the area around Lakes Calhoun and Harriet for recreation and housing. In 1880, the Motor Line was extended from Lake Calhoun to Lake Harriet. The following year, the company acquired a double-deck paddle wheel steamboat and began offering excursions on Lake Calhoun.

The Motor Line was built to a narrow, three-foot gauge. Power was originally provided by two small steam engines that were enclosed and resembled the passenger cars they pulled behind them. Both engines were built by the Baldwin Locomotive Works of Philadelphia and were delivered in 1879. They were painted black with gold trim, and the passenger cars were painted yellow. Several were open cars that allowed passengers to enjoy summer breezes.

In 1881, the railway was renamed the Minneapolis, Lyndale & Minnetonka Railway and resolved to tap the resort and tourist business on Lake Minnetonka. Additional equipment was acquired for the extension to Lake Minnetonka, including two steam motors and a conventional (2-6-0) steam locomotive, which could only be used between Lake Calhoun and Excelsior. The city of Minneapolis would not allow it on downtown streets.

Lake Minnetonka by this time was a national tourist destination. As it became accessible by rail, large hotels catering to wealthy guests were erected and advertised throughout the country. The most famous was James J. Hill's Hotel Lafayette at Minnetonka Beach. It opened in 1882 and was served by Hill's St. Paul, Minneapolis & Manitoba Railway. Other posh hotels on Tonka Bay and at Deephaven opened at about the same time. The Motor Line began service to Excelsior in 1882. It was the fourth and last railroad to reach Lake Minnetonka, and after a short time it would prove to be one railroad too many.

In 1884, the railway acquired land at 31st Street and Nicollet Avenue South. A roundhouse, shops, and offices were constructed on the site, which was later used for streetcars. (Today, the site remains in use as a Metro Transit bus garage.) That same year, the company built another line south along Nicollet to 37th Street then east to just beyond Hiawatha Avenue. From there it ran south parallel to the Chicago, Milwaukee & St. Paul Railway (the Milwaukee Road) tracks to Minnehaha Park, ending at the Milwaukee Road's depot (the "Princess" depot stands today). Two more steam motors and several passenger cars were purchased for this new service.

Regrettably, revenues, which came primarily from summer traffic, could not sustain the railway's expansion to Lake Minnetonka and

Minnehaha Park. Colonel William McCrory and the other original backers sold out to a new group of investors in 1885, among whom were Charles Pillsbury and James J. Hill. Hill's interest was primarily in using the Minneapolis, Lyndale & Minnetonka as part of an extension of his St. Paul, Minneapolis & Manitoba to Hutchinson by way of Hopkins and Excelsior. All service beyond Lake Calhoun was discontinued in 1886.

Complicating matters, residents began objecting to the use of steam motors on city streets. The company responded by experimenting with one of Charles Van Depoele's electric motor cars to tow the trains through downtown. Overhead trolley wire was strung and connected to a small steam-powered generator. There were three tests: one in December 1885 and others in January and February 1886. All of them were unsatisfactory. Van Depoele then personally invested $25,000 in an ill-advised effort to begin full operation, which had only limited success. There were mechanical problems and such extreme vibration that the car body was nearly shaken apart.

The company then turned to an experimental steam motor, which used steam generated by the addition of caustic soda to water at a very high temperature. These were the so-called soda motors and similarly proved troublesome and unreliable.

In 1887, Minneapolis passed an ordinance requiring the use of cable or some other source of power for the railway's operation within the city limits, but the railway did not have the financial resources to do so. Van Depoele's efforts were successful. The railway had just defaulted on its mortgage bonds and was almost out of money.

James J. Hill, Charles Pillsbury, and Thomas Lowry were the principal debt holders. In a move to reorganize, the railway proposed a refinancing plan that called for the issuing of $1 million in thirty-year, first mortgage bonds with the interest payments guaranteed by the Minneapolis Street Railway. Under the terms of a lease agreement, the Minneapolis Street Railway took over operation, effectively ending the Motor Line's separate identity. Calvin Goodrich was named general manager.

Thereafter, the Minneapolis Street Railway continued to make improvements. In 1887, it extended track south along Nicollet Avenue to the Washburn Home at 50th Street, resumed service to Lake Harriet, and built the first in what would be a series of large picnic and entertainment pavilions on the lake.

Electrification and the Great Merger

In 1888, on the eve of electrification, the then separate Minneapolis and St. Paul street railway systems were operating 110 miles of horsecar track and 17 miles of steam-powered motor line. Six miles of cable car track would be placed in service in St. Paul that year. The two systems owned some 360 horsecars and stabled 1,900 horses. By 1890, they would be transporting 27,677,000 passengers out of a population of 297,000—a yearly average of ninety-three rides per capita. At the time, the boundaries of the Minneapolis settled area were, roughly, Lowry Avenue on the north, Lake Street on the south, University Avenue–17th Avenue Southeast to the east, and Penn Avenue to the west. St. Paul had filled in from the Mississippi River to Lexington Avenue on the west, Maryland Avenue on the north, and Duluth Avenue on the east side. There was a small pocket of development near Robert Street and Concord Avenue across the river.

The Pillsbury and Washburn interests made Minneapolis a major grain market and flour-milling center. The completion of the Northern Pacific Railway to Tacoma and the growth of James J. Hill's St. Paul, Minneapolis & Manitoba gave St. Paul its standing as a gateway city and transportation hub. Major streets were paved, and municipal sewer and water systems were in place. Great stone mansions arose along Summit Avenue in St. Paul and along Park Avenue and in the Kenwood neighborhood in Minneapolis. New people arrived every day, and new businesses sprang up to provide them with jobs and services.

Regrettably, this urban progress was not reflected in the street railways, which continued to rely on the horse for motive power, despite other efforts to improve service and expand the system. New lines and track mileage were added in both cities. Larger horsecars and expanded carhouses and other support facilities came along as the system built into new neighborhoods.

Both Minneapolis and St. Paul operations represented large investments for their owners. Unfortunately, the returns on those investments were negligible due to the constant demands on resources to finance expansion. The low average speed and comparatively low passenger capacity of the cars, along with other inefficiencies associated with the use of horses, drove up operating expenses. Change was needed, but the technology was not there. The steam motors of the Minneapolis, Lyndale & Minnetonka Railway were unpopular nuisances. The Van Depoele demonstrations failed in 1886. The only alternative was the cable, which by then had come into extensive use in other cities.

Attaining the crest of Selby Hill at Summit Avenue, the cable cars passed the Norman Kittson mansion, future location of the Cathedral of St. Paul. Photograph by Truman Ward Ingersoll; courtesy of the Minnesota Historical Society.

The Minneapolis Street Railway and the St. Paul City Railway sponsored a tour of cable installations in 1887. Members of the Minneapolis and St. Paul city councils visited systems in Baltimore, Boston, New York, Cleveland, and Philadelphia to learn more about cable operations and how they might work in the Twin Cities. St. Paul officials were especially impressed.

The steep grades out of downtown St. Paul made the cable attractive to St. Paul city offi-cials, and they applied considerable political pressure to the St. Paul City Railway to proceed immediately with a cable system. Construction on the first line started in 1887. Beginning at 4th Street and Broadway downtown, it went out 4th Street, through Seven Corners and then up Selby Hill on a 16 percent grade between Pleasant and Summit Avenues. The line continued on Selby Avenue to St. Albans Street. A powerhouse and a carhouse were built at Selby and Dale. The line opened on January 21, 1888.

The East 7th Street cable line climbed this long 5 percent grade, viewed after electrification around 1905 from the top of the hill at Hope Street.

That same year the company started work on a second cable line that would tackle the stiff, 5 percent grade leading out of downtown on East 7th Street. Starting at Wabasha Street, it followed East 7th Street to Duluth Avenue, where another carhouse and cable powerhouse was constructed. This line began operation in June 1889 and replaced a horsecar line on the same street.

Construction costs for both lines were astounding: $1,564,809 in 1888 dollars. As a measure of the size of that investment, the bonding issued in 1887 to finance the lines was not fully paid off until 1947, even though the East 7th Street line and the Selby line were converted to electricity in 1893 and 1898, respectively.

Minneapolis city fathers watched the St. Paul construction and demanded improvements. Then in 1888, an outside group with considerable support from city residents petitioned the city council for an electric railway franchise. The Minneapolis Street Railway fought back, taking the position that electric technology was unproved. Eventually, given public pressure and threatened with a possible loss of its franchise, the company agreed to a council resolution passed in July 1889 requiring it to build three cable lines, as follows:

- Washington Avenue from 20th Avenue North to Cedar Avenue South;

- Bloomington Avenue from 32nd Street to Franklin Avenue, to 8th Avenue South, to 4th Street, to 1st Avenue (Marquette), to High Street; and

- Hennepin Avenue from Lyndale Avenue, to Central Avenue, to 6th Street Southeast to 3rd Avenue Southeast to Harrison Street, to 29th Avenue Northeast.

Further council action in August and September called for three more lines:

- A "loop" line on 1st Avenue South, High Street, Hennepin Avenue, and Washington Avenue;

- An extension on Cedar Avenue, to Riverside, to 27th Avenue South to 26th Street; and

- A line on 1st Avenue (Marquette), to Grant, to Nicollet, to 31st.

The ordinance stipulated that all lines were to be standard gauge (4 feet 8½ inches), double-tracked, and constructed to "high standards."

Meanwhile, city leaders in St. Paul, aware of the potential benefits of electric operation, began talks with St. Paul City Railway officials about converting to electric power, even though the two cable lines had been in service for little more than a year. Archbishop John Ireland met personally with Thomas Lowry in early 1889 and urged him to build several electric lines. Lowry was not enthusiastic, offering concerns that electric operation had not been perfected. He was further troubled by the large investment already made in the cable system and the prospect of similar large investments in the proposed Minneapolis cable lines. Lowry agreed because competing interests had made offers to the city council, and, as in Minneapolis, he did not want to lose his franchise or face competition. In any event, he must have made a good bargain because the city agreed to a bonus payment up front to protect the railway from financial loss once construction began.

Two lines were to be built:

- A line from 7th and Wabasha Streets on 7th, to Oakland Avenue, to Grand Avenue as far west as Cleveland Avenue; and

On February 22, 1890, the first electric streetcars in St. Paul began service on Grand Avenue. Thomas Lowry and Archbishop John Ireland occupied the front seat of the first car in this ceremonial procession. Photograph by Eclipse View Co.; courtesy of the Minnesota Historical Society.

• A line from 4th and Wabasha Streets on 4th, to 7th Street and Randolph Avenue, continuing on Randolph to Cleveland Avenue.

Minneapolis officials were similarly interested in electricity because, as part of the order to construct the cable lines, they reserved the right to designate one of the existing horsecar lines for experimental conversion to electricity. As a measure of their seriousness, they demanded the company post a performance bond of $225,000 for the cable lines and $25,000 for the electric line, forfeitable to the city if for any reason the lines were not built as scheduled.

Both cities wanted to be rid of the horse. Word of Sprague's successes with electrification in Richmond no doubt spread, especially after Boston's West End Street Railway Company, then the largest horsecar operation in the country, committed to electrification in mid-1888.

In September 1889, barely two months after passing the cable ordinance, the Minneapolis City Council passed a resolution directing the Minneapolis Street Railway to construct an "experimental" electric line on 4th Avenue South. Thomson-Houston Electric Company subsequently offered a proposal to build a demonstration line at its expense, providing the Minneapolis Street Railway purchase the line if the demonstration proved successful. The railway accepted the proposal and work began at once.

The line opened on December 24, 1889. Enthusiasm for it was so high that the city substituted electricity for cable power in a new resolution dated January 17, 1890. A month later, on February 22, 1890, St. Paul's first electric line opened on Grand Avenue. Then in September 1890 the Minneapolis City Council passed an ordinance requiring the conversion of all horsecar lines to electric power, the St. Paul City Railway already having such authority.

In December 1890, the cities were joined when the "interurban" electric line began operation between the two cities via University Avenue. Two years later the horsecars were gone.

Neither Minneapolis nor St. Paul had the first electric operation in Minnesota. That honor goes to the tiny Stillwater Street Railway, which opened an electric line in June 1889. Never a success, the company was in receivership by 1893. It ended operations altogether

Cedar Avenue at 5th Street on the West Bank in Minneapolis in the 1890s. The landmark Dania Hall (destroyed by fire in 2000) is at the right. The early center poles supporting the overhead wires were replaced with poles on the sidewalks and span wires. Photograph courtesy of the Minnesota Historical Society.

5196. MINNEAPOLIS PUBLIC LIBRARY.

5196. PUBLIC LIBRARY BLD.

One of the early single-truck streetcars, yet to receive a state-mandated enclosed vestibule to protect the motorman from the elements, passes the original Minneapolis Public Library on Hennepin Avenue at 10th Street in the early 1890s. The library was demolished in the 1960s, and the site remains vacant to this day. Photograph courtesy of the Minnesota Historical Society.

sometime during 1897 and was subsequently dismantled for scrap.

Few events in Twin Cities history in the nineteenth century can compete in significance with the electrification of the street railway system and its subsequent effects on growth and development. From 1890 to 1920, where people lived and where they worked were determined by proximity to a streetcar line. It also should not be overlooked that the system was built and sustained with private capital, nor should the amount of the investment be thought insignificant.

Electrification required a complete write-off of the investment in the horsecar and cable railway systems long before that investment was depreciated or (in the case of the cable lines) the bonds paid off. The cars, the track, virtually the entire infrastructure were obsolete. Between 1889 and the completion of electrification in 1892, the two companies would spend $6 million (in 1890 dollars) on electrification and a complete rebuilding of the two systems, resulting in a doubling of track mileage.

Raising such a large amount of capital was no small challenge. At that time street railway companies were deemed speculative investments. The quality and surety of the investment depended largely on the credibility of management, the overall economic health of the community, and timing.

That was the difficult task before Thomas Lowry in early 1891 when he approached conservative New York bankers for funds to complete a rebuilding of the Minneapolis and St. Paul systems. Initially, they were unreceptive, concerned that the assets of the two separate companies were insufficient, but Lowry pushed the issue, persuading them to consider financing a merged system serving the populations of both cities. Out of this the Twin City Rapid Transit Company was incorporated in New Jersey in June of 1891. It would acquire all of the capital stock of the Minneapolis Street Railway Company and the St. Paul City Railway Company. Lowry got his funds, but he was a very lucky man. Two years later, the Panic of 1893 would have made financing impossible and swept away everything that he had struggled so hard to build.

More Tracks to More Places

2

Growing the System

GREATER PICTURES
ANY SEAT 10 CENTS!

Panic

The Aberdeen Hotel sat at the corner of Virginia Street and Dayton Avenue in St. Paul. The finest hotel in the city, it catered lavishly to the comings and goings of St. Paul's wealthiest citizens and visitors. On the evening of June 9, 1893, it hosted a banquet honoring James J. Hill, who had just completed his Great Northern Railway all the way to Puget Sound. Among the invited guests alighting from their carriages were Marshall Field, George Pullman, and Minnesota's first governor, Alexander Ramsey. It is not known whether Thomas Lowry was invited. Hill did not like speculators, and he once described Lowry as a "flamboyant plunger," undoubtedly because of Lowry's leveraged real estate adventures, not to mention that he was also president of the Minneapolis, St. Paul & Sault Ste. Marie Railway (the Soo Line), a Great Northern competitor. But if Lowry was not there, other notables were missing as well—namely, the New York financiers who provided funds to build Hill's railroad. They, like Lowry, were distracted by one of the great

financial disasters of the nineteenth century, the Panic of 1893.

Wall Street brokers and bankers usually get blamed for nineteenth-century panics. The country's economy was simpler then, with very little regulation of the financial markets or the banking industry: it was laissez-faire capitalism at its worst and best. In the blink of an eye, speculators could make, and then lose, great fortunes. In 1893, western states wanted cheap money and espoused the free coinage of silver. Eastern industrialists and bankers wanted a high, protectionist tariff and a gold standard. Both factions got what they wanted, but not what they expected.

The Sherman Silver Purchase Act of 1890 mandated that the U.S. Treasury buy 4.5 million ounces of silver per month, a move that pleased the western interests and increased the amount of money in circulation. At the same time, eastern industrialists backed the McKinley Tariff Act, also passed in 1890, to protect onshore industries. Politicians thought they had hit upon a splendid compromise. On the one hand, the tariff pumped money into the treasury, reducing government debt. But

The Masonic Temple, now the Hennepin Center for the Arts, and the West Hotel filled the block of Hennepin Avenue between 5th and 6th streets, the bustling heart of the "prairie metropolis" of Minneapolis.

on the other, it also reduced the amount of money in circulation.

Meanwhile, the treasury was busily buying silver with treasury notes (paper IOUs) redeemable in silver or gold. When foreign finance ministers and other "cynical" holders of government debt caught on and demanded payment in gold, there was a raid on the treasury's gold reserve. By statute that reserve had to be maintained at a minimum of $100 million to protect the value of the nation's currency and credit. When it was breached in April 1893, the

bubble burst and the banking system collapsed. There was no money and no credit. Some 8,000 businesses went broke and shuttered their doors, 156 railroads fell into receivership, and 400 banks folded. A million people were out of work, roughly 10 percent of the workforce. Worse, there was no Federal Reserve Bank to manage the crisis, and as more businesses and banks failed, the money supply contracted even further. The economy was in shambles. There would be nothing like it until the crash of 1929.

Lowry faced ruin. Although he was a

wealthy man, with investments in banking and substantial land and property holdings, his personal assets were heavily encumbered and tied to the fortunes of TCRT. He had also invested in the schemes of Louis Menage, a local promoter and developer, and served as a vice president in several of Menage's companies. Menage went bankrupt and fled to Guatemala, deserting Lowry and other investors.

There were other embarrassments. Lowry was a partner in the Minneapolis Stockyards and Packing Company, which went under. Another investment, the new West Hotel, was in trouble. Worse, Lowry owed large sums to the

This Lake Minnetonka car is deadheading back to East Side Station. It is just gaining the east bank of the Mississippi River after crossing Nicollet Island.

Northwestern National Bank, where he served on the board of directors. Most at risk was TCRT. Before the panic Lowry concluded a $2 million loan with Kuhn, Loeb & Company. The loan was repayable in installments of $250,000 in 1895, 1896, and 1897, with a balloon payment of $1,200,000 in 1898. With all of TCRT as security, default of a single payment meant loss of the company and with it Lowry's entire fortune.

There were other complications. The bicycle became popular and people turned to it in large numbers, further driving down TCRT revenues. Net earnings in 1893 were $116,000, down from $241,000 the year before, not enough to meet the loan payments.

Lowry struggled. There was no chance for a fare increase to cover expenses because franchise agreements fixed the fare at a nickel. The only alternative was to cut costs. Calvin Goodrich, TCRT's general manager, ordered employee wages reduced 10 percent. Service was trimmed, despite public complaints, with overall car mileage cut by 12 percent. When these measures were not enough, layoffs were ordered in all departments. The result in 1894 was a $367,000 reduction in operating expenses and a $105,000 improvement in earnings; 1895 brought $103,000 in savings and a further $28,000 increase in earnings. That year, in another effort to strengthen his financial position and TCRT, Lowry successfully wooed British capitalists seeking control of the Pillsbury and Washburn flour mills to build a dam below St. Anthony Falls to generate electricity for the streetcar system. Lowry reasoned the dam would have the capacity to power the cars with enough left over to sell to local industries. He had proposed to pay $91,000 a year to lease the waterpower rights and recover that expense by selling the excess capacity for additional income. He would get cheap power, and someone else would pay for it. While the concept was sound and Lowry signed the lease on December 5, 1896, the desired outcome proved elusive, because TCRT's own power needs jumped dramatically in the next few years.

Lowry's next great coup was persuading these same investors to put up $1,130,000 in exchange for equal shares of 7 percent TCRT preferred stock. To make his case, Lowry used two reports from Frank Trumbull, a highly respected consulting engineer. Kuhn, Loeb commissioned Trumbull to evaluate the TCRT system and its operations. They were heavily invested in TCRT and wanted comfort with their investment. Trumbull's 1893 report was favorable, as was a second report published in 1894. Wisely, Lowry used both reports to convince them.

TCRT's recovery assured its reputation for sound management. In 1895, it made a 7 percent dividend payment on its preferred stock and would continue making payments. Moreover, its common stock began paying annual dividends in 1899, establishing a record of unbroken dividends that would continue until the Great Depression.

Growth and Prosperity

The next twenty-five years were the heyday of the streetcar in the Twin Cities, and they produced some altogether incredible statistics. By 1910, 510,000 people lived in Minneapolis and St. Paul, 212,000 more than in 1890, nearly doubling the developed areas in both cities. Many were recent immigrants.

Others came from eastern states and cities, attracted by jobs and business opportunities. Economic activity exploded. St. Paul banks cleared $56 million in financial transactions in 1880 and $560 million in 1910. Minneapolis banks reported $10 million cleared in 1880 and a staggering $1 billion in 1910. This era saw the rise of the department store, and downtown retailing prospered. Dayton's opened in 1901 at 7th Street and Nicollet Avenue. Donaldson's Glass Block added 350,000 square feet, taking in half a square block. Power's Dry Goods rebuilt its store at 5th Street and Nicollet Avenue in 1905–6. The same happened in St. Paul as

Hennepin Avenue was deserted in 1905 as a car stops to unload a couple of passengers at the Plaza Hotel, across from Loring Park. Lyndale Avenue approaches at left. The hotel has been replaced by Interstate 94 and the portal of the Lowry Hill Tunnel. Photograph by Charles J. Hibbard; courtesy of the Minnesota Historical Society.

Schuneman's, the Emporium, and the Golden Rule built new stores.

At a time when 76 percent of all ton-miles moved by rail, Minneapolis and St. Paul were one of the top ten rail centers in the nation. Minneapolis hosted corporate headquarters for the Soo Line and the Minneapolis & St. Louis. St. Paul was home to the Great Northern, the Northern Pacific, and the Chicago, St. Paul, Minneapolis & Omaha. The Great Northern and the Northern Pacific dominated passenger and freight traffic from the Twin Cities across North Dakota and Montana and on to the ports of Seattle and Portland. The Milwaukee Road (the Chicago, Milwaukee & St. Paul Railroad) and the Soo Line only feebly challenged them for western business. The former, in what proved to be a very unwise move, built to the Pacific in

the first decade of the twentieth century only to find itself overbuilt and bankrupt by 1925. The Soo Line wisely forged connections with the Canadian Pacific at Portal, North Dakota, sending its Pacific-bound traffic via Canadian Pacific rails to the port of Vancouver. Other midwestern roads—the Chicago & NorthWestern, the Chicago, Burlington & Quincy, the Rock Island, the Chicago Great Western, and the

The Twin City Rapid Transit Company ran scheduled sightseeing streetcars that toured both cities. One passes the Minneapolis Union Depot, which hosted trains of the Great Northern, Northern Pacific, Chicago Great Western, Chicago & North Western, Minneapolis & St. Louis, and Wisconsin Central. Located at the foot of Hennepin Avenue by the Mississippi River, it was replaced in 1914 by the larger Great Northern Depot across the street. The High Street loop, terminus for certain cars ending downtown, diverges at the right. Today's vestige of High Street is the traffic signal leading to the loading docks behind the main U.S. Post Office on 1st Street. Photograph by Charles J. Hibbard; courtesy of the Minnesota Historical Society.

Minneapolis & St. Louis—served markets to the east and south, connecting the Twin Cities with Chicago, Omaha, St. Louis, and Kansas City. Before there were paved roads, this rail network moved most of the freight and passenger traffic from farms and rural communities to larger urban centers.

The Twin Cities hosted two-thirds of all manufacturing jobs in the Upper Midwest and dominated roughly 55 percent of all the busi-

ness activity in the region. As the economy grew so did the boundaries of the developed area. Office buildings, hotels, banks, retail establishments, theaters, and factories gradually displaced residences near the downtown areas. Schools, hospitals, and libraries sprouted to serve the growing population. The University of Minnesota attracted students from across the state and the region. Park systems took form along the Mississippi River and around Lakes Phalen, Como, Cedar, Isles, Calhoun, Harriet, and Nokomis.

By the end of the 1920s, residential growth in Minneapolis had filled in all the way to 50th Street on the south, the Camden–Northeast–St. Anthony neighborhoods on the north, the France Avenue–Morningside–Bryn Mawr areas on the west, and the Mississippi River Parkway on the east. In St. Paul, the Midway area was largely filled in, as were the neighborhoods in and around Como Park, St. Anthony Park, and Macalester College. Residential neighborhoods extended along Summit, Grand, St. Clair, and Randolph Avenues all the way to the Mississippi River. The east side and the area up to the West St. Paul city limits at Annapolis Street were built up.

Suburban development was well under way. Hundreds of worker residences went up in South St. Paul, which had become the largest meat processor and livestock market west of Chicago. Robbinsdale and Columbia Heights attracted families and smaller middle-income residences, as did St. Louis Park and Hopkins. Streetcars served all of these neighborhoods and communities.

This growth, along with the relative scarcity of automobiles and the absence of paved roads, provided a strong traffic base for TCRT well into the 1920s. A major expansion of the system got under way once the Panic of 1893 receded and business conditions improved. Track mileage jumped from 224 in 1894, the year after the Panic of 1893, to 523 in 1931, early in the Great Depression. Three new intercity lines joined the Interurban. They were the Como–Harriet, opening in 1898; the Selby–Lake, opening in 1906; and the Snelling–Minnehaha line, which linked downtown Minneapolis and St. Paul via Minnehaha Park and Ft. Snelling. It opened in 1909. There were also new lines to Lake Minnetonka and Stillwater.

To speed up service on the new Selby–Lake intercity line, TCRT determined it should replace the last vestige of its cable railways with a tunnel through Selby Hill. Until 1891, Selby Avenue had been entirely a cable car operation from downtown St. Paul all the way to Fairview Avenue. The segment between Chatsworth and Fairview was electrified that year as part of an extension to Merriam Park. In 1898, the remainder of the line was electrified except for a portion that was retained and rebuilt with a counterweight system that used cable cars to assist streetcars up the 16 percent grade of Selby Hill between Pleasant and Summit Avenues. This system proved slow and expensive, and it was decided to proceed with a tunnel. Work began in 1906. By the time it was finished and opened for service, TCRT had exchanged $366,000 (1906 dollars) for the removal of 43,200 cubic yards of dirt and 2,100 yards of rock, as well as the purchase of 164 tons of steel rods and 12,000 barrels of cement. The result was a bore 1,500 feet long and fifty feet deep at its lowest point. The grade on Selby Hill was cut to 7 percent

These improvements allowed TCRT to better accommodate the thousands of new riders

Lake Street was still unpaved in 1906 as a car on the newly opened Selby–Lake line heads east toward St. Paul, crossing the Bryant line at Lyndale Avenue. Several buildings in this photograph are still standing. At this time, most power and telephone lines were above ground, creating a visual blight. Photograph courtesy of the Minnesota Historical Society.

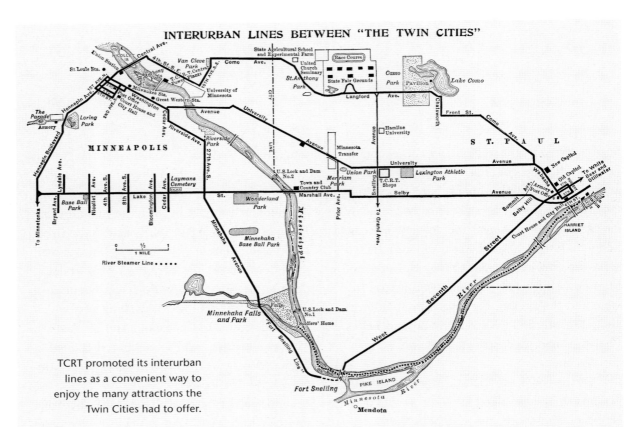

INTERURBAN LINES BETWEEN "THE TWIN CITIES"

TCRT promoted its interurban lines as a convenient way to enjoy the many attractions the Twin Cities had to offer.

More Tracks to More Places

that crowded its cars every day. Fifty-three million people rode the streetcars in 1900. By 1920, there were 238 million, a fourfold increase. Fares stayed relatively constant: a nickel in 1900 and six cents in 1921. The main traffic generators were in or near downtown Minneapolis and St. Paul, where most people worked and the major retail establishments, theaters, hotels, railroad stations, and hospitals were located. There was another strong traffic base near the city limits of Minneapolis on University Avenue extending along University through the Midway district of St. Paul. This strip hosted many manufacturing establishments whose workers rode the St. Paul–Minneapolis interurban streetcar. The Interurban also served the Minneapolis campus of the University of Minnesota. It was the busiest line in the system and, even today, is the busiest local bus line for Metro Transit and the likeliest route of the next light-rail line. The Interurban was so successful that the railroads, which were operating steam-powered commuter trains between Minneapolis and St. Paul, discontinued them shortly after it opened in December 1890.

Recreation also brought riders. There were baseball games at Nicollet Park in Minneapolis and Lexington Park in St. Paul. The rivalry between the two cities carried over into a heady competition between the Minneapolis Millers and the St. Paul Saints. TCRT really cleaned up when the teams played doubleheaders in both

Cars passed close by the Round Tower, one of the few surviving original structures of Ft. Snelling.

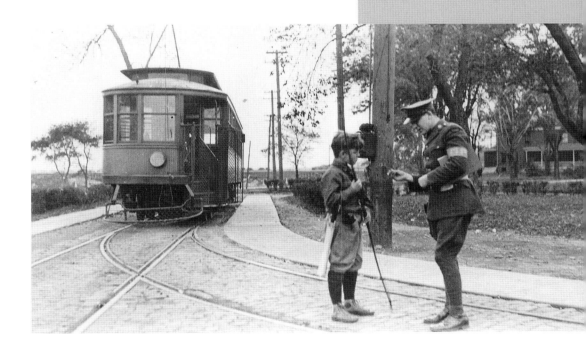

The double-ended Ft. Snelling shuttle car waits for its Minneapolis and St. Paul connections at the Ft. Snelling wye. The Mendota Bridge is visible in the background.

This site now lies within the replicated walls of the historic fort. Photograph by John W. G. Dunn; courtesy of the Minnesota Historical Society.

Como and Phalen Parks in St. Paul. The streetcar company sponsored evening band concerts at Lake Harriet. Visitors to the Twin Cities could tour the cities on a sightseeing car. Late in the summer the Minnesota State Fair attracted thousands upon thousands of riders to the streetcars. So many were pressed into service to handle the crowds that TCRT constructed special passenger facilities at the fairgrounds and a large yard to store streetcars between runs.

More Electric Power for a Growing System

In 1900, this small wood depot was constructed at 42nd Street and Queen Avenue next to Lake Harriet to serve the residential Linden Hills neighborhood. It was replaced in 1914 by a much larger chalet-style building by architect Harry Wild Jones. The 1900 depot was sold to the Park Board and moved to the lakeshore south of 42nd Street, where it served as a boat rental office. It was moved again next to the refectory and finally demolished in the 1950s. The Minnesota Streetcar Museum replicated it on its original site, where passengers may now board historic streetcars operating on a remnant of the Como–Harriet line. Photograph courtesy of the Minnesota Historical Society.

parks on the same day. On summer weekends thousands of people took the streetcars to Lake Minnetonka or to Wildwood Amusement Park on White Bear Lake, while others picnicked at

TCRT's expanding system needed more electric power. Two small plants were originally put in service at the start of electric

The Detroit Publishing Company took this view of the Como Park Station and published it as a postcard. Seen from Lexington Avenue, most of the infrastructure remains in place today, more than fifty years after the last streetcar departed. Photograph courtesy of the Library of Congress.

In 1917, Robbinsdale was still separated from the city by open country, and West Broadway was subject to drifting snow.

operations in 1889. In Minneapolis a simple 250-horsepower steam plant drove three 80-horsepower generators located in a building at 5th Avenue South and 1st Street. A similar installation in St. Paul at the St. Paul Gas Light Company powered the St. Paul lines. By the 1920s, with more than nine hundred cars in operation during peak hours, the power and distribution system had grown to include a large main steam plant, two hydro stations at St. Anthony Falls, multiple substations, and hundreds of miles of overhead and underground cables.

In 1890, the first large power station in Minneapolis was installed at 3rd Avenue North and 2nd Street North in a building that housed the company's general offices and a carhouse, a structure that stands today. The plant was steam powered and generated 2,955 kilowatts of direct current electricity that was fed directly to the trolley lines. A short section of underground conduit and feeder cable was laid from the plant along 3rd Avenue North, Washington Avenue South, and 1st Avenue South. A tunnel carried water for the boilers from the Mississippi River to the plant

A second power station opened in 1892 at 31st Street and Nicollet Avenue in Minneapolis. This was the site of the former roundhouse and shops of the Minneapolis, Lyndale & Minnetonka Railway, which TCRT had acquired a few years before. With electrification the facility became a carhouse and maintenance shop. The station generated 2,500 kilowatts of direct cur-

rent fed directly to the trolley wires, supplying the needs of all lines south of Washington Avenue and east of Nicollet. A powerhouse at West 3rd Street (now Kellogg Boulevard) and Hill Street fed the St. Paul system. It opened in 1891, replacing the first installation at the St. Paul Gas Light Company.

Lowry's 1896 contract with the St. Anthony Falls Water Power Company resulted in a dam and hydroelectric plant that produced alternating current at 3,450 volts, which was stepped up to 12,000 volts for long-distance transmission. Two smaller direct current generators were installed in the same building to directly feed some of the close-in car lines.

This 1885 building on 3rd Avenue North at 2nd Street was originally a horsecar barn and shop. It was intended to be the powerhouse for the never-built cable car system but instead became an electric carhouse and the first streetcar powerhouse in 1890, as well as the main offices of the Minneapolis Street Railway. By 1904, its powerhouse had been displaced by the Main Steam Station, and the general offices of TCRT had moved to the new office building at 11th Street and Hennepin Avenue. The building was sold soon thereafter, but survives today.

The Minnesota State Fair

TCRT loved special events. They brought in additional revenues and used equipment that might otherwise sit idle. Those coinciding with rush hours presented more of a challenge because cars and crews had to be stretched to meet the extra demand, but TCRT never turned away the business. Motormen and conductors never complained because the extra hours meant fatter paychecks. Besides the baseball extras for the Millers and Saints, there were Gopher football at the University of Minnesota, band concerts at Lake Harriet, the Shrine Circus, the Minneapolis Aquatennial, the St. Paul Winter Carnival, and Fourth of July fireworks at Powderhorn Park. There were church extras on Sundays and on Christmas Eve, as well as extras for cemetery observances on Decoration Day (known officially as Memorial Day after 1967). New Year's Eve brought out extra cars at midnight to take revelers home from the downtown bars and restaurants.

None of these events was as big as the Minnesota State Fair, however, or required as many extra cars and crews. For ten straight days through Labor Day, more than a hundred additional cars might be scheduled during off-peak hours. And that was just on the Como–Harriet–Hopkins and Snelling lines that directly served the fairgrounds. More cars were added to other lines to handle additional riders, especially on weekends and on the Labor Day holiday. Even after World War II, as automobile ownership grew, people continued to go

Streetcar service to the State Fair ended in 1953. Photograph by John Runk; courtesy of the Minnesota Historical Society.

to the fair by streetcar. It was almost as traditional as the fair itself and easily as enjoyable.

Service to the fairgrounds opened in 1898 with completion of the Como–Harriet line between downtown Minneapolis and St. Paul. Two storage yards and turning loops were built during 1904 on the fairgrounds in an area east of what is now the Coliseum. Separate loops and boarding areas were set up for cars going to and from Minneapolis and St. Paul. The storage yards, each with five tracks, were located within each loop. As an example, an extra car coming from Minneapolis would go into the Minneapolis loop, unload its passengers, continue around the loop to the yard lead, then back into one of the five yard storage tracks and wait there until it was called on for another trip. Como–Harriet cars running between Minneapolis and St. Paul would swing into the fairgrounds to drop off and pick up passengers and continue on to either city. In downtown St. Paul, fairgrounds cars would follow the Wabasha–5th–Robert St. route to turn around and return to the fair. Some Minneapolis extras would carry "Loop" signs and return via Hennepin, 1st Street North, 1st Avenue North to Hawthorne, then via 11th Street back to Hennepin Avenue and another trip to the fairgrounds. Still others might carry Oak–Harriet or Como–Harriet

In the late 1940s, fairgoers pour off the cars. Photograph courtesy of the Minnesota Historical Society.

Three substations were constructed at other locations to take the high-voltage alternating current and convert it to 600-volt direct current for the overhead trolley wires. Two of these substations were in Minneapolis: one in the original steam plant at 3rd Avenue North and 2nd Street; the other at 31st and Nicollet. A third was located at the Hill Street power plant in St. Paul.

The company wanted to make the three original steam plants backup units when these improvements were finished in 1897, but the demand for electric power was so high that it could not do so immediately, and all three

signs and run through downtown and out to southwest Minneapolis.

District supervisors were assigned to the fairgrounds to keep things moving. They were in regular contact by company telephone with station foremen at the Snelling, East Side, and Duluth Avenue carhouses to call out extra cars if they were needed. On very heavy days, North Side, Nicollet, and Lake Street cars would be called on to accommodate the crowds. Besides the supervisors, switchmen were stationed in the storage yards to line up switches so that cars could be directed to the proper tracks. Fare collectors were on the platforms to assist conductors in making change, collecting fares, and issuing transfers. The mechanical and overhead departments had crews and equipment at the fairgrounds in case they were needed. A breakdown or delay of any kind could be a disaster. TCRT even brought out a car, usually 1136, an original gate car that had never been modified with a front exit, for use as a supervisor–cashier's office.

Business slipped somewhat in the early 1950s, following the systemwide trend of declining ridership. The 1952 fair was the last one for streetcar service from both Minneapolis and St. Paul. The Como–Harriet intercity line was cut back to the

city limits at Eustis Street in July 1953. Passengers were then required to transfer to a Como–Stryker bus for the remainder of their trip into St. Paul. Track, however, was kept in place from Eustis Street to the fairgrounds, and Minneapolis cars were run through for the 1953 fair. All St. Paul service was provided by bus. Rail operations ended in Minneapolis in June 1954 and, with it, streetcar service to the Minnesota State Fair.

Streetcars served the Minnesota State Fair from 1898 to 1953 and carried the great majority of fairgoers. They were staged for the return trip in two large holding yards, one for Minneapolis and the other for St. Paul. Each city had its own boarding area and return loop to Como Avenue. The Grandstand, advertising "War of Nations To-night," has changed little since this photograph was taken around 1910.

were kept in service until the new Main Steam Station opened near St. Anthony Falls on the Mississippi River in 1904. This increase in electrical demand, despite the Panic of 1893 and the resulting economic depression, shows the strong connection between the expansion of the street railway system and the overall population and economic growth of the Twin Cities. By 1906, TCRT was generating 14,000 kilowatts of electricity at the Main Steam Station compared to the 3,500 kilowatts produced in 1889. In 1903 and 1904, the company spent almost $3 million on improvements to its power generation and distribution systems.

Construction on the new plant began in 1902. It would be TCRT's largest capital investment to date and represent a nearly tenfold expansion in generating capacity over the small plants that electrified the system fifteen years before. The building sat next to the St. Anthony

Water Power Station at 6th Avenue Southeast and the Mississippi River adjoining the Stone Arch Bridge. It was designed by Sargent and Lundy of Chicago and F. S. Pearson and built of brick on a limestone foundation. General Electric, Allis-Chalmers, and Babcock & Wilcox supplied generation equipment. The plant burned coal, which was brought in by rail and stored outside the plant. A conveyor system moved the coal inside, where it was crushed and fed to the boilers by automatic stokers. Improvements continued with the installation of steam turbines and turbo generators between 1907 and 1917. By 1917, the plant reached a capacity of 74,000 kilowatts of electricity, supplying power for the streetcar system as well as all of the company's shop and office buildings. Much modified, it remains in operation today as a steam plant for the University of Minnesota campus.

By 1910, all of the smaller inefficient plants were gone, and the power system looked much as it would at the end of streetcar operations in 1954. The two plants in Minneapolis (on 3rd Avenue North and at 31st and Nicollet) were closed, as was the Hill Street plant in St. Paul. Another plant in North St. Paul—acquired with the 1899 purchase of the St. Paul & Suburban Railway—was taken out of service along with a small facility at Wildwood, which had been built to handle the Stillwater extension. In addition, a small plant at Aurora and Dale in St. Paul was also closed. It had originally powered the Selby Avenue cable line but was temporarily converted to generate electricity when the company needed more capacity. The Main Steam Station, the St. Anthony waterpower plant, and a new waterpower plant on Hennepin Island remained (the last facility opened in 1908).

As part of the expansion, TCRT constructed a series of substations to convert the high-voltage alternating current to 600-volt direct current for the overhead trolley wires. These were cement brick buildings approximately fifty feet square, each containing several rotary converters.

The substations were as follows:

Minneapolis

- 11th Street and Hennepin Avenue (in the main office building)
- Lower Dam (in the waterpower station)
- Chicago Avenue and Lake Street
- Lowry Avenue and 3rd Street North (this building stands today)
- 4th Street and 2nd Avenue Southeast
- 27th Avenue South and 29th Street
- Girard Avenue and Lake Street

St. Paul

- College Avenue and Wabasha Street (in the St. Paul office building)
- East 7th and Hope Streets

These are rotary converters in the substation at 11th Street and Hennepin Avenue in Minneapolis. Alternating current from the Main Steam Station powered these units, which in turn supplied the 600-volt direct current to the overhead trolley wires. Photograph courtesy of Charles Camitsch.

The Minneapolis office building of Twin City Rapid Transit Company at 11th Street and Hennepin Avenue. Photograph by Sweet; courtesy of the Minnesota Historical Society.

- Snelling and University Avenues (in the Snelling carhouse)
- Concord and Isabel Streets (opened in 1917)

Suburban

- Wildwood (adjoining Wildwood Amusement Park on White Bear Lake)
- Stillwater (Owen Street; this building was still standing in 2005)
- Hopkins (Washington Avenue and 3rd Street)
- Excelsior (Division Street)

Terminal Houses

(These buildings contained equipment for switching high-voltage power to and from overhead transmission lines and to and from underground cables.)

- Como Terminal House (21st Avenue Southeast and Talmadge Avenue)
- Wildwood Terminal House (adjoining Wildwood Park)
- Harriet Terminal House (private right of way and Upton Avenue South)

Every electric substation in the system had a control panel like the one shown here at 11th Street and Hennepin Avenue in Minneapolis. From here substation operators controlled the rotary converters and routed power to the circuits that fed the overhead trolley wires. Photograph courtesy of Charles Camitsch.

TRANSMISSION LINES AND TROLLEY WIRES

By the close of the 1920s, some two hundred miles of underground cables and three hundred miles of overhead feeders carried electric power around the system. The underground cables were large-diameter wires bundled together and wrapped in thick insulation, which were then routed through a concrete conduit buried several feet below the street. Multiple

cables usually occupied a single conduit. Manholes at regular intervals gave access for maintenance. Underground cables transmitted the high-voltage alternating currents from the generators to the substations. Because underground construction was expensive and difficult to maintain, high-voltage lines, outside the downtown areas, were usually strung aboveground on cross arms fastened to the same poles that anchored the trolley support (span) and contact wires. These poles also carried the direct current feeder cables from the substations. At 500- to 1,000-foot intervals, the direct current feeders were hooked to the trolley contact wires through circuit breakers that could be opened to interrupt the flow of electric current.

TCRT at first suspended its overhead wires from ornamental poles placed in the middle of the street. These became traffic hazards, and they were replaced by capped iron poles set at the curb on both sides of the street. The span wires were strung across the street between them. The trolley contact wire was suspended from the span wires on insulated fittings called hangers. At intersections where tracks curved or where two lines crossed, special fittings and an elaborate web of wires called pull-offs kept the trolley wire in line above the tracks.

Along private right of way, TCRT commonly used cedar poles. It also experimented with concrete poles and installed a number of them along West Lake Street on the St. Louis Park line. In the downtown areas, span wires were usually anchored to adjoining buildings to

Typical conditions inside one of the early carhouses in St. Paul in the 1890s. They were wood structures, prone to fires, and TCRT replaced most of them by 1915 with much larger, fireproof buildings.

This south Minneapolis view, looking north on Minnehaha Avenue at 37th Street around 1905, illustrates the strengths of the street railway: it served growing new neighborhoods and was immune to the mud that mired all competitors. Photograph courtesy of the Minnesota Historical Society.

The switch rod, demonstrated here, was used to pry over the single-point switch, permitting a streetcar to change tracks. Photograph from the *Minneapolis Journal*; courtesy of the Minnesota Historical Society.

minimize the visual clutter. Section insulators in the overhead wire isolated one trolley circuit from another. Special protective devices such as lightning arrestors and surge protectors were installed in the overhead lines.

At busy track intersections, where routes diverged, a contactor on the trolley wire controlled the position of an electric track switch in the street. Motormen approaching these intersections had to take special care. If the controller was open and the car under power, the contactor would activate the track switch and send the car through the switch on a diverging route. If the controller was closed and the power turned off, the car would coast straight through the intersection. Signs were suspended from the span wires alerting motormen to the locations of these switches.

A special, electrified trolley guard (resembling a fishnet) was hung above the trolley wire at railroad grade crossings. This was an important safety feature. Motormen had to stop and make sure the tracks were clear and no train was approaching before proceeding. The guard kept the trolley wheel in place as the car crossed over the tracks.

A load dispatcher managed the power distribution system from the Main Steam Station, and all the substations had an operator who was responsible for maintaining the rotary converters and other equipment. A private telephone system tied everything together: the substations with the Main Steam Station and the carhouses with the general offices in Minneapolis and the St. Paul division offices on College Avenue and Wabasha Street in St. Paul. Call boxes were placed strategically throughout the system for motormen to call in and report problems.

Making Tracks

The larger streetcars that were put in service after electrification required a complete rebuilding of every mile of track in the system. Horsecar track, built to a gauge of 3 feet 6 inches, was ripped out, replaced by heavier rail set to the standard 4 foot 8½-inch standard gauge. Later, when the cities began paving streets, this track had to be taken up and relaid in the newly paved surface, all at TCRT's expense. The company's franchise agreement

When streetcars crossed railroad tracks, they often did so on a single track. This minimized the cost of maintaining and replacing the crossing diamonds, which was TCRT's responsibility because the railroad had arrived first. To prevent a de-wirement that could stall a streetcar on the crossing, an electrically charged wire trough was hung around the overhead wire. Even if the pole came off the wire, the car would still draw power and clear the crossing. This is the Camden neighborhood in north Minneapolis, where the Soo Line Railroad crossed Lyndale Avenue. Photograph by the *Minneapolis Star-Journal*; courtesy of the Minnesota Historical Society.

Early track was constructed to low standards—basically, laid in the dirt—and would be replaced by something much more solid and permanent. The St. Louis Park line was eventually double-tracked near the north shore of Lake Calhoun, which in 1902 was lined with icehouses. Photograph courtesy of the Minnesota Historical Society.

Workers filling potholes in the middle of Wabasha Street at Fillmore Avenue on St. Paul's West Side in 1912 were untroubled by traffic. The landmark bluff stair tower, still standing, is visible in the distance at right behind a street pole.

neers objected, pointing out that asphalt would eventually break up unless it had a firm foundation. The city ignored the advice and went ahead with the project. Once again the track was taken up and replaced. This time the rails were set on wooden ties spaced ten feet apart. The ties rested on a solid foundation of Portland cement with yet another layer of cement poured between the rails. Granite pavers were set alongside the rails and a layer of asphalt poured over the cement foundation. Forty-some miles of track were renewed at a cost of $34,000 per mile. Unfortunately, this method of construction turned out to be a costly failure. As predicted, the asphalt broke up after just a few years because it had no foundation. Moisture seeped in, and the freeze-thaw cycle did the rest. The streetcar tracks fared better because they had a cement foundation, but the rest of the streets became honeycombed with cracks,

with the city made it responsible for maintaining the portion of the street on which its tracks were laid plus two feet on either side of the outermost rails.

Before 1896, paving meant nothing more than wooden blocks set on pine boards or granite blocks on a sand base. When this proved unsuccessful, Minneapolis decided to try asphalt in the downtown business district. TCRT engi-

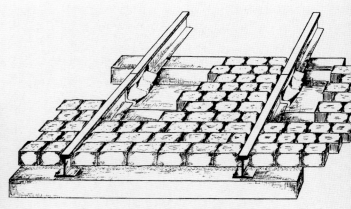

Track construction in downtown Minneapolis on 2nd Avenue South at 5th Street. Girder rails with built-in flangeways were spiked to wood ties on a gravel base, and then covered with concrete and granite Belgian blocks. Drawing is reprinted from *The Electric Railways of Minnesota*; courtesy of Russell L. Olson.

which turned into huge potholes. The city may have learned an expensive lesson, but TCRT ended up with a large chunk of the tab because, once again, it had to pull up its tracks and completely rebuild them.

Between 1896 and 1909, TCRT adopted new construction standards and improved methods to accommodate its larger, heavier, home-built streetcars. The result was a track structure that was not only the most expensive of any street railway system in the country but also the most durable. Most of TCRT's track lasted until the end of the streetcar era in 1954. Even today, hundreds of miles of track in Minneapolis and St. Paul lie buried under asphalt paving.

The track structure was put down in layers. First came the subgrade, which had to be solid and perfectly level. Then came six inches of crushed rock ballast compacted by steamrollers. The ballast supported the ties and provided drainage. White oak ties, six inches by eight inches by eight feet were set upon the ballast on two-foot centers. Sections of ninety-pound T rail rested on the ties and were spiked into place. (Note: Rail weight by the yard is a measure of the ability of the rail to withstand loads. The heavier the rail, the heavier the load it can carry. Much of TCRT's early track was forty to sixty pounds per yard. Some rail installed in later years, in downtown Minneapolis and St. Paul, weighed as much as 120 pounds per yard.)

Rail sections were welded together in a thermite process involving the mixing of aluminum and iron oxide in a mold or casting placed between the ends of each section. The resulting high temperatures fused the ends of the rails together. Rail welding provided for two things:

a smoother ride and a continuous ground, or return circuit, for the electric current.

The space between the ties was filled with six inches of cement (up to the level of the ties). Cut granite blocks (resting on an inch of sand) were put in place between the rails of each track and between double tracks and then grouted with cement. Paving brick was laid two feet on either side of the outermost rails and similarly grouted in place. In some locations, particularly new construction in later years, the granite blocks were not used and cement was simply poured all the way to the top of the rail. This method was probably cheaper and proved equally durable, especially when street improvements were made to accommodate automobile traffic.

The company priced the cost of its improved construction at $12.00 per running foot of double track or $60,000 per mile (in 1910

When the Selby Avenue cable line was electrified in 1898, a counterweight cable system was installed on Selby Hill, which was still too steep for streetcars to climb. Cable-powered counterweight cars, converted from former cable grip cars, assisted the electrics up and down the hill until the Selby Tunnel was completed in 1907.

The Selby Tunnel reduced the Selby Hill grade from 16 percent to 7 percent. The Cathedral of St. Paul looms in the background. The abandoned lower tunnel portal survives intact today.

dollars). Street intersections where car lines crossed or diverged were even more expensive. This "special work" included such things as crossing frogs (where pairs of rails met and crossed at right angles in the middle of an intersection), turnouts (track switches embedded in the street that allowed cars to take a different route), and grooved girder rail (used on curves and in switches wherever cars made sharp turns). Most special work was prefabricated in castings of hardened alloy steel. Curved girder rail was usually bent to the required angle before installation.

Shops and an Expanding System
SHOPS IN TRANSITION

For more than fifty years the Twin Cities street railway system distinguished itself among its peers. Not even larger systems, like Chicago or New York, could compete with its levels of service or the superb condition of its track, power system, and fixed facilities. But it was the streetcars that attracted the most attention and drew the greatest praise because they were so visible, so many people rode them, and they were so superbly maintained. All of them were built in the company shops to a standard design that was replicated more than a thousand times. The quality of work in these shops was such that streetcars built in 1906 were still running on the last day of service in 1954.

At the end of the horsecar era, TCRT owned seventeen buildings and stables, eleven in Minneapolis and six in St. Paul. There were also two cable carhouses in St. Paul and the former shops of the Motor Line at 31st Street and Nicollet Avenue (the latter were acquired with the purchase of the Motor Line in 1887). Four of the horsecar barns in Minneapolis were retained and converted to electric cars, including the building at 3rd Avenue North, which housed the main office and shops. Two St. Paul horsecar barns were retained and converted, as were the East 7th Street and Selby Avenue cable shops.

Major improvements to accommodate electric cars were made at the site of the Motor Line

Leaving the original Motor Line roundhouse along the Blaisdell Avenue side of the property, TCRT built the 31st Street Station and Shops along Nicollet Avenue. From 1898 to 1907, this facility manufactured the first 535 home-designed streetcars, twenty-two work cars, and six Lake Minnetonka express boats. Photograph by Edmund A. Brush; courtesy of the Minnesota Historical Society.

When the Minneapolis Street Railway purchased the Motor Line, it inherited this roundhouse at 31st Street and Blaisdell Avenue. Pressed into service for electric car storage and servicing, the facility was awkward at best. A separate carhouse, 31st Street Station, was built on the property in 1892, enlarged in 1898, and replaced with the new Nicollet Station in 1912. In 1916, much of the roundhouse was demolished. Photograph courtesy of the Minnesota Historical Society.

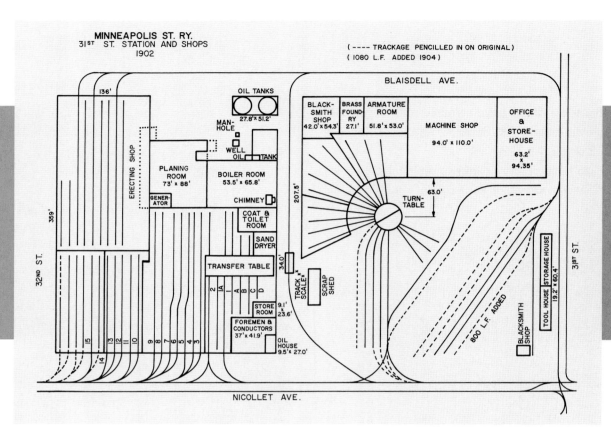

shops. In 1890, TCRT added an office–store-house building on the northwest corner at 31st and Blaisdell. In 1891, a fifty-car carhouse was constructed on the southeast corner, and the former roundhouse, left over from the Motor Line, was remodeled into a large general repair shop. Finally, in 1898, the company added an erecting shop on the southwest corner. That shop could build an entire streetcar or repair any of the rolling stock in the system. From 1898 to 1907, it built 535 streetcars, twenty-two work cars, and six Lake Minnetonka express boats. The new facilities were renamed 31st Street Station and Shops.

Three new carhouses built specifically for electric cars opened in 1891: East Minneapolis Station (East Side Station) on 1st Avenue Northeast between University Avenue and 4th Street Northeast, Bloomington Station on Bloomington Avenue and 32nd Street, and Midway Station on University Avenue, just east of Raymond

Avenue in St. Paul. The latter served the new interurban line on University that linked downtown Minneapolis and St. Paul.

East Side Station was the largest of the three and the largest in the system (at that time), with thirty tracks, all of them under roof, and a capacity of 150 cars. Its location, close to downtown Minneapolis, and its size combined to make for an efficient operation. Cars pulling out or in from East Side could access all of the major lines in Minneapolis with a minimum of "deadhead" time and mileage. In later years, however, its layout and stub-ended track arrangement caused serious problems. Cars pulling in from 1st Avenue had to back into the building. In 1891, this was not much of an issue, but by 1950, automobile traffic made this a challenging, if not hazardous, maneuver. Although smaller, Midway Station was laid out much like East Side, while Bloomington was set up for through movements. It had a transfer table inside the building, which allowed cars to be shuffled from one track to another. Because of their size, neither Midway nor Bloomington lasted long. Both were replaced by larger, more centrally located facilities: Midway in 1907, and Bloomington in 1911.

In 1904, TCRT had car storage and repair operations at seven locations. Three were in Minneapolis: 31st Street Station and Shops, Bloomington Station, and East Minneapolis Station. Four were in St. Paul: Midway Station, East 7th Street Station, Smith Avenue Station, and Selby Station. In Stillwater, a wood frame structure, built in 1899 on Owen Street, stored cars and several pieces of work equipment for that city's local lines.

All of the other shops and carhouses, including those TCRT retained during the conversion from horse-drawn to electric cars, were either closed down and sold or were being used to temporarily store out-of-service equipment. This included the offices, shops, and steam-generating plant at 3rd Avenue and 1st Street

North. It was replaced by the new office building at 11th and Hennepin, which opened in 1904, and the new power plant on the Mississippi.

SNELLING SHOPS

It was apparent to TCRT officials by 1904 that the growth of the system was outrunning its maintenance capabilities. The company needed more shop capacity, and it needed more street-cars. A farsighted management had earlier acquired sixty acres of suitable land on Snelling Avenue between University and St. Anthony Avenues in St. Paul, midway between the two cities on the St. Paul–Minneapolis car line. Work on a new shop complex started in September 1904 with the construction of a lead track off University Avenue onto the property to bring in construction materials. The Chicago, Milwaukee & St. Paul also extended a spur from its main line near Marshall Avenue. This too was originally built for construction materials and shop machinery, but it would later provide rail access for delivery of supplies to the shops.

East Side Station, located on 1st Avenue Northeast at University Avenue. It survives today (but probably not for long) as the Superior Plating Company.

The Snelling complex in the Midway district of St. Paul. University Avenue runs from upper left to lower right. Snelling Station, in the center of the photograph, hosted day-to-day streetcar operations. Snelling Shops is the complex of buildings to the right of the streetcar storage yard. The landmark Montgomery Ward Midway store and distribution center is at upper left.

Forty of the original sixty acres purchased were used for the shop complex. The remaining twenty acres were sold to Montgomery Ward sometime around 1920 for construction of its retail store and mail order warehouse. Portions of this land had earlier been used as an automobile racetrack, the Motordrome.

All of the buildings were constructed of brick built on a reinforced concrete foundation. Floors and roofs were also built of concrete. All brick and block was manufactured on the site. The Main Steam Station in Minneapolis supplied electricity to run the shop machinery. The

carhouse opened in 1907, as did the erecting shop and several other buildings. With completion of the Snelling carhouse, streetcars based at Selby Station, Smith, and Midway moved to Snelling. Selby, Smith, and Midway closed, and those properties were sold. A few additions and alterations came later, but by 1916, except for the wheel shop added in 1925, the complex was complete.

The carhouse building had six run-through tracks accommodating up to forty-two cars undergoing inspections or light repairs. On the ground floor there was a conductor and

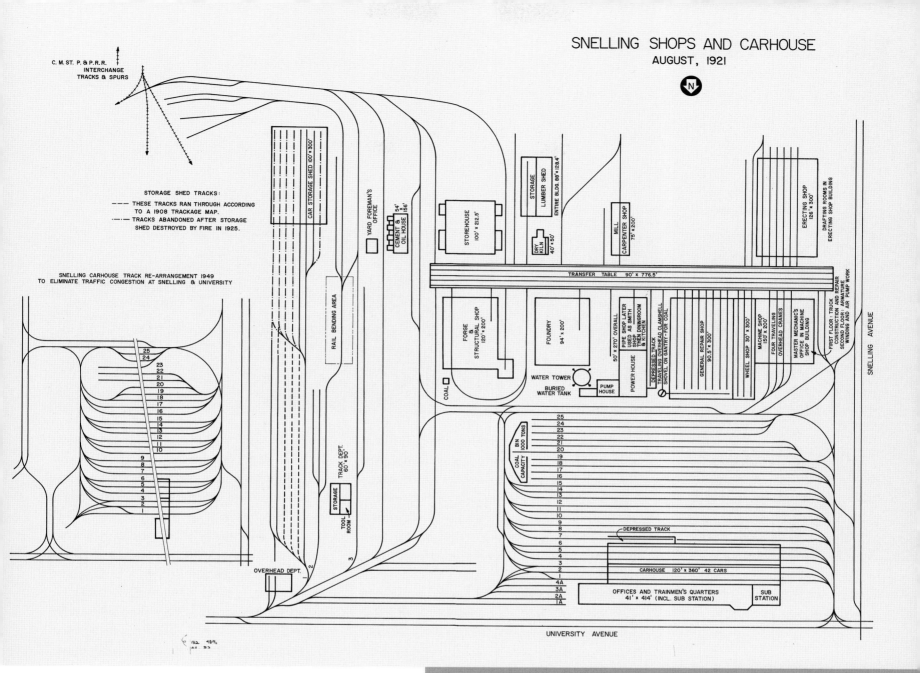

C. M. ST. P. & P. R. R.
INTERCHANGE
TRACKS & SPURS

STORAGE SHED TRACKS:
— — — THESE TRACKS RAN THROUGH ACCORDING
TO A 1908 TRACKAGE MAP.
— · — TRACKS ABANDONED AFTER STORAGE
SHED DESTROYED BY FIRE IN 1925.

SNELLING CARHOUSE TRACK RE-ARRANGEMENT 1949
TO ELIMINATE TRAFFIC CONGESTION AT SNELLING & UNIVERSITY

CAR STORAGE SHED 100' x 300'

YARD FOREMAN'S OFFICE

CEMENT & OIL HOUSE 54' 156'

RAIL BENDING AREA

STORAGE LUMBER SHED
ENTIRE BLDG. 88' x 128.4'

STORAGE

STOREHOUSE 100' x 212.5'

DRY KILN 40' x 50'

MILL CARPENTER SHOP 75' x 200'

ERECTING SHOP 126' x 300'

DRAFTING ROOMS IN ERECTING SHOP BUILDING

TRANSFER TABLE 90' x 776.5'

TRACK DEPT. 60' x 90'

STORAGE

FORGE & STRUCTURAL SHOP 120' x 200'

FOUNDRY 94' x 200'

50' x 270' OVERALL
PIPE SHOP LATER
USED AS SMITH
SHOP
THEN DININGROOM
& KITCHEN

POWER HOUSE

DEPRESSED TRACK
TRAVELING OVERHEAD CLAMSHELL
SHOVEL ON GANTRY – FOR COAL

GENERAL REPAIR SHOP 90.5' x 300'

WHEEL SHOP 30' x 300'

MACHINE SHOP 150' x 200'
FOUR TRAVELING
OVERHEAD CRANES

MASTER MECHANIC'S
OFFICE IN MACHINE
SHOP BUILDING

FIRST FLOOR: TRUCK
CONSTRUCTION AND REPAIR
SECOND FLOOR: ARMATURE
WINDING AND AIR PUMP WORK

COAL

WATER TOWER

BURIED WATER TANK

PUMP HOUSE

SNELLING AVENUE

25 24 23 22 21 20 19 18 17 16 15 14 13 12 11 10 9 8 7 6 5 4 3 2 1

BIN 1000 TONS
COAL CAPACITY

25 24 23 22 21 20 19 18 17 16 15 14 13 12 11 10 9 8 7 6 5 4 3 2
1A

DEPRESSED TRACK

CARHOUSE 120' x 360' 42 CARS

OFFICES AND TRAINMEN'S QUARTERS
41' x 414' (INCL. SUB STATION)

SUB STATION

4A 3A 2A 1A

OVERHEAD DEPT.

TOOL ROOM

UNIVERSITY AVENUE

trainmen's room with lockers, showers, and bathroom facilities. Offices for the operating foreman and his supervisors and clerks adjoined the trainmen's quarters. The company's employment bureau and its training department were in the building. There was also a locker room for car repairmen, a mechanical foreman's office, and a parts room. A second-floor lounge and rest area provided comfortable furniture and sleeping facilities for crews resting between work assignments. An electrical substation was located on the ground floor on the west side of the building. With a few

The Snelling complex was divided into three basic areas: Snelling Station, where daily streetcar service was based, includes the offices and trainmen's quarters and tracks 1A–25; Snelling Shops, where streetcars were manufactured and overhauled, is the group of buildings clustered on both sides of the transfer table; and the track and overhead wire departments were located along the tracks on the eastern edge of the property that run at right angles to the rest of the tracks. Drawing by Kent Dorholt is reprinted from *The Electric Railways of Minnesota*; courtesy of Russell L. Olson.

minor differences, the same layout and overall design and building materials would be used in the three new carhouses built in Minneapolis in the next several years.

Between the carhouse and the next row of shop buildings was a huge, eighteen-track yard that could hold up to 224 streetcars. Cars stored here were assigned to Snelling Station and the St. Paul lines. Several tracks were also used to store cars awaiting heavy repairs that were brought to Snelling from the other carhouses.

Across the storage yard and to the south there was a string of buildings arrayed on an east–west axis facing a transfer table that was used to move cars and shop supplies between buildings. The first large structure on the west (adjoining Snelling Avenue) was the machine shop. It was two stories high with a large open repair bay. Four traveling cranes rolled along below the ceiling. Each crane could lift a streetcar so that the trucks could be rolled away for repairs to the motors, framing, springs, or wheels. Because they were interchangeable, a repaired truck was usually put in place and the car set down so that it could be quickly returned to service. There was also a gallery area on the second floor where repairs were made to electrical equipment.

The general repair shop came next. It took on most of the heavy repairs to the cars and car bodies. Farther east was the powerhouse and pipe shop (a portion of which was later converted into a dining room). The powerhouse generated steam heat for all of the buildings in the shop complex.

Next door, the foundry made all of the company's castings, including the cast iron overhead wire poles. An adjoining forge and structural shop fabricated other metal parts. Between the forge and the eastern property line was another large open area, used by the track department for storage of rail, ties, and other construction materials. There was also a car storage shed, which until 1925, when it burned, stored out-of-service cars or seriously damaged cars awaiting repairs.

Returning west, the next building in line was the cement and oil house, which, as its name implies, was used to store cement and oil products, greases, and the like. Next to the cement and oil house and facing the transfer table was the main storehouse building, which served Snelling Shops and the entire system. Supply cars moved on a regular schedule between the storehouse and all company facilities. Next in line came a dry kiln, a lumber storage shed, and the carpenter shop where all of the company's wood parts were fabricated.

The last building on the west side, paralleling Snelling Avenue, was the erecting shop. It had six tracks under roof and a system of overhead cranes for moving parts and entire car bodies around the building. The shop could fabricate an entire streetcar body or rehabilitate an existing car.

During rehabilitation the car was flipped on its side, permitting workers easy access to all of the car's surfaces. Painting and finishing work were done in this shop. The second floor accommodated office space for the drafting and engineering departments.

All of the buildings and their position with respect to each other were carefully designed to optimize shop efficiency, just as all of the work going through the shop followed careful production plans. A full fire protection system was installed in 1925–26, following the catastrophic fire and loss of the car storage building. At its peak, more than five hundred people were employed at the Snelling Shops.

NEW CARHOUSES

The company turned to expanding and modernizing its carhouses once the Snelling Shops opened. The capacity problem in St. Paul had eased, and it was further improved during a 1905–7 reconstruction of the East 7th Street Station, which was originally a horsecar barn, then a cable car shop. In a 1913–14 rebuilding, all of the original structures came down, replaced by a carhouse with a two-story office wing. East 7th Street Station, renamed Duluth Avenue Station in 1919, could store and maintain 134 streetcars. Both Snelling and East 7th Street were extremely well sited with respect

to all of the lines in the St. Paul system. Their locations made for great efficiency and a minimum of deadhead mileage, saving the company many thousands of dollars in unnecessary operating expense.

The superb south Minneapolis location of 31st Street Station was not used efficiently, because much of the property was given over to shop buildings, many of them dating back to the Motor Line era. Bloomington Station was too small, and East Minneapolis was so hard pressed for space that an adjoining lot between University Avenue and 2nd Street Northeast

Looking west at Snelling Shops from the Montgomery Ward building. The transfer table in the center moved cars between buildings. The area in the foreground was used by the track and overhead wire departments.

had to be purchased in 1916 for use as a car storage yard. Neighborhoods east of Chicago Avenue were growing rapidly, and additional cars for the new intercity Selby–Lake line were overloading 31st Street, Snelling, and the small Bloomington Station.

To relieve them, a new car station on Lake

Duluth Avenue Station in St. Paul, located on East 7th Street at Duluth, was rebuilt about 1910–12 from the East 7th Street Station, which had been constructed as a cable car barn and powerhouse in 1892.

Street between 21st and 22nd Avenue South opened in 1910, replacing Bloomington Station. Lake Street Station was second only to Snelling in size and overall capacity. The carhouse was a single-story building with six run-through tracks, three with inspection pits. A two-story section of the same building faced Lake Street and housed offices for the operating department, crew quarters, maintenance offices, a parts room, and a locker room for car maintenance workers. The yard had twenty-five tracks running an entire city block and, with the carhouse, had a combined capacity of 180 cars. Streetcar lines that worked principally out of Lake Street over the years included Selby–Lake, Minnehaha–Plymouth, Kenwood–E. 25th St., 34th Ave. S.–N. Bryant, 28th Ave. S.–Robbinsdale, and Bloomington–Columbia Heights.

Next came 31st Street. Demolition of the former carhouse and repair shop on the south half of the site began in the spring of 1911, followed immediately by construction of the new building, which opened in November 1912. Renamed Nicollet Station, the new carbarn's of-

fice wing was two stories tall with a full basement. It faced eastward, stretching 305 feet along Nicollet Avenue. Large windows ran the length of the building on both floors, admitting ample natural light. Constructed of steel and reinforced concrete, the exterior was faced in light brown brick set in mortar colored to match. Window trim, belt courses, and coping were white unglazed terra-cotta.

Inside, on the north half of the first floor there was a large trainmen's room where conductors and motormen waited for assignments or copied schedules and read bulletins as they reported for work. Adjoining the trainmen's room were offices for the call clerks, cashiers, supervisors, and the operating foreman. The mechanical department worked out of the south half of the ground floor. There was a parts room, a small work area for the mechanical foreman, a lunchroom, and toilet and wash area for the car repairmen. The second floor provided additional space for parts storage as well as a rest area and clubrooms for crews. The basement became the headquarters for the underground-electrical

The Carhouse

The carhouse, or station, as TCRT called it, was at the center of a trainman's day. It was a home away from home, even a private club of sorts. If you were a motorman, it was where you reported for work to pull out your car. If you were a conductor, it was where you got your change supply or turned in your receipts at the end of the day. It was also a place to play cards with your buddies, talk to the foreman about a passenger complaint, and maybe get chewed out or suspended for a day or two, which in turn might prompt a talk with the union steward about filling out a grievance form. Or, it was a place to catch some sleep between a late-night run and an early pullout the next morning.

A motorman had to report for work ten to fifteen minutes before his car was scheduled to pull out. This was called plug-in time. The term was descriptive because reporting meant inserting a wooden peg, or plug, alongside the run number and car assignment written on a large chalkboard in front of the "cage." The cage was not really a cage but rather the dispatch, or foreman's, office. A clerk sat at a window looking out on the trainmen's room. The clerk's job was to watch the board and make sure all of the plugs were in place, indicating that the motormen had properly reported for work. This same clerk would be responsible for other clerical duties and, most important, would assign a motorman or conductor who might be waiting on call to fill a run if someone failed to report on time. A motorman or conductor who did not show up was said to have "scratched," and too many "scratches" would get you fired.

After plugging in, checking the bulletin board, and picking up a supply of transfers, a motorman would go out to the yard and look for the assigned car, which had been marked up by track number on the plug-in board. Having found the car, the first task would be to get on board and throw the master switch, then go into the electrical cabinet and turn on the lights, air compressor, and heaters. If the car was not electrically heated, you would have to step off and walk around to the side of the car and check the underfloor coal stove, which supplied hot-air heat. If the night maintenance crew had done its job, the stove would be good and hot. If not, a trip to the coal-bunker and some stoking were in order.

While outside, it was always a good idea to walk around the car and look for body damage, taking care to note any. That done and after getting back on board, it was time to walk through the car and look for any trash or newspapers the cleaners might have missed the night before. Along the way you would set the destination signs, then return to the front of the car. After jotting down the farebox readings on your trip sheet, it was time to go.

Two taps on the gong signaled departure. A whoosh of air would follow as the air brakes came off, then a slight jerk and the sound of metal on metal as the car rolled through the yard toward the street and another day on the line.

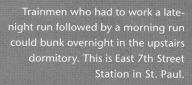

REST ROOM AT E. 7TH ST STATION

Trainmen who had to work a late-night run followed by a morning run could bunk overnight in the upstairs dormitory. This is East 7th Street Station in St. Paul.

The stations had some of the amenities of a men's club, including libraries, pool tables, and paid attendants who cut hair and performed other services for tips. This is Snelling Station. Photograph by Bruce Sifford Studio; courtesy of the Minnesota Historical Society.

Nicollet Station at 31st Street and Nicollet Avenue in south Minneapolis opened in 1912 on the site of the 1898 31st Street Shops (which were replaced by the 1908 Snelling Shops). Nicollet replaced the 31st Street Station and most of the old Motor Line roundhouse. The track department used the surviving portion of the roundhouse (visible beyond the streetcars) until 1953. Photograph courtesy of the Minnesota Historical Society.

them with full-length inspection pits. A series of skylights provided natural illumination augmenting the artificial lights. There were also transom windows above the carhouse doors. The doors were usually left open during clement weather to provide ventilation. An attractively landscaped garden fronted the main entrance to the building on 31st Street.

There were eleven storage tracks in the yard, oriented north and south, which could be accessed from both 31st and 32nd Streets. Several pieces of work equipment and 158 streetcars were based at Nicollet. A portion of the old roundhouse and stores building was kept on the northwest side of the property for use by the track department. Otherwise, all of the original buildings were taken down.

Nicollet furnished streetcars for the Nicollet–2nd St. N.E., Glenwood–4th Ave. S., Grand–Monroe, and Bryant-Johnson lines as well as extra, rush hour cars for the Selby–Lake line.

The system's last new carhouse, North

department and was used to store electrical conduit and cabling. A sloping track on the south side of the building led directly into the basement. Work cars could be backed inside for easy loading and unloading of cables and large electrical parts.

The car repair area was attached to the office wing. It had six run-through tracks, all of

Side, opened in 1914. Located in the city block bordered by Washington Avenue and 2nd Street North and 25th and 26th Avenues, North Side was built mainly to relieve overcrowding at Lake Street. Its layout was much like Lake Street's, with a two-story office wing that faced Washington Avenue and a single-story, six-track car repair shop. There were thirteen outside storage tracks, enough for 148 cars assigned to the Chicago–Penn and Chicago–Fremont, Broadway, 28th Ave. S.–Robbinsdale, and the 34th Ave. S.–N. Bryant lines.

There was also a pair of small satellite carhouses. The Owen Street Station in Stillwater housed the handful of local streetcars that served Stillwater and Bayport, plus a pair of the high-speed suburban cars that ran to St. Paul. The 1920 South St. Paul carhouse housed tripper cars that transported stockyard workers to and from work.

Of all the shop facilities that TCRT built during its great expansion between 1904 and 1914, only North Side remains, and it is no longer used to maintain transit vehicles. Converted to a bus garage in 1953, it was replaced by Metro Transit's Fred T. Heywood Office and Garage near downtown Minneapolis. The property was subsequently sold and redeveloped for other uses. Lake Street Station was closed and razed in 1954. Portions of the Snelling Shop complex, the erecting shop building, and the carpenter shop, were made part of a new bus garage in 1954; that garage was torn down in 2002. Nicollet Station, like North Side, became a bus garage in 1953, but was demolished to make way for a new bus maintenance facility in the late 1980s.

North Side Station, the last of four stations built to a standard design, was located at 26th and Washington Avenues in north Minneapolis. It survives today.

Trolleys to the Country

Lake Minnetonka and Stillwater

3

Nineteenth-century streetcar moguls could feel secure in their monopolies and were content to let the nickels simply roll into the fare box and on to their bottom lines. But they also knew that the streetcar was more than mass transportation and that with enormous investments in track, power systems, and rolling stock, it was good business to encourage traffic on weekends and holidays when equipment and operating personnel were idle. Selling the trolley ride as a recreational experience brought in extra revenues with little additional expense. What came to be called "streetcarring" was promoted and became popular, whether it involved a ride around town, a trip to the park, a band concert, or a picnic at the lake.

This was the era of the streetcar amusement park, and building them was a common way for companies across the country to encourage traffic on their suburban lines. Some well-known examples included the Philadelphia Transportation Company's Willow Grove, Capital Transit's Glen Echo Park in Washington, D.C., and the Monongahela Street Railway Company's Kennywood near Pittsburgh.

To attract riders, the Minneapolis Street Railway in 1887 built the first in a succession of large pavilions at Lake Harriet for summer picnics and concerts. TCRT made other public improvements at Como and Phalen Parks in St. Paul and at Minnehaha Park in Minneapolis. It also promoted Wonderland Park, a short-lived (1906–12) amusement venue at 34th Avenue and Lake Street served by the Selby–Lake line. But its attentions were mostly lavished on two large amusement parks that it built on its suburban lines to Lake Minnetonka and Stillwater.

Lake Minnetonka

Lake Minnetonka became a popular tourist attraction in the late 1870s and early 1880s, and three large railroad hotels were built on the lake between 1879 and 1882 to accommodate visitors. The first, the Minnetonka Lake Park Hotel, later the Tonka Bay Hotel, went up in 1879. The Hotel St. Louis in Deephaven followed in 1880, and the most lavish of them all, James J. Hill's Lafayette Hotel, opened in 1883. However, only the affluent and influential summered and partied at these elegant hostelries,

TCRT's expansion to Lake Minnetonka was made possible by purchasing and upgrading three steam railroads. The Great Northern's former Motor Line from Hopkins to Excelsior was straightened and double-tracked. The Milwaukee Road's Hopkins–Deephaven branch line received overhead wire and little else. From downtown Excelsior new streetcar tracks were built alongside the existing Minneapolis & St. Louis Railway to Manitou Junction. From there, TCRT leased and electrified the existing M&StL branch to Tonka Bay and built a short spur from it to the new Wildhurst Upper Lake steamboat dock.

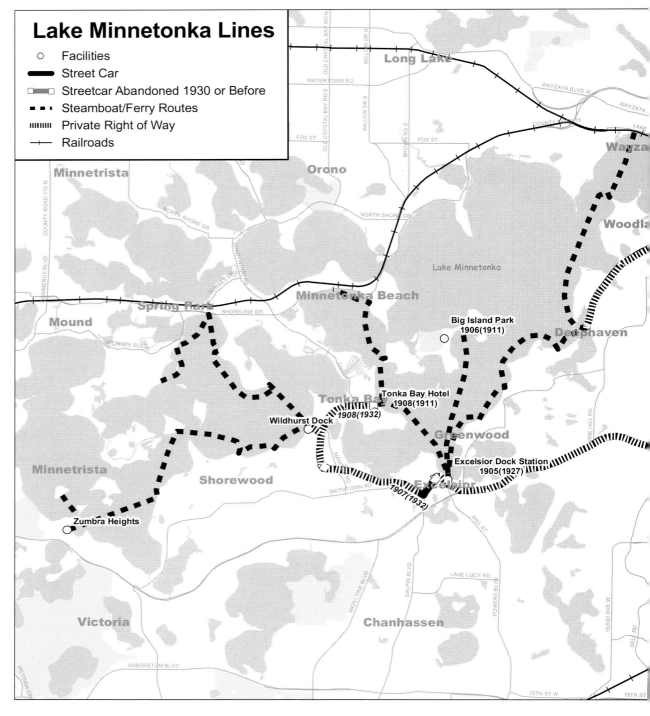

Lake Minnetonka Lines

○ Facilities
━━ Street Car
▭▭▭ Streetcar Abandoned 1930 or Before
▪ ▪ ▪ Steamboat/Ferry Routes
ııııııı Private Right of Way
┼─┼ Railroads

and they arrived in Pullman cars from faraway places. As these wealthy vacationers traveled farther west seeking the wonders of Yellowstone Park and the Rocky Mountains, the hotels withered, and Lake Minnetonka became a desirable weekend destination for the growing population of the Twin Cities.

The Motor Line ended service to the lake

in 1886 for lack of business, but TCRT saw fresh opportunities in 1904 and made plans to extend its line from Lake Harriet to Excelsior and Lake Minnetonka. To ensure that its extension had plenty of traffic, the plans included a large amusement park on Big Island and a fleet of express boats that would reach all points on the lake.

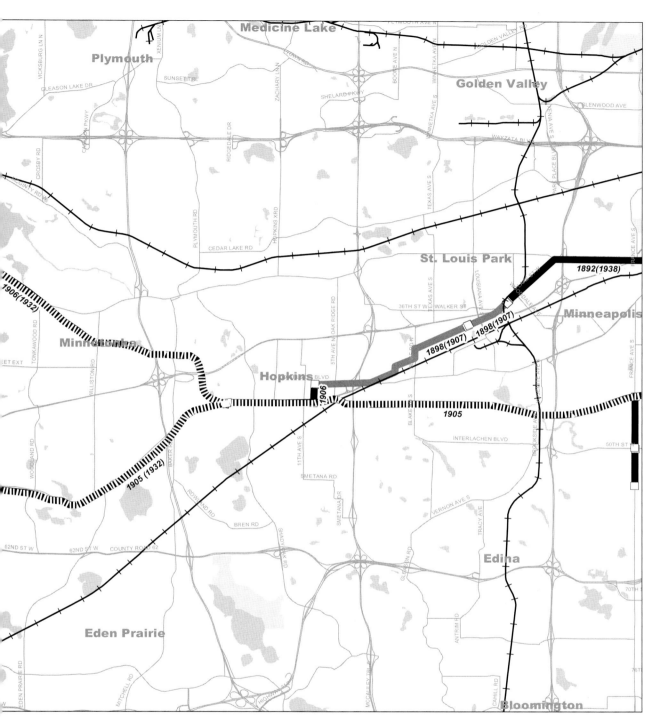

With approvals in hand from the communities of Hopkins and Excelsior, TCRT began work in the spring of 1905. Tracks followed the line of the former Minneapolis, Lyndale & Minnetonka Railway. Its right of way was extensively resurveyed and reengineered, curves eased, and the profile smoothed to permit high-speed operation.

The Great Northern Railway had earlier acquired the segment from Hopkins to Excelsior and used it as part of the branch line it built to Hutchinson, Minnesota. When it built a new line through Mound in 1900, this segment became redundant and was abandoned.

TCRT spared no expense. The line was laid with heavy, eighty-pound T rail. Span wires

CooLiNG The WHEELS OFF 1913

WELAND ME 211-26

A single track between Lake Harriet and Excelsior opened for service in September 1905. Construction resumed in the spring of 1906 on a second main track from Lake Harriet to Excelsior. A short, single-track branch was built into downtown Hopkins along 9th Avenue, terminating at a wye at Excelsior Boulevard. Both main tracks between Lake Harriet and Excelsior were put in service that October. At night electric arc lights, suspended from the span wires, lighted the right of way from 34th Street, just east of Lake Calhoun, in Minneapolis, all the way to Excelsior.

Final construction took place in 1907 with the completion of a single-track extension from downtown Excelsior westward parallel to the Minneapolis & St. Louis to a point called Manitou Junction. In 1880, the railroad had laid a short branch from there to Tonka Bay and the Tonka Bay Hotel. The branch came under TCRT lease in October 1907; it was electrified and opened in 1908. TCRT also built a loop track off the branch to Wildhurst, where it constructed a dock for passengers connecting with its excursion boats operating on the upper lake.

stretched between cedar poles on both sides of the right of way carried the overhead trolley wires above the tracks. High-tension electrical feeders and private telephone lines were strung on cross arms attached to the poles. Electric substations at Hopkins and Excelsior were constructed to power the streetcar line and the attractions at Big Island Park. Two large steel viaducts spanned the Chicago, Milwaukee & St. Paul and the Minneapolis & St. Louis tracks in Hopkins.

Nelson's Corner, Hopkins, Minn.

As work progressed on its Excelsior line, TCRT took control of the Chicago, Milwaukee & St. Paul's track from Hopkins to Deephaven, which it had built in 1887 to serve the Hotel St. Louis. Business at the hotel had fallen off. It closed in 1903 and would be razed in 1907. TCRT management saw the branch as another outlet for its Lake Minnetonka business and leased it from the Milwaukee Road in October 1905. Wires went up the following spring, and

The Excelsior Dock Station, opened in 1905, with the streetcar station in the right background. The steamboat Dispatcher and the Commodore of the Fleet were housed in its central tower. The dock station survived the end of steamboat service in 1926 and became part of the Excelsior Amusement Park, housing the bumper car ride. Photograph by Sweet.

In 1905, TCRT purchased the Milwaukee Road's branch line from Hopkins to Deephaven. The deal included the station and dock at the Deephaven end of the line, just down the hill from the Hotel St. Louis. TCRT electrified the line and provided hourly train service that made a timed connection with the Excelsior–Wayzata express boat. The station, moved and much modified, survives as a private residence up the hill from its original site.

The experimental Lake Minnetonka double-deck car 1145 at the 31st Street Shops. Thomas Lowry's idol was Abraham Lincoln, and in 1905 Lowry purchased the railroad car that transported Lincoln's body to Illinois for burial; it appears at extreme left, apparently being refurbished by the shop forces. Soon thereafter it was placed on display next to the Soo Line track crossing of Central Avenue, just south of 37th Avenue Northeast. The car was destroyed in a fire in 1911.

the tracks connected to the Excelsior line just west of what is now the intersection of Shady Oak Road and Excelsior Boulevard at a point called Deephaven Junction. Service to Deephaven commenced in June 1906.

For reference, the main line to Excelsior began at Lake Harriet where the Lake Harriet Trolley operates today. It followed what is now an alleyway on the north side of 44th Street to France Avenue. It crossed France Avenue at an angle, then swung to the south side of 44th Street, running parallel to 44th all the way to Brookside, where it struck out across a marsh fed by the waters of Minnehaha Creek. It ran south along the boundary of the current Morningside Golf Course, crossed Blake Road south of Blake School, crossed Washington Avenue (now Highway 169), then jumped over the former Milwaukee Road and Minneapolis & St. Louis tracks on a high viaduct. From there it continued west. Between Hopkins and Interstate 494, Excelsior Boulevard occupies the

right of way. Beyond 494, the right of way dips south of Excelsior Boulevard through an area that is now filled with housing. West of Highway 101, Highway 7 runs on the streetcar right of way all the way to Excelsior.

Today, some features of the line remain and can be followed, although most of it has been obliterated by roads or housing. The Lake Harriet trolley line occupies the original right of way between 36th Street and the Linden Hills bridge, continuing west as an alley and pedestrian path to the vicinity of Zenith Avenue and 44th Street. Beyond Zenith Avenue to Blake Road, the right of way has been taken over by residences. Between Blake Road and Washington Avenue, it is a paved bike trail. The right of way is also visible south of Excelsior Boulevard and east of Highway 101, where it crossed Purgatory Creek on a high fill. The fill can still be seen, as can the remains of a concrete abutment that once supported the bridge over Purgatory Creek.

Little of the Deephaven Line remains today; it, too, has largely been covered over by development. However, the remnants of Deephaven Junction can be seen at the intersection of Junction Road and Excelsior Boulevard just west of Baker Road. The line is also visible in a cut just north of Northome in Deephaven.

Today, the former Minneapolis & St. Louis line from Hopkins through Minnetonka and Excelsior is a bike path. Public streets have replaced portions of the branch line from Manitou Junction to the site of the Tonka Bay Hotel, which today is occupied by a privately owned marina.

CARS

In 1905, work orders went out to the 31st Street Shops to build twelve in what would eventually

be a series of forty-two high-speed cars for suburban service. They looked like any other TCRT car and were constructed with a steel frame and wood body. However, they were much heavier, weighing in at approximately 60,000 pounds compared to 45,000 pounds for a typical standard car. The additional weight allowed that at least a few them would eventually be rebuilt as double-deckers. Two were double-decked as an experiment and used briefly in 1906 and again in 1907, but were converted back to its original configuration because of concerns about top-heaviness. (It joined another car from an earlier series, number 1092, that had been double-decked as an experiment.) The rest of the weight was in the heavier trucks and larger, higher-horsepower traction motors. They were designed for high-speed operation—sixty miles per hour on private right of way—and regularly attained such speeds in scheduled service.

BIG ISLAND PARK

TCRT bought sixty-five heavily wooded acres on Big Island in Lake Minnetonka in 1905. The island was just a short distance offshore from Excelsior and was largely uninhabited and undeveloped except for a few fishing cabins. Work started on Big Island Park in 1906, and it opened for its first full season in 1907. The park featured multiple picnic pavilions, picnic kitchens and dining halls, an amusement building, carousel, a music hall and bandstand, and a roller coaster. John Philip Sousa's and other nationally known bands and orchestras were brought to the park for memorable concerts. Buildings were solidly constructed of steel and concrete in a Spanish mission theme. A two-hundred-foot tower, a replica of a similar tower in Seville, Spain, dominated the park and was illuminated at night by hundreds of decorative

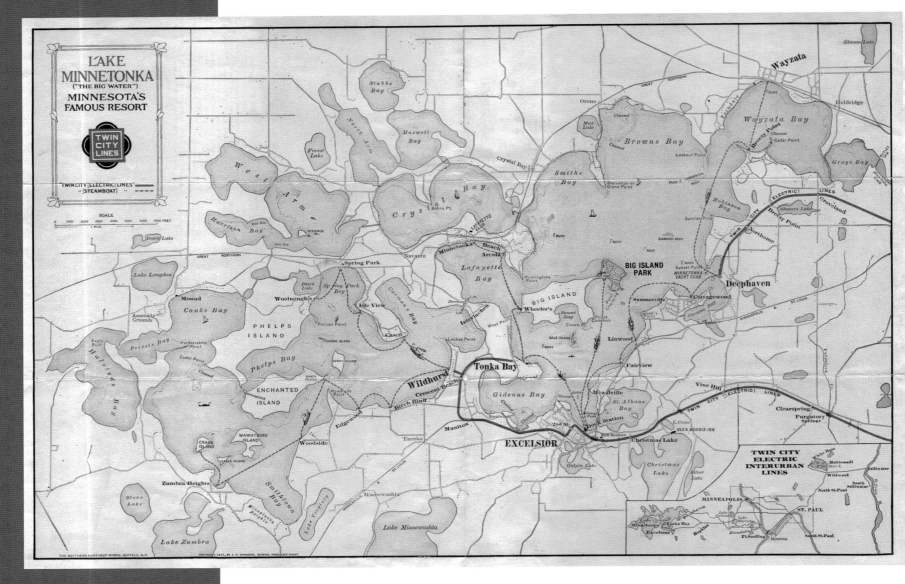

TCRT invested heavily in printed brochures promoting its service to Lake Minnetonka and Big Island Park. Passengers could reach many other destinations on the lake by boarding one of TCRT's express boats.

electric lights. Hundreds more lights covered the grounds, turning night into day.

The company promoted Big Island Park as the place for city families seeking a day at the lake and advertised it heavily in all of the local newspapers. Church and fraternal groups were especially encouraged to hold summer events on the island and, of course, travel there by streetcar. Special round-trip excursion rates were offered that included the streetcar ride, admission to the park, and transportation from the Excelsior Dock Station to Big Island on one of TCRT's large steamboats. Passengers could reach other destinations by boarding one of TCRT's express boats for a complete tour of the lake or a trip to

a favorite cabin or fishing spot. Before cars and paved roads, an express boat was the only convenient way to travel around the lake.

BOATS

Large steamboats appeared on the lake in the 1860s and 1870s, mainly to connect with the railroads and transport wealthy guests to and from the various resorts and hotels. Steamboats gradually disappeared as the passengers who used them went elsewhere for their summer holidays and the large hotels declined in popularity. By 1900, what was left was primarily a summer excursion business not unlike today's dinner cruises.

INTERIOR OF LAKE MINNETONKA EXPRESS BOAT
"TWIN CITY LINES"

The express boats were nicknamed "streetcar boats" because they so closely resembled streetcars, both inside and out. The colors, interior finishes, and seats were identical.

TCRT turned things in a fresh direction when it opened Big Island Park and moved into the summer recreation trade. It bought several of the larger independently owned boats and built three large double-ended paddle-wheeled ferryboats of its own—the *Minneapolis, St. Paul,* and *Minnetonka*—to transport visitors from the Excelsior docks to Big Island. At the same time, during the winter of 1905–6, TCRT built six, seventy-foot express boats at the 31st Street Shops and moved them to the lake on the streetcar line the following spring. They were sleek, steam-powered craft that looked like streetcars on water—which they were. TCRT designers took streetcar bodies and modified them to conform to the contour of a ship's hull. The car body became the ship's cabin. These streetcar boats, as they were called, connected with the streetcars at Excelsior and Wildhurst and operated a scheduled service to points on the lake. The boats were named for various locations in TCRT's system and each carried a crew of three: a pilot, purser, and an engineer. They were the *Como, Minnehaha, White Bear, Hopkins, Harriet,* and *Stillwater.* A seventh boat, the *Excelsior,* was constructed in 1914–15.

From May 15 to September 30 the express boats covered four routes with hourly service:

- Excelsior–Deephaven–Wayzata, serving public docks in Excelsior, Wayzata, and Deephaven and private docks at Meadville, Fairview, Linwood, Summerville, and Cottagewood.

- Excelsior–Minnetonka Beach, serving public docks in Excelsior, Tonka Bay, and Minnetonka Beach and private docks at Wheeler and Arcola.

- Wildhurst–Spring Park, serving public docks at Wildhurst and Spring Park and private docks at Casco, Isle View, and Woodnough.

TCRT's six Lake Minnetonka express boats were built at 31st Street Shops in 1905. They were placed on streetcar trucks and towed over the company's own tracks to Excelsior, where the engines were installed, the roofs completed, and the boats launched.

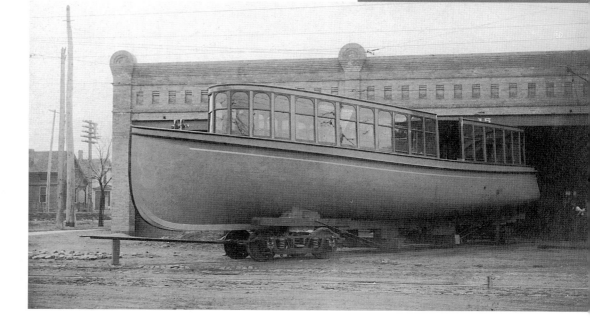

The express boat *Hopkins,* bound for Zumbra Heights in 1915, charges through the Narrows separating the upper and lower lake. Photograph by Charles J. Hibbard; courtesy of the Minnesota Historical Society.

- Wildhurst–Zumbra Heights–Mound (two-hour service), serving public docks at Wildhurst and Mound and private docks at Edgewood, Shady Isle, Woodside, Zumbra Heights, and Crane Island.

The routes and service would change over the years until the end of boat operation in 1926. In addition to the scheduled express and ferry boats, the company offered excursion tours of the lake using the large steamers it had purchased from previous Lake Minnetonka operators: the 1898, 70-foot *Mayflower;* the 1901, 85-foot *Puritan;* the 1901, 125-foot *Excelsior;* and the 1903, 75-foot *Plymouth.*

TONKA BAY HOTEL

The Tonka Bay Hotel came under TCRT control and management in 1907 and reopened in 1908 after extensive remodeling and refurbishment. It was the last addition to the company's Lake Minnetonka portfolio. A distinctive wood-framed building designed by L. S. Buffington,

In addition to the seven express boats and the three Big Island ferries, TCRT purchased five previously existing Lake Minnetonka steamboats and used them for excursions. The *Excelsior,* at right, is leaving its namesake port for a forty-mile tour of the lake, perhaps in the company of the *Puritan,* at left. Photograph courtesy of the Minnesota Historical Society.

the Tonka Bay was four stories tall with two hundred guest rooms and a large dining room that could seat five hundred. A classic Victorian resort hotel, it also featured verandas and enclosed porches offering cooling breezes and excellent views of the lake, as well as a combination roller-skating rink and dance hall. The Tonka Bay Branch of the Lake Minnetonka Line brought guests directly to the door. Built in 1879, the hotel was the first of the large resort hotels on Lake Minnetonka. By 1908 it was among the last. The others had either closed or had been demolished or burned down.

OPERATIONS

By 1908, Lake Minnetonka operations were in full swing. The summer season started in mid-May and lasted through the end of October. Seven classes of service operated, each with its own destination and stopping points:

- Lake Minnetonka: from downtown Minneapolis to 2nd Street in Excelsior; made all local stops.

- Excelsior Limited: limited service from Minneapolis to 2nd Street in Excelsior; no stops beyond Lake Harriet except at 9th Avenue in Hopkins.

- Excelsior Excursion: limited service from Minneapolis to Dock Station in Excelsior; no stops beyond Lake Harriet except at 9th Avenue in Hopkins.

- Tonka Bay: limited service from Minneapolis to Tonka Bay; cars operated through the Wildhurst Loop for boat connections.

- Deephaven: local service from Minneapolis to Deephaven.

- Hopkins: local service from Minneapolis to Hopkins.

- Como–Hopkins: local service from St. Paul via the Como–Harriet interurban to 9th Avenue and Excelsior Boulevard in Hopkins.

On weekdays, cars operated every half hour to Excelsior during rush hours and every hour to Tonka Bay and Deephaven. Como–Hopkins cars ran every half hour from downtown St. Paul via the Como–Harriet line. On summer weekends, the service expanded to handle the huge crowds. Scheduled cars left downtown Minneapolis every ten minutes with extra cars added as needed. Each car was referred to as a train because it often had several cars following close behind, which were part of the same movement. In such cases, all cars in the series carried

The Tonka Bay Hotel, built as the Lake Park Hotel in 1879, was reached by a branch of the Minneapolis & St. Louis Railway the following year. TCRT leased the hotel and the branch line from the M&StL in 1907. The company's steamboats also served the hotel, but it was financially unsuccessful and closed in 1911 on the same day as Big Island Park. Photograph by Sweet; courtesy of the Minnesota Historical Society.

Lake Minnetonka

Electric Lines

TWIN CITY LINES

Minneapolis
Hopkins
Excelsior
Tonka Bay
Deephaven

Patrons are invited to telephone, call on, or write to the General Passenger Agent for any information concerning the service of the Twin City Lines, or to make complaints or offer suggestions. Prompt attention and thoughtful consideration are assured.

J. J. CAUFIELD, General Superintendent
W. O. CLURE, General Passenger Agent
Room 308, No. 1 Eleventh St. S., Minneapolis
Telephone—N. W. Main 4580

a green marker indicating that more cars were following until the last car in the series passed displaying no marker. Up to sixty cars could be on the line at any one time.

Storage tracks were built at Excelsior to accommodate as many as forty cars awaiting their next runs. A train dispatcher was stationed in the dock station building at Excelsior along with the "commodore of the fleet," who was in charge of all boat operations. This dis-

patcher kept in communication with all cars on the line by telephone. Call boxes were located at strategic points, and conductors and motormen were required to call in and obtain necessary clearances before proceeding. To guard against the possibility of collisions, special electric block signals located at the entrances and exits to single-track lines indicated when a streetcar was on the track ahead.

The downtown depot and ticket office was located at 17 North 6th Street in Minneapolis. Inbound cars from Lake Minnetonka turned off Hennepin Avenue at 7th Street, then right to 1st Avenue North and another right to 6th Street. They unloaded their inbound passengers and awaited a return trip in front of the ticket of-

A public timetable issued by TCRT in 1920 for its Lake Minnetonka suburban services. Streetcars ran every thirty minutes during rush hours to Excelsior. From the collection of John W. Diers.

MINNEAPOLIS TO EXCELSIOR, AND TONKA BAY

WESTBOUND TRAINS	Fare Zones	Miles	4 Ex. Sun. AM	1 Ex. Sun. AM	2 Ex. Sun. AM	3 Daily AM	1 Daily AM	3 Daily AM	1 Daily AM	3 Daily AM	1 Daily PM	3 Daily PM	1 Daily PM		3 Daily PM		1 Sun. Only PM	1 Ex. Sun. PM	3 Sun. Only PM	3 Ex. Sun. PM	4 Ex. Sun. PM	1 Sun. Only PM	1 Ex. Sun. PM	3 Daily PM	3 Daily PM	3 Daily PM
Leave Minneapolis—Sixth Street Station		.00	5:30	6:00	6:30	7:00	8:00	9:00	10:00	11:00	12:00	1:00	2:00		3:00		4:00	4:10	5:00	5:15	5:40	6:00	6:15	7:30	9:30	11:30
" —Seventh Street		.14	5:31	6:01	6:31	7:01	8:01	9:01	10:01	11:01	12:01	1:01	2:01		3:01		4:01	4:11	5:01	5:16	5:41	6:01	6:16	7:31	9:31	11:31
" —Eleventh Street		.39	5:32	6:02	6:32	7:02	8:02	9:02	10:02	11:02	12:02	1:02	2:02		3:02		4:02	4:12	5:02	5:17	5:42	6:02	6:17	7:32	9:32	11:32
" —Twelfth Street		.47	5:33	6:03	6:33	7:03	8:03	9:03	10:03	11:03	12:03	1:03	2:03		3:03		4:03	4:13	5:03	5:18	5:43	6:03	6:18	7:33	9:33	11:33
" —Groveland Avenue		1.14	5:35	6:05	6:35	7:05	8:05	9:05	10:05	11:05	12:05	1:05	2:05		3:05		4:05	4:15	5:05	5:20	5:45	6:05	6:20	7:35	9:35	11:35
" —Douglas Avenue		1.23	5:36	6:06	6:36	7:06	8:06	9:06	10:06	11:06	12:06	1:06	2:06		3:06		4:06	4:16	5:06	5:21	5:46	6:06	6:21	7:36	9:36	11:36
" —Lagoon Avenue		2.53	5:42	6:12	6:42	7:12	8:12	9:12	10:12	11:12	12:12	1:12	2:12		3:12		4:12	4:22	5:12	5:27	5:52	6:12	6:27	7:42	9:42	11:42
" —Lake Street		2.59	5:43	6:13	6:43	7:13	8:13	9:13	10:13	11:13	12:13	1:13	2:13		3:13		4:13	4:23	5:13	5:28	5:53	6:13	6:28	7:43	9:43	11:43
" —Lake Harriet—42nd St.		4.33	5:50	6:20	6:50	7:20	8:20	9:20	10:20	11:20	12:20	1:20	2:20		3:20		4:20	4:30	5:20	5:35	6:00	6:20	6:35	7:50	9:50	11:50
" —Upton Avenue		4.63	5:51	6:21	6:51	7:21	8:21	9:21	10:21	11:21	12:21	1:21	2:21		3:21		4:21	4:31	5:21	5:36	6:01	6:21	6:36	7:51	9:51	11:51
" —Xerxes Avenue		4.83	5:51	6:21	6:51	7:21	8:21	9:21	10:21	11:21	12:21	1:21	2:21		3:21		4:21	4:31	5:21	5:36	6:01	6:21	6:36	7:51	9:51	11:51
" —City Limits	1st	5.45	5:54	6:24	6:54	7:24	8:24	9:24	10:24	11:24	12:24	1:24	2:24		3:24		4:24	4:34	5:24	5:39	6:04	6:24	6:39	7:54	9:54	11:54
Arrive Hopkins—9th Avenue		9.53	6:01	6:31	7:01	7:31	8:31	9:31	10:31	11:31	12:31	1:31	2:31		3:31		4:31	4:41	5:31	5:46	6:11	6:31	6:46	8:01	10:01	12:01
" Deephaven Junction	3rd	10.65	6:03	6:33	7:03	7:33	8:33	9:33	10:33	11:33	12:33	1:33	2:33		3:33		4:33	4:43	5:33	5:48	6:13	6:33	6:48	8:03	10:03	12:03
" Mayview		11.83	6:05	6:35	7:05	7:35	8:35	9:35	10:35	11:35	12:35	1:35	2:35		3:35		4:35	4:45	5:35	5:50	6:15	6:35	6:50	8:05	10:05	12:05
" Glen Lake	4th	12.64	6:06	6:36	7:06	7:36	8:36	9:36	10:36	11:36	12:36	1:36	2:36		3:36		4:36	4:46	5:36	5:51	6:16	6:36	6:51	8:06	10:06	12:06
" Clearspring		14.77	6:09	6:39	7:09	7:39	8:39	9:39	10:39	11:39	12:39	1:39	2:39		3:39		4:39	4:49	5:39	5:54	6:19	6:39	6:54	8:09	10:09	12:09
" Vine Hill		15.89	6:11	6:41	7:11	7:41	8:41	9:41	10:41	11:41	12:41	1:41	2:41		3:41		4:41	4:51	5:41	5:56	6:21	6:41	6:56	8:11	10:11	12:11
" Christmas Lake		17.26	6:13	6:43	7:13	7:43	8:43	9:43	10:43	11:43	12:43	1:43	2:43		3:43		4:43	4:53	5:43	5:58	6:23	6:43	6:58	8:13	10:13	12:13
" Excelsior—Steamboat Dock		17.91	6:15	6:45	7:15	7:45	8:45	9:45	10:45	11:45	12:45	1:45	2:45		3:45		4:45	4:55	5:45	6:00	6:25	6:45	7:00	8:15	10:15	12:15
" " —1st Street		18.05	6:16	6:46	7:16	7:46	8:46	9:46	10:46	11:46	12:46	1:46	2:46		3:46		4:46	4:56	5:46	6:01	6:26	6:46	7:01	8:16	10:16	12:16
" " —2nd Street		18.13	6:16	6:46	7:16	7:46	8:46	9:46	10:46	11:46	12:46	1:46	2:46		3:46		4:46	4:56	5:46	6:01	6:26	6:46	7:01	8:16	10:16	12:16
" " —3rd Street		18.24	6:17	6:47	7:17	7:47	8:47	9:47	10:47		12:47	1:47	2:47		3:47		4:47	4:57	5:47	6:02	6:27	6:47	7:02	8:17	10:17	12:17
" " —George Street	5th	18.56	6:17	6:47	7:17	7:47	8:47	9:47	10:47		12:47	1:47	2:47		3:47		4:47	4:57	5:47	6:02	6:27	6:47	7:02	8:17	10:17	12:17
" Manitou	6th	19.48	6:20	6:50	7:20	7:50	8:50	9:50	10:50		12:50	1:50	2:50		3:50		4:50	5:00	5:50	6:05	6:30	6:50	7:05	8:20	10:20	12:20
" Crescent Beach		20.19	6:22	6:52	7:22	7:52	8:52	9:52	10:52		12:52	1:52	2:52		3:52		4:52	5:02	5:52	6:07	6:32	6:52	7:07	8:22	10:22	12:22
" Wildhurst—Steamboat Dock		20.46																								
Arrive Tonka Bay	7th	21.26	6:25	6:55	7:25	7:55	8:55	9:55	10:55		12:55	1:55	2:55		3:55		4:55	5:05	5:55	6:10	6:35	6:55	7:10	8:25	10:25	12:25

fice, which was across the street from the former Masonic Temple Building. Waiting shelters were provided at other points on the line, but none of them had an agent. Two drugstores, one in Excelsior and one in Hopkins, sold passes and commutation tickets. Agents were also on duty at Excelsior to expedite fare collection and assist in the boarding of passengers.

Besides its passenger service, TCRT operated a baggage-express car on a regular schedule, leaving the ticket office in Minneapolis at 8:48 a.m. and again at 2:33 p.m. (except Sundays). The car worked its way to and from St. Paul in between the Lake Minnetonka trips. No passengers were carried, just luggage, handbags, and trunks destined for the Tonka Bay Hotel or private residences on the lake, as well as items intended for retail stores in Excelsior and supplies for Big Island Park. TCRT also had a contract with the postal service to carry pouch mail on its regular cars and on the baggage car.

DECLINE

In 1907, Big Island Park took in $44,000 against expenses of $48,000. Revenues declined for each of the next five years. The Tonka Bay Hotel covered its operating expenses the first year, but every year thereafter it lost money. TCRT closed the hotel and the park in 1911. Both turned out to be terrible disappointments. Salvagers took down most of the park during World War I, and the final remnants were carted away in 1924. The property was allowed to return to nature after that, and the land was finally sold in 1941 to the board of governors of the Big Island Veterans Camp. The veterans camp erected a few structures for its own use, but only a few isolated foundations, amid the weeds, or an eroded walking path remain as a

reminder of the thousands of people who once rode the streetcars to Big Island Park.

The Tonka Bay Hotel sat empty for two years but was finally pulled down in 1913. The adjoining dance hall and roller rink was moved to Excelsior and became part of the Excelsior Amusement Park. All of the property was eventually sold, and the last parcels were disposed of in 1944–45.

The streetcar service did better. Some 2 million passengers rode the Lake Minnetonka lines in 1907, the year the park opened. That number was at 3.7 million in 1911, the year it closed, and it kept growing until the all-time peak year of 1921, when 5.2 million passengers took the cars to Lake Minnetonka. By then paved roads ringed the lake, and automobile competition started taking its toll. The last year of profitable operation was 1924. That year TCRT sold its Excelsior lakefront property and the dock station to another company, which in

TCRT built three double-ended ferries in the winter of 1905–6 to carry the large crowds between the Excelsior Dock Station and Big Island Park. The boats' decks were built too low and took on water in windy conditions, and the paddlewheel housings prevented easy maintenance. They were completely rebuilt the following year and looked like the *Saint Paul,* here gliding up to Big Island.

The boats served some small docks, where the water was too shallow to use the midship gangway. Instead, passengers boarded by way of a front window with the upper sash removed. Photograph by Frederic Wommer; courtesy of the Minnesota Historical Society.

turn built Excelsior Amusement Park, opening for business in 1925. In 1928, TCRT closed the downtown ticket office and opened a new ticket office in the bus depot at 7th Street and 1st Avenue North. Excelsior Amusement Park was served by streetcar until 1932, when Lake Minnetonka service to Excelsior, Tonka Bay, and Deephaven was discontinued. Buses continued to serve Excelsior.

The express boat service was reduced during the 1925 season and discontinued at the end of the season in 1926. Three of the boats were stripped of all usable material then scuttled that year. One was sold in 1927; the remaining three were dismantled and scrapped in 1928.

Several factors were responsible for the demise of Big Island Park, the boats, and eventually the entire Lake Minnetonka operation. Local competition was one. The Twin Cities

population could support a single large amusement park, but TCRT owned two, the other being Wildwood Park on White Bear Lake. The public park systems in both cities were accessible by local streetcar lines and offered similar amenities for picnickers. Competing railroads, the Great Northern and the Minneapolis & St. Louis, offered their own outings to Lake Minnetonka. For those who wished to visit the St. Croix River Valley, the Northern Pacific had excursion packages to Taylors Falls and Stillwater.

General economic conditions were another factor. The country suffered a financial panic in 1907, not as grave as 1893, but enough to slow the economy and put people out of work. Then there was the forty-eight-hour workweek. Some businesses closed at noon on Saturdays, but that still left Sunday as the only free day of the week. Paid vacations or days off were rare, and, except for summer holidays like Memorial Day, the Fourth of July, or Labor Day, people did not have that much leisure time. Minnesota's short summer season and occasional outbreaks of bad weather during that short season created other problems. An operation like Big Island needed weeks of sustained high attendance and good weather. A three or, at best, three-and-a-half-month season simply was not enough.

Stillwater

Stillwater's location provided easy access to the vast timber resources of the St. Croix River Valley, and from its founding in 1848 until the mid-1880s, the town was at the center of one of the largest lumber-producing regions in the United States. Unfortunately, the railroads

The St. Paul & White Bear Railroad was an independent predecessor company that electrified the line from the east side of St. Paul to Mahtomedi. It was purchased by TCRT as part of the 1899 expansion to Stillwater. The branch around the south and west side of White Bear Lake followed in 1904, and the Bayport extension in 1905.

built their main lines through Minneapolis and St. Paul, and Stillwater was left somewhat isolated. The Northern Pacific arrived in Stillwater in 1870 via its branch line from White Bear Lake. The Milwaukee Road and the Omaha (the Chicago, St. Paul, Minneapolis & Omaha) built north from their main lines at Hastings, Minnesota, and Hudson, Wisconsin, respectively. By the turn of the century, Stillwater hosted three railroads. All of them were branch lines, however, and only the Northern Pacific offered direct passenger service to St. Paul.

Locally, Stillwater achieved distinction as having the first electric railway in the state of Minnesota. The Stillwater Street Railway built two lines in 1889 and ran its first electric car

on June 25, but the operation was undercapitalized and starved for lack of business. It was sold for scrap in 1897.

Stillwater's isolation, and the prospect of additional business, were undoubtedly on the minds of TCRT officials when they acquired the St. Paul & White Bear Railroad in 1899. The St. Paul & White Bear was a successor to

In 1925, officials turn out in Bayport to welcome the newly delivered lightweight cars built for the Stillwater local lines.

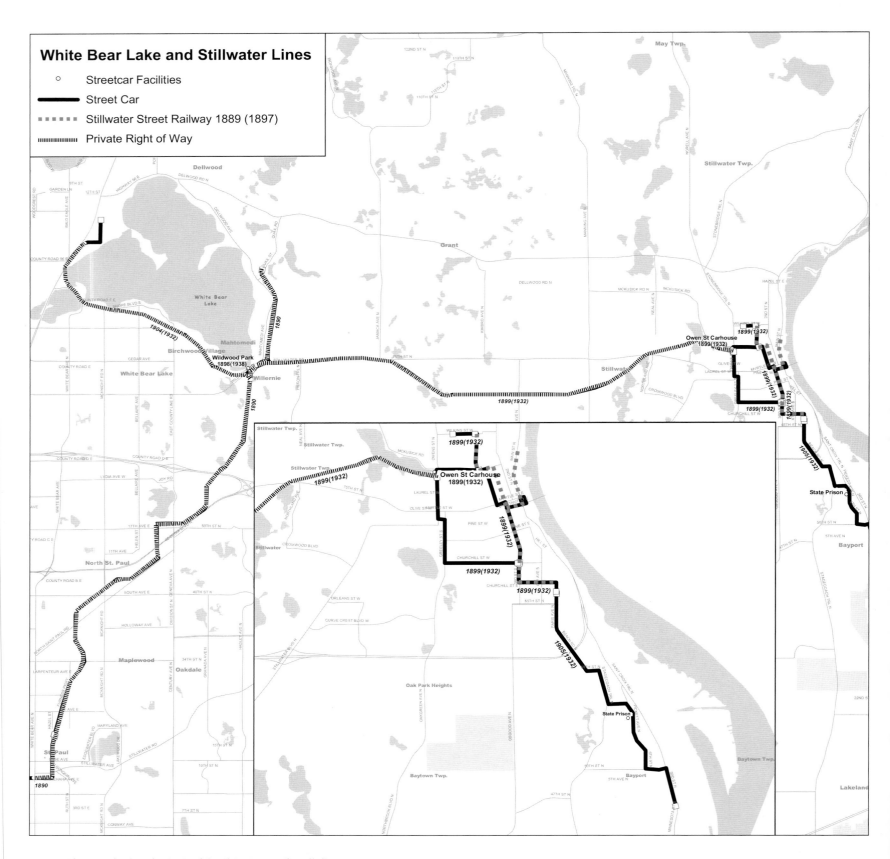

White Bear Lake and Stillwater Lines

○ Streetcar Facilities

━━━ Street Car

▪▪▪▪▪ Stillwater Street Railway 1889 (1897)

▥▥▥▥▥ Private Right of Way

After purchasing the St. Paul & White Bear Railroad's line
to Mahtomedi in 1898, TCRT built its Stillwater extension
in 1899. This included three local lines within Stillwater.

In 1904, a new branch opened around the south and west sides of White Bear Lake. At the Ramaley's Pavilion dock near Highway 61 and Highway 96, passengers could transfer to the steamer *White Bear.* Photograph by Sweet.

The local line from Stillwater to Bayport served the front door of the Minnesota State Prison. Special cars were chartered to transport prisoners, chained to the brass seat handles. Photograph by John Runk; courtesy of the Minnesota Historical Society.

the North St. Paul Railroad Company, which earlier, in 1889–90, had constructed a narrow gauge steam-powered railroad from East 7th and Newcombe Streets in the city of St. Paul to North St. Paul. Following its reorganization as the St. Paul & White Bear Railroad in 1892, the line was standard-gauged and converted to electricity, and extended to Mahtomedi. At the same time the company built a small amusement park adjoining its line on the south shore of White Bear Lake. It named the park Wildwood.

In the summer of 1899, TCRT completed track from a point at Willernie just east of Wildwood Park and a junction with the line to Mahtomedi through open country to Stillwater. The local streetcar lines in Stillwater were built at the same time. Power transmission lines and trolley wire went up, and a substation and small (wooden) carhouse were erected where the

right of way trackage entered Owen Street. The three local lines were Owen St., Wilkin St., and South 3rd St. The line from St. Paul and all of the local lines met at the Stillwater Union Depot on Water Street.

Full service began in August 1899, and two branches were added in 1904 and 1905. The first began at Wildwood and ran along the south shore of the lake into White Bear Lake, terminating at 6th Street and Banning Avenue. The second began at Oak and Orleans Streets in Stillwater and continued to South Stillwater, now named Bayport, a distance of approximately three and a half miles. Along the way it stopped at the front door of Minnesota State Prison, which chartered streetcars from time to time to transport prisoners from St. Paul.

OPERATION

Unlike the Lake Minnetonka Division, the White Bear–Mahtomedi–Stillwater lines were all single-tracked north of Ivy Avenue and the right of way in Hazel Park. Multiple sidings were provided at various locations to permit opposing cars to pass.

All movements were governed by time-table and train orders. Each car (train) had a schedule requiring it to meet and either take the siding or proceed at specific locations. A car approaching a train order semaphore with a stop indication would be expected to stop, and the motorman would then call the dispatcher for further orders. Similarly, a northbound car expecting to find a southbound car on a siding where a meet was scheduled, but not finding the southbound car, would not proceed further; instead, its motorman would call the dispatcher for orders.

As on the Lake Minnetonka line, a series

In the wide-open country beyond North St. Paul, near Long Lake, streetcars could attain speeds up to sixty miles per hour.

Trolleys to the Country

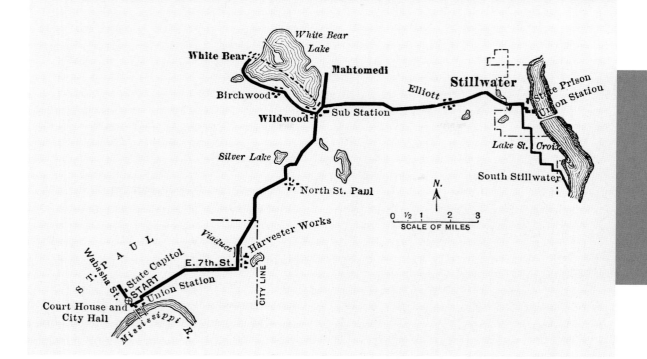

of perhaps five or six separate cars would operate together as sections of a single "train" running on the same schedule. Each car carried a green marker or signal at the front indicating that another car was following close behind it.

Base service on the Stillwater line was every thirty minutes from downtown St. Paul to Stillwater. During rush hours or at times of heavy traffic, separate cars were operated to North St. Paul, White Bear, and Mahtomedi

as sections of the Stillwater "train." A wye at Wildwood allowed extra cars from St. Paul to be turned and stored. A separate shuttle car operated between Mahtomedi and White Bear Lake for passengers wishing to transfer from the Stillwater line.

The local lines in Stillwater ran every thirty minutes, making connections with each other at the Union Depot and with St. Paul cars, as well as passenger trains of the Chicago &

Stillwater offered the most challenging hills in the metropolitan area, and the streetcars that served it had lower gearing to climb them. North 4th Street was one of the two steepest grades. A St. Paul–bound car is passing the Stillwater Public Library.

All Stillwater cars ended at the imposing Stillwater Union Depot on the St. Croix riverfront. Despite its impressive architecture, the depot served only branch line trains to nearby destinations: the Northern Pacific to White Bear Lake; the Chicago & NorthWestern to Hudson, Wisconsin; and the Milwaukee Road to Hastings. Photograph courtesy of the Minnesota Historical Society.

NorthWestern, Milwaukee Road, and Northern Pacific.

Streetcar revenue on the Stillwater Division sagged steadily after 1923. Losses mounted in each consecutive year, worsening abruptly after 1929 and the onset of the Depression. The company filed for abandonment of the Stillwater local lines, the Stillwater line beyond Wildwood, and the White Bear branch, proposing to substitute buses. The Railroad and Warehouse Com-

mission gave permission, and rail service ended in August 1932.

WILDWOOD

TCRT inherited Wildwood Park from the St. Paul & White Bear Railroad and spent large sums upgrading its facilities. In 1910, after ten years of ongoing improvements, it boasted a beautiful wooded picnic grove along the shore of White Bear Lake with tables, benches, and pavilions. There was a refreshment center in the main pavilion that sold sandwiches, ice cream, coffee, and soft drinks, or even fully catered lunches for large groups. Playground equipment was provided for children. There was an indoor baseball facility as well as a regulation baseball diamond with bleachers for competitive events. Rowboats were available along with fishing tackle and bait. Steamboats and motorized launches gave rides on the lake. There was a miniature steam-powered train. A sandy swimming beach with a large bathhouse offered private changing rooms, swimwear for rent, and equipment for water sports. There was a water chute and diving tower and on rainy days a fully equipped bowling alley.

The Fourth of July, 1912, on Chestnut Street in downtown Stillwater.

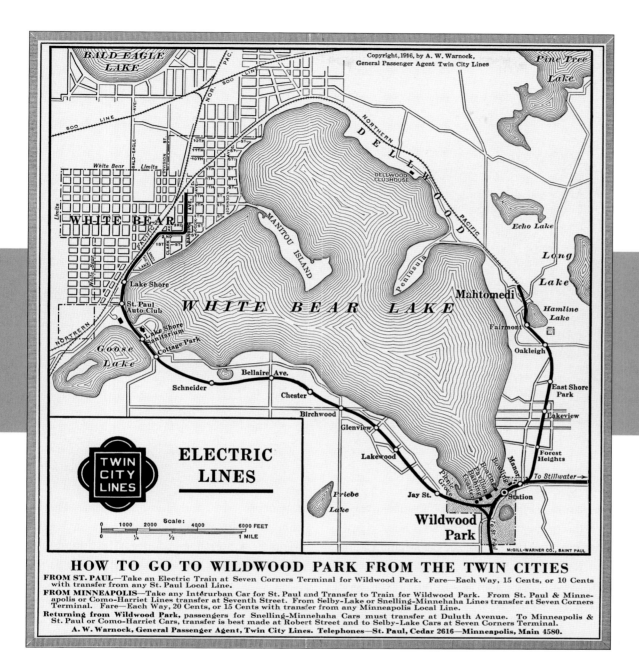

Copyright, 1916, by A. W. Warnock,
General Passenger Agent Twin City Lines

TWIN CITY LINES

ELECTRIC LINES

Scale:
1000 2000   4000   6000 FEET
0   ¼   ½   1 MILE

McGILL-WARNER CO., SAINT PAUL

HOW TO GO TO WILDWOOD PARK FROM THE TWIN CITIES

FROM ST. PAUL—Take an Electric Train at Seven Corners Terminal for Wildwood Park. Fare—Each Way, 15 Cents, or 10 Cents with transfer from any St. Paul Local Line.

FROM MINNEAPOLIS—Take any Interurban Car for St. Paul and Transfer to Train for Wildwood Park. From St. Paul & Minneapolis or Como-Harriet Lines transfer at Seventh Street. From Selby-Lake or Snelling-Minnehaha Lines transfer at Seven Corners Terminal. Fare—Each Way, 20 Cents, or 15 Cents with transfer from any Minneapolis Local Line.

Returning from Wildwood Park, passengers for Snelling-Minnehaha Cars must transfer at Duluth Avenue. To Minneapolis & St. Paul or Como-Harriet Cars, transfer is best made at Robert Street and to Selby-Lake Cars at Seven Corners Terminal.

A. W. Warnock, General Passenger Agent, Twin City Lines. Telephones—St. Paul, Cedar 2616—Minneapolis, Main 4580.

Brochures such as this one promoted excursions to TCRT's popular Wildwood Park on White Bear Lake.

Amusements included a large roller coaster, a carousel, and a penny arcade. The dance hall had a promenade over the lake and brought in name bands and orchestras. The main pavilion offered an excellent restaurant with à la carte service.

Unlike Minnetonka's short-lived Big Island Park, Wildwood had a long history. The park remained under TCRT management through the 1920s, and the company continued to invest in it

even as attendance and revenues softened and rail ridership and revenues declined. Following abandonment of the Stillwater and White Bear lines, it leased the property to a series of amusement companies that struggled to keep it going for several more years. By the mid-1930s, revenues from the lease could not cover real estate taxes and insurance, much less pay for minimal maintenance. Wildwood's last summer was 1938. It closed for good that fall, and

In the interest of safety, at Wildwood Park station and other major boarding locations like Excelsior, Como Park, and Lake Harriet, fences were placed between the tracks, and pedestrians crossed by means of underpasses or bridges. Photograph by Sweet; courtesy of the Ramsey County Historical Society, St. Paul, Minnesota.

the scrappers moved in; TCRT subsequently sold the property. Today the area is all private homes, and not a trace of the park remains.

Rail service to Mahtomedi and Wildwood Park continued. The Mahtomedi line was through-routed with the local Randolph Street line in St. Paul, becoming the Randolph–Hazel Park–Mahtomedi. Service to Mahtomedi ended in 1951, followed shortly thereafter by the abandonment of most local streetcar service in St. Paul in 1952.

There are vestiges of the Stillwater, White Bear, and Mahtomedi lines, although more of them disappear every year as development intrudes on the landscape. Parts of the Stillwater right of way are visible east of Willernie along County Road 12 and Manning Avenue. The former Stillwater substation on Owen Street survives as a private residence. The Mahtomedi line is visible in places east of Highway 244 on the east side of White Bear Lake. Other stretches can be seen through North St. Paul. The bridge over the former Chicago & NorthWestern (now Union Pacific) tracks at Duluth Avenue and East 7th Street is now a pedestrian walkway and bicycle path. West of Wildwood, what is now Birchwood Road is built on top of the streetcar right of way. Other bits and pieces are visible in the backyards of private residences.

Statistical information on the performance of the Lake Minnetonka and Stillwater operations is presented in Appendixes B and C.

Wildwood Park, with a St. Paul–
bound car in the distance at right.

From Profit to Penury
The Trolley Vanishes

The System Matures

T homas Lowry died on February 4, 1909, just twenty-three days short of his sixty-sixth birthday. In poor health for a number of years, he eventually succumbed to the tuberculosis he had once fought off as a young man. Lowry was entombed in the family mausoleum at Lakewood Cemetery in south Minneapolis. His passing was noted in the *New York Evening Post* of February 13, 1909:

> In a day when mere connection with a public utilities company is so often viewed as an a priori ground for suspicion, and when the management of street railways, in particular, has been the object of so much attack, the position that Mr. Lowry held was unique. It was through him that St. Paul and Minneapolis were welded together by a railroad system which its patrons did not look upon with angry derision, but were wont to boast of as the best in the country.

Longtime friend, brother-in-law, and business partner, Calvin Goodrich, Twin Cities Rapid Transit's general manager at the time of Lowry's death, succeeded him as president of the company. When Goodrich died in 1915, Lowry's son Horace took over as head. Horace Lowry inherited a well-managed, profitable street railway company that was highly regarded by its peers.

Unfortunately, the street railway industry was confronted by changes that would challenge its survival, and TCRT was caught up in them as well. Two forces were at work: the inability of companies to earn enough revenue to cover operating expenses, pay off debt, and finance improvements; and the public's growing attachment to the automobile.

TCRT suffered from a prosperity it could not afford. There were more riders, but the company could not recover enough of its operating expenses to accommodate them. The cities of Minneapolis and St. Paul set fares, and there was absolutely no support for a fare increase, even though the nickel fare had been in force since horsecar days. The public and local politicians reasoned that TCRT held a transportation monopoly, and the nickel fare symbolized that monopoly even though people were buying more automobiles and those automobiles, after 1920, would start making inroads on ridership.

In a way not anticipated by the photographer, this photograph contrasts the postwar allure of the automobile with the then-dowdy image of the streetcar. The location is a Lincoln showroom at 13th Street and Hennepin Avenue, then the center for automobile sales in Minneapolis. Photograph by Norton & Peel; courtesy of the Minnesota Historical Society.

SERVICE

Your transportation company must be ready at all times to meet any emergency for the great majority depend upon street cars.

During April, the Street Car Company cleaned snow from 4,705 miles of track, more than ten times the distance from Minneapolis to Chicago.

With summer just around the corner, street sweeping and sprinkling machines take up the work of the public service. Our share of this expense is $75,000.00 a year.

These services are included in our whole-hearted effort to make Twin City transportation complete. Only by service, fully accomplished, can there be mutual pride and good will.

TWIN CITY LINES

THE TRADE MARK OF A FRIEND

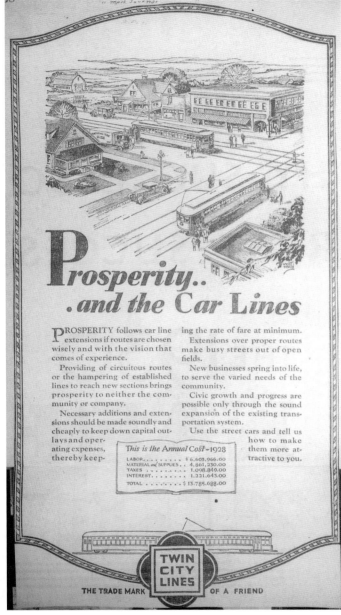

Prosperity.. and the Car Lines

PROSPERITY follows car line extensions if routes are chosen wisely and with the vision that comes of experience.

Providing of circuitous routes or the hampering of established lines to reach new sections brings prosperity to neither the community or company.

Necessary additions and extensions should be made soundly and cheaply to keep down capital outlays and operating expenses, thereby keeping the rate of fare at minimum.

Extensions over proper routes make busy streets out of open fields.

New businesses spring into life, to serve the varied needs of the community.

Civic growth and progress are possible only through the sound expansion of the existing transportation system.

Use the street cars and tell us how to make them more attractive to you.

This is the Annual Cost—1928	
LABOR	$ 6,605,966.00
MATERIAL and SUPPLIES	4,861,230.00
TAXES	1,098,849.00
INTEREST	1,221,643.00
TOTAL	$ 13,785,688.00

TWIN CITY LINES

THE TRADE MARK OF A FRIEND

In these advertisements from the 1920s, TCRT tried to educate the public about the financial vise it was in, unable to raise fares despite declining ridership, yet compelled to fund ever more expensive street improvements and maintenance.

In September 1917, a committee of workers confronted Horace Lowry and TCRT, demanding increased wages and improved working conditions. Motormen and conductors were compelled to work up to twelve hours a day. There was no paid time off, and they were compensated only for time actually worked. When the company denied the request, citing increasing costs and inadequate revenues, the workers sought help from the Minneapolis Trades and Labor Assembly. Learning of this appeal, company officials retaliated and fired those involved. Those employees then engaged the International Amalgamated Association of Street and Electric Railway Employees and organized under its banner. A strike began on October 6 that lasted four days. Service in Minneapolis continued uninterrupted except for some sporadic demonstrations at North Side Station. Striking employees attracted less support from fellow workers in Minneapolis, but in St. Paul, the *Pioneer Press* reported rioting and vandalism. Mobs roamed the streets attacking any streetcar that moved, and the entire St. Paul system was forced to shut down. Governor Joseph Burnquist was persuaded to call out federal troops from Ft. Snelling, allowing service to resume the next day. Following intervention by the Minnesota Commission of Public Safety, the strike ended on October 10 with a commitment from the company to rehire the fired employees, improve working conditions, and increase wages by 10 percent, but it was an empty promise because the issues remained and continued to fester. The company took an increasingly confrontational stand, organizing its own union and forbidding, on penalty of discharge, the wearing or displaying of any union buttons other than those authorized by the company. Amalgamated members defied the company and refused to comply. Eight hundred employees were locked out as a result of the company's actions and were eventually fired.

Over the next several months there was more violence, the worst on December 2 causing Governor Burnquist to call up units of the National Guard to restore order in what the press termed "The War of St. Paul." Although the company eventually triumphed over the strikers and suppressed the organizing drive, its standing in the public mind was destroyed, especially among working people. TCRT's reaction is understandable given World War I, the "Red Scare," and the activities of the Industrial Workers of the World (IWW). Not all of the employees joined the strikers, many of whom were notorious radicals with IWW ties. TCRT also could not afford what the employees demanded without relief through the fare box. Its 1918 annual report, citing wartime inflationary pressures, noted increased expenses of 20 to 40 percent for materials and 60 percent for wages. Nonetheless, the fare adjustments needed to cover these increases were bitterly opposed by the cities. Voters turned down a service-at-cost franchise, negotiated with the city of Minneapolis in 1919, at the same time demands were

Horace Lowry, son of Thomas and TCRT president from 1916 to 1931. Photograph by Lee Brothers; courtesy of the Minnesota Historical Society.

being made for improved service in both Minneapolis and St. Paul.

In 1920, TCRT won an emergency fare increase from five to six cents, but it prevailed in 1921 when it persuaded the legislature to pass the Brooks Coleman Law, which transferred the authority to regulate fares from the cities of Minneapolis and St. Paul to the Minnesota Railroad and Warehouse Commission. The law established a formula for setting fares that would allow a prescribed return on the value of the company's assets. That same year it engaged A. L. Drum and Company to conduct a valuation study, which was submitted to the commission in June of 1923. After contentious hearings and considerable negotiations, in 1925 TCRT accepted a finding that set a 7.5 percent return on the value of the property and a cash fare of eight cents or six tokens for forty cents. This

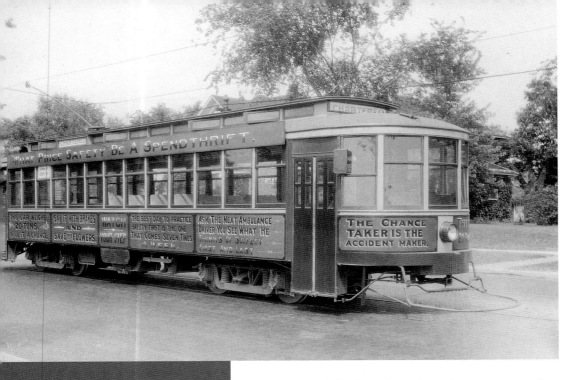

Increasing automobile traffic in the 1920s led to more collisions, and TCRT responded with this car, covered with exhortations to drive safely.

marked the first time that tokens were used as a discount fare.

The company won "The War of St. Paul" and its fare increases, but its obstinacy did nothing to improve its fortunes, as more and more streetcar riders became automobile owners.

The Evolution of the Bus

The automobile came into its own as TCRT's rail system reached its zenith. At first an expensive and unreliable novelty for those who could afford it, the automobile became plentiful and popular as mass production reduced its cost and technical improvements turned it from a summer toy into an all-season vehicle that anyone could buy on credit. The first automobile dealerships appeared around 1910, one being the Pence Auto Company at 8th Street and Hennepin Avenue, just three blocks from TCRT's corporate headquarters.

Thirteen years later, in 1923, the automobile was more than a frivolous nuisance. Not only was it taking away riders, the congestion it created on downtown streets slowed the streetcars and increased the company's operating expenses. More autos also meant many more collisions, an additional source of red

ink. Automobiles needed good roads, and as Minneapolis and St. Paul made improvements to accommodate them, TCRT was compelled to remove and reinstall its tracks as part of city repaving projects. Ironically, it received no compensation for this work even though improved streets encouraged automobile competition at the same time that Minneapolis and St. Paul were demanding that TCRT extend its lines and expand service.

There were thirteen million cars on the road in 1920, and that year another 3.7 million would emerge from U.S. auto plants. Half would be Henry Ford's Model T, available on credit for only $290. By then, it had occurred to street railway companies that motor vehicles, without the expensive track and power infrastructure, just might be a less expensive way to provide service and perhaps make money. The automobile was not going away, and its cousin, the bus, was getting bigger and more reliable. After years of disdaining motorized competition and snubbing buses as inferior vehicles, the street railways stopped complaining and started buying. The stately streetcar was in very serious trouble.

Early buses were nothing more than a box mounted on an auto or truck chassis. The first bus in revenue service is credited to the German engineer Karl Benz, who put a five-horsepower single-cylinder gas engine on a carriage body in 1895. That vehicle accommodated eight passengers and made scheduled trips between the German town of Siegen and the villages of Netphen and Deuz. In 1902, the Mack brothers of Brooklyn, New York, turned out this country's first bus. It resembled an oversized touring car and could carry up to fifteen passengers at a brisk twenty miles per hour. It was never

SHOP BEST BY STREET CAR

Your shopping tours will be far more pleasant if you go by Street Car. For these clean, roomy, and comfortably heated cars take you direct to the entrance of your favorite store. You avoid the danger and fatigue of driving and parking. Use what you save in transportation to buy other gifts.

Shop often this year. The downtown stores offer a wealth of new and attractive merchandise at prices that double the pleasure of shopping.

For Convenience Shop Between 9 and 4.

TWIN CITY LINES

In the 1920s, many women had not yet learned to drive, so TCRT marketed to them. Note the encouragement to "Shop Between 9 and 4," avoiding the crowded rush hours.

intended for point-to-point transportation but did find work as a sightseeing vehicle. Transit buses appeared in 1905, when the Fifth Avenue Coach Company imported fifteen De Dion Bouton double-decker buses from France and placed them in service in New York City.

The first challenge to the streetcar came with the jitney craze of 1914–16. Jitneys were

Development along the outer blocks of the 4th Ave. S. line in south Minneapolis is sparse and scattered in this aerial view from 1929. The southbound streetcar has just passed 47th Street and Field Elementary School. Photograph courtesy of the Minnesota Historical Society.

automobiles owned by unregulated entrepreneurs who made a business of skimming passengers off streetcar routes. At the peak of the craze in 1915, there were 60,000 jitney operators in direct competition with the streetcar companies, enough to popularize a trade journal, *Jitney Bus*. Enraged at losing business, the streetcar companies retaliated, demanding that cities suppress jitney competition. Compliant city governments, beholden to the streetcar companies for franchise revenues and street maintenance, fell into line, passing ordinances that compelled jitney operators to buy liability bonds, follow

designated routes, and charge prescribed fares. By 1916, jitneys were mostly banished from the streets, although their memory was enough to convince the street railway industry that motor vehicles had enormous potential for local transit service. *Motor Bus* magazine editorialized, prophetically, in September 1915:

> Most of the buses at this time are ordinary
> touring cars. The touring car, however, is
> being superceded by the regular motorbus.
> While the streetcar companies are showing
> hostility, not unnatural to the competitor who

For a brief time in the mid-1920s, TCRT owned Yellow Cab and had a near monopoly on public transportation in the Twin Cities. Appropriately, these taxis are parked in front of the Hotel Lowry at 4th and Wabasha Streets in downtown St. Paul.

In 1923, new bus 51, with a White chassis and Minneapolis-built Eckland Brothers body, poses on St. Peter Street in front of the Hamm Building in downtown St. Paul. Photograph by Brown's Studio; courtesy of the Minnesota Historical Society.

is materially reducing their profits, we venture to predict that inside of a few years the present-day streetcar interests will have huge investments in the more economic means of transportation. It should be remembered that (the streetcar) interests' business is the carrying of passengers. If a more economic method of transporting passengers were discovered, they would be foolish to persist in their obsolete system. Never again, however, can the traction interests have a monopoly of public transportation. They must learn to compete as other businesses compete.

Bus technology still had a long way to go before it could take on the streetcar. But, unlike the streetcar, which made only slight technical progress between 1915 and 1935, buses improved considerably. The Fageol brothers marketed the first true bus, the Fageol Safety Coach, in 1922. It used a four-cylinder Hall-Scott engine and could accommodate twenty passengers. As in an automobile, passengers boarded the bus through a series of doors along the side. Later models featured a single entrance door and aisle seating. The Fageol proved popular, particularly among the pioneering intercity operators, one of them being E. Roy Fitzgerald of

Eveleth, Minnesota, who would go on to found National City Lines, a company that owned and managed dozens of transit systems around the country, some in major cities such as Los Angeles, Baltimore, and Philadelphia. Time passed and other manufacturers appeared: Twin Coach, White, Flxible, Reo, Pierce-Arrow, Studebaker, Dodge, and Yellow Coach began turning out hundreds of buses every year. Eckland Brothers of Minneapolis became a major supplier of bus bodies for Greyhound, partnering with C. H. Will Motor Corporation, which itself was partially owned by Greyhound. Twin Coach introduced its Model 40 in 1927, the first true transit bus with entrance doors ahead of the front wheels. Yellow Coach pioneered the monocoque (single unit) body in 1931. Diesel

engines came into use following the pioneering work of General Motors' Charles Kettering, who perfected the two-cycle engine. By the late 1920s, there were more than one hundred companies involved in the production of buses, engines, and bus chassis. Only five major streetcar builders remained.

Meanwhile, the automobile onslaught continued. Electric starters became available in 1911. Pneumatic tires replaced solid rubber wheels. Cadillac Motor Company introduced the V-8 engine in 1914, the same year that Henry Ford gave his employees a five-dollar, eight-hour day, doubling the average wage and making the Model T affordable for Ford's assembly line workers. In 1916, President Woodrow Wilson signed the Federal Aid Road

Automobiles created traffic congestion, reducing streetcar speed and reliability and increasing operating costs. This is Marquette Avenue between 6th and 7th Streets in downtown Minneapolis. Photograph courtesy of the Minnesota Historical Society.

Act, which committed the federal government to pay half the cost of new highway construction. Four-wheel hydraulic brakes were introduced in 1920. In 1923, John D. Hertz, president of Yellow Cab, founded Hertz Rent-A-Car. Safety glass appeared in 1926. By 1927 sales of replacement vehicles were exceeding sales to first-time buyers, and used car lots were popping up everywhere.

First Encounters

None of this was good news for the traction companies. The electric interurbans that ran between cities were early casualties, losing riders to improved roads and the autos and the bus companies that used them. The year 1915 saw the last addition of any significant mileage to the national interurban network. In 1917, abandonments exceeded new construction and revenues fell off drastically. The years between 1925 and 1929 were especially bad. Even with the national prosperity of the Roaring Twenties, 45 percent of all companies still in business were in deep deficit by 1929. People were buying automobiles; they were not riding the interurban. The Great Depression brought about a complete collapse.

YEARS	MILES ABANDONED
1914–19	412
1920–24	915
1925–29	3,285
1930–34	5,116
1935–39	2,612
1940–44	1,031
1945–49	925
1950–54	964

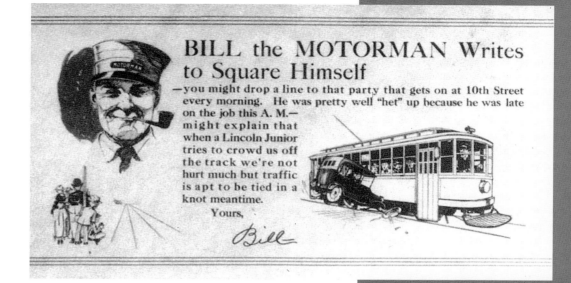

BILL the MOTORMAN Writes to Square Himself

—you might drop a line to that party that gets on at 10th Street every morning. He was pretty well "het" up because he was late on the job this A. M.— might explain that when a Lincoln Junior tries to crowd us off the track we're not hurt much but traffic is apt to be tied in a knot meantime.

Yours,

Bill

By 1960, only five of the early interurbans remained in operation, and they were shadows of themselves. In California, the Metropolitan Transit Authority operated Pacific Electric's last line to Long Beach. It was converted to freeway buses in 1961. In the Midwest, the Chicago North Shore & Milwaukee, between Chicago and Milwaukee and the Chicago South Shore, and South Bend, between Chicago and South Bend, Indiana, continued to operate commuter services. The North Shore was abandoned in 1963. Only the South Shore and two suburban lines in the Philadelphia area, the former Philadelphia and Western and two lines of the former Philadelphia Suburban Transportation Company, known as the Red Arrow, remain today, and they are all part of public transit authorities.

Minnesota followed a similar course. The Minneapolis, Northfield and Southern, which used gas-electric cars rather than overhead trolleys, discontinued passenger service on its Richfield–Bloomington branch line from 54th Street and Nicollet Avenue via Auto Club Junction and Savage to Northfield, Minnesota, in 1922. Remaining Northfield service from Auto Club Junction via Edina and St. Louis Park to Glenwood Junction and the downtown Minneapolis depot at 7th Street North and 3rd Avenue North ended in 1942. The Mesaba Railway, serving Iron Range communities,

Bill the Motorman was a fictionalized spokesman for TCRT from the 1920s through the 1940s. His friendly face and commonsense, often humorous, advice on matters of importance to the company appeared in newspapers and in advertisements aboard the cars. In the 1920s, automobiles were competing with streetcars for passengers as well as space on the street. Collisions were common, as were delays, and TCRT often was blamed, even when it wasn't at fault. Reproduced courtesy of Forrest Johnson.

"I Like to Read on My Way Home"

RIDE · READ · RELAX

TWIN CITY LINES

"Ride, Read, Relax": The "why drive and fuss with traffic when you can ride and read?" message rings true today.

ceased operations in 1927. The St. Paul Southern Electric Railway, between St. Paul and Hastings, quit in 1928.

Some systems survived by substituting buses or making them part of their operations. The Minneapolis, Anoka & Cuyuna Range abandoned its electric passenger service between downtown Minneapolis and Anoka in 1939, replacing it with buses; freight service continued.

City transit systems held out much longer. In 1914, they were all rail. Streetcar ridership peaked, nationwide, in 1920 with 13.8 billion passengers, but as the 1920s moved along, buses grabbed a larger share of the business. In 1924, the *Electric Railway Journal* published the results of a survey of street railway properties. The survey asked how many buses they were using, and how they were being used. It found 1,200 in service on U.S. and Canadian systems, representing a threefold increase over 1922 and 30 percent more than 1923. They were divided among 121 street railway companies. In addition, thirty systems not using buses stated they were planning bus operations for 1925. The survey compared these findings with figures from 1923, when only fifty street railway systems reported bus operations of any kind. Interestingly, at the time of the survey only six properties, all of them in smaller towns, had completely replaced their streetcars with buses. The majority used them to start up new service or as extensions or feeders to streetcar lines. The consensus of streetcar management at the time held that "the bus cannot replace streetcars in ordinary service," and "most railways find it unsuitable for regular service."

Events soon demonstrated the fragility of that consensus as more properties turned to buses to replace their streetcar lines. In 1929, 20 percent of systems were all bus operations. By 1937, 50 percent exclusively used buses. In Minnesota, Mankato switched to buses in 1930, St. Cloud in 1936, and Winona in 1938. Duluth Superior Traction ended all streetcar service in September 1939, substituting electric trolley buses on its heavier lines and using gas buses on the rest.

This trend had nothing to do with the streetcar itself but everything to do with the economics of streetcar operations. A well-maintained streetcar on good track gave far superior service to a motorbus of that era. Streetcars were much larger vehicles. As an example, TCRT's standard cars were forty-six feet long and nine feet wide. Typical bus bodies were twenty-five feet long and seven feet wide. A streetcar could comfortably seat fifty passengers with another sixty standing. Buses could squeeze in twenty to twenty-five seated passengers and perhaps a dozen standing. A fully loaded streetcar, especially one of the new PCCs introduced in 1936, accelerated faster than a fully loaded bus and, on private right of way, had a higher operating speed. Streetcar passengers enjoyed a smooth ride on good track. Bus riders were at the whim of every crack and pothole in the street. Streetcars could move large numbers of people at a much lower labor cost because of their high unit capacity—if the people were there. Unfortunately, in later years they were not, and the streetcar became a victim of its own efficiency.

Streetcars came with a large fixed investment in track and in electric power systems. The cost of that investment had to be spread over a large number of passengers. The more passengers they carried, the lower the cost per rider and the more cost effective the operation. Buses did not have these fixed costs, but their limited capacity and lower overall speed made them less efficient people movers on heavily used lines in large urban transit systems. Streetcars held sway as long as the passengers were there, but they became vulnerable as ridership declined and track and power infrastructure came due for replacement.

The Bus and TCRT

TCRT took notice of the jitney operators swarming over its streetcar lines and, like any worthy monopoly, resolved that the best way to deal with competitors was to buy them out. In 1918, its subsidiary, the Minnetonka and White Bear Navigation Company, paid $150,000 to acquire thirty-nine jitney buses and related tools and facilities in an agreement with the Associated Commercial Clubs of Minneapolis and the Minneapolis Jitney Bus Association, thereby wiping out all jitney competition in the city of Minneapolis. It also began using buses as feeders to its streetcar lines. One example was a shuttle that opened in 1921 on Marshall Avenue from 30th Street and Grand Avenue Northeast (the end of the 2nd St. N.E. line) to the end of the Washington Ave. N. line at Camden. Others were crosstown routes such as the Lowry Avenue Crosstown, which traveled on Lowry Avenue between Xerxes Avenue North and Stinson Boulevard. By 1926, TCRT had acquired all the urban bus operators in Minneapolis and St. Paul and merged them into the Twin City Motor Bus Company, which, prior to 1924, had operated as an independent company under separate ownership.

The Interurban line on University Avenue found itself with competition in 1918: buses that made limited stops every mile or so between the downtowns. TCRT eventually bought them out and ran them as part of its system. Here the westbound competitors approach Fairview Avenue. Photograph courtesy of the Minnesota Historical Society.

By the end of World War II, buses and bus operations had grown in importance in TCRT's overall business. Some twenty-four million passengers rode TCRT buses in 1946, bringing in revenues of $2.3 million. From 4 percent of all passengers carried in 1929, buses carried 12 percent of TCRT riders in 1946. The company owned 221 buses plus four garages, two large facilities, in downtown Minneapolis and St. Paul, and two smaller suburban garages in Excelsior and White Bear Lake. Portions of the Nicollet carhouse in Minneapolis were modified to store and service buses, and a bus overhaul shop had been added to the Snelling complex in St. Paul.

Detailed records of other early bus operators in the Twin Cities are few and scattered, but it is known that at least six companies were doing business by 1923. They included Como Transportation Company, Minneapolis–St. Paul

Bus Line Inc., Kenney Bus Company, American Auto Transit of St. Paul, Gopher Coach Line, and the Twin City Motor Bus Company.

Como Transportation Company provided bus service along Como Avenue between Minneapolis and St. Paul. It was incorporated in 1923 and subsequently acquired by Minneapolis–St. Paul Bus Line Inc., which took over its operations. Como Transportation owned two White buses (eighteen-passenger and sixteen-passenger), two Locomobile Model 648 automobiles, and a White Town Auto. All of them went to Minneapolis–St. Paul Bus Line, which subsequently purchased five Macks, three in 1924 and two in 1925. Como Transportation and Minneapolis–St. Paul Bus Line were acquired by TCRT in 1925 and merged into the Twin City Motor Bus Company in 1926.

Kenney Bus Company was incorporated

From Profit to Penury

in South Dakota in 1923. Its president, W. T. Kenney, had earlier begun a bus service from Minneapolis to the Glen Lake Sanitarium. That service was extended to Waconia briefly in 1923 but was promptly cut back because of financial losses. Kenney was also an owner of the American Auto Transit Company, which was incorporated in South Dakota in 1919. It began service to South St. Paul from downtown St. Paul in 1919, followed by service to Minneapolis via Dayton and Marshall Avenues in 1923 and lines to White Bear Lake, Bald Eagle, White Bear Beach, and Ft. Snelling in 1924. In 1925, its intercity route was changed to one by way of Central and University in St. Paul and Franklin Avenue in Minneapolis. American Auto Transit acquired Kenney Bus Company in 1923, and it in turn was bought out by TCRT in 1925 and merged into the Twin City Motor Bus Company in 1926. Prior to its acquisition by TCRT, American Auto Transit of St. Paul owned forty-seven buses, a mixture of Macks and Whites, twenty- to twenty-five-passenger units with Eckland bodies. Gopher Coach Line operated two routes: one ran from Minneapolis–St. Paul to Taylors Falls, the other to Duluth. The route to Taylors Falls was sold to Twin City Motor Bus in 1923; the Duluth route went to Mesaba Motor Company the same year.

The Twin City Motor Bus Company, once it was acquired by TCRT and became a subsidiary, operated all the services of its predecessors plus a number of new routes that were established under TCRT control. These included the short shuttles that preceded some streetcar extensions. Streetcar lines subsequently converted to buses came under the Minneapolis Street Railway or the St. Paul City Railway, not Twin City Motor Bus.

The Great Depression

The market crash of 1929 and the Great Depression that followed thoroughly savaged the street railway industry. Streetcar commuters disappeared along with their jobs as factories closed down and unemployment soared. People without incomes stopped taking the streetcar to shop or go see a movie. Those who could afford an automobile kept right on driving. Dozens of streetcar systems became insolvent and filed for bankruptcy protection. United Railways, operator of the Baltimore, Maryland, system, lost $2 million in 1932 and fell into receivership. St. Louis Public Service, already weakened, saw its revenues plummet by 20 percent in 1932 and was forced into reorganization in 1933. Chicago's street railways and its elevated railway system, torn asunder by years of political infighting and financial shenanigans, failed. Other systems, among them Cleveland, Indianapolis, and Detroit, accepted New Deal

With the creation in 1946 of the new Lyndale Avenue North bus line from downtown Minneapolis to the Camden neighborhood, buses were reintroduced to North Side Station. Photograph courtesy of Forrest Johnson.

reconstruction funds to pay for car and track maintenance. Service reductions, wage cuts, layoffs, deferred maintenance, and the substitution of buses became commonplace.

Amid the chaos, TCRT staged an orderly retreat. Horace Lowry, the last member of the Lowry family to lead the company, passed away in 1931 and was succeeded by T. Julian McGill. Lowry's legacy of efficient management, along with a civic-minded board of directors, had prepared it for lean times. TCRT carried a debt load of roughly $22 million in 1927, mostly borrowings to fund system expansion around the turn of the century. During the prosperous 1910s and 1920s, it had managed to reduce operating expenses, keep up maintenance, and pay dividends, while positioning itself to pay down this

T. Julian McGill, TCRT president from 1931 to 1936. Photograph by Harris & Ewing; courtesy of the Minnesota Historical Society.

debt. It also enjoyed respect in the community, even though as the streetcar company and a public monopoly it had a lot of leftover baggage from the 1917 encounter with organized labor. Local politicians loved to beat up on TCRT, but it was mostly empty rhetoric. The streetcars were superbly maintained and ran on time. President McGill stated, "We are commended as one of the best street railway systems in America, and are noted for our fine property and the courteous and efficient handling of our patrons."

TCRT brought $1.2 million to its bottom line in 1929. That fell to a mere $41,000 in 1932, and in 1933 it lost $23,000. Ridership had been in a steady slide throughout the 1920s, from a high of 238 million in 1920 to approximately 168 million in 1929, all because of automobile competition and despite the expansion of streetcar lines into new neighborhoods. Between 1929 and 1933, the Depression took away another 68 million, reducing total ridership to 100 million, its lowest point since 1906 and, after the World War II surge, its lowest point until 1953.

A fare increase from eight to ten cents in January 1929 preceded the October market crash, softening the effects of the subsequent loss of riders and income and giving TCRT time to make adjustments to its operations. The most significant and controversial was the abolition of conductors on all but the heaviest streetcar lines. The cities of Minneapolis and St. Paul protested, citing safety concerns. Union members at Lake Street Station staged a brief strike in 1938, but the one-man cars stayed.

There was more: August 1932 brought an end to the suburban rail lines to Lake Minnetonka, Deephaven, White Bear Lake, and Stillwater. Several bus routes disappeared as well. Service was trimmed across the system to

Edina's Country Club neighborhood was a planned streetcar suburb, with entrances at the Grimes, Wooddale, and Browndale stops, which featured waiting shelters. It would be the last such suburb; subsequent developments would be built around the automobile, ignoring public transit. Here, the camera is looking southwest. The streetcar line and 44th Street run next to each other from the bottom center of the photograph to the right edge. The original Motor Line right of way is also visible as the rear boundary of the mostly vacant lots along the north side of Sunnyside Road in the lower center. Photograph courtesy of the Edina Historical Society.

bring car miles into line with ridership by cutting the number of "extra" cars used at rush hours. Annual revenue car miles fell from twenty-nine million in 1929 to twenty-two million in 1933 and bus miles from 4.4 million in 1929 to 3.9 million in 1933. Employees were hit, too. Motormen's wages were reduced from fifty-five cents an hour to fifty cents an hour in 1932, followed by another 10 percent across-the-board cut for all employees in 1933. Shop employees were given two unpaid days off per month for seven months in 1933. The "allowed time" paid in runs to bring them to an eight-hour minimum was also eliminated. No employees were furloughed, but the conversion to one-man cars along with service reductions forced hundreds of conductors and motormen off regular paid runs and on to the extra board, where work was scarce. Many went from a full week's work to only two or three days of work per week, often less.

President McGill tried to smooth things over, expressing to employees that this was "difficult" and "regrettable," then adding, "It is therefore obvious that we are giving our employees preference in the division of our earnings. We must pay our bond interest and when conditions justify we must pay a fair return to our preferred and common stockholders, who have invested $25,000,000 in this property, but in the meantime during this Depression we are first taking care of our employees." Such soothing words did not go down well with workers who had to provide for themselves and their families. In 1934, they voted to join the Amalgamated Association of Street, Electric Railway and Motor Coach Employees of America. Nor did they mollify dissident shareholders. A group led by J. F. Fitzpatrick, his son P. W. Fitzpatrick, and J. A. Solmes took "alarm at the present situation of the Company" and warned of "destruction and bankruptcy" unless a new deal was secured. Their proxy circular announced that "in this company the stockholder is truly the FORGOTTEN MAN, there being no dividends paid since 1929." It went on, charging management with paying employees "prosperity wages," keeping 570 excess employees on the payroll, maintaining streetcars on an "extravagant scale," wasting hundreds of thousands of dollars in repair shops that "belong to a by-gone era," and setting aside funds for employee benefits and pensions without

As Christmas 1944 approached, this streetcar at Snelling Shops urged citizens to divert their holiday dollars to war bonds. Photograph from the Minneapolis Star and Tribune News Negative Collection; courtesy of the Minnesota Historical Society.

board approval. They proposed installing P. W. Fitzpatrick as vice president of operations and making him a director. Wisely, most shareholders disagreed and turned away the dissident group's charges in favor of the incumbent management, which had retained Stone & Webster, a respected transportation engineering firm, to study the company's operations. Its report refuted all of their allegations. Fifteen years later another dissident shareholder, Charles Green, would revive the charges. His efforts to address them would bring about an altogether different outcome.

World War II Brings Temporary Prosperity

By the mid-1930s, operating expenses had come down from $8.4 million in 1931 to $6 million in 1935, turning a $23,000 operating loss in 1933 to a profit of $472,000 in 1935 and a $649,000 profit in 1936. None of this increase was sustainable, however, because it all came from operating economies, not more riders. Passenger revenues and ridership kept right on tumbling. From $10.6 million in 1931, revenues dropped to $8.6 million in 1935. From 130.8 million riders in 1931, the number declined to 107.3 million in 1935. There would be a temporary flood of business during World War II, until the surrender of Japan in August 1945 brought peace, more automobiles, and, with them, the end of TCRT's prosperity.

TCRT ridership and automobile ownership closely paralleled national trends until the middle of the 1920s. Thereafter, automobile registrations sprinted ahead. In Minneapolis and St. Paul, there were already 4.5 persons per automobile in 1928 compared to 5.3 nationally in 1929. A study in 1940 found only eight out of thirty cities surveyed with populations over 300,000 had more automobiles per capita. The Twin Cities trend was as follows:

YEAR	AUTOMOBILES LICENSED	PERSONS/ AUTO	TCRT RIDERS
1920	75,053	8.2	238,388,782
1924	115,382	5.7	209,252,949
1928	159,480	4.5	179,493,116
1932	170,945	4.2	113,032,559
1936	203,606	3.8	115,195,524
1940	220,266	3.5	104,313,619
1944	*	*	185,222,547

* Data for these categories are not available.

This relentless growth in the number of automobiles, even during the Depression years, underscores TCRT's shrinking market and its poor long-term prospects. Riders who had flooded the streetcars and buses during World War II flocked to automobile dealerships once the war ended.

The entry of the United States into World War II following the Japanese attack on Pearl Harbor on December 7, 1941, found TCRT's rolling stock and fixed facilities in good shape. The company never reduced maintenance during the Depression, and, even though most of its streetcars were over thirty years old, its five-year rebuilding program kept them all in superb condition. A typical streetcar averaged three and half years since it had last gone through the Snelling Shops. All of this was reflected in the reliability of both the system's streetcars and its buses, the latter receiving similar care. In 1941, streetcars averaged 17,680 miles per maintenance breakdown, buses 15,100 miles.

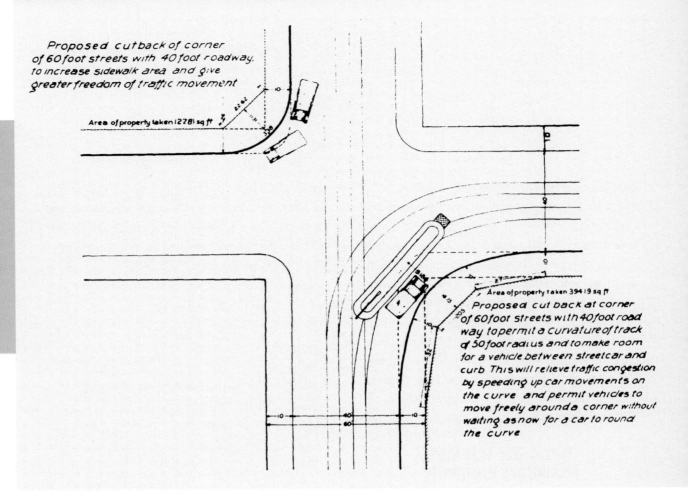

Proposed cutback of corner of 60 foot streets with 40 foot roadway. to increase sidewalk area and give greater freedom of traffic movement

Area of property taken 1278 sq ft

Area of property taken 3941.9 sq ft

Proposed cut back at corner of 60 foot streets with 40 foot road way to permit a curvature of track of 50 foot radius and to make room for a vehicle between streetcar and curb This will relieve traffic congestion by speeding up car movements on the curve and permit vehicles to move freely around a corner without waiting as now for a car to round the curve

As automobiles proliferated, they set in motion a trend without end, the widening of streets to serve their ever-increasing numbers. This diagram shows how to widen the radius of an intersection so that turning autos need not wait for a streetcar to clear the corner. Courtesy of the Ramsey County Historical Society, St. Paul, Minnesota.

Both numbers far exceeded industry norms. Similar attention was given to track and power infrastructure. Twenty-seven miles of track were completely renewed between 1936 and 1940. Trolley overhead wire replacement averaged 21,000 feet per year. A new high-pressure boiler capable of burning either coal or natural gas was installed at the Main Steam Station.

TCRT reduced its bonded debt during the 1930s despite the Depression, mainly by omitting stock dividends, a strategy that would subsequently prove very troublesome. In 1942, its operating cost, at 24.91 cents per mile, was the lowest of eighteen systems in an American Transit Association survey. That survey included major cities such as Philadelphia, St. Louis, Chicago, Cincinnati, Los Angeles, New Orleans, Detroit, and San Francisco. By the start of the war, TCRT had taken its first steps toward bus substitution, replacing streetcars on the Kenwood, Bryn Mawr, St. Louis Park, Franklin, and 6th Ave. N. lines in Minneapolis

and the Jackson–South Robert, Western, Merriam Park, and Hope lines in St. Paul. All of them had low ridership compared to the rest of the system or required track work that could not be justified economically. The 6th Ave. N. line, in Minneapolis, for example, would have needed a complete reconstruction as part of 6th Avenue's transformation into Olson Memorial Highway. In 1940, no highway money was available to assist with such work.

TCRT had plenty of capacity for new riders immediately after Pearl Harbor. There were 704 streetcars and 160 buses on the roster at the start of the war. One year later, even with staggered work hours, it could barely handle the passenger volume. Additional buses had been authorized by the War Production Board and were subsequently acquired to transport war workers to the New Brighton Army Ammunition Plant. Bus garage space was created at Nicollet Station in 1942. TCRT also discontinued the two intercity bus lines on University and Marshall

Avenues to free equipment. But there were no more streetcars. Regrettably, more than three hundred of its oldest wood-framed cars stored during the Depression were scrapped between 1934 and 1939. The cars it owned just had to work harder. By 1943, they were averaging 50 percent more miles per car than in 1934 and 27 percent more miles per car than in 1941. Total annual car miles went from twenty million in 1941 to twenty-five million in 1943. Electric power consumption jumped from an average wintertime load of 40,310 kilowatts in 1941 to 45,510 in 1943.

Finding new employees to operate and maintain the streetcars and buses became an equally serious problem as hundreds of its conductors, motormen, and car repairmen were drafted into military service. The company reduced its minimum hiring age to eighteen. For the first time it hired women as motormen and conductors (dubbing them "motorettes" and "conductorettes"), as well as car cleaners. Even high school students were recruited as conductors. The average number of hours actually worked by operating employees went from Depression lows of twenty-five to thirty hours to a scheduled minimum of forty-eight hours per week, creating a dispute with the union about overtime pay. Local 1005 won wage increases in 1941 that cost the company $250,000. Additional demands were made in late 1942, including a requirement for overtime pay after forty-four hours of work, all of which led to an extended tug-of-war involving the company, the union, and the Regional War Labor Board, the latter created by the federal government to referee issues involving wartime wages and hours. Finally, to drive home its point, the union barred all of its employees from working any overtime for three

Motorman's Tales: Adventures of a Teenage Trainman

In the spring of 1943, I heard they were hiring over at Snelling Station. I was only fifteen years old, but I got up enough courage to apply. On July 28 I found myself in training at East Side Station as a conductor. After a few months I returned to high school at De La Salle on Nicollet Island and found I could still take both a morning and evening rush hour run from nearby East Side.

There was always a hassle around the cage where we all "plugged in" on the assignment board. If someone missed, there was a quick scramble to cover the one-man runs. We high school student conductors would sneak a motorman's spot if we could. I waited for a year to try it, and got my Como–Harriet car out to the 44th Street loop at France Avenue before the inspector caught up.

The worst run, always left to new men, was #66, which hit all the theater closings on Saturday night and caught the last ride for sailors avoiding AWOL/curfew at the University. We often had head counts exceeding two hundred. Then totaling up the cash forced me to miss the owl car home, which meant sleeping overnight at the station. Sleeping upstairs at East Side was nothing short of traumatic. There were no sheets, just gray blankets on army cots thoroughly stained by the snoose chewers. The old wooden barn would shudder as each car rumbled in or out, and the thought of all those trolley poles still on the wire, with the fire warnings, made sleep impossible.

Our pay was sixty-six cents per hour with all the free rides we wanted.

—William J. Olsen

During the war, TCRT changed its hiring policies to handle skyrocketing ridership and the loss of male employees to military service. Five hundred women were hired, plus high school boys who worked as conductors. Photograph from the Minneapolis Star and Tribune News Negative Collection; courtesy of the Minnesota Historical Society.

D. J. Strouse, TCRT president from 1936 to 1949. The last of the traditional company heads, he was ousted during the Charles Green takeover. Photograph courtesy of the Minnesota Historical Society.

weeks during the 1943 November–December holidays, resulting in a 22 percent reduction in peak hour service. In January the company relented and restructured its schedules to provide for a forty-four-hour week.

Following settlement of the 1941 labor contract, the company applied for and was granted a fare increase of six tokens for fifty cents by the Minnesota Railroad and Warehouse Commission. From 1929 through 1941, the base fare had been ten cents cash or six tokens for forty-five cents. This higher rate of fare was in effect until April of 1943, when (amazingly) the commission determined that the increased wartime ridership and revenues no longer justified the higher fare and directed a reduction to the Depression era fares in effect prior to 1941. This arbitrary decision completely ignored escalating wartime prices and material shortages and was driven by politics, not economic facts. However, it was typical of transit regulatory bodies that still felt the public needed protection from the streetcar monopoly even though that monopoly had ended with the advent of the Model T some thirty-five years before. It was a bad move and would lead to bad things after the war. Twenty-five million additional passengers came aboard the cars in 1942, joined by another forty-five million in 1943, thirty-five million in 1944, and eight million each in 1945 and 1946. In four years TCRT regained all the riders it had lost to twenty years of auto competition and the Depression and, at 201.5 million passengers, was back to the same number of riders it carried in 1925. But four years later, two-thirds of them would be gone, and by 1954, its final year of streetcar operations, TCRT was down to 86.5 million passengers, roughly the same number it carried in 1904.

None of this came as a surprise to D. J. Strouse, who succeeded T. Julian McGill as TCRT's president following McGill's death in 1936. An extremely competent and knowledgeable transit executive, Strouse had been with the company since 1903. He knew that people would return to their automobiles once the war was over and wrote in the 1942 annual report:

> The management of the company is not unmindful that the present sharp upturn in passenger revenue is the result of the decreased use of private automobiles caused by gasoline and tire restrictions and an accelerated business activity generated by the war. When tire and gasoline rationing is discontinued the company will again be confronted with intense automobile competition. The management is apprehensive that the share-your-ride campaigns and other group transportation practices will continue after this emergency. Your company is furnishing the best possible service and hopes to retain a large number of these new patrons. The degree of success in that respect cannot be foreseen, and will not be known until after the present emergency.

What Strouse did not know, nor did anyone in the company know, nor could the transit industry foresee at that time, was the speed at which people would abandon streetcars and buses. Much depended on the direction of the national economy. Some economists were concerned that the wartime boom would turn to a postwar depression. Others rightly predicted that the Depression and the war years would loose a flood of pent-up demand and inflation. Strouse recognized that large expenditures would be needed for renewals and improvements if the company were to keep providing good service and attract riders. He also knew the board would ask tough questions before it committed company resources to capital improvements, especially after it had deferred shareholder dividends for fifteen years. To be sure, Strouse had good answers to what would be tough questions. He hired W. C. Gilman and Company, a New York transit engineering firm, to make a comprehensive evaluation of TCRT and its operations.

Gilman was directed to make a complete assessment of the property to include fixed facilities—carhouses and garages, track, power generation and distribution equipment and systems—along with all revenue and non-revenue rolling stock. It was to evaluate the organization, its structure and personnel, and all policies, procedures, shop methods, and maintenance programs, together with operating practices, schedules, staffing levels, and accidents. Gilman was to thoroughly examine the financial condition of the company, including its most recent income statements, consolidated balance sheets, profit and loss, funded debt, and additions and retirements. The evaluation was to project postwar operations, taking into account ridership levels, revenues, and operating expenses and recommending capital improvements that would be needed after the war.

The Gilman report went to Strouse in August 1944. It found a property in above-average condition, its overall operating practices and procedures sound, and its finances in good order. In making its projection for postwar business, Gilman recommended "the carrying out of a reasonable program of conversion of streetcars to motor buses or to some other type of equally efficient and flexible vehicle." It went on to project that the postwar ratio of revenues to expenses would approximate those of 1940, resulting in an operating ratio of 87.5 percent, and that rides per capita would increase slightly.

The report acknowledged "the Company contemplates that new passenger equipment will be purchased in the future from available funds, and the management has indicated that because of possible future developments in motor bus design the type of equipment to be purchased will be motor buses rather than streetcars or trolley coach units."

It estimated a ten-year capital expenditure of $6,650,000 that would allot:

- $650,000 for a replacement 15,000-kilowatt generator at the main power plant;
- $5,000,000 for 525 motor buses for conversion and/or replacements;
- $750,000 for garage facilities; and
- $250,000 for miscellaneous equipment.

There was no mention of new streetcars.

The Gilman report's assessment of TCRT's situation at the end of the war was on the mark, but its postwar projection of ridership, revenues, and expenses was much too optimistic and may have persuaded TCRT's management to invest in new streetcars rather than converting to buses. It is unclear what the Strouse management actually recommended to the board or whether there was any internal debate or discussion. It is known that the 1944 annual report stated that management "contemplates purchasing annually a number of modern, light weight, noiseless, streamlined cars to replace present equipment. This program will be continued upon a reasonable basis throughout the coming years."

Five years later there were 141 brand-new streamlined PCC cars in service, but not a single dollar in shareholder dividends had been paid and TCRT was losing riders and money fast. For one shareholder the consequences of the board's decision presented an opportunity.

Turmoil

Charles Green liked to make money. He had no special interest in, or fondness for, the street railway industry. In fact, as his behavior would demonstrate, he knew absolutely nothing about the business. Today his talents and tactics might be legitimized and even admired, but Green, ever street smart, characterized himself best when said that he was just "always ready to make a fast buck."

During the war he prospered by wholesaling appliances to army post exchanges through his Green Sales Company. All of his wartime cash needed a new home, so he started shopping around for undervalued stocks and came upon TCRT. On paper the company looked ripe: assets of $60 million, positive earnings, money in the bank, not a lot of debt, low stock price. Never mind that it had not paid dividends since 1929—so much the better. Green did not really care; dividends were for widows and orphans. Green saw his chance to make another "fast buck," so he bought six thousand shares and slipped into the weeds.

Time passed. When the TCRT board bought new streetcars and did not pay dividends, Green decided to stir things up and began making noise about shareholders' rights. Green knew that TCRT was worth more dead than alive and told D. J. Strouse so to his face. When Strouse would not back down, Green, along with Bigham D. Eblen, a Detroit attorney and a large TCRT shareholder, made his next move. At the March 1949 board of directors meeting, Green and Eblen attempted to unseat Strouse, but they did not have the votes and failed. Strouse hung on but had to concede two seats on the board to Green's candidates. One seat went to Eblen, the other to James A. Gibb, an Eblen client and former general manager of the Lansing, Michigan, transit system.

Gibb, a former National City Lines executive, knew something about the transit business and did not like what he saw at TCRT. The company was hemorrhaging cash. Two fare increases were not covering operating expenses, and thirteen million riders had departed since the end of the war. Once again Green demanded that Strouse resign, and, again, he re-

Ignoring all the signs that it was a bad investment, TCRT extended the Nicollet Avenue line in 1947 from 58th Street to 62nd Street, the Richfield city limits. The area had recently built up with postwar housing, and the streetcar loop became a park-and-ride lot, perhaps the first in the Twin Cities.

As late as June 1950, TCRT was investing in more physical plant, replacing the single track on Snelling Avenue at University Avenue with double track. It would be abandoned in two years.

fused. By then Green and Eblen decided they needed some local help. Green's stockbroker suggested they meet another shareholder with similar concerns: he introduced them to Isadore Blumenfeld, more popularly know as Kid Cann, a former bootlegger and racketeer turned club owner and legitimate transit investor. They met at a Minneapolis nightclub to talk things over. Blumenfeld offered the name of Fred Ossanna, a local attorney who he believed would help their cause. Green subsequently met with Ossanna and Blumenfeld, and the three of them concocted a takeover strategy. It would not be difficult. TCRT lost almost a half million dollars in 1949, and the majority of its shareholders wanted change. At a November 1949 shareholders meeting, Strouse and his directors were forced out. Green became company president, Ossanna

its legal counsel, and James Gibb its operating vice president.

Green and his associates had their hands full. Another twenty million passengers went away in 1949, bringing the total ridership loss to forty-five million in just three years. The new PCC streetcars, all 141 of them, were not luring returning GIs, who were buying cars and moving into new homes in places like Richfield, Falcon Heights, and St. Louis Park, addresses well beyond the end of the nearest streetcar line. A third fare increase in October 1949 did not offset expenses, and riders continued to leave the system. The Strouse management had made attempts to trim expenses by cutting the annual miles of streetcar operation from twenty-six million in 1946 to twenty-four million in 1949. However, it increased the miles of bus operation from 6.3 million in 1946 to 9.9 million

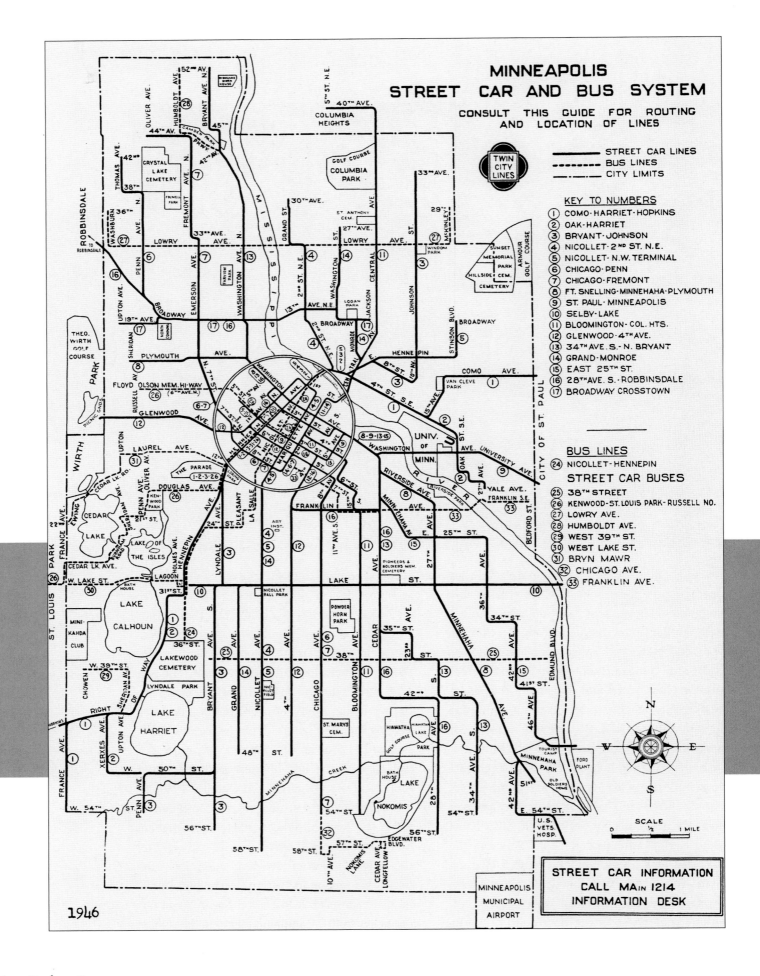

From Profit to Penury

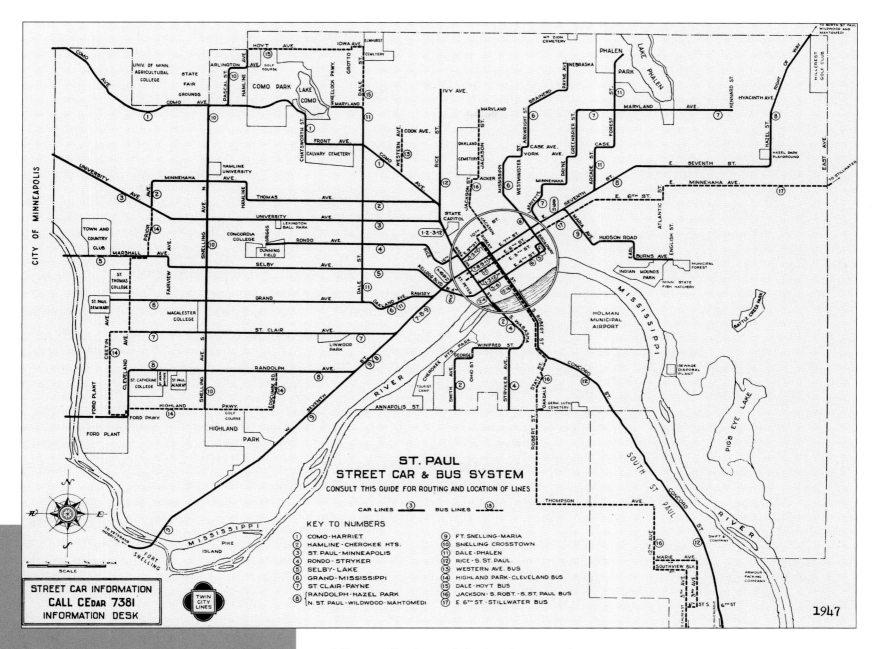

ST. PAUL
STREET CAR & BUS SYSTEM
CONSULT THIS GUIDE FOR ROUTING AND LOCATION OF LINES

CAR LINES ───③───   BUS LINES ──⑱──

KEY TO NUMBERS

① COMO·HARRIET
② HAMLINE·CHEROKEE HTS.
③ ST. PAUL·MINNEAPOLIS
④ RONDO·STRYKER
⑤ SELBY·LAKE
⑥ GRAND·MISSISSIPPI
⑦ ST. CLAIR·PAYNE
⑧ RANDOLPH·HAZEL PARK
N. ST. PAUL·WILDWOOD·MAHTOMEDI

⑨ FT. SNELLING·MARIA
⑩ SNELLING CROSSTOWN
⑪ DALE·PHALEN
⑫ RICE·S. ST. PAUL
⑬ WESTERN AVE. BUS
⑭ HIGHLAND PARK·CLEVELAND BUS
⑮ DALE·HOYT BUS
⑯ JACKSON·S. ROBT.·S. ST. PAUL BUS
⑰ E. 6TH ST.·STILLWATER BUS

STREET CAR INFORMATION
CALL CEdar 7381
INFORMATION DESK

TWIN CITY LINES

1947

Going somewhere by streetcar? Need
information? In the 1940s you could
look at these maps in the Minneapolis
and St. Paul telephone directories or
call MAin 1214 or CEdar 7381 and talk
to one of TCRT's information clerks.

in 1949, offsetting any reductions in streetcar
mileage. Some of this additional mileage is at-
tributable to conversion of the Rondo–Maria
line in St. Paul and the Robbinsdale line in
Minneapolis from streetcar to bus operation.
The Northwest Terminal streetcar line on East
Hennepin Avenue and Stinson Boulevard in

Minneapolis also switched to buses, and more
suburban feeder routes were added. However,
the company also expanded its streetcar trackage, building an extension on Nicollet Avenue
in Minneapolis from 58th Street to 62nd Street
and adding a second track on France Avenue
from 50th Street to 51st Street. By 1949, it
was clear that too many miles of operation
and expense were chasing too few passengers.
Something had to be done.

The choices were simple but intensely political: either increase fares to bring revenues in
line with expenses, or reduce service to bring
expenses in line with riders and revenues. The

alternative was insolvency. Green had it right when he told shareholders in the 1949 annual report: "It is recognized that the rendering of courteous, rapid & convenient service to the public, which provides the company's revenues, is the first essential of a local mass transportation company. However, it is self-evident that this important public service cannot be provided by a private industry on a basis, which results in a financial loss to the owners."

The Minnesota Railroad and Warehouse Commission would not allow TCRT an adequate fare, and public ownership in 1949 Minnesota was inconceivable. Therefore, expenses had to be reduced if the operation was to survive, and that is exactly what the Green management set out to do. The Railroad and Warehouse Commission did not oversee or have any control over maintenance, nor did the Minneapolis and St. Paul city councils, so Green shut down the Snelling Shops and fired most of the employees. Green was not concerned about the aging streetcars, since he planned to convert the entire system to buses. He hired Booz, Allen & Hamilton to do an organizational study. TCRT's organizational chart (see Appendix L) was a warren of streetcar-era departments and management employees, and Green intended to thin them out.

Next he went after schedules and service, abruptly lopping off three million miles of streetcar and bus operation. Public protests and hostile editorials did not worry Green. They just made him mad. When pressed by the city councils and the Minnesota Railroad and Warehouse Commission, he announced that he would wring a profit out of the system even if he had to "auction off all the streetcars and buses and sell the rails for scrap iron."

When St. Paul officials countered that TCRT, as a public utility, had no right to ignore its public responsibilities, Green said he would shut down and liquidate the St. Paul City Railway unless it starting making money.

Green, the market player, instinctively knew what was wrong and what had to be done, but he did not understand transit finance or transit operations and would not listen to those who did. A careful, thoughtful, planned approach would have won public support and cooperation. His robber baron tactics just made more enemies for the company when it desperately needed friends. His approach worried his associates who had different agendas. Green was a speculator. Their plans were far more ambitious, and Green was not a part of them.

Ossanna had been working behind the scenes and warring with Green on policy matters for some time, and he wanted Green out. On May 12, 1950, Ossanna persuaded the board to silence Green and make him the company spokesman. This led to even more acrimony, most of it public. That June, Eblen, with Ossanna's encouragement, approached Green about buying out his stock. Eblen claimed that some of his Detroit friends would purchase Green's stock, giving Green a profit, if he would agree to step aside. Green consented and sold the stock, only to learn that the buyers were not from Detroit but instead were associates of Ossanna and Blumenfeld.

Things became even more tangled when Leonard E. Lindquist, the new chairman of the Minnesota Railroad and Warehouse Commission, vetoed the company's request for yet another fare increase. Lindquist strongly disapproved of the service cuts and was deeply troubled by rumored irregularities. He was also angered by Ossanna's threats to shut down the entire system within forty-eight hours if Lindquist did not approve the increase. Lindquist had talked with Green, who, still feuding with Ossanna, had given up enough information to convince Lindquist and other commission members to make a full investigation into Ossanna and his associates. Ossanna, in rather unusual and ill-tempered remarks, called Lindquist a "cheap politician who would do or say anything to gain a vote." He went on to declare Lindquist a "liar" for alleging that "gangster elements" were taking over the company.

This contretemps so alarmed TCRT's executive committee that they and three other local board members, who were not part of the Ossanna clique, voted to dismiss Ossanna as legal counsel and revoke his status as company spokesman. Undaunted, Ossanna, Blumenfeld, and others kept buying stock until they had enough to assure control. Chairman Lindquist reported to Governor Luther Youngdahl and the Kefauver Crime Committee that not only had Ossanna and Blumenfeld sharply increased their holdings, but the "others" now included Tommy Banks, a convicted bootlegger, and six of his associates, all with reputed underworld connections. Lindquist observed that "over twenty-five per cent of the Twin City Rapid Transit stock is held by persons of questionable character. It is obvious that this is a strong enough faction to control management votes."

Meanwhile, Green, in testimony before Lindquist's panel, alleged that Ossanna wanted to set up a secret slush fund to pay off city council members by arranging kickbacks from companies that did business with TCRT. Under his scheme, TCRT would buy materials and supplies at inflated prices from "friendly" vendors. They in turn would return the difference, which would then be set aside for payoffs. This arrangement caught the attention of the Hennepin County grand jury, which subsequently indicted Ossanna on perjury charges in conjunction with the alleged slush fund.

By mid-1950, the courts and several regulatory bodies were investigating Ossanna and the activities of his associates. They included the Minnesota Railroad and Warehouse Commission, the Ramsey County and Hennepin County grand juries, the Federal Securities and Exchange Commission, the New York Stock Exchange, and the ethics committee of the

The automobile suburbs had not yet appeared in 1951, yet the battle for the streetcar's stronghold had begun, in this case at the intersection of 4th and Minnesota Streets in downtown St. Paul. Besides easier mobility, the automobile offered continuously updated styling, whereas the streetcar had remained unchanged since World War I. Photograph courtesy of the Minnesota Historical Society.

Hennepin County Bar Association. Governor Youngdahl had assigned officers from the State Bureau of Criminal Apprehension to protect Green, who had purportedly received death threats. Chairman Lindquist and his wife were also under guard after receiving threatening phone calls.

At a December 1950 stockholders meeting, Ossanna and his faction attempted to take over but were blocked by Green, who had obtained a court order temporarily halting the election of new officers. Green alleged that Ossanna's committee of stockholders had made "false and misleading statements" in its proxy circular. Green, however, was so fearful for his personal safety that he came armed with a pistol. Minneapolis police frisked Green and relieved him of it.

Green's maneuvers did not stop Ossanna,

who kept buying stock and waited for the next opportunity. In January 1951, a judge dismissed the perjury indictment for insufficient evidence. Lindquist's investigation raised questions but did not find anything substantive, and the commission closed its hearings. Green and Ossanna made peace (the terms were not disclosed), and at the March 1951 annual meeting Green willingly stepped aside. Emil Aslesen became president, and Ossanna was appointed chairman of the board. This arrangement lasted but a short time, and within a few months Ossanna took full control as president.

Prophetically, Lindquist warned in his final report to the governor that "the activities of this group both before and after taking control, give good reasons to fear that it may exploit the transit company for improper purposes." Nine years later he was proved right. Ossanna was convicted of fraud in federal court in August 1960 and sentenced to four years in prison.

Conversion

A *Minneapolis Tribune* photographer caught Charles Green clearing out his desk after the TCRT board, at the behest of Fred Ossanna, ousted him as president of the company. A controversial figure, Green reduced service, fired employees, and threatened to sell off the entire St. Paul operation in an effort to cut costs and return the company to profitability. Ossanna and the new management group had other plans, and Charles Green was not going to be part of them. *Minneapolis Tribune* photograph by Peter Marcus; courtesy of the *Star Tribune/* Minneapolis-St. Paul.

Between the March 1951 stockholders meeting and June 1954, Ossanna and his associates presided over the dismantling of all rail operations. It was inevitable and necessary given the loss of riders, TCRT's deteriorating financial situation, and the public's preference for the automobile. But the dismantling was not done as a matter of public good or in the interests of the community or even, as it would turn out, in the best interests of the stockholders. Instead, it became an exercise in greed for those who ultimately would profit personally from the changeover, and at first that changeover did not seem possible.

TCRT did not have the cash in 1951 to buy buses, nor could it borrow local capital to finance conversion. It appeared that at least a few streetcars might be around for the next several years. That changed when General Motors stepped forward with an offer to finance 525 buses. GM had a very marketable product. Its new buses were diesel powered and equipped with automatic transmissions. Both the engine and transmission had been proved worthy in military vehicles in World War II. The bus could carry fifty passengers in comfort, as many as a PCC streetcar. It was extremely rugged and could withstand the rigors of stop-and-go transit service. It was also cheaper to operate than a streetcar. Transit systems were snapping buses up as fast as GM could turn them out. GM realized that the reduced operating costs and savings would allow the buses to pay for themselves in short order. GM may have had its suspicions about TCRT's management, but it was not worried about the company's financing arrangements.

With buses on the way, TCRT needed an expert, and Ossanna hired Benson (Barney) Larrick, a former employee of National City Lines and a veteran of bus conversions in Los Angeles. Larrick took charge and mapped out a plan. He would make streetcars disappear as rapidly as the buses were delivered, starting with St. Paul. The St. Paul lines had lower ridership than Minneapolis. St. Paul's downtown streets were narrower and more congested, and traffic engineers wanted to convert them to one way as soon as possible. The removal of streetcars would speed that along, but there were some obstacles. TCRT had to negotiate agreements with both St. Paul and Minneapolis to cover costs of street repaving. It also had to

negotiate job protection agreements with the union and retrain several hundred motormen as bus drivers, as well as modify shop and maintenance facilities.

The first new buses, 125 GM 5103s, were delivered in the spring of 1952. TCRT also purchased 53 used buses, 1947 and 1948 vintage Mack C-41 models from Los Angeles; Springfield, Massachusetts; McKeesport, Pennsylvania;

The men of TCRT responsible for converting the streetcar system to buses. Left to right: Benson (Barney) Larrick, vice president and general manager; James Towey, secretary and treasurer; Fred Ossanna, president; and Dr. David Ellison, vice president and medical director.

in February 1953, and sixteen months later it was done.

Charles Green shut down the Snelling Shops in 1950, making most of the buildings and car repair facilities surplus, although portions would be needed and useful until conversion was completed. Surplus streetcars began filling the Snelling yards in 1952, either for scrapping or to be stripped of their trucks and electrical equipment, and their bodies sold. The Transportation Sales Company was set up to dispose of the bodies, and 239 of them eventually became chicken coops, fishing and hunting cabins, and storage sheds. As this work progressed, the shop buildings were cleared of all streetcar repair equipment and tooling. Anything marketable was sold. The rest of it went for scrap. There was no need to do any repairs on the old cars. Enough of them were surplus that any that broke down were taken to

Schenectady, New York; and Sioux Falls, South Dakota. Another 25 new buses, C-50s, were purchased from Mack. By May 1952 it had sufficient buses on hand to begin converting St. Paul car lines. It finished the job in November. GM began delivering its newest Model 5105 air-suspension buses in early 1953 and continued through June of 1954. The changeover in Minneapolis began

From Profit to Penury

Snelling and burned. The former erecting shop building was modified to service buses in the spring of 1952. The other shop buildings would be used to store buses during the winter of 1952. The Snelling carhouse remained in use for the St. Paul–Minneapolis line until November 1953. Then, once streetcar operations ended in June of 1954, the carhouse and yards were used to store and scrap all of the remaining streetcars. Dozens of buses were stored outside or in the empty shop buildings for several months, but by the summer of 1955, a large bus storage facility had been constructed adjoining the erecting shop on the site of the former transfer table, extending around and enclosing the former carpenter shop. All of the buses were then moved inside the new storage building, and the other buildings on the site were left empty and abandoned. They would be torn down within the year and replaced by the Midway Shopping Center.

The conversion to buses is under way in 1953. The buses are parked all around the Snelling Shops, and the transfer table pit has been partially filled.

More than two hundred car bodies were sold for use as cabins or outbuildings. Car 1268 went to Sacred Heart Catholic School in Robbinsdale, where it served as a playhouse for children for many years.

Other facilities were either adapted for
bus service or closed and sold. The Nicollet
and North Side carhouses in Minneapolis
were rebuilt for buses during the summer of
1953. The rail shop equipment was removed
from the buildings, the yard tracks ripped up,
and the overhead wire taken down, and a large
bus storage building was built over the former
streetcar storage yard. The Duluth Avenue
carhouse in St. Paul closed in May 1952 and
subsequently was torn down and the property
sold. Lake Street Station in Minneapolis closed
in December 1953 after its lines had been con-

verted to buses that were assigned to Nicollet
and North Side in Minneapolis or, in the case of
the Selby–Lake, to Snelling Garage in St. Paul.
For a short time, surplus streetcars were stored
at Lake Street prior to scrapping. The building
was then demolished and the site cleared for a
shopping center. East Side Station closed out all
rail service in the Twin Cities, and the building
was sold to Superior Plating.

Northern States Power bought the Main
Steam Station in July of 1954. The substation
buildings were sold and subsequently torn
down. All of their equipment went for scrap

together with the entire power distribution system, including underground and overhead cables, trolley wire, and support poles. The St. Paul office building at College and Wabasha was sold. The headquarters building at 11th Street and Hennepin Avenue stood until 1960. It came down after TCRT moved all of its offices to the second floor of the Nicollet Garage. Tracks on private right of way were immediately pulled up for scrap. Those in the streets were removed or paved over by the cities.

The 141 PCC streetcars found new homes at other transit systems. Twenty were sold in January 1953 to Shaker Heights Rapid Transit in Cleveland, Ohio. Newark, New Jersey's Public Service Coordinated Transport took thirty of them in March 1953. The remainder went to Mexico City.

Management Goes to Jail

Fred Ossanna left TCRT in December 1957. He and several associates came under scrutiny by federal authorities for fraudulent activities in conjunction with the conversion from rail to bus. There had been strong suspicions about Ossanna and his earlier dealings, but never enough solid proof to discredit him or cause state or federal authorities to intervene. There would undoubtedly have been a different outcome if the governor had stepped in or if Chairman Lindquist's investigation had stirred more activity, but there was very little enthusiasm for such things, particularly when transit had such a low public priority.

Ossanna was convicted on August 6, 1960, on thirteen counts of mail fraud and interstate transportation of property taken by mail fraud. He was sentenced to four years in prison and given an $11,000 fine. Barney Larrick, TCRT's vice president, was given a two-year sentence and a $3,000 fine. Others convicted included Harry and Fred Isaacs (father and son) of American Iron and Supply Company and Mid-Continent Construction and Development Co., and Earl Jeffords, of J & C Holding Co., a Minneapolis real estate firm. The Isaacses and Jeffords were involved in various kickback schemes. Isadore Blumenfeld was indicted and tried but found not guilty on all charges.

TCRT filed a civil suit against Ossanna and the others, seeking restitution for losses from assets that were sold at below-market prices in exchange for kickbacks and payoffs. Those losses involved the sale of cable and scrap metal at below-market prices to American Iron and Supply Company and the sale of eleven parcels of real estate to Mid-Continent Construction and Development below their market value, the difference paid back to the defendants. Charges against Jeffords included payment of unearned real estate commissions for sale of the Snelling property and a $250,000 kickback and discounting scheme on the ninety-one PCCs that were sold to Mexico City. Those convicted pocketed over $1 million in TCRT's assets in 1950 dollars.

Remnants

After fifty years there are few physical remnants of the streetcar and the Twin City Rapid Transit Company. The Lowry Avenue substation in Minneapolis and the

Concord Street substation in St. Paul stand, as does the Main Steam Station, now owned by the University of Minnesota. The Metropolitan Transit Commission used the former North Side Station as a bus garage until 1984. It is now privately owned and leased to several small businesses. Superior Plating owns East Side Station. Midway Station is still in use as an office building, and the former Stillwater substation is a private home. The South St. Paul carhouse is a trucking company garage. The old carhouse/general office building on 3rd Avenue North and 2nd Street still stands.

Three of TCRT's homebuilt streetcars have been preserved and restored by the Minnesota Streetcar Museum. Two operate during the summer on a portion of the former Como–Harriet right of way between Lake Harriet and Lake Calhoun in south Minneapolis. The third is kept at Excelsior and runs in conjunction with the streetcar steamboat *Minnehaha,* another TCRT relic rescued from the

The system's only rolling stock with resale value was the 141 PCC cars, only five to eight years old in 1953. They were sold to New Jersey Public Service in Newark, Shaker Heights Rapid Transit in Cleveland, and Mexico City. Car 414, repainted in its new owner's cream and green, is prepared for the trip to Mexico City.

bottom of Lake Minnetonka and operated by the Museum of Lake Minnetonka. Recently, one of the former PCC cars was brought back from Cleveland. It has now been restored and operates at Lake Harriet. Other former TCRT PCCs survive in San Francisco and are being restored for service on Market Street. Another TCRT car is owned by the Seashore Trolley Museum in Kennebunkport, Maine. It has been completely restored to its original appearance and is in operating condition. More than two hundred streetcar bodies were sold and scattered around Minnesota and Wisconsin. Most of them are slowly disappearing.

Vestiges of TCRT's extensive private rights of way can still be located and followed. The Como–Harriet line between Lake Harriet and Calhoun is used by the Minnesota Streetcar Museum. Another portion along the bluff above Lake Calhoun between 34th and 36th Streets is a walking path, as is a segment near Blake Road in Hopkins. Excelsior Boulevard uses the old Lake Minnetonka right of way between Shady Oak Road and Baker Road. Highway 7 does the same between Vine Hill Road and the Excelsior exit. In St. Paul the right of way through Como Park has, as an added attraction, the former streetcar waiting station, which was only recently restored by the St. Paul Parks Department. The east portal of the Selby Tunnel just below the Cathedral near the Minnesota History Center can still be seen. The Mahtomedi line's bridge over the Omaha Railroad near Maryland and Hazel survives for pedestrians. Elsewhere there are bits of the Lake Minnetonka and Stillwater lines that can still be discerned among all the new streets and housing projects.

The Metropolitan Transit Commission kept most of TCRT's corporate records. Former TCRT employees and private collectors saved others. Russell Olson, a TCRT historian and longtime member of the Minnesota Transportation Museum and the Minnesota Streetcar Museum, worked extensively to catalog them for the Minnesota Historical Society, where they now reside.

Made in Minnesota

The "Tom Lowrys"

5

I f the rapid growth and decline of the electric railway industry exemplify the pace of technological change in the twentieth century, then the rise and fall of the number of suppliers to the industry are indicative of the pace of change in the industry itself. In 1900, there were at least fifteen major companies building streetcars and interurbans. Names like J. G. Brill Company, American Car Company, McGuire-Cummings Manufacturing Company, St. Louis Car Company, Niles Car Company, Jewett Car Company, and Pullman competed for orders from hundreds of street railway properties. Those manufacturers in turn sustained dozens of independent companies making motors, wheels and trucks, control equipment, seats, trolley wheels, valves, and a long list of other components that went into the building of a streetcar. Other companies supplied construction materials such as rails ties and wire and insulators, while consulting and engineering firms sold their technical expertise.

Just thirty years later all but four or five of the major streetcar builders had succumbed to merger, diversification, or outright insolvency. Most of the small suppliers were gone, too. The market for street railway equipment began drying up in the 1920s. Small systems, flirting with bankruptcy, stopped buying new cars, keeping their old equipment until the bitter end. Others shopped for used equipment from systems that had already converted to buses or gone out of business altogether. Only the larger street railway companies pursued modernization and bought the PCC (Presidents Conference Committee) cars that became available around 1936. The last streetcars built by an American manufacturer came from the plant of the St. Louis Car Company in 1952; they were delivered to the San Francisco Municipal Railway.

The industry was slow to accept standardization. There was no such thing as an "off the shelf" car. Each property had its own design and its specifications and demanded that builders follow them. Builders, similarly, had widely differing designs in their catalogs. Major components such as motors and controllers, supplied by firms like Westinghouse or General Electric, were interchangeable, but body design and other appointments were highly customized. Every system had a slightly different car, even if it came from the same manufacturer.

No doubt this individuality persisted in part because of local pride, but there was something else, something much more fundamental. Most streetcar bodies were constructed entirely of wood. Steel frames appeared around 1900, but wood exteriors and wood interior trim persisted. Car building was an art, the craftsmanship amazing, and the product beautiful and highly durable. Many of the early cars are still operating in museums a century after they were built. It would take several years before economics forced companies to accept a standard design, and even more years would pass until a truly modern streetcar evolved and came into mass production. Unfortunately, by then the industry was in full decline, and bus technology had im-

proved to the point that it was competitive with the streetcar.

TCRT took this individuality much further and added its own twist when it developed a distinctive car specifically for service in the Twin Cities and built all of them in its own shops. Except for its very first electric cars and the 141 PCC cars delivered from 1945 to 1949, TCRT never placed an order with any of the major builders. Between the years 1898 and 1927, a total of 1,362 passenger cars and sixty-nine pieces of nonrevenue work equipment came from the 31st Street and Snelling shops, including 190 passenger cars built for other electric railway systems. The company adopted standardization and mass production, but it did so on its own terms. In some cities, streetcars were known as "rattlers"; in Minneapolis and St. Paul, they were "Tom Lowrys."

The cars made a commanding presence on the streets of Minneapolis and St. Paul. Nine feet wide and forty-six feet long, they were among the largest in the industry. Ample windows added to the feeling of spaciousness. On hot days they were breezy; in winter they were tight and warm. Passengers could board, pay their fare, and take a seat inside, or stand and gossip with the conductor on the rear platform as he made change, punched transfers, called out streets, and chased away the occasional errant youngsters who tried to pull the trolley pole off the wire. The rear platform was a popular hangout where smokers (and there were lots of them in that era) could light up a cigar or a pipe. An obliging company made it convenient by fixing brass match strikers to the window posts.

The earliest electric cars in the Twin Cities were single trucked and of all-wood construction, about twenty-five feet long with a capacity

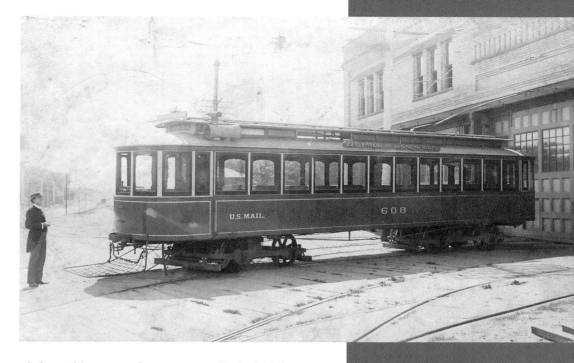

of about thirty seated passengers. Typical of the era, they resembled horsecars. In fact, when it needed more passenger-carrying capacity, TCRT converted a few of its original horsecars to trailers and coupled them to a motorized car to handle the increased business.

In 1893, the city of Minneapolis ordered that open cars be used during the summer months. TCRT obliged, despite its financial troubles, and purchased 105 from American Car Company and sixty from LaClede Car Company. Deliveries in the 1890s from the Northern Car Company of Robbinsdale, Minnesota, Thomson-Houston, and American Car Company were larger and accommodated more passengers. Still, company officials became increasingly unhappy with the performance of cars supplied by outside builders. They were small, which meant that two cars were often required to do the work of one, driving up operating expenses. They were underpowered and could get bogged down with a large number of passengers, making it difficult to keep schedules. They were not rugged enough to withstand the rigors of day in, day out operation in Minnesota's extremely cold winters and hot summers. Something better was needed.

American Car Company built the first production double-truck closed cars in 1892, introducing what would become the look of the TCRT standard cars: a rounded front, deck roof, and large rear entrance/exit with wire gates.

Early Homebuilts

🚋

The first three Twin City Rapid Transit cars emerged from the 31st Street Shops in 1898. The original design is credited to TCRT's master mechanic, W. M. Brown. One of the three was Thomas Lowry's specially outfitted private car. Designed for touring the system, it featured an observation room and was furnished with wicker chairs, an upholstered davenport, and a large mahogany table for holding business meetings. Brussels carpet was used throughout. There was a bathroom, and a full kitchen provided meal service. The liquor cabinet and the cigar humidor were well stocked when President William McKinley joined Lowry aboard the car on a visit to the Twin Cities in 1901.

The other two cars went into regular passenger service and were joined by twenty more that same year and another 358 by 1905. Cars in this group, numbers 739 through 1111 (except 789–96, which were not built by TCRT but acquired in 1898 from the St. Paul & Suburban Railway), were similar in overall appearance and interior features. There were differences, but they were all built to the same design. The

TCRT president Thomas Lowry toured his domain in this private streetcar, the first product in 1898 of the company's new car-building program. Furnished with wicker armchairs and heavy curtains, and staffed by an attendant, the car burned in a fire at Snelling Shops in 1925.

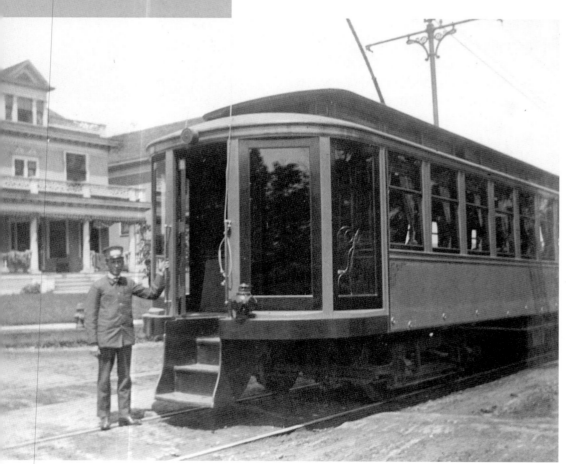

first major improvement came in 1902, when TCRT introduced air brakes. Earlier cars with hand brakes were then given air brakes when they went through the shops for rebuilding. With the exception of some minor variations in the various building programs, these early cars were forty-three feet long, eight feet nine inches wide, double trucked, and could accommodate forty-eight seated passengers, on seven pairs of forward-facing transverse seats and two longitudinal bench seats at the rear. The seats were covered with rattan in a natural finish. Car interiors were wood with a cherry finish. Passengers boarded and exited at the rear through a double set of gates. A small exterior door on the right side at the front provided entrance to the motorman's compartment. With few exceptions, all of TCRT's streetcars were single ended, meaning the motorman's controls were always at the front of the car. Upon reaching the end of the line, the motorman pulled the car forward across the intersection and then, with assistance from the conductor, backed around the corner and onto a short section of track on the intersecting street. When it was time to go, the car pulled forward around

the corner and headed back on its route in the opposite direction. There were more than eighty "wyes" of this kind in Minneapolis and St. Paul, with about a dozen more on the suburban lines. Where cars were not turned on wyes, they circled a city block or made a semicircle through an off-street turning loop.

A stove in the motorman's compartment provided hot-water heat. As cars were rebuilt in later years, a hot-air system supplied by a coal stove under the car floor came into general use. Some cars were converted to electric heat.

Car exteriors were painted chrome yellow, with brown and olive trim, and a red oxide roof. Everything below the floor line, including trucks and underbody equipment, was a moss green. Numbering and striping were in aluminum with bronze highlighting around the numbers. With some variation this exterior scheme persisted for the next fifty years.

TCRT had a disposal problem as more of its homebuilt cars went in service and displaced its original equipment. Some of the older cars were sold to other street railway systems or converted to work equipment. Most of them, though, were retired and scrapped between 1902

An early homebuilt car lays over at the Lake Harriet loop, just east of the Linden Hills business district. Beginning in 1894, all TCRT streetcars featured a U.S. Mail box attached to the rearmost post by the entrance gate. Mail was probably off-loaded in the downtowns near the main post offices. The practice ended in the early 1900s. Photograph courtesy of the Minnesota Historical Society.

and about 1912. A 1902 Minneapolis newspaper article noted that many were being dumped in a lot at 31st Street and Bryant Avenue South. People were encouraged to chop them up for free firewood. The company planned to return and burn the remainder to recover the scrap metal. Other cars had a different fate and survive today in a totally unique form. It seems that a resident of Mahtomedi was going to build a house and asked the company for three car bodies. TCRT obliged, but instead of three it took twenty-two of the old cars out to Mahtomedi, built a short spur track to the property, and pushed all of them off the tracks. The resident complained, but TCRT refused to take the cars back. So, fifteen bodies were incorporated into the house and the rest were sold. The house stands today, and although you cannot see the streetcars from the outside, their various wood features are visible inside the home.

TCRT's original horsecar and Thomas Lowry's private car were preserved but were sadly destroyed in 1925 when a car storage shed at Snelling Shops burned to the ground.

The Next Step

Car 1112 came out of the 31st Street Shops in August 1905. It resembled its predecessors, but there was a steel frame beneath the wood exterior and the car was wider, at approximately nine feet, and longer, roughly forty-six feet. TCRT organized all of its cars into various classes, depending on individual specifications. They looked the same, but there were subtle differences among the various classifications even as they were being built. Those differences would become more numerous and

complex as the cars aged and went through a series of rebuilding programs.

Forty-two suburban cars, numbers 1112–23, 1145–63, and 1255–65, were the heaviest and most powerful cars built by TCRT. They weighed 60,000 pounds, were equipped with four seventy-five horsepower motors, and were geared for high-speed operation on the Lake Minnetonka and Stillwater suburban lines. They could make a mile a minute. Motormen were given a special clamp to put on the controller to prevent it from being placed in a high-speed position. That clamp could not be removed until the car had left city streets and was on private right of way. Two new suburban cars and one of the earlier homebuilt cars were experimentally outfitted with a second deck. This increased passenger-carrying capacity, but there were concerns about stability as well as vertical clearance. The decks were removed, and the experiment was never repeated.

Electric motors, air compressors, controllers, and trucks varied between and among the various classes of cars, depending on when they were built. Generally, the older cars (those preceding 1112) came with lower-horsepower motors. Some of the very earliest models had only one motorized axle per truck, making them slow and eventually relegating them to lighter service. For the most part, all of the motors and truck assemblies were interchangeable and were often shifted between and among the various cars. For example, the high-speed suburban cars lost their motors and controllers to the snowplows each winter and were then given smaller motors and operated in local service during the winter months. Fast city cars with fifty-horsepower motors typically filled in on the suburban lines. As a rule, a "fast" car was any car with four fifty-horsepower motors. Depending on the gear ratio, a fast car was good for a top speed in the range of forty miles per hour. A "slow" car with lower-horsepower motors could do at best twenty-five miles per hour. By the late 1920s, most of the cars built after 1905 with steel frames were given the higher-horsepower motors.

Form Follows Function

The last steel-framed standard car, number 1855, came out of the Snelling Shops in June 1917. Eleven hundred and thirty-nine cars preceded it on the roster, including the wood-framed standards built between 1898 and 1905. In 1917, TCRT rostered 1,134 homebuilt streetcars, all of them were "muzzleloaders," a term coined in the industry to describe a streetcar with only one common entrance and exit, usually at the rear.

This arrangement proved inefficient. With cars stopping at every block, passengers at the front of the car had to work their way to the rear,

often past standees, and then exit through the rear gates at the same time people were boarding. Congestion on the rear platform was always troublesome. Some people needed change from the conductor or had to ask for, or turn in, a transfer. Inevitably there were questions or fare disputes. The car could not move until everyone was aboard and the motorman got the proper bell signal from the conductor. If all of this was happening downtown at the height of the rush hour there might be seven or eight cars behind waiting to move up to the loading zone or car stop. One car with a heavy load ended up delaying others and disrupting their schedules.

The solution was to add a front exit allowing passengers to board at the rear, pay their fare, and exit at the front of the car. From 1920 through 1924, Snelling Shops rebuilt 526 cars, numbers 1329–1854 with front exits. Another sixty-four cars were rebuilt in 1928. These cars came to be known as "gate cars" because they kept their semienclosed rear platform and rear gates but had a narrow folding exit door at the front.

This photograph captures 50 years of streetcar development. St. Paul City Railway horsecar 1 was preserved by TCRT as a historic artifact. It appeared in parades and other special functions. Here it sits at Snelling Shops with a standard car that has recently received a folding front exit door. The horsecar was lost in a fire in 1925.

ASK FATHER HE'LL REMEMBER.

FIRST HORSE CAR
OPERATED IN TWIN CITIES
JULY 15 1872
SEATING CAPACITY-14.

ONE HORSE-POWER
HAY MOTOR.
1822

200 HORSE-POWER
ELECTRIC MOTORS.
1921

The view from the rear platform of a gate car.

The automobile and the Great Depression brought other changes. Fewer people were riding, and TCRT determined that it could significantly lower operating costs by discontinuing the use of conductors on all but its busiest lines. The measure was opposed by the employees and by the two city governments, citing safety concerns and the ability of a single employee to perform the duties of conductor and motorman. That argument had merit in 1920, when 238,000,000 passengers dropped their coins in the fare box, but not in 1930, when ridership had fallen by a third and was still slipping.

TCRT compromised and redesigned its cars for either one-man or two-man operation. Large folding double-stream doors replaced the rear gates, completely enclosing the rear platform. The single front door became a double-stream door. All doors were equipped with a safety device, a "sensitive edge," that both sounded an alarm and automatically caused the door to open if anything became wedged between the two halves. The motorman's controls were given "dead man" safety features, and a backup control box was installed on the rear platform that allowed a motorman to turn the car around at a wye without assistance from a conductor.

Other modifications were made to the heating systems and interior appointments. Because the rear platform was now enclosed, the bulkhead and sliding doors that separated the rear platform from the interior were removed and a concrete-like mastic floor was applied to the front and rear platforms. A conductor's station was retained at the rear of the car for use on lines where passenger loading justified a conductor, in which case passengers boarded at the rear and exited at the front. With one-man

Even then, many of the original cars remained "muzzleloaders." Mainly they were wood-framed cars approaching thirty years of age. Most of them remained in service through the 1920s and into the early 1930s. A few lost their motors and control equipment and were paired with another powered car as a trailer, forming a two-car train. The suburban cars would never receive front exits, and still other steel-framed cars would be rebuilt directly to one-man operation. Two cars, 1129 and 1230, were rebuilt for double-ended operation on the Merriam Park, Deephaven, and Ft. Snelling shuttles. They joined several wood-framed cars in the 800–900 series that had been converted to double-ended operation for use as shuttle cars on new line extensions that were still single tracked. (A double-ended car has motorman's controls at both ends; it does not require turning at the end of the line.) By the end of the 1930s, all of the wood-framed cars from the low-numbered 1100s were surplus and had been scrapped, including the double-ended cars.

operation, all boarding and fare collection took place at the front of the car.

The conversion to one-man operation began in 1931 and continued at a steady pace as gate cars came due for scheduled overhaul. A total of 527 cars were converted between 1931 and 1942. When the program ended, the 144 gate cars that remained saw service only on Selby–Lake, Como–Harriet, St. Paul–Minneapolis, Nicollet–2nd St. N.E., Chicago–Penn–Fremont, and the Inter-Campus, the last lines in the system that still used conductors. One gate car was subsequently converted to a supply car and another donated to the Seashore Trolley Museum. The remaining cars were scrapped between the end of World

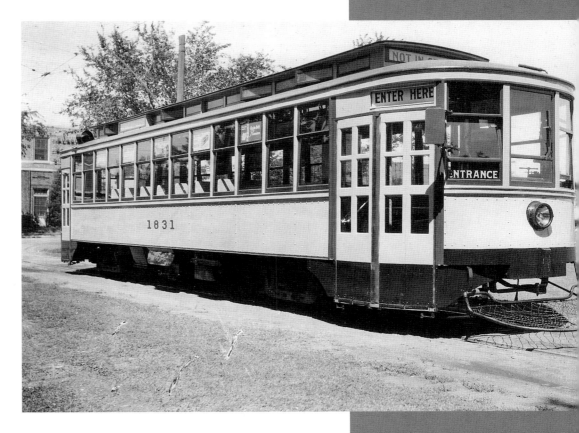

During the period from 1931 to 1942, 527 cars were rebuilt for one-man/two-man operation, with air-operated doors controlled by the motorman. During subsequent shoppings, 287 cars had rotting exterior wood wainscot covered with sheet steel.

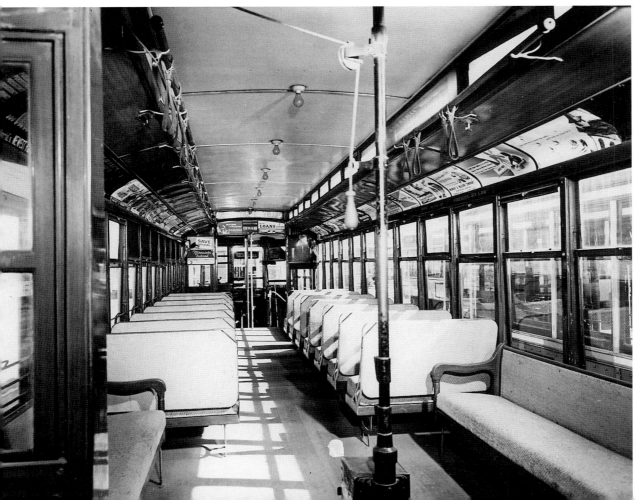

Despite rebuildings and the reconfiguring of the seats, the basic look of the TCRT standard streetcars remained unchanged for fifty-six years. Spacious front and rear platforms swallowed crowds of boarding passengers, permitting the car to start moving while they fished out their fares. The seats were rattan, originally varnished but later painted a creamy yellow. The large windows, including those in the roof clerestory, let in plenty of light. In the summer, the lower sashes could be lowered into wall pockets, admitting fresh air and summer breezes. Exterior storm windows were hung for winter.

War II and the completion of the conversion to buses in 1954.

Lightweight Cars and Other Experiments

Shortly before World War I, the street railway industry became interested in lighter-weight cars. They were cheaper to buy because they were mostly built to a standard design, something the industry was learning to accept. They were also cheaper to operate, because they required less electric power, were easier on track, and were set up for one-man operation. One popular design was the Birney Safety Car, named after its inventor, engineer Charles O. Birney. The Birney came in a small single-trucked version, ideal for lightly traveled lines, and a larger double-trucked model with greater passenger capacity. Unfortunately, these cars helped market automobiles as effectively as paved roads and being able to buy on credit. They were horrible—worse, in fact, than some of the primitive buses of that era. Noisy and rough riding, their light construction offered little passenger comfort, especially on poorly maintained track, which by then was all too common. The best that can be said is that they provided convenient transportation to the nearest Ford dealership.

TCRT never bought a Birney. Instead, in 1916 its master mechanic, Walter Smith, came up with a design that had all the features of a TCRT standard car but weighed 28,000 pounds, half as much. Most of the weight savings came out of the trucks, allowing a lighter, smaller motor. The first example rolled out of the Snelling Shops as a fully motorized two-car train. All of the axles on the second car were powered and were controlled by the motorman in the lead unit.

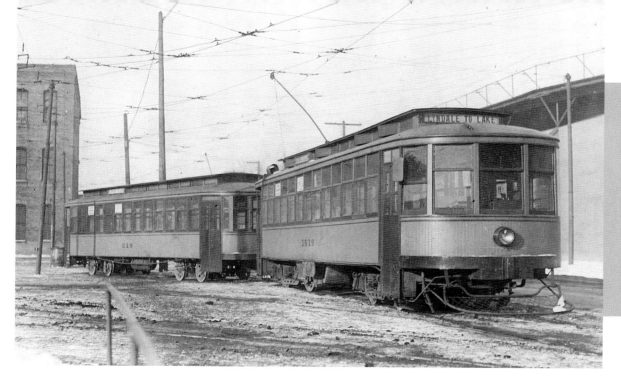

Increasing ridership prompted the creation of twenty-five trailer trains in 1921. The unpowered trailers were created from old wood cars. The trains were withdrawn when the Depression of the 1930s cut ridership in half. This train is leaving the Nicollet Station yard along the 31st Street wall of Nicollet Park, home of the Minneapolis Millers baseball team.

Around the same time, TCRT experimented with removing the motors on one of its older cars, turning it into an unpowered trailer that could be towed behind a powered car. Ridership was increasing, and TCRT needed the additional capacity of two-car trains on some of its lines. This became a test to determine which of the two versions worked best. The trailer arrangement won out, and, in 1921, twenty-five additional old cars were demotorized and paired with powered units. The two-car trains were used until 1932, when falling ridership eliminated the need for their extra capacity. The trailers were taken out of service and stored. They were scrapped in 1936.

TCRT also continued work on fully powered two-car trains. A second set with multiple-unit controls emerged in 1921 in a more modern-looking car body. A third and final set followed in 1926. All three sets were eventually rebuilt so that each car in the paired train could operate singly or in multiple units. TCRT constructed twenty-five more in 1927 and 1928. None of them, however, were equipped for multiple-unit operation. Regrettably, the lightweight design was not completely successful, and the cars quickly gained a bad reputation among motormen more accustomed to the rapid acceleration and hard-

braking characteristics of the heavier standard cars. Motormen complained that they lacked power and were unresponsive. They disliked the band brakes, which were slippery, especially on wet track. This slipperiness caused skids, which flattened wheels, creating more work for shop forces. Because their traction motors were only two to three inches above the pavement, the cars could not move through standing water or deep snow without moisture getting into the motors, shorting them out.

All of these problems quickly relegated the lightweight cars to less demanding schedules or rush hour service. They were usually found on the Snelling Avenue, Rondo–Maria, St. Clair–Payne, and Grand–Mississippi lines in St. Paul and the Broadway, Grand–Monroe, and 34th Ave. S.–N. Bryant lines in Minneapolis. Not surprisingly, they were the first cars sidelined during the conversion to buses, and they were among the first cars scrapped. All of them were gone by 1952.

Despite its shortcomings, Smith's design drew the interest of several investors who proposed to build it for other systems and compete with the Birney, then at the height of its popularity. TCRT's managers did not have the same enthusiasm. They were aware of the design's

One of the twenty-five production lightweight cars on Snelling Avenue passes the Old Main of Hamline University.

early problems and believed it unwise to invest corporate funds in production when much development work remained. It was just too risky. Undiscouraged, its backers incorporated the Light Weight Noiseless Electric Street Car Company with offices in Chicago. Its president was A. L. Drum, a consulting engineer whose firm, A. L. Drum and Company, did considerable work for TCRT. Lacking its own facilities, the company negotiated a contract with TCRT's subsidiary, the Transit Supply Company, for production of the cars at the Snelling Shops. Transit Supply would build the cars at cost plus a 10 percent profit for itself. Between 1924 and 1927, the

company won orders and built a total of ninety-three cars for Chicago; Grand Rapids, Michigan; Duluth, Minnesota; Chattanooga and Nashville, Tennessee; and Evansville, Indiana. Among these were four cars for TCRT. After 1927, there was no further business and the company quietly disappeared. TCRT continued to supply spare parts.

Another innovation taking root in the industry was the trolley bus, a streetcar on rubber tires. For the most part, these vehicles came into use at street railway properties that wanted to rid themselves of the expense of maintaining track but were heavily invested in a newer power system that could not be written off the books. Management at other systems that adopted the trolley bus did so out of skepticism that the motorbus lacked the durability to sustain itself in heavy service. At the time, they were probably right. TCRT never pursued the technology except as a brief experiment on the Bloomington Avenue streetcar line in south Minneapolis, which in 1922 ended at 38th Street. Residential development south of there justified service but

A car built for Chattanooga, Tennessee, at Snelling Shops by tenant Light Weight Noiseless Electric Street Car Company was posed on Como Avenue by the Minnesota State Fair grounds in 1926.

apparently not enough for a track extension. Instead, TCRT extended a double trolley contact wire from 38th Street to 48th Street. One wire was "positive," the other "negative." TCRT then purchased one trolley bus from the J. G. Brill Company of Philadelphia and built another at the Snelling Shops. Both used rubber tires and drove like a regular bus. South of 38th Street the single trolley pole, which carried two separate contact wheels, was positioned such that one wheel made contact with the live wire, the other with the neutral or ground return. When the buses operated north of 38th Street, to and from the Lake Street carhouse, only one trolley wheel was used for current pickup. Ground return was provided by a shoe, which was lowered to make contact with the streetcar rail. This experiment lasted for about a year until tracks were extended to 48th Street. Afterward, both vehicles were stored until 1934, when they were sold for scrap. The experiment was never repeated.

Presidents Conference Committee Cars

James H. McGraw sold books. He never ran a street railway system, but he had published the *Electric Railway Journal* since buying it in 1886, two years after he graduated from high school. In the 1920s, he and his editor, Charles Gordon, set out to save the electric railway industry from itself. Their issue was standardization, and their cause was to convince reluctant managers to develop and buy a modern streetcar that could beat the automobile and the bus. It would not be easy given the attitude of most properties, best expressed by Frank R. Phillips of Pittsburgh Railways in remarks at the 1921

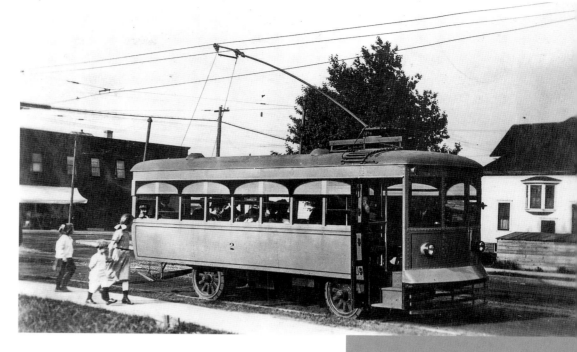

convention of the American Electric Railway Engineering Association. Phillips said that he "could see no valid reason for spending so much time in standardizing things that require changing so frequently. Even if a standard car was ultimately adopted, most railway men would still adhere to the types which they already had in service."

Opinions change, and by 1928 some in the industry were coming around. The prevalence of bankruptcy and abandonment provided sobering incentives. Speaking before a similar audience that year, Charles Gordon leveled sharp criticism at managements who made cosmetic improvements to older cars that "are still awkward in appearance, noisy, slow, and excessively costly to operate." He was similarly very critical of car builders for being contractors rather than marketing standardized designs, "which could be sold as other manufactured products are sold." The sharpest comments were aimed at properties that kept huge shops busy by building and rebuilding their own cars. That, he said, was an "expensive luxury" that drove up costs and took away the incentives for builders to pursue new technology. "Electric railways," Gordon admonished, "must compete

TCRT experimented briefly in 1922 with electric trolley buses. They ran on Bloomington Avenue from 38th Street to 48th Street. One bus, pictured here at 38th, was purchased from commercial builder J. G. Brill. The other was built at Snelling Shops. Some cities, such as Duluth, converted to trolley buses. Photograph courtesy of the Minnesota Historical Society.

Eager to test a PCC car, in late 1944, TCRT received one car diverted from an order destined for Pittsburgh and already painted in that city's red and cream. This is one of its first runs, captured at 5th Street and Hennepin Avenue in Minneapolis, now the site of the light rail Warehouse District Station. It was repainted, re-numbered 299, and lasted until 1953, when it was sold to Mexico City. Photograph from the Minneapolis Star and Tribune News Negative Collection; courtesy of the Minnesota Historical Society.

with individual automobile transportation" and "create the desire to ride them (streetcars) . . . for the public has become automobile-minded (and) . . . the very existence of the industry is dependent on developing equipment to meet the demands of the times."

The following year Gordon and Dr. Thomas Conway, an industry general manager, presided over the creation of the Electric Railway Presidents Conference Committee, a group of railway executives and suppliers charged with developing a modern streetcar that would compete with the automobile and banish the bus. What evolved from their work was the hugely successful Presidents Conference Committee car, generally known as the PCC, a streetcar that would be built in the thousands for transit systems around the world.

Initially, TCRT shunned the PCC. It chose not to participate in the work of the design committee, nor did it buy any of the cars until 1945, even though the first production models were available in 1936. This decision may have been a function of industry "politics," since TCRT

was a widely respected operation and would have been a natural leader in the development of a new design. Or, it may have reflected a firm conviction on the part of a conservative management that, contrary to Charles Gordon, TCRT's homebuilt standards, along with a thorough maintenance and rebuilding program, were better for the company's bottom line and its customers. Sixty years' hindsight would question the wisdom of that view, but when TCRT did buy PCCs it bought the best and most modern examples of the design, even though that investment came after thousands were in service in systems such as Los Angeles, Philadelphia, Chicago, and New York.

PCCs were lightweight, incredibly fast, modern appearing, quiet, and comfortable. Passengers loved them, as did operating and maintenance personnel. At 38,000 pounds, they were 20 percent lighter than some of the older, TCRT standard cars. The carbody was of a modular or "unibody" design constructed of corrosion-resistant "Corten" steel. Not only were the trucks lighter, the use of rubber composite materials wherever there would have been metal-to-metal contact dampened shock and vibration. Wheels were "resilient," a sandwich of steel and rubber that sharply reduced the metal-to-metal noise of steel wheel on rail. The PCCs came with four fifty-five horsepower motors, which, along with the lightweight trucks and an improved motor control system, produced remarkable acceleration and overall performance. A PCC could run away from anything on the street, especially the lumbering gas and diesel buses of the 1940s. Inside, passengers had such amenities as hand-cranked windows, soft indirect lighting, electric heat, and fully upholstered seats. Speed and braking

Running "Not in Service" for testing or for operator training, a new PCC car sits on the wye at Hamline and Hoyt Avenues in St. Paul, the north end of the Snelling Avenue line. Note the recently built postwar houses.

were pedal controlled, freeing the motorman's hands to make change or punch transfers. The cars were all electric: everything from door controls to the braking system was electrically controlled. They appeared in TCRT's traditional livery of chrome yellow with moss green trim and a moss green roof.

After testing and purchasing a single car diverted from a Pittsburgh order, TCRT bought 140 all-electric PCCs from the St. Louis Car Company between 1946 and 1949 and would probably have bought more. However, financial problems followed by an abrupt change in management that chose to convert the entire system to buses precluded any future purchases.

PCCs were initially assigned to the Snelling, Duluth Avenue, Nicollet, and East Side stations and worked TCRT's best and most popular lines. In Minneapolis, the cars were put on the Glenwood–4th Ave. S., Bryant–Johnson, Nicollet–2nd St. N.E., and Grand–Monroe lines.

In St. Paul, they appeared on the Grand–Mississippi, St. Clair–Payne, and Hamline–Cherokee Hts. lines. The St. Paul–Minneapolis interurban was the first line to get PCCs and ran as a 100 percent PCC operation until it went to buses in November 1953. After the entire St. Paul system converted to bus operation, surplus PCCs served for a short time in Minneapolis on the Como–Harriet and the Bloomington–Columbia Hts. lines. As buses took over, TCRT put the PCCs up for sale, and Cleveland, Ohio (Shaker Heights), Newark, New Jersey, and Mexico City snatched them up. So durable were these cars that the last twenty-five of them were retired from the Newark subway in 2002. Eleven have been purchased by San Francisco for continued use. One has been preserved and restored and operates on the Minnesota Streetcar Museum's Como–Harriet line in south Minneapolis. Still others await restoration at different museums.

The early snowplows were simply all-purpose work cars with plows attached. They weren't up to the job and were replaced by much heavier, more powerful cars designed for that task alone. This location is 31st Street and Nicollet Avenue in Minneapolis.

Work Equipment

As of January 1944, TCRT rostered seventy-eight work cars, all built at 31st Street and Snelling shops specifically for the company's needs. Multiple cars of the same type, such as snowplows, work flats, and wire cars, were assigned to carhouses around the system. Still others were unique and assigned to specific departments for specific jobs. The latter were stored at Snelling or Nicollet stations when they were not needed. (See Appendix H for list.)

Maintenance

Maintenance performed at the carhouses involved mechanical inspections and the routine repair of minor defects detected on inspections or reported by motormen. Cars in heavy service one day were given rush hour (tripper) assignments the next day. They were then scheduled for wheel and brake inspections between their morning and evening runs. Still other inspections and lubrication were completed at night. All cars were swept and dusted daily and their exteriors washed, usually dur-

ing the evening hours. Floors were scrubbed every nine days, and every seventy days a car was brought in for an intensive hand-washing of all interior surfaces. During the winter months, cars with underfloor stoves had their fires tended in the yards at night.

All heavy electrical, mechanical, or body repairs were done at the Snelling Shops, which also completely rebuilt cars every five years, or sooner if their condition warranted. It was during this rebuilding that they were given improvements or, as happened in the 1920s and 1930s, rebuilt with front exits or converted to one-man operation. Cars brought to Snelling Shops for rebuilding were parked on a receiving track where they were stripped of all interior parts and fittings. Seats, window sashes, window shades, and light fixtures were removed and sent to the appropriate shop for renewal and/or replacement.

The car was then placed on the transfer table and shunted into the erecting shop.

The municipal operating franchises required TCRT to sprinkle dirt streets, using a special homebuilt car.

Its wing extended, a streetcar plow was capable of clearing an entire street in two passes, if parked cars were absent. This is Nicollet Avenue south of 26th Street. Photograph from the Minneapolis Star and Tribune News Negative Collection; courtesy of the Minnesota Historical Society.

TCRT needed gravel for track ballast and sand for winter traction. It built spurs to online quarries on Concord Street in South St. Paul (shown here), on Como Avenue across from the fairgrounds, and on Johnson Street Northeast in Minneapolis. Photograph courtesy of the Minnesota Historical Society.

The three shop shifters moved cars around the Snelling Shops complex. Their short length allowed them to fit on the transfer table at right, while pushing or pulling a dead car. The oldest equipment on the roster, they were rebuilt from 1890 vintage cable cars, later employed on the Selby Hill counterweight from 1898 until 1907.

There it was lifted off its trucks, which were then moved to the truck shop, where the traction motors were removed and rebuilt along with the frame, wheels, axles, springs, and journals. In the erecting shop the car body was tipped on its side and positioned so that workers could access all interior and exterior surfaces. Anything that showed excessive wear, decay, or corrosion was removed and replaced. This included all electrical cabling and wiring, which was inspected and replaced if found defective. Once this work was completed the car's interior and exterior were refinished and repainted, it was reunited with its trucks and motors, and the parts removed during stripping were restored after rebuilding in the various shops. When returned to service the car was virtually new. Between heavy overhauls, car exteriors were repainted every two to three years. A TCRT car never looked dirty, faded, or worn.

Besides repairing and rebuilding cars, Snelling Shops manufactured or remanufactured most of the parts used in the cars. This included everything from trolley wheels and brass fittings to stoves, seats and seat frames, and destination signs. There was not much that went into a Twin City Rapid Transit car that Snelling Shops could not, or did not, build. TCRT persisted in this self-sufficiency for fifty years, throwing off criticisms that such practices were not cost effective. Repeated studies, its own and those conducted by outside engineering firms, showed that the Snelling Shops were competitive with and often cheaper than outside suppliers. Doing its own work gave TCRT firmer and much more predictable control over the cost and quality of parts used in the maintenance of its cars. It also preserved the knowledge base and skill sets of its employees and assured continuity in its shop practices.

Today, when the economic life of a transit bus is determined to be twelve years and a railcar twenty-five to thirty, it is a tribute to TCRT and its employees that the company's homebuilt streetcars were doing the same, dependable work on the last day of service in 1954 as they were when they rolled out of the Snelling Shops almost fifty years before.

A streetcar body was turned on its side as part of the regular five-year rebuilding.

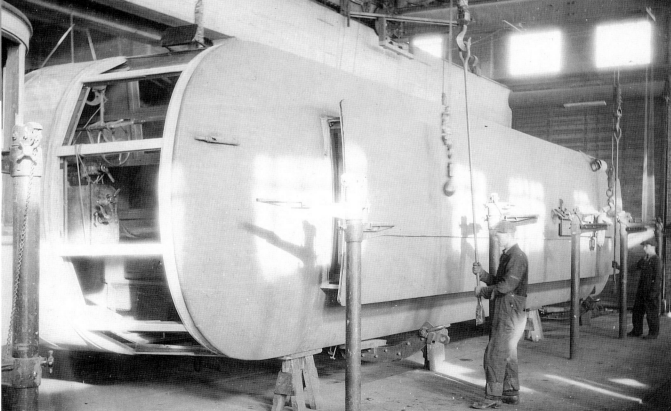

Service, Courtesy, Safety

Working for the Company

6

The Twin City Rapid Transit Company in the 1920s was typical of street railway companies in the early twentieth century. It was a hierarchical, vertically integrated, and functionally directed organization with well-defined authority and responsibility for each department and every employee. What we would today describe as "corporate culture" did not really exist in those days. One simply worked for the company, and those who did not work up to expectations, or who made the same mistake twice, got fired.

This structure was patterned after the military and was adopted after the Civil War by the hundreds of Union and Confederate officers who went on to build and operate railroads and other large industrial organizations. It was an efficient and familiar form for them to apply in managing the activities of large groups of employees. The system had worked during the war and was easily adapted for business purposes after the war. The emerging street railway industry modeled its operating rules and personnel practices after those of the railroad companies.

There was little ambiguity about who was in charge at TCRT. The board of directors made

company policy, which was then carried out by the president. The general superintendent, division superintendents, superintendents, engineers, the master mechanic, and the foremen were in charge. Employees addressed company officials by their first initials and last name; preceded by the salutation "Mr." There was no "team approach" to running the company that one often sees in modern management. Suggestions and ideas were appropriately considered and rewarded, but they had to work their way through the chain of command. Company officials knew the employees and consulted with many of them on a first-name basis, but it was a one-way familiarity.

In the early 1900s, jobs with the streetcar company were sought after with the same fervor as well-paid technical jobs are today. A job with TCRT gave one special standing, even status, in the community. This was especially true for the young men recruited as motormen and conductors, often from farms and small towns, some of them recent immigrants. Management felt that men from rural areas, or newcomers to the country, had better work habits and were more disciplined than their city cousins. For

There was some prestige to being a motorman or conductor. Commercial photographers regularly visited the carhouses and took portraits such as this one.

Musical groups were organized at all five stations in 1914. A few years later, they were consolidated into the Twin City Lines Trainmens Band. The band appeared in parades and at company functions until 1929, when TCRT withdrew its financial support.

nations, and protocols for hiring, evaluating, or promoting employees did not exist. A record of loyalty, deference to company rules, and seniority were more likely to result in promotion. Rulebooks provided direction on operating policies and procedures, but there were no employee guidebooks or manuals that defined a worker's rights or outlined a procedure for filing a grievance.

TCRT issued a book of general rules in 1916 that described in considerable detail the organization and workings of each of the eleven departments in the company and the duties of their employees. It began with a simple two sentence declaration: "The object of these rules is the betterment of the service rendered by the Twin City Lines, and the guidance of all concerned in the performance of their duties. The safe and prompt operation of cars and the

many of these men, it was their first and best job in the big city. They were proud of their brass-buttoned uniforms and their responsibilities aboard the cars. TCRT embodied this image in a fictionalized spokesman, "Bill the Motorman," whose kindly face promoted the company's motto of service, courtesy, and safety in its advertisements for more than forty years.

Those applying for work went to the employment bureau; the human resources department as we know it today did not exist. Formal job descriptions, postings, competitive exami-

Especially in its early years, TCRT hired numerous immigrants. This photograph was taken at the Americanization Day graduation exercises held at Snelling Station in 1919 for St. Paul employees. Company president Horace Lowry and the mayor of St. Paul spoke. Photograph by Charles J. Hibbard.

In every streetcar station trainmen's room, a card game was in progress—here, at Lake Street Station in 1938. Photograph by *Minneapolis Star Tribune*; courtesy of the Minnesota Historical Society.

were scheduled to work. Some of the clerks worked as cashiers. Conductors (as well as motormen and bus operators in later years) made change and sold tokens. Passenger fares went through the fare box and were counted, then returned to the conductor to renew the change supply. At the end of the day these receipts, along with any transfers collected, were given to the cashiers, who confirmed that the money turned in matched the fare box readings recorded by conductors on their trip sheets. These clerks also collected and secured any lost articles found by the trainmen.

Trainmen (TCRT referred to its motormen and conductors as trainmen) were trained for and assigned to a specific station and to lines that worked out of that station. Those with enough seniority could choose particular lines and specific runs on those lines. Obviously, senior trainmen picked better work in terms of pay hours and day versus night work. The typi-

cal workday for a regular (or scheduled) run was ten hours. A few runs were one piece, that is, continuous or straight runs. They were very desirable and could be held only by the most senior employees. Most runs consisted of two or three segments or pieces distributed over a spread of fourteen hours. A motorman, as an example, might pull out a car at 5:00 a.m., work through the morning rush hour until relieved at 9:00 a.m., be off until 11:00 a.m., then relieve another motorman and work until 3:00 p.m., be off from 3:00 to 5:00 p.m., and finish the day with a two-hour assignment from 5:00 to 7:00 p.m. Time between assignments was unpaid.

The hours of operation shaped the picked runs. "Day runs" went to work before the morning rush hour, generally from about 4:00 to 7:00 a.m., and were usually held by trainmen with the highest seniority. They were relieved on the line by the "sunshine" runs during the early afternoon. "Night runs" pulled out of the

Long benches, counters, and display cases ran the length of the trainmen's room. Inside the cases was a copy of every trainman's current assignment, showing the scheduled departure times for every time point in a day's work. The trainmen copied them by hand. Photograph from the Minneapolis Star and Tribune News Negative Collection; courtesy of the Minnesota Historical Society.

rush hour trippers and other extra service that might be needed for major civic events such as the state fair. Pay was allowed only for the hours actually worked, termed platform time. In the early years, until the mid-1930s, there was no overtime pay and no paid days off. However, employees on the extra board were allowed a minimum of two dollars per day providing they made themselves available for all work assignments that might come up on that day. During the Depression, the union negotiated a provision that rotated the extra board each day to give everyone an equal chance at all work. This had the unintended consequence of making extra board employees work around the clock in the course of a couple of months.

Motormen and conductors came under the supervision of district supervisors, reporting to the division superintendent, who were responsible for all of the lines in their respective districts. In the Minneapolis Division in 1916, there were four districts encompassing the following lines:

• East Side Station

Como–Harriet–Hopkins
Oak & Xerxes
Hennepin Local
Kenwood & Johnson
Western & 2nd Street
Bryn Mawr
Minnetonka–Deephaven
Robbinsdale & St. Louis Park
Calhoun Beach

• Nicollet Station

54th St. and Col. Heights
Marquette and Grand
Monroe and Bryant
4th Ave. S. and 6th Ave. N.

stations in the late afternoons, before the evening rush hour, and worked until midnight or so. The much smaller number of "owl" runs relieved the night runs and remained on duty through the morning rush hour. With few exceptions, there was no such thing as conventional 8:00 a.m. to 5:00 p.m. hours.

Employees without sufficient seniority to hold a regular run were assigned to the extra board. The extra board was an employee pool used to cover absences and provide crews for

The Motorettes

As World War II ground on, TCRT found itself in a tough situation. Up to nine hundred of its male employees were potentially fit for military duty, and many had already left for the service. At the same time, ridership was soaring and the streetcars were terribly overcrowded. Like so many other industries, TCRT turned to women to fill the jobs. Ads appeared in the newspapers, and the women responded. Nearly five hundred were hired as trainmen, forty-seven as car cleaners, plus a number in other jobs, including mechanics. Some followed family members onto the cars. Marcella Anderson joined her father, an East Side motorman with over thirty years' seniority. Adeline Lundquist joined her husband, a North Side motorman. Elvita Verite filled the job at Lake Street vacated by her husband when he went off to war. Helen Chamberland Zarembo and her sister Bonita Jodell Rudeen applied for jobs in the lost and found, only to be told that they were needed more on the cars. Neither had a driver's license, but they were put to work anyway. Many of the women commented that they felt they were helping the war effort by working.

Since the title "motorman" wouldn't do, the company substituted the awkward "motorette." Three hundred and eight-one of them were hired from July 1943 to November 1945. The first of 126 "conductorettes" was hired in on April 15, 1945. Though the women generally were well received within the company, the public wasn't always so accepting. Several motorettes told of passengers refusing to ride with a woman and waiting for the next car. In 1945, conductorette Florence Hill was beaten by a drunken returning serviceman who accused her of taking a job from a man. The motorettes also had their share of derailments and collisions, and a number were injured on the job. Noella Sitzman backed into a Cadillac after missing her switch at Rice Street and Como Avenue. Marcella Anderson's PCC car jumped the tracks at 51st Street and Bryant Avenue and ended up in a front yard. Other experiences were merely humorous. The St. Paul paper told of a novice motorette who mistook a police call box for a company telephone and asked the cops where to park her streetcar at pull-in. Maxine Magnuson found two mice on her streetcar

and dutifully turned them in to the lost and found. They were unclaimed, so she took them home for her children. A kid put candy in Arlyne Taylor's changer. Conductorette Catherine Ruley thought that her car was stopping to allow her to flag a railroad grade crossing in North St. Paul, so she got off. Her motorette was actually stopping to pick up a passenger and took off, leaving Catherine standing there for forty-five minutes.

TCRT initially outfitted the women in tailored jackets along with vests and trousers and hats that were softer and smaller in diameter than a man's hat, with a braided hatband. The initials TCL were intertwined to form a new logo that was displayed on the cap and coat lapels. Wartime shortages apparently doomed the new look, and soon women were wearing the same uniform as the men, but often providing their own trousers. Skirts were never worn.

Up to 183 women were employed at any one time. Their tenure was usually short. Most worked less than one year and left soon after the war ended in August 1945. By the end of 1946, there were forty-six left. By 1950, this had dwindled to twenty-five, partially because of a layoff in 1948. A handful made the switch to buses. Ruby Peterson was the last one, working run number 1 on Selby–Lake for many years and retiring in 1980. No other women were hired to drive streetcars or buses from 1945 until the early 1970s.

Some of the first motorettes, hired to replace men during World War II, get their car assignments in 1943.

Mayme Bilek was hired during World War II to clean streetcars. She worked the overnight shift at Snelling until 1971.

Motorettes Marie Hagen, Bernice Nelson, and Verna Fox.

• Lake Street Station

Plymouth and Bloomington
Minnehaha Falls
Lake Street to 36th Ave. S.
Franklin Ave.–11th St.
East 25th Street

• North Side Station

Chicago and Fremont
Chicago and Penn
Lake Nokomis–Camden
Broadway and 20th Ave. N.
Cedar Ave. Extension

In the St. Paul Division in 1916, the districts and lines were as follows:

• Interurban

Minneapolis and St. Paul
Selby–Lake
Snelling–Minnehaha
Fort Snelling Stub

• Snelling Station

Selby Avenue
Merriam Park
Payne–Phalen
Hamline–Union Depot
Como Local
Dale & Forest
Western & South Robert

• 7th Street Station

Jackson and Stryker
Rondo and Maria
Burns Ave. Extension
Rice St.–So. St. Paul–Inver Grove
Miss. & Cherokee Hts.
St. Clair–Hope St.
Snelling Ave.–E. 7th St.

• Stillwater

St. Paul and Stillwater
Wildwood
White Bear
Mahtomedi
Hazel Park
Owen Street
So. Stillwater

A corps of line inspectors reported to each district supervisor. They monitored daily operations, checked schedule adherence, and dealt with problems and special situations. Besides the district supervisors and line inspectors,

There were some problems inspectors could not solve. The stalled auto at the left has backed up streetcars down Wabasha Street in downtown St. Paul. The inability to detour easily around an obstruction was a real drawback—and a definite advantage for buses.

the operating department stationed fixed post supervisors, called "starters," at critical locations in downtown Minneapolis and St. Paul. They were expected to observe all lines passing through the central business district and correct any problems affecting the service. A starter was always on duty at Hennepin and Washington Avenues in Minneapolis (later 5th Street and Hennepin) and 7th and Wabasha Streets in St. Paul. Working out of a small shelter, starters had direct telephone connections with the carhouses and the general offices. As supervisors, they were authorized to deal with service irregularities or emergencies on the spot. For example, an outbound car running ten minutes late on a line with three-minute service during the afternoon rush hour might be directed to turn around at a wye short of the end of the line, then fall in place and leave on time on its inbound trip.

There was a small cadre of special inspectors, not well known and deliberately so, who reported directly to the general superintendent. Their job was to observe the work of employees suspected of discrepancies, especially involving the handling of money. A special inspector would board a car as if he were a regular passenger and make a point of watching the work of the conductor, making sure that fares and transfers were properly handled and recorded.

A Streetcar Odyssey

On a winter rush hour evening of 1947–48, I was stationed as a street fare collector on the corner of 7th and Wabasha Streets in downtown St. Paul. For some reason there had been an interruption in eastbound service on the St. Clair–Phalen line for more than half an hour. The waiting riders were becoming restless, for they were used to service of less than ten minutes headway during the rush hour. As the delay lengthened, they sent their delegates across the street with increasing frequency to complain to the starter (inspector) and demand that he do something about it.

At first, the starter confined his efforts to looking for pull-in cars of the St. Paul–Minneapolis Interurban line, and he asked the trainmen of several such cars if they would run a fill-in. Each time the crew refused when asked. (Prewar crews were *told* and would have complied.) As the complaints became more frequent and more vocal, the starter began making the same request of regular Interurban crews, and again he received refusals. That was real desperation—to even think of pulling an Interurban from a scheduled run!

Finally a Como–Harriet gate car came along with its pull-in "East Mpls. Station" sign, and the same request was made. Both conductor and motorman responded that they wouldn't mind at all except they didn't know anything about St. Paul routes. I was asked if I would ride along to show the motorman the route, and I said OK.

The front destination sign was rolled to blank. As soon as I called out "Payne Avenue," the cold passengers swarmed across the street to the car, so we had standees even before we swung eastward onto 7th from Wabasha. At each downtown corner, I stepped down from the front steps and announced the destination. We probably set some record for a passenger count since I was squeezing them in through the front door while the conductor was doing the same through the rear gates.

I pointed out the route to the motorman and called out the street names to the passengers. The riders seemed more jovial than annoyed, and the crew seemed to be enjoying themselves, too. When we arrived at Maryland Avenue and Duluth Street, the motorman wanted to continue up the single track to Kennard just for the sightseeing, but I talked him out of it. We backed around the wye and rolled the destination sign to "East Mpls. Station."

The trip back to downtown was uneventful. I directed them onto the Cedar Loop track and left the car at 9th Street and Wabasha.
—Earl Anderson

Load dispatcher Charles Camitsch at his desk in the control room at the Main Steam Station in 1939. From here, 74,000 kilowatts of electricity were directed around the system to power TCRT's cars. Photograph courtesy of Charles Camitsch.

They became less affectionately known as "snoops."

THE AUDITOR'S OFFICE AND THE TREASURY

The auditor's office and the treasury were headquartered at the main offices at 11th Street and Hennepin Avenue in downtown Minneapolis. They were responsible for overseeing income, primarily from passenger fares, and authorizing disbursements for company expenses, the largest being payroll. The departments also prepared financial statements and reports, administered contracts and leases, monitored budgetary expenses, and were involved in any major capital projects or purchases concerning the company. More than a hundred people, the majority of them clerical workers, were employed in both departments. In an era before machine data processing, this clerical army went through the hundreds of trip sheets and time cards that were turned in every day, making certain that all of the miles, hours, and revenues were properly posted and accounted for.

THE POWER AND EQUIPMENT DEPARTMENT

The power and equipment department was responsible for the generation and distribution of electric power for streetcar operations. That included the Main Steam Station, the Lower Dam Water Power Station, substations, and a network of underground and overhead transmission lines and the trolley overhead. It also maintained the company's private telephone system in the shops and offices and the dozens of call boxes scattered throughout the system that were used by motormen and conductors to call in problems on the line. The power and equipment department maintained a testing laboratory. It was formally divided into the following subdepartments:

- Office of engineer (headquartered in the General Office Building)
- Steam station–construction and operation (headquartered in the Main Steam Station)
- Electrical operation (headquartered in the Lower Dam Power Station)
- Overhead construction and maintenance (headquartered in the General Office Building)
- Underground construction and maintenance (headquartered in Nicollet Station)
- Electrical construction (headquartered in the General Office Building)

- Laboratories and testing (headquartered in the Snelling Shops)

Employees in these various subdepartments were scattered around the system at the Main Steam Station, substations, and, in the case of maintenance crews, at each of the carhouses. Two hundred employees worked in the power and equipment department.

The majority of the jobs in the power and equipment department required special skills and included electrical and mechanical engineers, chemists and laboratory technicians, equipment operators and riggers, plant maintainers, electricians, linemen, and draftsmen. Employees reported to the engineer of power and equipment.

TCRT power engineers developed an ongoing plan and program for upgrading and renewing its equipment. Turbines and boilers at the Main Steam Station were taken off line for inspection and maintenance at times of low power demand. The power distribution system, including the transmission lines and the trolley contact wires, were inspected on a regular schedule. Engineers were ever vigilant for faults in the ground return circuit and took special measurements whenever or wherever trouble was suspected. Separate crews performed under-

ground and overhead maintenance. It was hazardous duty, and employees were thoroughly trained for their jobs. Underground maintainers had to be watchful for stray currents, as well as deadly sewer gas and explosive natural gas leaks.

Work on the overhead lines was usually done from a wire car—a work car with a long, flat bed and a small cabin up front for the motorman and the repair crew. At the rear of the car there was a tower with an insulated platform that could be raised to the level of the trolley wire. Linemen working from this platform could make

In later years the power department discovered the advantages of line trucks that could repair the overhead with fewer delays to scheduled service. This is Como Avenue just west of Eustis Street.

repairs on "live" wires, thereby permitting uninterrupted streetcar service. The wire car also carried spools of cable and wire for emergency repairs. Every carhouse was assigned a wire car and a maintenance crew. In later years the wire cars were supplanted by wire trucks, which carried similar equipment but had the advantage of greater mobility. Besides routine work such as replacing stretches of worn trolley contact wire, linemen were called out for any number of mishaps: broken wires, accidents involv-

ing damage to the overhead, fires in adjoining buildings, and severe weather involving wind damage, lightning strikes, and perhaps their least favorite, ice and sleet storms.

THE PURCHASING AND STORES DEPARTMENT

The purchasing and stores department procured and distributed all of the equipment, spare parts, supplies, and consumables used in the operation of the system. The department reported to the general storekeeper, whose offices were in the main stores building at the Snelling Shops. Besides purchasing and inventory management and control, the department performed cost accounting and related functions for all of the departments in the company, particularly the mechanical departments and the Snelling Shops, which manufactured many of the spare parts for the streetcars as well as the streetcars themselves.

Each day the supply car, rebuilt from an old streetcar, left the Snelling Shops Storehouse and transported needed parts and materials to the other carhouses. Here it leaves the Lake Street bridge and enters Minneapolis on its way to Lake Street Station.

The department was organized under the Transit Supply Company and acted as a fiscal agent and clearinghouse for all purchasing and inventory functions. Its workforce was made up of purchasing agents, clerks, cost accountants, and material handlers. Each carhouse and shop facility had a stores department under the direction of a storekeeper. A central inventory was maintained of all shipments received at the stores building at the Snelling Shops. Every day a special car left the stores building and made the rounds of all the shops and carhouses, dropping off supplies and picking up parts for return and rebuilding at the Snelling Shops.

THE TRACK DEPARTMENT

The engineer of maintenance of way headed up the track department, which was responsible for the construction and maintenance of all track, bridges, roadbed, and fixed facilities in the system. It also was responsible for snow removal from the streets, private right of way, and yards.

Some 350 people worked in the track de-

partment. Additional laborers were hired for special construction or renewal projects or in the event of emergencies such as heavy winter storms. Track crews were based at the various shops and carhouses around the system.

A central inventory of track materials—rail, ties, ballast, paving stones—was kept in the yards at Snelling along with most of the

All across the Twin Cities, when dirt streets were paved, TCRT had to replace and upgrade its track structure. This is Penn Avenue North at Lowry Avenue. Note the prefabricated temporary track at far right, which carried the cars around the construction.

heavy work equipment used for major track construction.

Work cars and equipment assigned to the track department included trolley work flats for transporting rail, ties, and ballast, and crane cars for lifting rail and special work (switches and crossovers) into place. A sprinkler car was used to water down unpaved streets. During winter storms, snowplows came out along with cars that spread salt to keep ice from building up in flangeways. Curves and special work were inspected regularly. Tight curves were greased on a regular schedule to reduce wheel and track wear. A rail-grinding car (a former passenger

car modified for this work) made the rounds of the system. This car had special abrasive blocks that smoothed out irregularities (flat spots or corrugations) on the surface of the rails.

Besides these routine jobs, emergency crews could be called out whenever there was a major fire adjoining one of the car lines. Unlike buses, which can be detoured, streetcars had to either proceed through such scenes or be cut back and turned at the nearest wye. To maintain service, hose jumpers were secured to the tracks and the fire hoses routed through them. Streetcars could then cross over the hoses and proceed on their route.

Rail grinding restores the rail's profile, producing a smoother ride. This very early grinder is being deployed on University Avenue at Syndicate Street in front of Brown and Bigelow's office and printing plant in St. Paul.

Maintenance work at Snelling Shops. The shop man is adjusting brakes in the pit.

THE MECHANICAL DEPARTMENT

The mechanical department, under the direction of the master mechanic, was the second-largest department in the company. Over three hundred people worked at the Snelling Shops, which built all of the company's rolling stock and performed heavy repairs and reconditioned all of its equipment. Additional shopmen worked at the carhouses, inspecting and cleaning cars and doing routine, preventive maintenance. TCRT's shops and its maintenance programs were considered the best in the industry.

Wages, Hours, and Working Conditions

🚋

Before 1934, the company set wages and benefits. After 1934, wages and benefits for nonsupervisory employees were bargained with the Amalgamated Association of Street, Electric Railway and Motor Coach Employees Local 1005 (since 1964 the Amalgamated Transit Union). ATU advocated arbitration in lieu of strikes, and many of the improvements it won for employees came about through arbitration. TCRT generally agreed to arbitration, even though it was rarely in its best economic

TCRT upholstered its seats in woven rattan, very common in streetcars and steam railroad commuter coaches. Originally sealed with clear varnish, the rattan snagged women's stockings when hemlines rose in the 1920s. The solution was to apply a thicker cream-colored paint that smoothed the rough edges. Seats were reupholstered as needed during the regular five-year overhaul received by all streetcars.

The day-to-day washing of streetcar exteriors was performed manually overnight by a small army of car cleaners.

TCRT officials hated this sort of collision the most—there was no one to file a claim against. This misunderstanding occurred at Rice Street and University Avenue in St. Paul. Photograph by *St. Paul Pioneer Press-Dispatch*; courtesy of the Minnesota Historical Society.

By far the biggest and heaviest vehicle on the street, this Bryant Avenue car has tangled with a fire truck at 44th Street. This is on Bryant at 44th Street in south Minneapolis. Although the front platform was demolished, none of the other windows was broken. Photograph courtesy of the Minneapolis Public Library, Special Collections.

Service, Courtesy, Safety

interests to do so, because its fares and most aspects of its operations were subject to regulation by elected governmental bodies that it could ill afford to antagonize by frequent, lengthy work stoppages.

TCRT's ten-hour workday, within a spread of fourteen hours, was not unusual in the street railway industry of 1915. Railroad operating employees worked up to sixteen hours. For locomotive firemen that meant shoveling coal sixteen hours at a stretch. Paid time off was a rarity and overtime pay nonexistent. TCRT's office employees fared somewhat better. In 1915, their day ran from 8:00 a.m. to 5:00 p.m. with an hour off for lunch. On Saturdays it was 8:00 a.m. until noon. There were six paid holidays: New Year's, Washington's Birthday, Memorial Day, the Fourth of July, Thanksgiving Day, and Christmas. Office employees received two

weeks of paid vacation after one year's service. Department heads were authorized to allow up to one month paid leave to "employees whose services are of such a nature that their value to the company is not entirely determined by the actual hours of service." These benefits were extended to salaried management employees

Other than sheer mass, there was little to protect the motorman in a severe crash. The window glass and wood became flying knifelike shards and splinters. The motorman's best option was to set the air brake and retreat to the passenger compartment.

As part of its five-year overhaul, the streetcar was jacked up and the trucks removed for repairs to the wheels, motors, gears, and brakes.

A Dissenting View from Labor

In 1951, distrust ran high and old wounds continued to fester. The Amalgamated Association of Street, Electric Railway and Motor Coach Employees (now the Amalgamated Transit Union) eventually won the right to represent and bargain for TCRT employees, but the company did everything it could to frustrate their efforts, resisting any attempts by employees and their union to secure improvements in wages, hours, and working conditions. Old-timers who worked for TCRT before and after World War II would often say that working for TCRT was like "working for Hitler." It must be kept in mind, however, that TCRT, like every privately owned transit company in the country, was in a life-or-death battle with the automobile, and with over 90 percent of its operating expense going to labor, and its solvency at stake, it had to do whatever it could to drive down costs.

John Seidel was the president and business agent of Local 1005 in 1951. On May 15 of that year he sent union members a strongly worded response to an earlier letter from company president E. B. Aslesen, who, on behalf of a management group led by Chairman Fred Ossanna, was trying to rekindle goodwill among TCRT employees. Charles Green had just departed as president of TCRT after eliminating the jobs of some eight hundred employees. Ossanna and his associates wanted no trouble from labor as they moved ahead with bus conversion and the elimination of still more jobs.

Excerpts from John Seidel's reply reveal a deep cynicism and mistrust of management's motives: "They speak of the home folks who again own and manage this transit company, and they add and I quote, 'It may be our mutual pleasure to witness the rekindling of that fine, friendly spirit of cooperation among the employees which for years was of such great importance in securing for the company a place of outstanding rank in the transit industry of America. . . .'

"That fine, friendly spirit of cooperation, which they make reference to, was the kind of spirit that prevailed during the days of slavery, before there was an organization on this property, when the boss was able to hold the whip over the workers. He does not mention that during the years he speaks of that we worked seven days a week, thirteen hours or more a day, spread time from 5:00AM until 1:00AM the following day, with no such thing as overtime or penalty time. . . . If the foreman even suspected that you were not happy with the then prevailing conditions he would send you to the Superintendent's office and he would inform you: 'We don't need you anymore.' And if you asked why he would tell you it was for the good of the service. . . .

"It was also a fine, friendly spirit of cooperation when they arbitrarily reduced the pension payment to those already on a pension from $50.00 to $30.00 a month and that's what some of the old timers are getting today after having worked for these fine, friendly people for thirty to forty years. But they, the company officials, took care of themselves with a pension of at least five to six hundred dollars a month. . . . I refer specifically to the former president D. J. Strouse. When the union tried to negotiate a pension, Mr. D. J. Strouse told Brother Wigstrom the employees would get a pension over his dead body. . . .

"In the same paragraph reference is made to the company having secured a place of outstanding rank in the transit industry . . . It is true they were outstanding, especially so in their efforts to defeat attempts to organize time after time with the aid of the old labor-hating Citizens Alliance. . . .

"I am sure many of you will recall the 1917 strike, when they were able to get the governor to call out the National Guard and place soldiers with bayonets on the cars to prevent the workers from being organized. Yes, they were outstanding in the transit industry to the extent that other transit companies could point to the Twin City Lines as an example of low wages and long hours and profit thereby to keep conditions bad and wages low on their properties."

and hourly office employees in all departments. Arguably, some of these benefits, particularly paid leave, were discretionary rather than contractual; even so, they were rather progressive for supervisors and office workers in 1915.

Operating employees in the mechanical, operating, power, and maintenance of way departments did not enjoy the same paid leave as those in office positions. They did receive benefits, however, through the Employees Mutual Benefit Association, a company insurance program that provided medical coverage, life insurance, and pensions to all employees who were contributing members—with a portion of the plan funded by the company. Conductors and motormen with twelve years of service who for health or other reasons could no longer work a full day were eligible, and could apply, for the "Bonus List." These employees were guaranteed minimum pay but were only expected to work morning and afternoon rush hour trip-

Streetcar traction motors and deep water do not mix. A good rainstorm and a clogged catch basin could put an entire line out of business, as it has here at the Milwaukee Road 36th Avenue South railroad underpass. A TCRT maintenance crew is trying to unplug things. Photograph from the Minneapolis Star and Tribune News Negative Collection; courtesy of the Minnesota Historical Society.

pers. Assignment to the "Bonus List" was at the discretion of the general superintendent and required a medical certificate and recommendation from the division superintendent and station foreman.

Improvements to employee wages and benefits came slowly, made difficult by the company's financial situation. Two-thirds of its operating expenses went to labor. Thirty years of expansion and improvements to rolling stock and fixed facilities were purchased with borrowed money, and after 1922 its only source of revenue—passengers—was increasingly lured away by automobiles. Finding the revenues to offset the additional expense became more and more of a challenge. Anger erupted in 1917 when operating employees struck for union recognition and improved wages and working conditions. The strike failed. The Depression brought wage cuts and shortened work hours. TCRT did not lay off employees, but the amount of work available to them declined. In 1934, employees voted to join the Amalgamated Association of Street, Electric Railway and Motor Coach Employees, which over several years fought for and won wage increases, shortened work hours, and improved benefits. The Fair Labor Standards Act of 1938 brought further improvements.

The abolition of conductors on most lines and the conversion to one-man operation increased tensions, even though no employees were furloughed as a result of the change. A work stoppage occurred in 1938 over the elimination of conductors. Negotiations in 1936 resulted in a three-year contract, which provided for a six-day workweek with overtime after forty-eight hours. Runs were capped at nine and a half hours and the spread of hours reduced from fourteen to thirteen and a half. Motormen and conductors were guaranteed six hours off between night and day work. The base wage for motormen on one-man cars was set at sixty-seven cents an hour and sixty-two cents an hour with a conductor.

Employees won better wages and working conditions during and after World War II, but it would never be (and still is not) a nine-to-five job. For motormen, conductors, and bus drivers—even mechanical employees—the rate of pay, the hours and lines worked or the job held, days off, and vacations were all determined by and picked according to seniority. You were not an "old-timer" or a member of the club until you had twenty-five years. Then maybe you could pick a summer vacation or get a Saturday and Sunday off.

Trolleys in Your Neighborhood

Everywhere by Streetcar

Getting around by Streetcar

Thomas Lowry understood the connection between transportation and development. His vision and the street railway system it created meant that Minneapolis and St. Paul did not have to be a hodgepodge of factories piled on top of shops and homes. Land use could be planned and zoned, with residential neighborhoods organized near open spaces such as parks and lakes, and industry and manufacturing near transportation (the river or railroad lines). The Twin Cities and Lowry's streetcar system grew up together. Wherever the streetcars ran, people, neighborhoods, and businesses followed.

A streetcar line took the name of the street it traversed, a particular local feature or landmark, or its end destination. The name was a bond with the neighborhoods it served, an identity that was as much a part of the urban geography as the neighborhoods themselves. And unlike the freeways, constructed fifty years later, which either destroyed or isolated neighborhoods, the streetcar brought neighborhoods together in a greater community by gathering people with different ethnic backgrounds, education, wealth, and social standing, for a common journey on all their separate errands.

Board a streetcar and there could be accountants and lawyers, shop owners, bankers and stockbrokers, women in fancy hats headed for the office, or laborers smelling of whiskey and tobacco. A salesman, making calls, might swing on the back platform, put down his bulky sample cases, greet the conductor, light up a cigar and pass a flask, exchanging lies with other salesmen. Inside, gentlemen in fine suits would sit alongside workers with lunch buckets. Friends and neighbors would discuss the events of the day. A newsboy might slip past the conductor without paying, and then try to sell a few papers before the conductor caught up with him. Wives would be on shopping trips, perhaps to the produce market, the bakery, or the butcher shop, or all the way to downtown Minneapolis to Witt's grocery store or the Great Northern Market, or to Schunemans or the Golden Rule in downtown St. Paul.

A streetcar trip began with a short walk to the nearest stop. Knowledgeable riders kept an

In the late 1930s, the neighborhood fills the stands for a fall football game at Minneapolis Central High School. Barely noticed, a pair of 4th Avenue streetcars meet at 36th Street. Photograph by George Luxton; courtesy of the Minnesota Historical Society.

To save a minute in the crowded hour

Bill the Motorman Says:

"Some folks remind me of a man with a stiff neck—they can see only one car at a time."

Bill the Motorman spoke to the riding public, gently and humorously urging them to be considerate of others and understanding of the company's operating challenges. Human behavior baffled Bill—why does everyone try to pile on the first streetcar in line? Reproduced courtesy of Forrest Johnson.

eye on the overhead trolley wires. Any movement signaled that a car was approaching, even though it might be on the other side of a hill or around the corner. The wait was never long. Unless it was very late at night or in the wee hours of the morning, a car would appear in a few minutes, its approach announced by a distant hum and then a roar as it came closer. That roar would be replaced by the hiss of compressed air and squealing brakes as the motorman brought it to a stop.

If this were a "one-man" car, you would board through the front door, drop your fare in the box, and ask the motorman for a transfer if you planned to change to another line. Having the exact fare was never a problem because the motorman made change and sold tokens. On a "two-man" car, you would board through the rear doors (or gates, if it were a gate car) and do business with the conductor on the rear platform. By the late 1940s, finding a conductor was rare because only the busiest lines, among them Selby–Lake, Como–Harriet, Chicago, St. Paul–Minneapolis, Nicollet, and the Inter-Campus Special still used them.

Once you were aboard, the ride could be an adventure, if you watched the work of the motorman and the conductor, or mundane, if,

like so many riders, you opened a newspaper or a book or simply stared out the window. A motorman on a one-man car on a busy line always wished for an extra arm. The left hand was usually on the controller, which regulated the speed of the car, and the right hand on the brake valve. As a safety feature, the brake valve was spring-loaded: letting go applied the brakes. An experienced motorman learned how to rest his right knee against the valve, freeing his hand for punching transfers and cranking fares through the fare box, which counted the money and returned it to the motorman.

Streetcars ran everywhere. On hot summer nights they could take you to a band concert at Lake Harriet or for a ride to the country and back just to cool down. Before television, streetcars took people to evening movies, plays, concerts, and lectures. They were there for a picnic at Minnehaha Park or a tour of the cities. They ran to baseball games for the Minneapolis Millers at Nicollet Park in Minneapolis or the Saint Paul Saints at Lexington Park in St. Paul. They took thousands of Gopher football fans to Memorial Stadium on the University of Minnesota campus in southeast Minneapolis. Fairgoers rode them every year to the Minnesota State Fair.

Most destinations in Minneapolis or St. Paul were accessible by streetcar, either directly or by transferring to another line downtown, or to one of the crosstown lines on Lake Street or Broadway Avenue in north Minneapolis or Snelling Avenue in St. Paul. As important streetcar corridors, these crosstown lines attracted intense commercial and retail activity. Lake Street in south Minneapolis became one continuous shopping strip from Hennepin Avenue all the way to 36th Avenue South. At Chicago

Avenue and Lake Street, the Sears department store and warehouse stood at one of the busiest streetcar intersections in Minneapolis. In north Minneapolis, Broadway and Central Avenues filled in with small shops and businesses. In St. Paul, the crossing of the Snelling Avenue and St. Paul–Minneapolis car lines at Snelling and University Avenues turned that intersection into the heart of the Midway business district, dominated by the huge Montgomery Ward department store just east of TCRT's Snelling Shops. Every neighborhood had a drug store, market,

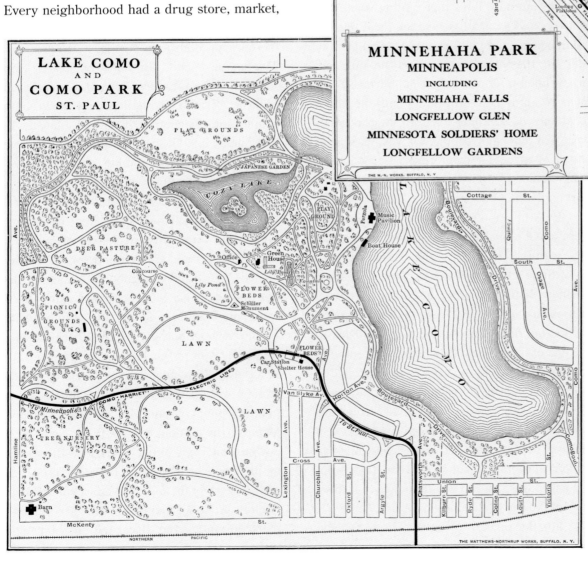

St. Paul and Minneapolis each had urban parks served by the streetcar that remain popular destinations today, including Como Park and Minnehaha Park (now served by the Hiawatha Light Rail). These maps are from pre-1920 TCRT tour brochures.

bakery, or five-and-dime at busy streetcar stops or at the end of a streetcar line. Neighborhood streetcar riders shopped at these local businesses much as we use convenience stores today.

Serving the Neighborhoods

By the time the system matured in the 1920s, there were forty-one streetcar lines in the TCRT system. They included the four intercity lines that ran between Minneapolis and St. Paul, seventeen local lines in Minneapolis, and another twelve local lines in St. Paul, the Inter-Campus, plus the long suburban lines to Tonka Bay, Deephaven, White Bear, Mahtomedi, Stillwater, and the three local lines in Stillwater itself. At its peak there were 523 miles of track, and it was possible to travel by streetcar from Tonka Bay on Lake Minnetonka all the way to Stillwater and Bayport on the St. Croix River.

In Minneapolis and St. Paul, the lines were about a quarter mile to a half mile apart, and, with the exception of the crosstown lines, all of them ran to and through the downtown business districts. Earlier, just after electrification, most cars entered the downtowns, looped around on major streets, and then ran back to the end of the line. By 1910, most were running through downtown, then out to another side of the city. This made for speedier scheduling and a more fluid operation, with fewer streetcars standing on congested downtown streets. It also reduced both revenue and nonrevenue miles on pullout and pull-in (not in service) trips from the carhouses, as well as unproductive layover time at the end of the line.

For these reasons, pairing lines became

a common practice, not just in the Twin Cities, but in other cities as well. When pairing lines from opposite sides of the city, TCRT's schedulers considered the round-trip cycle time of each line, the number of riders, and the frequency of service that would be required to accommodate them. The objective was to balance each side of the line, thereby assuring uniform service and an equal spacing of cars while trimming unproductive time in the schedule.

Over time, route pairs might be rearranged as travel patterns changed. For example, in 1891, the Bryant line in south Minneapolis was paired with Monroe in northeast Minneapolis. Thirty years later, Bryant was joined with Johnson, becoming the Bryant–Johnson, and Monroe was paired with the Grand line in south Minneapolis, becoming the Grand–Monroe. In the line-by-line descriptions that follow, line pairings are listed, beginning with the conversion to electricity in 1890–92.

Although done for economic and operational reasons, this pairing of lines must have created an interesting exchange of cultures. Slavic and Italian, Catholic northeast Minneapolis ("Nordeast") neighborhoods served by the 2nd St. N.E., Monroe, and Central lines were paired with predominantly Scandinavian, Lutheran neighborhoods in south Minneapolis. In St. Paul in the 1940s, the primarily African American neighborhoods along Rondo Avenue were paired with Italian and Mexican neighborhoods along South Wabasha Street, forming the Rondo–Stryker line. Near both downtowns from either direction, there was an inevitable overlap of people and cultures as passengers got on and off. Motormen and conductors no doubt found some diverse reading material among the discarded neighborhood newspapers as they took their layover at the end of the line.

Service frequencies (headways) were determined by passenger demand. A line with five-minute service at rush hours might have fifteen-minute service in the middle of the day or hourly service in the wee hours of the morning. Headways were similarly adjusted, depending on passenger demand, between points on the same line. At the outskirts of the city, where there was less development, there might be fifteen-minute service, while a more developed area three miles closer to downtown had seven-minute service. Some cars traveled all the way to the end of the line. Others turned back closer to downtown. Time and mileage were money, and TCRT, conscious of its bottom line, always attempted to maximize revenue passengers carried per car mile, while at the same time providing good service. Streetcars did not earn revenues when they were standing still. Nor did they cover expenses when there were empty seats, although empty seats were rare until automobiles became more common.

Between 1954, the year the system was finally abandoned, and the present day, all or significant portions of several streets once used by streetcars, along with the neighborhoods the streetcars served, either disappeared or were significantly altered by development and/or highway construction. Examples are 4th Avenue South, north of 28th Street in Minneapolis, displaced by Interstate 35, and Rondo Avenue in St. Paul, displaced by Interstate 94.

This was a large system nuanced by decades of changes that mirrored, and in some cases contributed to, the changing patterns of growth and development in the Twin Cities themselves. It is impossible, therefore, to convey the flavor of the system and the neighborhoods by map alone. The text sections that follow are an accompaniment to the system maps in this chapter, the individual line maps, and the track maps in Appendix J. They provide more detail and include a description and summary of each line's history and the characteristics of the neighborhoods they served, together with a list of the lines they were paired with over the years. Each text section has its own map.

Some lines were more significant than others because of the places they served and the number of people that used them, and, while the objective is to present as complete a picture as possible of the entire system from the horse-car era until conversion to buses in 1954, the relative importance of a line and its standing in the system may be reflected in the text and the length of the description. For the same reason, some lines were rarely photographed, and, therefore, only one or two photographs were available to accompany the text.

Readers are directed to the Minneapolis and St. Paul track maps appearing in Appendix J. These maps show important track intersections, wyes, loops, and sections of single track in the system as well as the location of TCRT facilities.

The next section of this chapter takes up the intercity streetcar lines that operated between Minneapolis and St. Paul. This is followed by a description of routings and operations in both downtowns. The streetcar lines in Minneapolis are considered next, followed by the lines in St. Paul. In both cities, the line descriptions begin at the western city limits and proceed clockwise around the map. The service frequencies noted in the line descriptions are generally typical

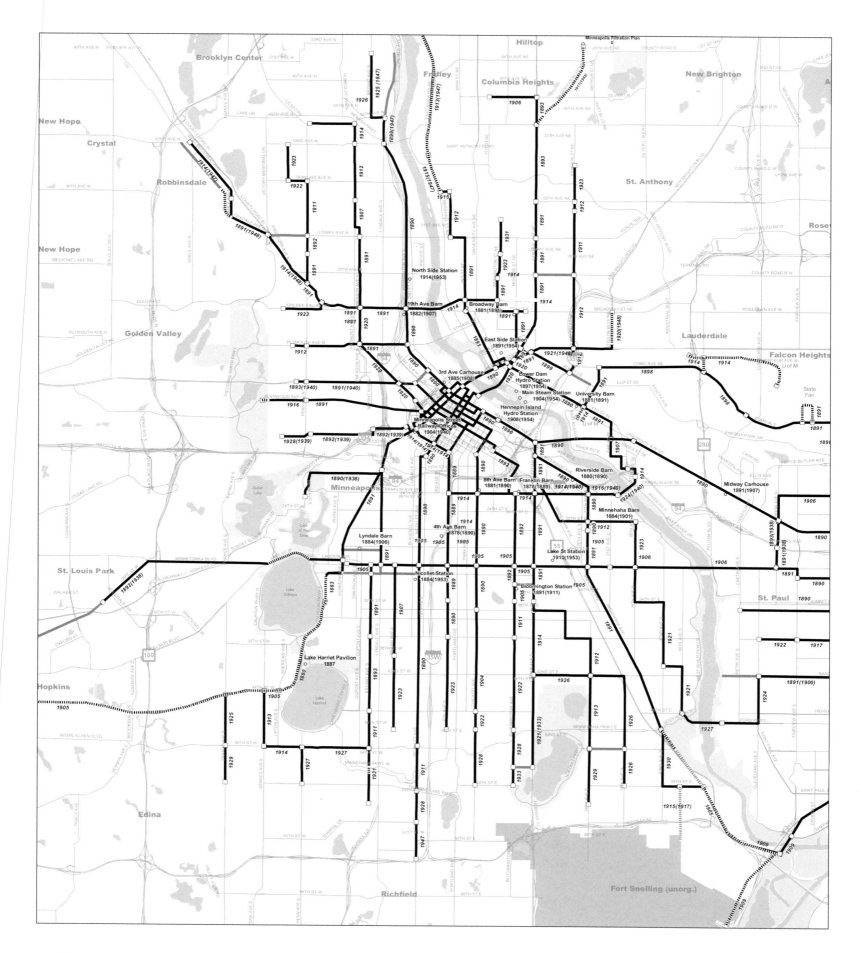

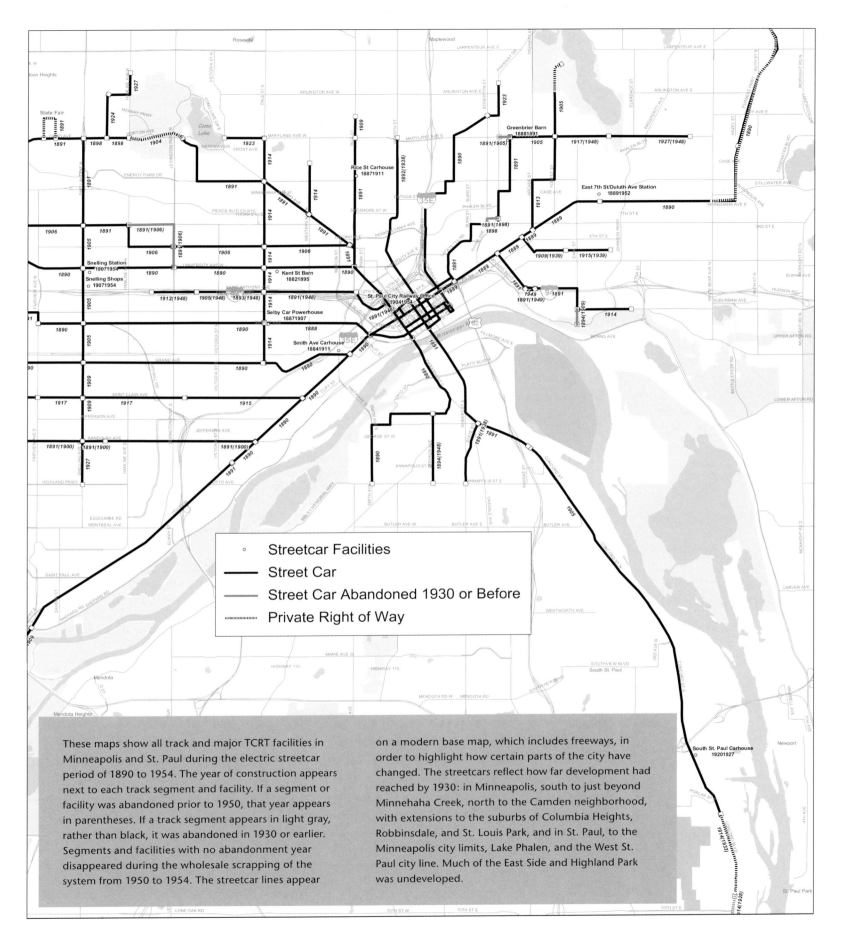

Streetcar Facilities

Street Car

Street Car Abandoned 1930 or Before

Private Right of Way

These maps show all track and major TCRT facilities in Minneapolis and St. Paul during the electric streetcar period of 1890 to 1954. The year of construction appears next to each track segment and facility. If a segment or facility was abandoned prior to 1950, that year appears in parentheses. If a track segment appears in light gray, rather than black, it was abandoned in 1930 or earlier. Segments and facilities with no abandonment year disappeared during the wholesale scrapping of the system from 1950 to 1954. The streetcar lines appear on a modern base map, which includes freeways, in order to highlight how certain parts of the city have changed. The streetcars reflect how far development had reached by 1930: in Minneapolis, south to just beyond Minnehaha Creek, north to the Camden neighborhood, with extensions to the suburbs of Columbia Heights, Robbinsdale, and St. Louis Park, and in St. Paul, to the Minneapolis city limits, Lake Phalen, and the West St. Paul city line. Much of the East Side and Highland Park was undeveloped.

of the late 1930s through the immediate post–World War II years. The start dates shown are for electric or cable operation. For earlier line routings, see the horsecar maps in chapter 1.

While TCRT was strongly committed to the streetcar, it began substituting buses on some of its lines in 1932. First to go were the lines to Lake Minnetonka and Stillwater. By the mid-1930s, TCRT had implemented several new bus routes to serve neighborhoods beyond the ends of its streetcar lines. A common device was to connect the ends of two adjacent lines by shuttle bus. There also were several special or experimental bus routes that were short lived because the need for them disappeared, as in the case of the wartime service to the New Brighton Arsenal, or because they failed to attract sufficient riders and were discontinued. Buses were a small part of TCRT's overall business before the systemwide conversion, but they were nonetheless a part of its operations. Maps of the TCRT bus routes are shown in Appendix K.

Intercity Lines

In the 1940s and 1950s, three lines—the Como–Harriet–Hopkins, the Selby–Lake, and the St. Paul–Minneapolis—provided a one-seat ride between Minneapolis and St. Paul. Two, the E. 25th St. line in Minneapolis and the Randolph line in St. Paul, met at the Ford plant just across the Mississippi River in St. Paul. Connecting passengers changed cars. From 1909 until 1936, a fourth line provided intercity service. Ft. Snelling cars ran from Minneapolis to St. Paul as the Snelling–Minnehaha (1909–21), 7th St.–Minnehaha–Plymouth (1921–32), and

Minnehaha–7th St.–Hope St. (1932–36) lines. After 1936, passengers changed cars at Ft. Snelling. The two halves of the former intercity line are described separately.

Como–Harriet–Hopkins

Years of operation: 1891–1954
Como paired with: Bryn Mawr (1894–1902), Kenwood (1902–5), Lake Harriet (1898–1954)
Lake Harriet paired with: Downtown only (1891–92), Central Avenue (1892), Downtown only (1892–1902), Como (1898–1954)
There was some overlapping of lines and service during 1898–1905 on both the Como and Lake Harriet ends of the line. Before 1932, Lake Minnetonka cars also provided service to Hopkins. See chapter 3 for more information.
Service frequency: Ten minutes off-peak; three minutes peak

Oak–Harriet

Years of operation: 1891–1954
Paired with: Downtown only (1891–95), Bryn Mawr (1895–1902), Kenwood—part of service combined with Lake Harriet (1902–10), Lake Harriet (1910–54)
Service frequency: Ten minutes off-peak; five minutes peak

The Como–Harriet–Hopkins and Oak–Harriet lines were separate but shared many miles of track. Both lines served southwest Minneapolis, using Hennepin Avenue to 31st Street, then via private right of way past Lake Calhoun and Lake Harriet. Como–Harriet cars ran south on France Avenue from the private right of way at 44th Street to 54th Street. Como–Hopkins cars continued west on the private right of way to Hopkins. Oak–Harriet cars diverged at Xerxes Avenue South and ran south on Xerxes to 50th Street, then east on 50th to Penn Avenue.

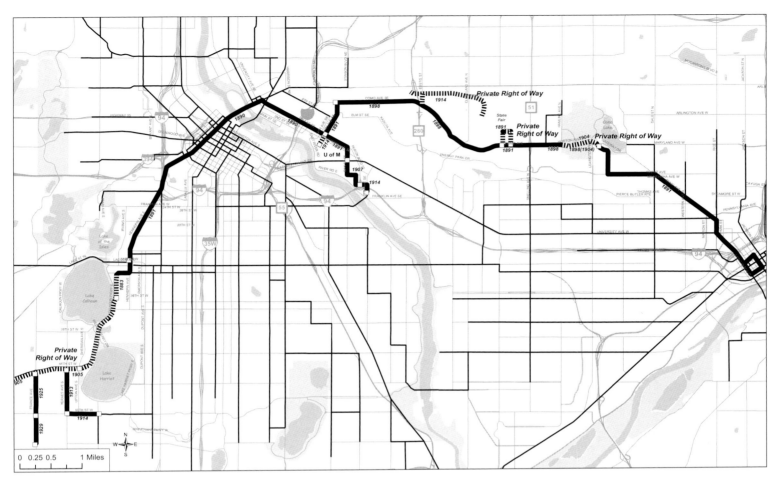

Como–Harriet–Hopkins line
Oak–Harriet line
Inter-Campus line

From downtown Minneapolis, eastbound Como–Harriet and Como–Hopkins cars used 4th Street Southeast through Dinkytown near the University of Minnesota, then turned on 15th Avenue Southeast to Como Avenue and on to St. Paul. Eastbound Oak–Harriet cars used 4th Street Southeast but, rather than turning on 15th, continued out 4th to Oak Street, then on to the end of the line at 27th Avenue and Yale Street Southeast.

Como–Harriet–Hopkins was the longest line in the TCRT system and the most scenic, traversing some of the most beautiful neighborhoods in the Twin Cities. While many people rode the Como–Harriet just for the experience, many more people took it to work downtown or to classes at the University of Minnesota. At rush hour there would be more than fifty cars on the line, enough to move more than six thousand people at any one time.

Electric streetcars began running out Hennepin Avenue to Lake Harriet in 1891, replac-

ing steam-powered trains of the old Motor Line, which had used Nicollet Avenue and 31st Street to reach private right of way at 31st and Irving Avenue. The new route on Hennepin was faster and more direct. Before 1898, Lake Harriet cars turned around in downtown Minneapolis— except for a few months in 1892 when they were through-routed with Central Ave. In 1898, they were extended out 4th Street Southeast to 15th Avenue Southeast and Como Avenue, to the city limits at Eustis Street, then all the way to downtown St. Paul. TCRT started work on its line to Lake Minnetonka in 1905, laying track westward from Lake Harriet beyond France Avenue and the western city limits. In 1906, Como–Hopkins cars began running from Excelsior Boulevard and 9th Avenue in Hopkins through Minneapolis all the way to St. Paul. Branches were added on Xerxes Avenue (1913) and France Avenue (1925). The Xerxes branch became the Oak–Harriet line.

The Como–Harriet connected with the

Viewed from the pedestrian overpass, a St. Paul–bound car emerges from under Lexington Avenue and approaches the Como Park station.

Shortly before service ended in 1954, an eastbound car turns from 15th Avenue Southeast onto Como Avenue, with the remains of an unused wye in the foreground.

Selby–Lake crosstown and all of the major lines in downtown Minneapolis and in downtown St. Paul. The line operated around the clock seven days a week, with reduced service at night.

Along the way, the Como–Harriet also served Como Park, Luther Theological Seminary in the St. Anthony Park neighborhood of St. Paul, the temporary postwar student Quonset housing at 29th Street and Como, Marshall–University High School, the Walker Art Center, West High School, the Uptown area of south Minneapolis, Southwest High School, and downtown Edina at 50th Street and France Avenue.

The line was truncated on the right of way at 44th Street and Brookside in 1951, ending service to Hopkins. Edina initiated a repaving project along France Avenue in 1952, forcing removal of the tracks and the substitution of shuttle buses. In July 1953, buses took over

in St. Paul from the city limits at Eustis Street to downtown, forcing through passengers to transfer at Eustis. The Como–Harriet–Hopkins and Oak–Harriet switched to buses on June 19, 1954. They were the last streetcar lines to operate in Minneapolis and St. Paul.

Two landmarks along Como Avenue at 22nd Avenue Southeast: the Northern Pacific Railroad overpass and Manning's restaurant.

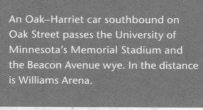

An Oak–Harriet car southbound on Oak Street passes the University of Minnesota's Memorial Stadium and the Beacon Avenue wye. In the distance is Williams Arena.

One of the first two horsecar lines in Minneapolis terminated here, 14th Avenue and 4th Street Southeast, the heart of Dinkytown near the University of Minnesota. A pair of Como–Harriet cars pass the Varsity Theater and Gray's Campus Drugs. Photograph by *Minneapolis Star Journal*; courtesy of the Minnesota Historical Society.

Today the west side of Hennepin along Loring Park is a noisy freeway. Long gone are the Plaza Hotel and Downtown Chevrolet, watched over by the Basilica of St. Mary. Photograph by Norton & Peel; courtesy of the Minnesota Historical Society.

The Oak–Harriet line ended at this wye at Yale and 27th Avenues in southeast Minneapolis near the east end of the Franklin Avenue bridge in Prospect Park. Red & White neighborhood food stores were common.

At 31st Street and Irving Avenue, Como–Harriet cars left the city streets and entered the private right of way that once extended to Lake Minnetonka. Photograph by *Minneapolis Star Journal Tribune*; courtesy of the Minnesota Historical Society.

This is the "bottleneck," where Lyndale and Hennepin Avenues crossed next to the Hennepin Avenue Methodist Church in the background (the large church in the left foreground is St. Mark's Episcopal Cathedral). Como–Harriet, Oak–Harriet, St. Louis Park, and Kenwood cars continued up the hill on Hennepin; Bryant cars angled left onto Lyndale. Photograph courtesy of the Minnesota Historical Society.

Hennepin Avenue at Dupont Avenue, near the summit of Lowry Hill.

A Como–Harriet car crosses Lake Street in Uptown, passing the Granada Theater, now the Suburban World. Photograph courtesy of the Minnesota Historical Society.

Until the end of streetcar service, Lakewood Cemetery had a second public entrance, this turreted stone streetcar stop on the southeast side of Lake Calhoun. It survived until the end of service in 1954. Photograph courtesy of the Minneapolis Public Library, Special Collections.

The Minnesota Streetcar Museum's restored Como–Harriet line still passes under the William Berry Parkway bridge between Lakes Calhoun and Harriet. At the bridge is the Cottage City streetcar stop, named for a neighborhood on the south side of Lake Calhoun platted with twenty-five-foot lots for summer cabins. The stop was restored by the museum in 2005. Photograph from the Minneapolis Star and Tribune News Negative Collection; courtesy of the Minnesota Historical Society.

There is little evidence of it today, but the streetcars crossed over West 36th Street on a bridge that featured steps to the street and a boarding platform. Lake Calhoun is in the distance.

The Como–Harriet line crossed 42nd Street near Lake Harriet, where museum streetcars operate today. The 1914 chalet-style station, designed by local architect Harry Wild Jones, housed a confectionery and a holding cell for the Minneapolis Park Police, and was the boarding point for returning concertgoers.

An Oak–Harriet car rolls south on Xerxes Avenue at 48th Street.

The right of way west from Lake Harriet, now a public alley, split the Linden Hills business district. The Upton Building now houses a children's toy store. Streetcars connected here with the West 39th Street bus line.

West of Brookside Avenue, the line to Hopkins and Lake Minnetonka rode a fill across Meadowbrook Lake, south of the municipal golf course.

This car is on the wye at 50th Street and Xerxes Avenue, facing south. Most cars continued on to 50th and Penn Avenue. With the track centered in the street, there was little room for autos to both park and pass.

The streetcars reached downtown Edina at 50th Street and France Avenue in 1925. Note the Edina Theater at left. Photograph by Lee Brothers; courtesy of the Minnesota Historical Society.

The great S-curving Hopkins viaduct vaulted over three different rail lines where Highway 169 crosses today. Photograph courtesy of Forrest Johnson.

Inter-Campus Line

The Inter-Campus Line between the Minneapolis campus of the University of Minnesota and what was then the "Farm School," the St. Paul campus, opened in 1914 and, until its last day of service in 1954, carried thousands of students between the two campuses. Oddly, that wasn't the original intent. The university needed a better way to move coal and other bulky materials to the St. Paul campus from a nearby railroad yard. It had been hauling by horse and wagon, which meant unloading a car at the yard, transferring the contents to a wagon, and unloading again. A railroad spur was the best alternative because it would allow direct shipments. It then occurred to university officials, undoubtedly after discussions with TCRT, that if the spur were connected to the Como–Harriet streetcar line and electrified, its students could travel by streetcar between the Minneapolis and St. Paul campuses, thereby eliminating the need for duplicate classes on the same subjects on both campuses and resulting in a considerable savings to the university.

The legislature appropriated funds for the line in 1913, and university engineering students surveyed the right of way that spring. Grading was completed in the fall, and TCRT crews moved in to lay track and put up wire in 1914. The work was finished in November, and the line opened for service.

On the Minneapolis campus, cars originally turned on a wye behind the Mechanic Arts building, later on a turning loop inside a traffic circle on 15th Avenue Southeast in front of Eddy and Nicholson Halls. (That traffic circle is there to this day, as are the streetcar rails, which periodically emerge from the asphalt overlay covering them.) The line then proceeded north on a landscaped median passing Folwell Hall, crossing University Avenue and joining the Como–Harriet line at the intersection of 15th Avenue and 4th Street Southeast. Continuing along 15th Avenue Southeast to Como Avenue, it followed Como to Eustis Street. At Eustis, it turned north for a short distance, then swung east on a private right of way that brought it all the way to the St. Paul campus

The private right of way was entirely single tracked. The university owned it along with several sidings.

One siding adjoined the storehouse building on 15th Avenue Southeast, and others served various buildings on the St. Paul Campus. There was also a short freight interchange track with the Minnesota Transfer Railway near Larpenteur Avenue.

Base service operated every fifteen minutes on weekdays and every thirty minutes on Saturday afternoons. No service was provided in the evening or on Sunday. This schedule was adjusted from time to time, depending on the needs of the university.

Students wait in front of Folwell Hall on the Minneapolis campus as an Inter-Campus car negotiates the turnaround loop. The two-block extension into the campus was built by the university. Photograph courtesy of the University of Minnesota Archives

Inter-Campus cars traveled the grassy median of 15th Avenue, entering the street at University Avenue. At left is the University of Minnesota YMCA.

The Inter-Campus was completely separate from the Twin Cities system. The cars were leased by the university and assigned from a separate pool out of the East Side Station. TCRT supplied crews at a fixed hourly rate and performed all maintenance on the cars as well as on the track and electrical overhead.

The university set fares, and cash, tokens, or commutation tickets were all accepted. The last were good for multiple rides and were sold by the university at the bursar's office. No transfers from other car lines were honored. If a student didn't have funds, the conductor would issue an IOU, which the student would sign and return to the conductor. The fare would then be deducted from the student's deposit.

Some freight was moved on the line. The university owned a switch car, built at Snelling Shops, with a large, enclosed cab on the front end, for handling express shipments, and an open flatbed on the rear for coal or similar bulk commodities. The car had standard railroad couplers and could shift boxcars or other railroad freight cars as needed. Appropriately, it was painted maroon and gold.

One of the last two lines in service, the Inter-Campus was converted to bus on June 18, 1954. Parts of the Inter-Campus line are still visible. Cleveland Avenue passes over a segment just north of the campus. Driving southbound and looking off to the right it can be seen in a deep cut. Several of the intermediate stations between the St. Paul campus and Eustis Street remain, but they are covered by brush and weeds.

Approaching the St. Paul Campus, Inter-Campus Specials made a broad arc along the southwest edge of the test fields, passed the livestock barns, and ended in a loop at Buford Street. Photograph by Don Mac Bean; courtesy of the Minnesota Historical Society.

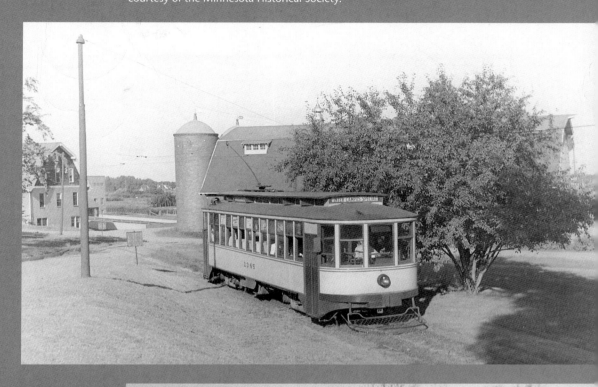

After passing the agricultural test plots along the north edge of the St. Paul campus, westbound Inter-Campus cars stopped at this modern shelter before passing under Cleveland Avenue. Photograph courtesy of the University of Minnesota Archives.

The Inter-Campus line was unique for hauling railroad freight cars of coal and other supplies to the St. Paul campus from this interchange with the Minnesota Transfer Railway near Highway 280 and Larpenteur Avenue. The locomotive, painted in the University of Minnesota's maroon and gold, was built at Snelling Shops in 1914.

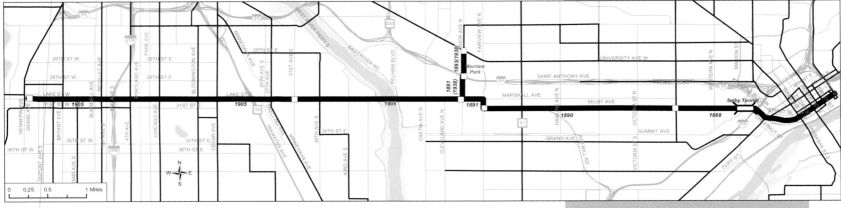

Selby–Lake line

Selby–Lake

Years of operation: 1888–1906 as Merriam
Park; 1906–53 as Selby–Lake
Service frequency: Seven minutes off-peak;
three minutes (or less) peak

Signs and open pits between
the rails served to keep autos
from entering the Selby Tunnel's
west portal at Nina Street.

The camera is looking east at a Selby–Lake car approaching Snelling Avenue. The bank building at far left still stands, although with a different facade. This was a major transfer point with the Snelling Avenue crosstown line. Photograph courtesy of the Minnesota Historical Society.

In 1887, after considerable arm-twisting by the city council, the St. Paul City Railway agreed to build a cable car line up Selby Hill. The council was taken by the success of cable lines elsewhere and wanted better, more direct service to the prosperous neighborhoods between Summit and Marshall Avenues. The line opened in January 1888 from 4th and Broadway Streets downtown, to Selby Avenue and St. Albans Street. In 1890, it was extended out Selby to Fairview Avenue. Electric cars replaced the cable a year later between Chatsworth Street and Fairview, and the line was extended to the newly developed Merriam Park neighborhood. Following electrification of the entire line in 1898, the cable installation over Selby Hill was converted to a counterweight system, and the cable cars were used to assist streetcars up and down the 16 percent grade. In 1906, a new bridge opened carrying Lake Street/ Marshall Avenue over the Mississippi River, and the Lake Street and Selby Avenue lines were joined, forming the Selby–Lake. A final improvement came in 1907 with the opening of the Selby tunnel, permitting abandonment of the counterweight system. From June 1906 until October 1907, Selby–Lake cars ran all the

way to downtown Minneapolis via Hennepin Avenue, terminating at Hennepin and 1st Street North. This downtown-to-downtown service was withdrawn as additional cars were added to the Como–Harriet–Hopkins and Oak–Harriet lines, increasing frequencies along Hennepin south of Lake Street.

The Merriam Park service continued as a separate line with cars operating from downtown St. Paul via Selby Avenue to Prior and University Avenues. From 1920 until 1932, Merriam Park was paired with Mississippi and through-routed as the Merriam–Mississippi line. After 1932, a shuttle car was substituted along Prior, connecting with the Selby–Lake at Marshall, although some trips continued to run directly to downtown St. Paul during rush hours. In 1938, all rail service along Prior was abandoned, and

Lake Street at Blaisdell Avenue, looking east toward the major transfer point at Nicollet Avenue. Only one building in this photo survives, but the relocated Yukon Club is still open a couple of blocks to the west. Photograph by Norton & Peel; courtesy of the Minnesota Historical Society.

An eastbound Selby–Lake car approaches 27th Avenue South, the junction of the Minnehaha–Ft. Snelling line. The building sporting the large "M" in the distance is the Minneapolis-Moline tractor plant.

Looking west at 36th Avenue South and East Lake Street, where the E. 25th St. line crossed.

Uptown in the 1920s. Selby–Lake cars terminated on the wye at Lake Street and Girard Avenue at right. The final block of tracks to Hennepin Avenue were used to deadhead cars to and from the Como–Harriet line. The Calhoun Theater was a dental academy for many years and is now a restaurant.

the line became part of the Highland Park bus route.

Selby–Lake was a huge people mover and the most important crosstown line in the system, intersecting every north–south line in the city of Minneapolis. Along Lake Street, which had turned into a busy commercial strip because of the streetcar, the line carried more passengers per mile than any in the system. East of the river, along Marshall and Selby Avenues in St. Paul, it traversed mainly residential neighborhoods, crossing the Snelling and Dale car lines. Traffic generators lined the route. Among them were St. Paul Central High School, Concordia College, Minneapolis West High School, the Minneapolis–Moline tractor plant at Hiawatha

Avenue and Lake Street, and the huge Sears store at Chicago Avenue and Lake Street. With sixty or more cars on the line at rush hours, there were often two, or even three, streetcars moving together from one block to the next as the traffic signals changed along Lake Street.

St. Paul–Minneapolis (Interurban)

Years of operation: 1890–1953
Paired with: 6th Ave. N. (1918–39)
Service frequency: Seven minutes off-peak;
three minutes (or less) peak

A horsecar line was built on University Avenue as far as Dale Street in 1881. Then in December 1890, the Minneapolis Street Railway and St. Paul City Railway companies completed an

St. Paul–Minneapolis line

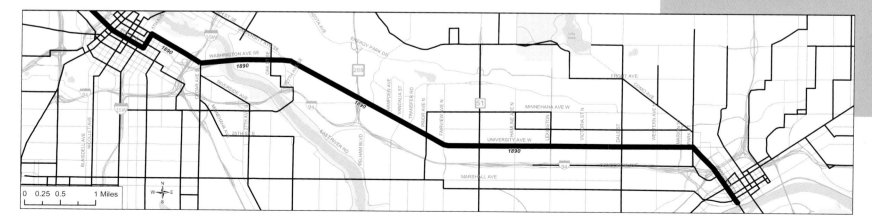

The great retail rivals, Montgomery Ward and Sears Roebuck, broke with normal department store practice and constructed enormous stores and distribution centers far from downtown. These locations combined first-class streetcar service in front of the building with direct freight railroad delivery to the back of the building. This is Ward's Midway store on University Avenue in St. Paul. Photograph courtesy of the Minnesota Historical Society.

The University Avenue retail strip began at Rice Street, just west of the State Capitol, viewed here in 1932. Photograph by John W. G. Dunn Jr.; courtesy of the Minnesota Historical Society.

In 1948, in what became an ill-timed expenditure, TCRT renewed long stretches of track and paving as part of a Minnesota Highway Department rebuilding of University Avenue, then U.S Highway 12. University Avenue hosted the Interurban, whose trademark PCC cars, bull-nosed safety islands, and fast frequent service made it the premier streetcar line in the Twin Cities. Here, a westbound car approaches waiting passengers in front of the Prom Ballroom just west of Lexington Avenue. After 1953, these passengers would be boarding buses at the curb.

Interurban cars on University Avenue passed from St. Paul into Minneapolis at Emerald Street. City franchise regulations required that all passengers crossing the city limits pay a second fare. Photograph courtesy of the Ramsey County Historical Society, St. Paul, Minnesota.

Viewed from the Prospect Park water tower, a University Avenue car rolls toward the St. Paul city limits, with the grain elevators of southeast Minneapolis in the distance. Photograph by Charles P. Gibson; courtesy of the Minnesota Historical Society.

As auto traffic increased, it became more dangerous for passengers to walk out from the curb and board in the middle of the street. The solution, fully implemented only on University Avenue in St. Paul, was the safety island, bull-nosed to withstand a direct collision. This is University and Cromwell (near what is now Highway 280), looking toward Minneapolis. Photograph by St. Paul Dispatch & Pioneer Press; courtesy of the Minnesota Historical Society.

To accommodate the large number of servicemen returning from the war and entering college on the GI Bill, the University of Minnesota erected a series of temporary classroom buildings, such as this one at Washington Avenue and Church Street. Interestingly, the passing streetcar is not in service but is towing a disabled car to Snelling Shops. Photograph from the Minneapolis Star and Tribune News Negative Collection; courtesy of the Minnesota Historical Society.

The St. Paul–Minneapolis Interurban line gracefully curves through Seven Corners in Minneapolis. The tracks diverging to the right carry the Ft. Snelling, E. 25th St., and 28th Ave. S. lines onto Cedar Avenue. Photograph from the Minneapolis Star and Tribune News Negative Collection; courtesy of the Minnesota Historical Society.

On several rickety old bridges over the Mississippi River, streetcar speed was limited to twenty miles per hour. One of them was the Washington Avenue bridge, seen here with the University of Minnesota in the background.

electric line between downtown Minneapolis and St. Paul on University Avenue. The electric streetcars were so successful that by April 1891 the Great Northern and the Chicago, Milwaukee & St. Paul announced reductions in their commuter train services between Minneapolis and St. Paul. The Milwaukee Road, in particular, indicated that it might have to drop all local trains then providing hourly service via its "short line" route through the Midway district because the streetcars had taken over half the business. The streetcar line was so successful that its name, "the Interurban," was adopted by the electric railway industry to describe all intercity electric lines.

From 1890 until November 1953, when it converted to buses, the St. Paul–Minneapolis was among the busiest streetcar lines in the entire TCRT system. It carried large numbers of passengers, had excellent earnings per mile, and offered frequent service. The Midway district along University Avenue became a thriving commercial and industrial corridor mainly because of the St. Paul–Minneapolis car line. From 5th and Wabasha Streets in downtown St. Paul to 5th Street and Hennepin Avenue in downtown Minneapolis, there was never an empty seat, even with three-minute service. Extra cars had to be added regularly from Minneapolis to the city limits to accommodate the heavy traffic to and from the University of Minnesota campus. At 5th and Hennepin, it was not uncommon to see five cars in a row move eastbound on 5th Street, all signed for St. Paul–Minneapolis (or "University to City Limits"). By the time they cleared Marquette Avenue all of them would be full.

There were very few route changes over the years. Before 1914, cars looped around in downtown Minneapolis via a number of different street combinations involving Washington Avenue, Hennepin, 1st Avenue North, 5th Street, 6th Street, Marquette Avenue, and 2nd Avenue. From 1914 to 1918, a wye was used at 5th Street and 5th Avenue North. Then, the St. Paul–Minneapolis was combined with the 6th Ave. N. line and some cars began running out 6th Avenue to Russell Avenue. In 1940, 6th was rebuilt into Olson Memorial Highway. Buses appeared, and all St. Paul–Minneapolis cars returned to the wye at 5th and 5th. In downtown St. Paul, cars made a continuous loop on Wabasha Street, 5th Street, Robert Street, and 9th, then back to Wabasha. There was a wye at the city limits, University Avenue and Emerald Street, for turning back extra cars running from downtown Minneapolis to the University of Minnesota campus. From 1946 until bus conversion in 1953, PCC cars operated all services.

Intercity Bus Services

Marshall–Lake Express Bus

Originally operated by an independent company, the Marshall–Lake route was absorbed by TCRT in 1926. From downtown Minneapolis, buses ran out Bloomington Avenue to Lake Street, then across the Lake Street bridge to Marshall Avenue and into downtown St. Paul. The service was discontinued during World War II. After buses took over from streetcars, rush hour express trips from Lake and Hennepin to St. Paul continued as part of the Selby–Lake bus route.

University Avenue Express Bus

This was a limited-stop service operated by an independent company in direct competition with

TCRT's St. Paul–Minneapolis streetcar line. It was purchased by TCRT in 1924. Discontinued during World War II, the service resumed after the war. The service became rush hour only following conversion of the St. Paul–Minneapolis line to bus operation.

University Avenue Supplemental Bus Service

Service commenced in February 1943 from the University of Minnesota campus to downtown Minneapolis to relieve extreme crowding on streetcars. Service ended in June 1943. Supplemental, rush hour local bus service began on University Avenue from Snelling Avenue to downtown St. Paul in March 1943. It ended after the war.

The Downtowns

At the end of World War II, the two downtowns were the centers of urban life, the suburbs a developer's daydream. Bloomington was a village. France Avenue south of 66th Street was a gravel road. A farmer raised hogs on what is now the Best Buy office complex at Interstate 494 and Penn Avenue. Elsewhere, Falcon Heights was all truck farms and gravel pits. Corn grew in Highland Park on the site of the Highland Park High School. There were no freeways as such, just a short stretch of Highway 100, the "Belt Line" (or Lilac Drive, if you prefer), which had been upgraded to four lanes and given a few cloverleaf interchanges through

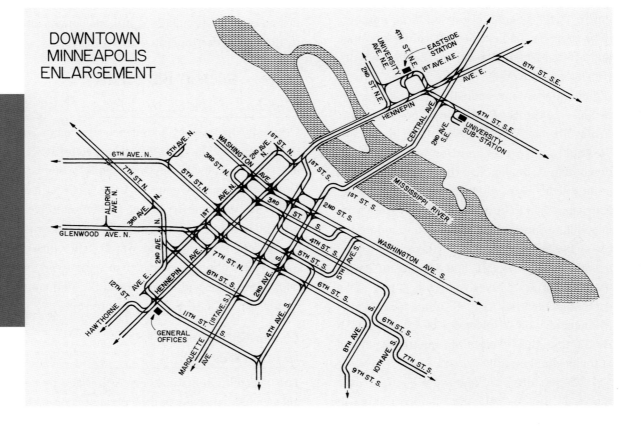

Reprinted from The Electric Railways of Minnesota, *this map shows the details of streetcar tracks in downtown Minneapolis during the mid-twentieth century. Each line on the map represents a track. When two lines are present, the street had a track in each direction. Illustration by Kent Dorholt; courtesy of Russell L. Olson.*

St. Louis Park and Golden Valley. People used to drive out and picnic at the interchanges thanks to an obliging highway department that put up tables and grills. Department stores, theaters, hotels, good restaurants, and jobs were mostly downtown, and to get downtown you took the streetcar.

Fourteen car lines and five bus routes converged on downtown Minneapolis; eleven car lines and three bus routes converged on downtown St. Paul. In Minneapolis, all of them, with the exception of the St. Paul–Minneapolis, ran through downtown to the other side of the city. In St. Paul, Selby–Lake cars turned around at 4th and Broadway Streets near St. Paul Union Depot. Everything else ran through. The Como–Harriet and the St. Paul–Minneapolis looped through downtown on Wabasha Street to 5th, Robert, and 9th Streets to return to Minneapolis. Rush hour trippers usually started or ended their runs downtown, but in the morning rush hour, as an example, inbound cars would unload passengers downtown and immediately return to the carhouse. In the afternoons, a car would pull out, go directly downtown, fall in place on its line, and start its run. As a matter of scheduling policy, layovers were always built into the schedule at the outer end of the line, never downtown. The only exceptions to this were late-night "owl" runs, which came into Minneapolis every hour and queued up at 8th Street and Hennepin Avenue, 5th Street and Hennepin, and Washington and Hennepin Avenues, where they waited five minutes to exchange passengers and then left. The same happened at 7th and Wabasha Streets and at 4th and Wabasha Streets in St. Paul. These "lineups," as they were called, are a practice that Metro Transit continues today.

Listed below are the principal downtown streets in Minneapolis and St. Paul and the names of the streetcar lines that used them in 1946.

Downtown Minneapolis Lines

- Hennepin Avenue: Como–Harriet–Hopkins, Oak–Harriet, Bryant–Johnson, Kenwood–St. Louis Park–Russell N. (bus), Excelsior-Glen Lake (bus)
- Nicollet Avenue: Nicollet–Hennepin (bus)
- Marquette Avenue: Nicollet–2nd St. N.E., Grand–Monroe, St. Paul–Minneapolis Express (bus)
- 2nd Avenue: Chicago–Penn, Chicago–Fremont (between 8th and 6th Streets), Bloomington–Columbia Hts. (from 1st Street North to 4th Street), Minneapolis–St. Paul Express (bus)
- Washington Avenue: 34th Ave. S.–N. Bryant, Minnehaha–Ft. Snelling (northbound on 3rd Street)
- 5th Street: St. Paul–Minneapolis, Plymouth–E. 25th St., 28th Ave. S.–Robbinsdale
- 6th Street: Glenwood–4th Ave. S.
- 7th Street: Franklin–N. Lyndale Ave. (bus)
- 8th Street: Chicago–Penn, Chicago-Fremont

Looking north on Marquette Avenue across Washington Avenue in the mid-1930s, with the recently constructed Minneapolis Main Post Office in the distance. The streetcar has a long run ahead of it, to downtown St. Paul via Ft. Snelling, then out the Hope Street line to East 4th and Atlantic Streets on St. Paul's east side. Photograph courtesy of the Minnesota Historical Society.

Powers and Penney's department stores bracketed 5th Street at Nicollet Avenue, where light rail has returned. Photograph by Norton & Peel; courtesy of the Minnesota Historical Society.

The block of 1st Avenue North between 4th and 5th Streets has changed little in the century since this photo was taken about 1910. Photograph by Sweet; courtesy of the Minnesota Historical Society.

On a bitter day, a 4th Avenue car on 6th Street passes the landmark Farmers and Mechanics Bank at Marquette Avenue. Photograph courtesy of the Minnesota Historical Society.

Several car lines crossed the Mississippi River and Nicollet Island on the Hennepin Avenue bridge. The Great Northern depot is in the background.

The landmark 620 Club presides over what is now called Block E, on the north side of Hennepin between 6th and 7th Streets.

The west end of the Warehouse District was the five-legged intersection of 7th Street, 1st Avenue North, and Glenwood Avenue (in foreground). The Jewelers Exchange Building on the right has been replaced by Block E. The Produce State Bank, named for the nearby City Market, is now the Target Center. Photograph from the Minneapolis Star and Tribune News Negative Collection; courtesy of the Minnesota Historical Society.

Looking east on 8th Street from Hennepin Avenue. The back of Dayton's department store looms at left. Photograph by *Minneapolis Star Tribune*; courtesy of the Minnesota Historical Society.

Trains departing south from the Milwaukee Road depot crossed over the streetcars on the notorious Washington Avenue viaduct, shown here in 1941. Its low clearances were forever wedging trucks, and it flooded regularly, cutting off the streetcars. Photograph by *Minneapolis Star-Journal*; courtesy of the Minnesota Historical Society.

Looking north at bustling Hennepin Avenue from 10th Street toward the Orpheum and State theaters. Photograph courtesy of the Minneapolis Public Library, Special Collections.

The Glenwood–4th Ave. S. line passed the 6th Street side of Donaldson's department store at Nicollet Avenue. The Nicollet Mall was still a decade in the future. Photograph courtesy of Forrest Johnson.

When Nicollet Avenue street-cars reached the south edge of downtown, they shifted a block east onto Marquette Avenue, shown here at 10th Street. Although it was the retail heart of downtown, Nicollet never saw streetcars. Visible surviving buildings include (left to right) the Young-Quinlan, Medical Arts, Northwestern National Bank, Rand Tower, Roanoke, and, of course, the Foshay Tower.

Interurban PCC cars passed through the Warehouse District on 5th Street, crossed the viaduct over the railroad corridor, and ended just beyond the downtown Honeywell plant, originally Ford Motor Company's first Twin Cities assembly plant.

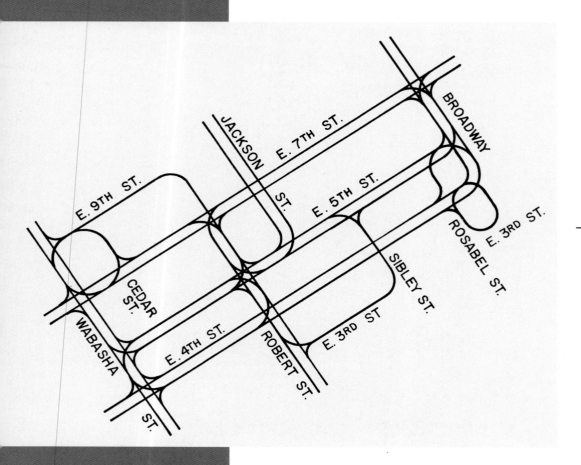

- Wabasha Street: Como–Harriet–Hopkins, St. Paul–Minneapolis, Hamline–Cherokee Hts., Rondo–Stryker, Rice–South St. Paul
- 7th Street: Ft. Snelling–Maria, Randolph–Hazel Park, St. Clair–Payne, Stillwater (bus), Dale–Phalen
- St. Peter Street: St. Paul–Minneapolis Express (bus)
- 4th Street: Grand–Mississippi, Selby–Lake
- Robert Street: Jackson–South Robert (bus), St. Paul–Minneapolis, Como–Hopkins–Harriet, Rice–South St. Paul

Over the years numerous minor changes occurred to the streetcar routings in the two downtowns. They were sufficiently complex that they are difficult to show on a map. Instead, this map reprinted from *The Electric Railways of Minnesota* shows the individual tracks in downtown St. Paul as they were during the 1930s and 1940s. Illustration by Kent Dorholt; courtesy of Russell L. Olson.

Documenting a World War I Liberty Bonds billboard, the photographer has also captured streetcars on 4th Street passing Rice Park, the St. Paul Hotel, and the St. Paul Public Library. Photograph courtesy of the Minnesota Historical Society.

Both cities sported an intersection called Seven Corners, where multiple streets met in a perfect storm of traffic, since pruned by traffic engineers. In St. Paul, Kellogg Boulevard, 4th Street, 7th Street, and Main Street all converged. This view today would face the Xcel Energy Center. Photograph courtesy of the Minnesota Historical Society.

The length of Robert Street, from 8th Street in the foreground to the Mississippi River bridge in the distance, is compressed by a telephoto lens. The Minneapolis–St. Paul Interurban, passing the Emporium department store in the company of an inbound South St. Paul bus, will travel beyond downtown Minneapolis to the end of the 6th Ave. N. line at Russell Avenue. Photograph from Northern Pacific Railroad Company Records; courtesy of the Minnesota Historical Society.

When the Mississippi River flooded in 1952, the south approach to the Robert Street bridge was underwater, forcing all traffic to Wabasha Street. Streetcars were stuck in traffic on the Wabasha Street bridge. Photograph by *St. Paul Pioneer Press-Dispatch*; courtesy of the Minnesota Historical Society.

7th and Wabasha Streets, the heart of downtown St. Paul, looking north on Wabasha. Photograph by *St. Paul Pioneer Press-Dispatch*; courtesy of the Minnesota Historical Society.

Until the 1940s, a residential neighborhood lay just beyond the base of the State Capitol steps. This entire scene was converted to expansive lawns and landscaping, and eventually Wabasha Street itself was removed.

Lined with department stores such as the Golden Rule and numerous five-and-dimes, 7th Street was the retail center of downtown St. Paul. Photograph by *St. Paul Pioneer Press-Dispatch*; courtesy of the Minnesota Historical Society.

A Grand–Mississippi car, on tracks shared with the Selby–Lake line, passes the St. Paul downtown library on 4th Street.

Wabasha Street at College Avenue. TCRT's St. Paul office building is at right. Photograph by *St. Paul Dispatch & Pioneer Press*; courtesy of the Minnesota Historical Society.

The fact that seven lines shared 7th Street leading toward the East Side could result in long strings of streetcars working their way through downtown. Photograph courtesy of the Minnesota Historical Society.

Loading passengers on 4th and Wabasha Streets in the snow in 1952.

Trolleys in Your Neighborhood

The Robert Street bridge, from high in the First National Bank Building. Photograph by Charles P. Gibson; courtesy of the Minnesota Historical Society.

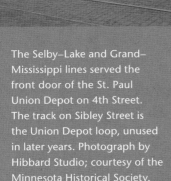

The Selby–Lake and Grand–Mississippi lines served the front door of the St. Paul Union Depot on 4th Street. The track on Sibley Street is the Union Depot loop, unused in later years. Photograph by Hibbard Studio; courtesy of the Minnesota Historical Society.

Minneapolis Lines

Bryn Mawr

Years of operation: 1892–1939
Paired with: Como (1894–95), Oak (1895–1906), 8th St. S.E. (1902–12), part of service via downtown loop (1906–12), Downtown only (1912–39)
Service frequency: Thirty minutes off-peak; twenty minutes peak

Bryn Mawr began in 1880 as a horsecar line from 12th Street and Hennepin Avenue via Hawthorne Avenue to Lyndale Avenue North. The line entered the Bryn Mawr neighborhood on a long viaduct, crossing over the Lyndale

Bryn Mawr line

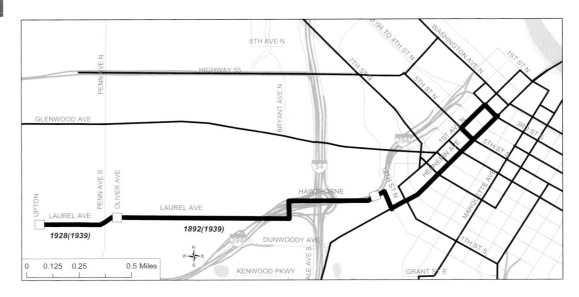

Few photographs show the group of lines abandoned by TCRT in the 1930s. Bryn Mawr crossed the Great Northern and Minneapolis & St. Louis railroads on the spindly Laurel Avenue bridge. These photographs look both ways from the west end of the bridge. Originally this was double track, reduced to a single track in 1901. Eastbound cars ran against the flow of autos, a particularly exciting prospect when topping the bridge.

Yards of the Great Northern Railway. Bryn Mawr was strikingly rural in appearance as late as the 1920s, but it gradually filled in and became a small residential enclave. Never a great traffic generator, the line was roughly half single track. Only one car could go through at a time, which limited the frequency of service to every fifteen minutes at most.

The Bryn Mawr Bus Extension shuttle bus debuted in 1927. It ran from the end of the car line at Laurel and Upton Avenues to 22nd and Ewing Avenues. The shuttle service became part of a new through bus route when the streetcars were discontinued in 1939 because of deteriorating track and the poor condition of the Laurel Avenue viaduct.

Glenwood

Years of operation: 1891–1954 (before 1927 as Western Avenue)
Paired with: 2nd St. N.E. (1891–1919), 4th Ave. S. (1919–54)
Service frequency: Ten minutes off-peak; five minutes peak

The Glenwood line passed through an industrial zone on the western edge of downtown. The Northwestern Knitting Works, later Munsingwear, at Glenwood and Lyndale Avenues became a major employer and traffic generator along with any number of small factories and lumberyards. Of note was the Ripley Memorial Hospital at Penn Avenue. Passenger traffic, through the 1920s, was so heavy that TCRT operated two-car trains during rush hours. One car was powered, the second car being an unmotorized trailer. Glenwood Park also drew recreational riders and picnickers on weekends. The wood waiting shelter at the end of the line in Wirth Park survives to this day.

An eastbound Glenwood Avenue car at Penn Avenue passes the former Ripley Memorial Hospital, which has been converted to condo housing.

Trolleys in Your Neighborhood

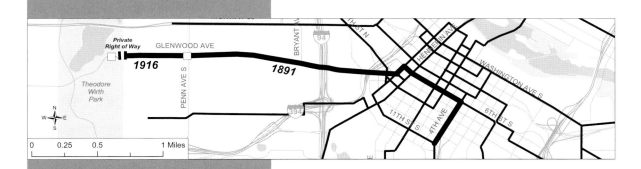

Glenwood line

Taken four months after abandonment in 1954, this is Glenwood Avenue at Lyndale Avenue, with the landmark Munsingwear plant (now International Market Square) at right. Photograph by Norton & Peel; courtesy of the Minnesota Historical Society.

The Glenwood Avenue line ended with a block of private right of way inside Wirth Park.

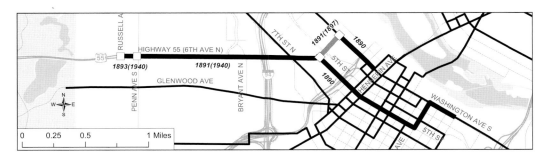

6th Ave. N. line

6th Ave. N.

Years of operation: 1891–1940
Paired with: 4th Ave. S. (1892–1918),
    St. Paul–Minneapolis (1918–39),
    E. 25th St. (1939–40)
Service frequency: Fifteen minutes off-peak;
    five minutes peak

The largely working-class neighborhood along 6th Avenue North, with its small shops and

A few years after this 1936 view looking east at Emerson Avenue, 6th Avenue North was bulldozed and replaced by Olson Memorial Highway, one of the state's first four-lane divided roads. The commercial buildings were all removed and replaced by the Sumner Field low-income housing projects, which in turn were demolished shortly after 2000.

The intersection of 6th Avenue North and Bryant Avenue.

4·14·36

Plymouth

Years of operation: 1891–1953
Paired with: Downtown only (1891–94), Bloomington (1894–1919), Minnehaha Falls (1919–21), Ft. Snelling (1921–27), Ft. Snelling–Hazel Park through service to Hazel Park (1927–32), Ft. Snelling–Hope St. (1932–36), Ft. Snelling—through service to St. Paul permanently discontinued (1936–46), E. 25th St. (1946–53)
Service frequency: Fifteen minutes off-peak; ten minutes peak as Plymouth–E. 25th St.

Plymouth Avenue was the center of the Jewish community on the near north side, and during most of the streetcar era it was a neighborhood of small shops and businesses. In 1921, it was joined with Ft. Snelling, and in 1927 service expanded beyond Ft. Snelling via West 7th Street through downtown St. Paul, out East 7th Street to Duluth Avenue, then on private right of way all the way to Hazel Park. This twenty-two-mile 7th–Minnehaha–Plymouth routing made for one of the longest streetcar trips in the entire system. In 1932, cars were switched from Hazel Park to Hope Street as the Minnehaha–7th–Hope St. line. Through service to St. Paul ended in 1936.

businesses, was wiped out by the construction of Olson Memorial Highway and the Sumner Field housing projects, taking with it the 6th Ave. car line, which then became the Kenwood–Russell Ave N. bus route. TCRT had no money to reconstruct its rail line, and, given neighborhood changes and the loss of its traffic base, a rail line would have been economically unjustifiable.

Plymouth line

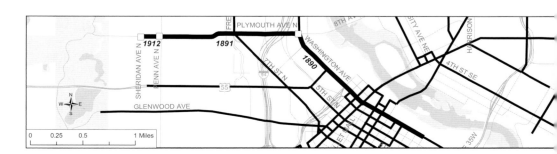

Homewood Drugs marked the end of the Plymouth Avenue line at Sheridan Avenue.

Broadway

Years of operation: 1914–50
Service frequency: Fifteen minutes off-peak;
extra service provided during rush hours

Broadway was a crosstown line serving north and northeast Minneapolis, and, like the Selby–Lake in south Minneapolis, a prosperous commercial and shopping strip filled in along its length from Penn Avenue on the west to Washington Avenue on the east. It never developed the traffic volumes of Selby–Lake, however, mainly because it was short (only 3.45 miles long) and much of its trackage was shared with other lines (Robbinsdale, Chicago–Penn–Fremont, Monroe) that ran downtown. It traveled along 13th Avenue Northeast because the Broadway bridge through the middle of the Grain Belt Brewery complex over the Mississippi emptied into 13th rather than Broadway Street. The streetcar is the reason for the commercial development along 13th at 2nd Street and University Avenue Northeast. Despite its function as a crosstown route, the Broadway line ended at Jackson Street, the base of the ramp leading up to the intersection with the Central line and a major potential transfer point. The intersection was constructed entirely on a bridge over the railroad tracks, and presumably that was the reason for stopping the line short. However, a streetcar junction of the Como, Oak, and Inter-Campus lines was built at the intersection of 4th Street and 15th Avenue Southeast, the only other intersection in the city located on a bridge. On its west end, the Broadway line was extended through a developing residential neighborhood along 19th Avenue North, later named Golden Valley Road.

Broadway line

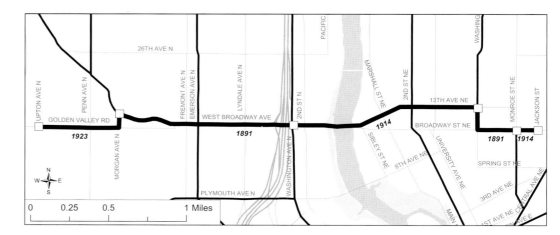

The Robbinsdale and Broadway lines both served this stretch of Broadway Avenue at Dupont Avenue in north Minneapolis. *Minneapolis Star Journal* photograph; courtesy of the Minnesota Historical Society.

In the 1940s, the east end of the Broadway bridge over the Mississippi River emptied not onto Broadway Street but onto 13th Avenue Northeast. The first experimental lightweight, car 2000, descends the ramp and will soon bisect the Grain Belt Brewery complex.

The Broadway line, running on 13th Avenue Northeast, crosses the 2nd St. N.E. line. Never well patronized, it was a perfect home for one of the short ex-Stillwater lightweights.

The north Minneapolis business district at Broadway and Fremont Avenues on the Broadway and Robbinsdale lines, viewed in 1946. Photograph by *Minneapolis Star-Journal*; courtesy of the Minnesota Historical Society.

Robbinsdale

Years of operation: 1891–1948

Paired with: Downtown only (1906–10), shuttle car from Penn and 32nd Avenue North (1910–14), St. Louis Park (1914–20), Downtown only (1920–35), Franklin (1935–40), 28th Ave. S. (1940–48)

Service frequency: Thirty minutes; extra service provided during rush hours

An independent company, the North Side Street Railway, built the portion of the Robbinsdale line outside the city of Minneapolis in 1891. Its streetcars shuttled passengers to a connection with the Minneapolis Street Railway at the city limits. TCRT acquired the company in 1906 and established through service. The portion north of Oakdale and France Avenues was rebuilt in

A Robbinsdale-bound car on West Broadway Avenue passes Sheridan Avenue.

The Robbinsdale line ended at 42nd Avenue, behind the photographer. The one off-center track required southbound streetcars to run in the northbound lane, against the flow of traffic. Photograph from the Minneapolis Star and Tribune News Negative Collection; courtesy of the Minnesota Historical Society.

1914 and relocated from the private right of way and Hubbard Avenue to parallel Broadway, the main street of Robbinsdale. Along its route, the Robbinsdale line served the warehouse-industrial area and scrap yard district along Washington Avenue, ran the length of the Broadway commercial strip, and ended in the small downtown of Robbinsdale. The portion of the route outside Minneapolis was technically part of the TCRT subsidiary Minneapolis & St. Paul Suburban Railroad Company.

Beginning in 1942, a feeder bus met the Penn Avenue streetcars at a terminal at 42nd and Thomas Avenues and traveled to Robbinsdale via 42nd, Abbott, 41st, Shoreline, 40th, Noble, 39th, and Vera Cruz Avenues. Later in 1942, the route was extended to 42nd and Broadway Avenues, where it met the Robbinsdale streetcar.

At the 42nd and Hubbard terminus of the North Side Street Railway was the factory of streetcar manufacturer Northern Car Company. Previously known as Robinson & Moen, it was located in Waterloo, Iowa, and built more than one hundred horsecars and steam motor trailers between 1880 and 1890, when it became Northern Car and moved to Robbinsdale. The company built at least several dozen electric cars for Minneapolis and St. Paul. A fire put the company out of business in 1892.

Penn

Years of operation: 1891–1953

Paired with: Downtown only (1891–1902), Nicollet Avenue (1902–10), 8th Ave. (Chicago) (1910–53). (During 1920,

part of the service was paired with Lake Nokomis.)

Service frequency: Ten minutes off-peak; five minutes peak

Emerson–Fremont

Years of operation: 1891–1953

Paired with: Downtown only (1891–94), Cedar (1894–1910 and 1921–26), Chicago (1910–53), E. 25th St. (1920–21), 28th

Penn line
Emerson–Fremont line

Ave. S. (1921–50). (Part of the Emerson and Fremont service was paired briefly with East 25th St., then with Cedar as the Cedar–Emerson and later as the 28th Ave. S.–N. Emerson line operating to and from downtown via Broadway and Washington Avenues.)
Service frequency: Ten minutes off-peak; five minutes peak

Penn, Emerson, and Fremont were the northern legs of the Chicago–Penn–Fremont line and served a primarily working-class neighborhood and the West Broadway Avenue commercial strip, as well as North and Patrick Henry high schools. Passenger volumes were so heavy that as many as seventy-five streetcars were in service on the Chicago–Penn–Fremont line. In a major construction project in 1920, TCRT built a new line into downtown Minneapolis from Broadway and Emerson Avenues via Emerson and along 7th Street to 3rd Avenue North to 8th Street. This speeded travel time to downtown compared to the old route via Broadway and Washington Avenues, eliminated duplicative service, and brought service closer to the neigh-

In 1949–50, the city of Minneapolis replaced the wood-and-steel North 7th Street viaduct that carried the Chicago–Penn–Fremont line over the railroad throat on the north edge of downtown. To the right of 7th Street is the Great Northern's refrigerator car yard where perishable shipments were unloaded. Next to it is the Northland Greyhound bus garage. Both were replaced by the Hennepin County garbage incinerator. *Minneapolis Star Journal* photographs; courtesy of the Minnesota Historical Society Society.

The camera is looking west on the 6th Ave. N. line. The Penn–Fremont crosses it on North 7th Street.

The commercial corner of Broadway and Emerson Avenues in north Minneapolis featured a good example of complex overhead wire that many felt to be unsightly and another reason to replace streetcars with buses. Photograph by Norton & Peel; courtesy of the Minnesota Historical Society.

Thomas Avenue at 39th Avenue North, near the end of the Penn Avenue line. Photograph by Norton & Peel; courtesy of the Minnesota Historical Society.

borhoods south of Broadway. As more homes were built and the neighborhood north of 44th Avenue filled in, a shuttle bus service was established that met the Fremont cars at 44th and Oliver Avenues and continued on to 52nd and Oliver Avenues.

A Chicago–Penn car traverses the curving section of West Broadway Avenue at Morgan Avenue. Broadway tracks diverge at the bottom of the photo. Photograph courtesy of Forrest Johnson.

Turning from northbound Fremont Avenue onto westbound 44th Avenue.

Most streetcar lines ended at wyes, like this one at 44th and Oliver Avenues in north Minneapolis. The streetcar pulls into the side street, then backs up into the middle of 44th in front of the Fairway Foods store (to the left, but not visible here), to wait until its next departure time. Scenes like this were repeated across the Twin Cities thousands of times daily.

Washington Ave. N.

Years of operation: 1890–1953
Paired with: Downtown only (1890–94),
    Nicollet (1894–1910), Cedar (1910–26),
    34th Ave. S. (1926–50), Ft. Snelling
    (1950–53)
Service frequency: Fifteen minutes off-peak;
    ten minutes peak

Always an industrial area, warehouses, light manufacturing, and scrap metal yards brack-eted Washington Avenue north from downtown Minneapolis all the way to the Camden neighborhood. To the east a warren of railroad yards and freight houses filled in between Washington Avenue and the Mississippi River. Industrial workers provided most of the traffic. TCRT's North Side Station was located at

The point of this newspaper photograph was to contrast new and old automobiles, but it unintentionally shows us the Franklin Creamery on Washington Avenue North at 21st Avenue. Photograph from the Minneapolis Star and Tribune News Negative Collection; courtesy of the Minnesota Historical Society.

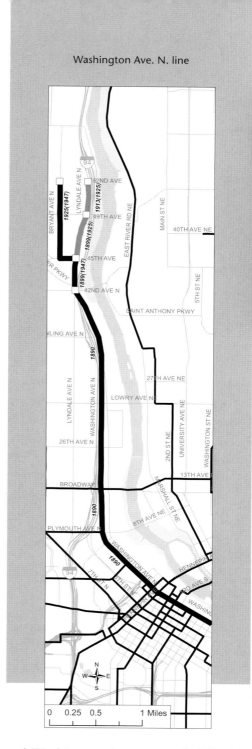

Washington Ave. N. line

TCRT ran a series of short shuttle bus routes that acted as extensions of the streetcar lines. Some were later replaced by streetcars. This particular bus began at 49th and Humboldt Avenues North, and fed passengers to the North Washington Avenue cars at Camden. Bus 1 was built by Eckland Brothers at 28th Street and Lyndale Avenue South in Minneapolis.

Washington Avenue North at Lowry Avenue, where passengers could transfer to the Lowry Avenue crosstown bus. All the houses on the west side of the street have been replaced by Interstate 94.

26th and Washington Avenues, and, following the morning and preceding the afternoon rush hour, a parade of streetcars either leaving or going in service could be seen moving along Washington between North Side and downtown Minneapolis.

North of the Camden business district, the line originally continued north on Lyndale to 52nd Avenue to serve the old Minneapolis Workhouse. In 1925, it was diverted to Bryant Avenue north of 45th Avenue to serve a residential neighborhood that did not develop completely until after World War II.

A feeder bus route was established in 1921 connecting the end of the 2nd St. N.E. car line with the Washington Ave. N. line at 42nd and Washington Avenues. The Humboldt bus, as it was called, operated via the Camden bridge. In 1922, it was extended west on Webber Parkway to a connection with the Fremont line and north

The Camden business district grew up around the six-legged intersection of Washington Avenue, 42nd Avenue, Lyndale Avenue, Webber Parkway, and the Camden bridge, the most northerly Mississippi River crossing in the city. Note the Camden Theater at left. Photograph courtesy of the Minnesota Historical Society.

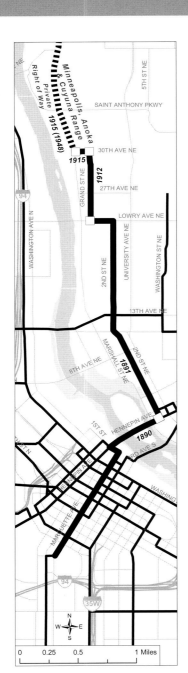

2nd St. N.E. line

on Humboldt Avenue to 52nd Avenue in 1924. The line across the Camden bridge was abandoned in 1926; in 1948, it was extended to 51st and Upton Avenues.

During World War II, the huge Northern Ordnance munitions plant in Fridley operated a shuttle bus across the Camden bridge to the Washington streetcar line. This service was notable for employing unusual-looking buses that had been custom built for the 1939 New York World's Fair.

2nd St. N.E.

Years of operation: 1891–1954
Paired with: Western (Glenwood)
(1891–1919), Nicollet (1919–54)
Service frequency: Ten minutes off-peak;
five minutes peak

As the northern leg of the Nicollet line, 2nd St. N.E. was among the busier lines in the system. Its traffic came from the primarily Polish and Italian neighborhoods of "Nordeast" Minneapolis; its riders headed for errands or jobs

downtown or the industrial area along the Mississippi River. The line served residential neighborhoods broken up with railroad corridors and industries, including the Grain Belt and Glueck breweries and the Northern States Power Riverside Power Plant. It had more railroad grade crossings (four) than any other line.

From 1915 until 1939, when it ended rail operations, cars of the Minneapolis, Anoka & Cuyuna Range Railway used the 2nd St. N.E. line on their run from Anoka to downtown Minneapolis. A short segment of the Anoka line was revived between 1943 and 1948 to shuttle employees from 30th and Marshall Avenues, the end of the 2nd St. N.E. line, to the Northern Ordnance defense plant on East River Road in Fridley. Hundreds of war workers used the 2nd St. N.E. line and the shuttle every day.

The 2nd St. N.E. line made a jog at Broadway, passing the Little Sisters of the Poor Convent.

Grand Street, shown here at 28th Avenue Northeast, is the center of a slender neighborhood sandwiched between railroad tracks on the east and the Mississippi River on the west.

A Minnesota Railfans Association excursion passes the large mill and crosses the Northern Pacific's "Mulberry Line" at 18th Avenue Northeast.

TCRT inaugurated a feeder bus extension in 1940. Operating from a connection at 30th Avenue and Grand Street Northeast, the bus route followed California Street, St. Anthony Boulevard, Main Street, 36th Avenue, and 3rd Street, to 37th Avenue Northeast. It was extended in 1947 to 44th and Madison Avenues in Columbia Heights. The route became part of the Nicollet Avenue bus line when streetcar service ended in March 1954.

Monroe

Dates of operation: 1891–1954
Paired with: Bryant (1891–1920), Grand
(1920–52), Nicollet (1952–54)
Service frequency: Fifteen minutes off-peak;
ten minutes peak

Monroe, like 2nd St. N.E. and Central, was an important line serving the northeast Minneapolis neighborhoods—a mixture of working-class housing and light industry. Traffic was very heavy all along Monroe Street to and from downtown Minneapolis, but also to and from industries in the area. The Shoreham Shops of the Soo Line Railroad were located at the end of

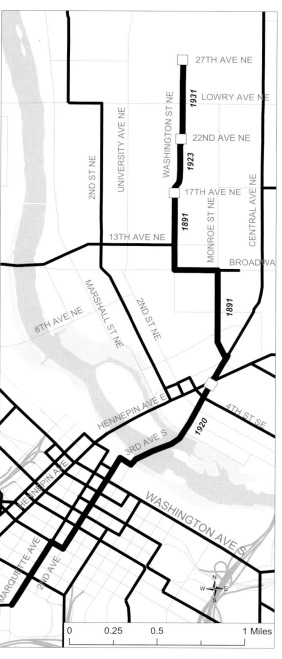

Monroe line

Minneapolis, Anoka & Cuyuna Range Railway

From the fur trade to lumber and flour milling, Anoka's history reflected the changing face of Minnesota's nineteenth-century economy. Founded in 1843 as a fur trading settlement at the confluence of the Mississippi and Rum rivers, the town's proximity to waterpower attracted lumbermen, who put a dam across the Rum River and built a sawmill there in 1853. Then the St. Paul & Pacific Railroad arrived in 1864, and Anoka was linked to Minneapolis and the developing farm regions to the north and west. Access to eastern markets and North Dakota wheat prompted the Washburn interests to build a flour mill in 1880, rebuilding it in 1885 after a disastrous fire the year before. By the turn of the century, Anoka industries were busy processing potatoes, turning wheat into flour, and making shoes—eight hundred pairs a day—at a local factory.

This prosperity stimulated discussions about the need for improved transportation between Anoka and Minneapolis, and several proposals were put forward to construct a new railroad between the two cities. One of them took hold. The Minneapolis & Northern Railway was incorporated in Maine in 1912. It subsequently acquired the franchises of a predecessor company, the Anoka–Minneapolis Suburban Railway, which lay moribund since its incorporation in 1909, unable to secure financing for construction. By July 1913, the company had completed its own line to 34th Avenue Northeast and Marshall Street in Minneapolis and obtained trackage rights over the Soo Line's Mississippi River bridge to 42nd Avenue North and Washington (Camden Place), where it met TCRT's streetcars.

The Minneapolis & Northern opened passenger service with two gas motorcars supplied by the McKeen Motor Car Company of Omaha, Nebraska. These cars were fifty-five feet long and resembled electric interurban cars; unlike interurban cars, which drew power from an overhead trolley, these were self-contained, powered by a gasoline engine and a direct mechanical drive. The McKeens proved unsuccessful on the Minneapolis & Northern, and their enumerable mechanical problems undoubtedly contributed to the company's financial woes and its eventual receivership in January 1915.

Its successor, the Minneapolis, Anoka & Cuyuna Range Railway, took over operations in March 1915. With new financing and renewed ambitions, it proposed building north to the Cuyuna Iron Range and electrifying the line. It never reached the Iron Range, nor did it go beyond Anoka, but it did electrify the line and acquire several cars from TCRT and a used streetcar dealer in Cleveland, Ohio. It also built a track connection to TCRT's 2nd St. N.E. line at 30th and Grand Street Northeast, which gave it an entrance to downtown Minneapolis via trackage rights. A ticket office was located in rented space in a building at 517 2nd Avenue South. Later it shared a depot on North 7th Street with the Dan Patch line and the Luce line.

A 1916 timetable showed seven weekday round trips between Minneapolis and Anoka with extra service provided on Saturdays and Sundays. Schedule speed was only seventeen miles per hour, owing largely to the amount of street running in Minneapolis. The running time would increase over time as track deteriorated. Derailments became more frequent. Near the end of service, the line was known as "Old Rock and Roll."

The Minneapolis, Anoka & Cuyuna Range Railway worked hard to attract freight business and had some moderate success. It took over switching chores at the Lincoln Mill of the Pillsbury–Washburn Flour Company and brought in carload freight for other local industries, handling some 3,278 carloads in 1926.

Unfortunately, the freight business was not enough to stave off troubles, and the heavier freight car loadings increased the wear and tear on track and roadbed. The company entered a second receivership in July 1926. Although its freight business improved slightly, passenger losses offset any gains, and the company suffered a 40 percent drop in total revenues. On August 29, 1929, it was sold at public auction, becoming the Minneapolis, Anoka & Cuyuna Range Railroad Company.

The name change did not help given that automobile and truck competition kept right on eating away at the line's remaining business. The Lincoln Mill closed in 1932. That and the economic effects of the Depression foreclosed any hope for the future. All maintenance on track and equipment was

The Northern Pump shuttle car waits at the corner of Marshall Street and 30th Avenue Northeast, opposite the Northern States Power Company's Riverside Station power plant.

Trolleys in Your Neighborhood

The optimistically named Minneapolis, Anoka & Cuyuna Range Railway made it from Minneapolis to Anoka and no farther. It paralleled Coon Rapids Boulevard and East River Road, entering Minneapolis over the 2nd St. N.E. line. Known in its later years for deplorable track, the railway last ran passengers to Anoka in 1939.

discontinued, and conditions grew so bad that cars literally fell apart. One car had its air compressor fall off while it was standing on an Anoka street.

A tornado ripped through Anoka in 1939, destroying most of the trolley wire in the downtown. Lacking funds to make repairs, the company substituted buses and ended all rail passenger service on August 23, 1939. Freight service continued until 1943, when the line was sold to Northern Ordnance, Inc. It rebuilt the line from 30th Avenue Northeast and Marshall Street to its defense plant adjoining the East River Road in Fridley and began a shuttle service from the end of the 2nd St. N.E. streetcar line to the plant. TCRT rebuilt three former Anoka cars for the shuttle service. The service was only for Northern Ordnance employees and was discontinued in 1948. All track between the Northern Ordnance plant and Anoka was dismantled for scrap in 1943.

Although the wire came down and the cars were scrapped in the early 1950s, this remnant of the Minneapolis, Anoka & Cuyuna Range lasted until 1967, serving Northern Ordnance. The Great Northern Railway purchased the line and in 1971 removed all the track except for two spurs serving the Minneapolis Waterworks that remain in service today.

The Minneapolis, Anoka & Cuyuna Range Railway was part of the electric interurban craze that swept the country in the early twentieth century. The dot-com bubble of that day, the interurbans tended to be cheaply built and financially leveraged. Cleaner and more convenient than the steam railroads, they were quickly eclipsed by the automobile. The line terminated at the Anoka depot, located on the north side of Main Street next to the Rum River. If car 1 looks familiar, it was built at TCRT's Snelling Shops in 1915. Photograph courtesy of the Minnesota Historical Society.

The Monroe line crosses four of the railroad corridors that slice across northeast Minneapolis. This is the Northern Pacific's "Mulberry Line" at 18th Avenue.

The Monroe Street line ended on Washington Street Northeast at 27th Avenue, the southern edge of the Soo Line's Shoreham rail yards and shops.

the line at 27th Avenue and Washington Street Northeast and were a dependable source of passenger traffic.

In 1935, TCRT experimented with a short crosstown bus from Broadway and Monroe Streets via Monroe, 18th Avenue, Central Avenue, and 19th Avenue to Stinson Boulevard. It was discontinued in 1936.

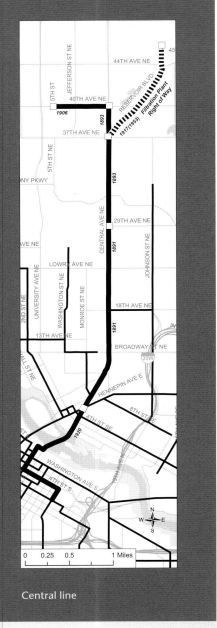

Central line

The mighty 3rd Avenue bridge, S-curving over St. Anthony Falls, was opened in 1920, bringing streetcars past the Exposition Building for the first time. Exposition Building subsequently gave way to a Coca-Cola bottling plant. La Rive Condominiums currently occupy the site.

Central

Years of operation: 1891–1953
Paired with: Lake Harriet (1891–1892),
    8th Ave. (Chicago) (1892–1910), Nicollet
    (1910–19), Bloomington (1919–53)
Service frequency: Ten minutes off-peak; five
    minutes peak

Central Avenue became a busy commercial-industrial strip, the retail spine of northeast Minneapolis, thanks to the streetcar service. Columbia Heights became an early residential suburb for the same reason. Columbia Heights was developed and heavily promoted by Thomas Lowry and is an example often cited to show the relationship between residential development and the expanding street railway system. Students from Edison and Columbia Heights high schools, the Northrup King seed plant and the Shoreham Shops of the Soo Line Railroad bolstered ridership.

Eastbound on 40th Avenue Northeast at Quincy Street in Columbia Heights.

A Columbia Heights car has just crossed the Mississippi on the 3rd Avenue bridge and is now on Central Avenue at University Avenue, viewed from the Exposition Building. Photograph by Joseph Zalusky; courtesy of the Minnesota Historical Society.

Although taken a few months after abandonment, this photograph captures the heart of the Central Avenue business district at Lowry Avenue. Photograph by Norton & Peel; courtesy of the Minnesota Historical Society.

Minneapolis Filtration Plant Railway

In 1913, Minneapolis needed a dependable source of clean water for its new industries and growing population, and it began work on a new water treatment plant in Columbia Heights. The location it selected was close to the Mississippi River and one of the highest points in the area, an important feature for a gravity-fed system. Chemicals and sand were needed to filter and treat the river water, and it was determined that a rail connection was the best way to bring carload shipments to the plant.

The city chose to involve TCRT in the project and entered into an agreement with the company. Under its terms the city would operate the line; TCRT would supply electric power and maintain any electric locomotives or cars that would be used in the operation.

F. W. Cappelen, the Minneapolis city engineer, designed the line, and city crews graded the right of way. TCRT furnished labor and materials to lay the track and put up the overhead. The line ran from a connection with the Soo Line Railway at a point where it crossed Central Avenue south of 37th Avenue Northeast. There it followed Central Avenue for few hundred feet on its own tracks, parallel to TCRT's. At Reservoir Boulevard it turned northeast and ran alongside the west side of the boulevard to the filtration plant at 49th Avenue Northeast. The line was 1.5 miles long, making it one of the shortest electric railways in the entire country.

The city purchased a car from McGuire-Cummings Mfg. Co., a major builder of electric railway rolling stock. It had a passenger-carrying car body that could accommodate a seated load of thirty-six passengers and was fitted with standard railroad couplers that allowed it to move a single loaded freight car up the grade to the plant. When the line opened in 1917, the area along Reservoir Boulevard in Columbia Heights had few residences, but in anticipation of future growth it was determined that several additional passenger trips should be provided for online passengers, even though the majority of riders were workers going to and from the plant.

Periodically the car had to go to Snelling Shops for repairs. Because there was no direct track connection, the car was run down the hill to Central Avenue to a point where it crossed TCRT's tracks. There, first one truck, then the other, was derailed and than rerailed on TCRT's tracks for the trip to Snelling. This totally bizarre operation was just one more oddity.

Why the line was built and operated by the city of Minneapolis is an even more interesting question. The city could have simply contracted with TCRT, as the university did for the Inter-Campus, or it could have arranged with the Soo Line to build a branch line to the plant and switch the cars. It is possible the city and the company were not on the best of terms. The city regulated the Minneapolis system, and there was an ongoing dispute at the time over a proposed fare increase. Things may have been just too tense politically for the parties to make an operating agreement.

Another possibility has to do with TCRT's corporate structure. The Minneapolis Street Railway operated solely within the city limits of Minneapolis. Because the filtration plant was in Columbia Heights, the operation would have been under the Minneapolis & St. Paul Suburban Railroad Company, a subcorporation of TCRT over which the city had no jurisdiction. As for the Soo Line, it no doubt would have used steam locomotives, which would have been very unpopular in a developing residential area, especially on washdays.

As it was, the Minneapolis Filtration Plant Railway offered a charming form of incidental transportation for residents along Reservoir Boulevard through May 1948, when passenger service ended. It also provided lifetime employment for its only motorman until he retired shortly before the line quit in 1953 and the city started trucking supplies to the plant.

The Minneapolis Filtration Plant Railway was built to carry freight and employees to the plant, which is located in Columbia Heights. It also ran an infrequent scheduled service for the public, meeting Columbia Heights cars at 37th and Central Avenues Northeast.

The Filtration Plant Railway followed the western edge of Reservoir Boulevard, which climbed a steep grade from Central Avenue to the plant. Car 1 was unusual because it was designed to haul freight cars and carry passengers.

Johnson

Years of operation: 1911–53
Paired with: Shuttle to Central Avenue
(1911–12), Kenwood (1912–18), Grand
(1918–20), Bryant (1920–53)
Service frequency: Ten minutes off-peak;
five minutes peak

There was no service on Johnson Street before 1911. TCRT originally built a line on 8th Street Southeast from Central Avenue to 14th Avenue Southeast in 1899. In 1902, it was paired with the Kenwood line, then with Bryn Mawr in 1906. In 1911, a new line was built from Central and 18th Avenue Northeast via 18th Avenue to Johnson, then north on Johnson to 28th Avenue Northeast. A shuttle car provided service from Central Avenue. The following year

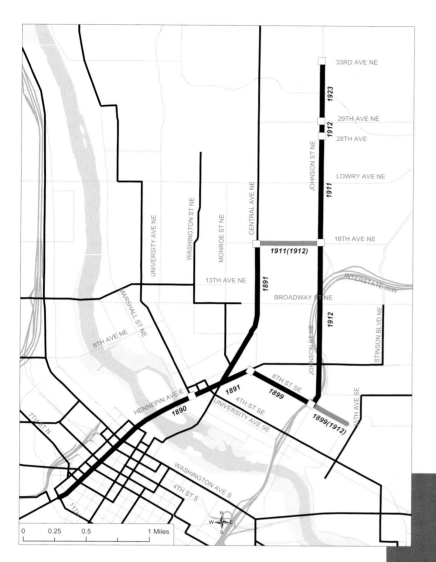

Johnson line

Johnson Street turned into 10th Avenue Southeast at this Great Northern Railway underpass. This was the route of State Highway 36. Photograph courtesy of Forrest Johnson.

Newspaper photographs of service disruptions provide a glimpse of locations that would otherwise have eluded attention, such as Johnson Street north of Broadway, a place of quarries rather than residential development. The halted streetcars and the onlooking crowd suggest a traffic mishap of some sort. Photograph from the Minneapolis Star and Tribune News Negative Collection; courtesy of the Minnesota Historical Society.

the shuttle was abandoned, and a new line opened from Hennepin and 8th Street Southeast via 8th Street to 10th Avenue Southeast, to Johnson Street and north on Johnson to 29th Avenue Northeast.

Johnson Street did not begin filling in until 1910–25. There were a few industries in the adjoining neighborhoods, but unlike Central Avenue, which was lined with businesses and retail shops, Johnson was mostly residential with a few neighborhood businesses at scattered intersections, most notably at 29th Avenue. Between Broadway and 18th Avenue Northeast, there was a sand and gravel mine. TCRT built a spur into it to load sand. Today's Quarry shopping center is a reminder of that former land use.

There is a geographic divide within northeast Minneapolis. The flat neighborhoods west

Looking north on Johnson Street at 22nd Avenue Northeast. Photograph by Lee Brothers; courtesy of the Minnesota Historical Society.

of Central Avenue, closer to the river, were settled first and tended more toward worker housing. East from Central there is a high glacial ridge centered on Johnson Street. It attracted more expensive housing, but that housing filled in at a much slower pace, and the new construction often came with garages for automobiles. The higher incomes, lower densities, and automobiles, along with the lack of commercial traffic generators, resulted in lower ridership on Johnson than on Central.

Northwest Terminal

Years of operation: 1920–48
Paired with: Nicollet (1920–48)
The Northwest Terminal line was originally routed via East Hennepin to 8th Street Southeast, then via 8th to Johnson Street Northeast to East Hennepin. In 1921, new track was built on East Hennepin between 8th Street and Johnson (see map for details).
Service frequency: Thirty-minute off-peak service with some extra trips during rush hours; rush hours only after World War II

While the zoning of industrial districts was nothing new, the concept of an "industrial park" first appeared in Minneapolis along Stinson Boulevard between East Hennepin Avenue and Broadway Street. Constructed just after World War I, the Northwest Terminal was a large industrial warehouse and manufacturing complex that housed multiple businesses. It was the first such facility designed for both rail and truck access. The buildings fronted on broad

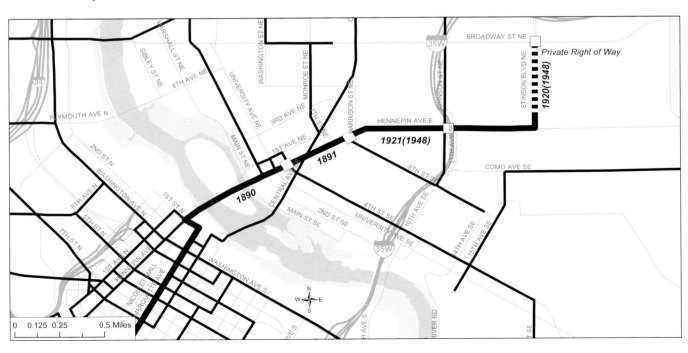

Northwest Terminal line

lawns. Stinson Boulevard was landscaped, and the streetcar tracks were put down in an attractive, tree-lined median strip. Streetcars turned around at Stinson Boulevard and Broadway Street on a wye in front of the landmark Cream of Wheat building, now converted to residential use.

Unfortunately, the complex attracted more automobile drivers than streetcar riders. In 1946, TCRT introduced a shuttle bus operating from a connection with the end of the Northwest Terminal streetcar line and from there along Stinson Boulevard to Lowry Avenue and McKinley Street, where it met the Lowry Avenue crosstown bus. Frustrated with poor ridership, TCRT ended rail service on January 10, 1948, replacing it with an extension of the Bryn Mawr bus line from downtown Minneapolis via East Hennepin to Stinson Boulevard to Lowry and McKinley. The shuttle was discontinued.

Franklin–11th

Years of operation: 1914–40
Paired with: Ft. Snelling (1914–21),
    Robbinsdale (1935–40)
Service frequency: Twenty minutes off-peak;
    extra service provided during rush hours

Much of this lightly patronized line duplicated or crossed other lines, and its 11th Street route along the edge of downtown Minneapolis

placed it several blocks from the heart of the central business district. The new Franklin Avenue bridge opened in 1924, and an extension was built across the bridge to 27th Avenue Southeast and a connection with the Oak line at 27th and Yale Avenue Southeast. The line became a bus operation in November 1940. At that time it was rerouted to a new terminal at

Franklin Avenue and Bedford Street Southeast, which better served the hilltop Prospect Park neighborhood. In 1951, the Franklin bus added a branch down East River Road to St. Anthony Avenue, the St. Paul city limits.

E. 25th St.

Years of operation: 1912–53
Paired with: Shuttle from Cedar and Minnehaha (1912–14), Downtown only (1914–18), Kenwood (1918–20), Emerson and Camden (1920–21), Kenwood (1921–38), Downtown only (1938–46; cars operated via Washington to 5th Avenue South, to 5th Street, to the wye at 5th Street and 5th Avenue North; some trips during 1939–40 were extended out 6th Avenue North until the 6th Ave. N. line was converted to buses in 1940), Plymouth Avenue (1946–53)
Service frequency: Fifteen minutes off-peak; extra service provided during rush hours

Franklin–11th line

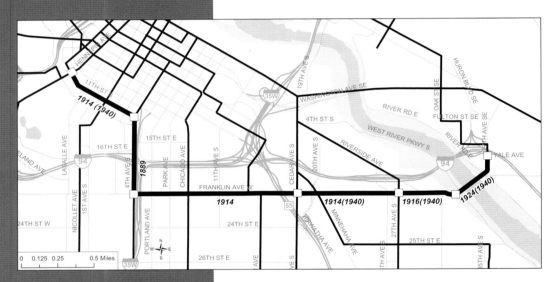

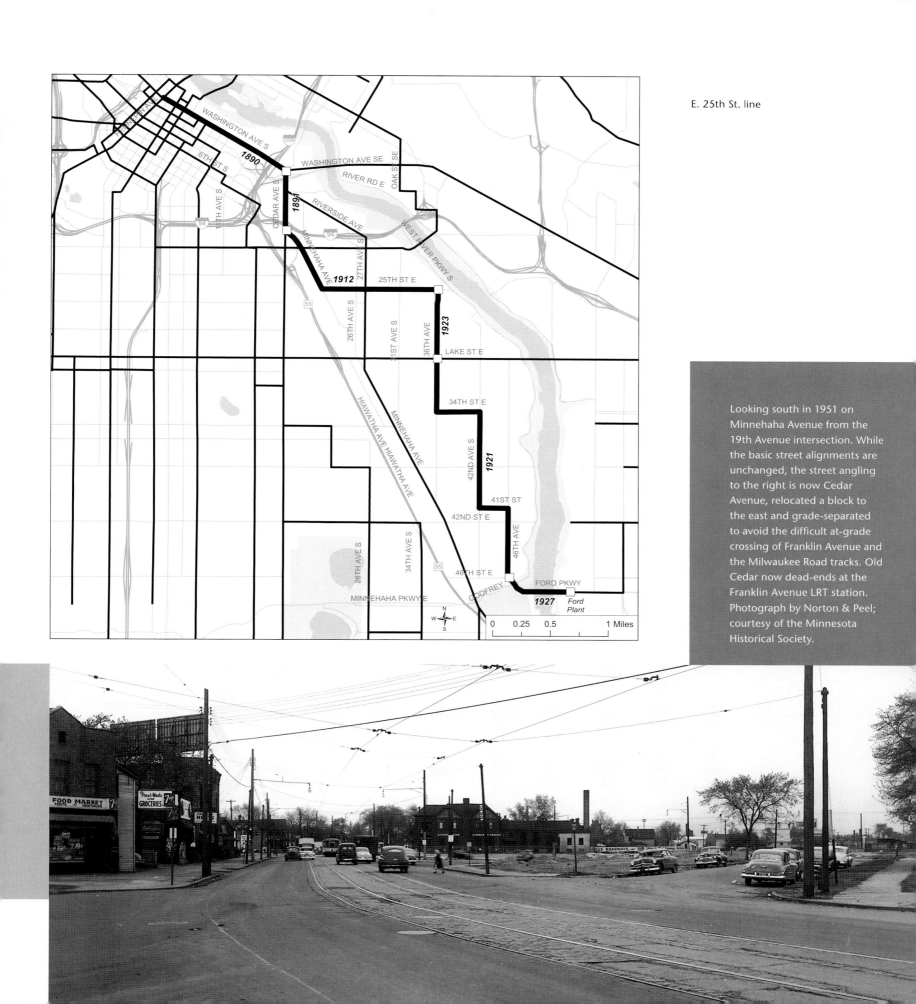

E. 25th St. line

WASHINGTON AVE S
FRANKLIN AVE
6TH ST S
WASHINGTON AVE SE
RIVER RD E
OAK ST SE
CEDAR AVE S
RIVERSIDE AVE
19TH AVE S
1890
1891
MINNEHAHA AVE
1912
27TH AVE S
WEST RIVER PKWY S
25TH ST E
26TH AVE S
31ST AVE S
36TH AVE
1923
LAKE ST E
HIAWATHA AVE HIAWATHA AVE
MINNEHAHA AVE
34TH ST E
42ND AVE S
1921
41ST ST
42ND ST E
28TH AVE S
34TH AVE S
46TH AVE
46TH ST E
MINNEHAHA PKWY E
GODFREY
FORD PKWY
1927
Ford Plant

N
W E
S

0   0.25   0.5   1 Miles

Looking south in 1951 on Minnehaha Avenue from the 19th Avenue intersection. While the basic street alignments are unchanged, the street angling to the right is now Cedar Avenue, relocated a block to the east and grade-separated to avoid the difficult at-grade crossing of Franklin Avenue and the Milwaukee Road tracks. Old Cedar now dead-ends at the Franklin Avenue LRT station. Photograph by Norton & Peel; courtesy of the Minnesota Historical Society.

This E. 25th St. car is exiting the east end of the Ford Parkway bridge across the Mississippi River. Shortly, it will enter the double-track loop in front of the Ford plant, where passengers can transfer to the Randolph car to downtown St. Paul.

Headed for the Ford plant in St. Paul's Highland Park, a southbound E. 25th St. car on 42nd Avenue South turns east onto 41st Street.

On its way to the Ford bridge, the E. 25th St. line zigzagged, its turns designed to center the line in the Longfellow neighborhood and minimize walking distance for passengers. To maintain this optimal spacing, it used 34th and 41st Streets, which were otherwise not arterial streets. This is East 41st Street, looking toward 46th Avenue.

The E. 25th St. line served the residential Seward and Longfellow neighborhoods between Minnehaha Avenue and the Mississippi River. Its southeasterly course required it to zigzag toward the river in such a way as to minimize the walking distance to it. To achieve this, it turned five times. In 1927, cars were routed over the new Ford Parkway bridge to a connection with the Randolph line at the new Ford plant in Highland Park. The E. 25th St.

line was built very late. Automobiles were appearing in considerable numbers, and many of the small bungalows that went up in the 1920s along 42nd and 46th Avenues came with detached garages. Business to the Ford plant surged during World War II, but only a handful of passengers typically made the trip thereafter. By the time an E. 25th St. car crossed the Ford Parkway bridge in the early 1950s, it was usually empty.

The Randolph car from St. Paul meets the E. 25th St. car at the Ford plant loop. The two motormen from different stations chat during their layover.

Minnehaha Falls– Ft. Snelling

Years of operation: 1890–1953
Originally served by the Motor Line (1884–1891)
Paired with: Downtown only (1891–1919), Ft. Snelling cars routed via Franklin–11th St. 1914–21), Plymouth Ave., Minnehaha Falls cars only (1919–21), all cars paired with Plymouth Ave. (1921–46), Downtown only (1946–50), Washington Ave. N. (1950–53), Downtown only (April-December 1953)
Service frequency: Fifteen minutes off-peak; extra service provided during rush hours. (Between 1909 and 1936, through interurban service was provided to downtown St. Paul and the city's east side, first to East 7th Street and Duluth Avenue [1909–27], then Hazel Park [1927–32] and, finally, the Hope Street line [1932–36].)

Fort Snelling did not receive direct streetcar service from Minneapolis until 1905. Before then it relied on the steam trains of the Chicago, Milwaukee & St. Paul Railroad, which had built its Mendota–Minneapolis line along the bluff below the fort in the 1860s and extended a spur to the fort to bring in supplies and an occasional troop train. Presumably, the absence of development south of Minnehaha Park made TCRT reluctant to extend its Minnehaha line to the fort until that comparatively late date. Service from St. Paul would have to wait until 1909, the year a new bridge opened across the Mississippi

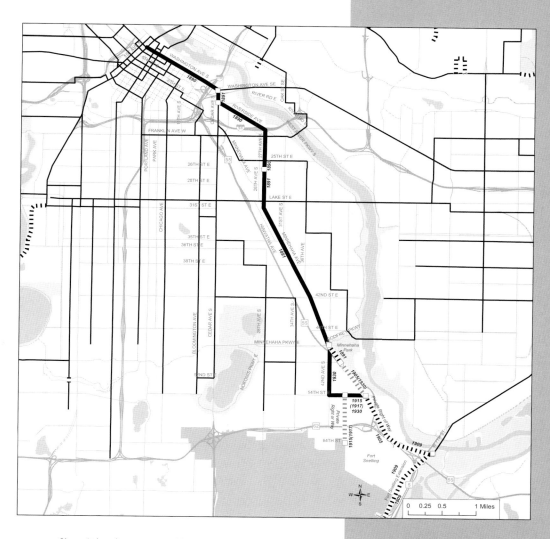

Since it has been severed by the freeway, it is easy to forget that Riverside Avenue, shown here near Cedar Avenue, is the extension of 4th Street, but the Minneapolis city hall in the distance makes that clear.

Minnehaha Falls–
Ft. Snelling line
Ft. Snelling Shuttle

The more direct route alignment to Ft. Snelling was replaced by this 1930 diversion on 42nd Avenue shown at 52nd Street. This is a good example of an oil-and-dirt unpaved street.

Looking north toward the Princess Depot, this track is a remnant of the original line from Minneapolis to Ft. Snelling. It was abandoned south of the Soldiers Home bridge in 1930 in favor of a new route via 42nd Avenue and 54th Street to serve a developing residential neighborhood and the Veterans Administration Hospital. This segment was retained to serve the home and to handle special movements to Minnehaha Falls Park, such as the annual Svenskarnasdag and Syttende Mai celebrations. These were some of the last center overhead wire poles, once common throughout the system, to survive.

A southbound car on Minnehaha Avenue at 43rd Street. Photograph courtesy of the Minnesota Historical Society.

The Twin Cities Speedway opened in 1915 just southwest of the site of the VA Hospital, on land that is now part of the airport. TCRT built a one-mile spur line to serve it, including a large staging yard, similar to the one at the State Fair. The speedway was a financial failure, closing in 1917 after only a handful of races. The photo shows streetcars waiting in the yard. Note the trainmen standing on the car roofs to the right watching the race. Photograph courtesy of the Peter Bonesteel Collection.

from West 7th Street, replacing an earlier wagon bridge that was too narrow and lightly constructed to accommodate streetcar traffic.

Minnehaha Falls was first served by an 1884 branch of the Motor Line that ran from Nicollet Avenue across 37th Street to a private right of way west of Minnehaha Avenue, then south to Minnehaha Falls, stopping at the Minnehaha Falls depot of the Milwaukee Road. This service ended in 1891 when the horsecar line on 27th Avenue was electrified and extended out

Minnehaha Avenue first to 37th Street in 1890, then all the way to Minnehaha Falls in 1891. Another extension via a long stretch of private right of way brought the line to Ft. Snelling in 1905. In 1915, track was laid from 51st Street and the right of way to a motor speedway (auto racetrack) at 46th Avenue and 60th Street. The speedway closed in 1917, and the track was abandoned. In 1930, new track was laid through a new residential neighborhood on 42nd Avenue from Minnehaha Park to 54th Street and east on 54th

Between the world wars, Ft. Snelling was the sleepy, green "country club of the Army." The highways from Minneapolis and St. Paul passed directly through the site of the historic fort, passing the Round Tower. Streetcars from both cities met the shuttle to Officers Row on the wye track at left. Photograph courtesy of the Minnesota Historical Society.

The Ft. Snelling Shuttle

The Spanish-American War brought a surge of activity to Ft. Snelling. The Chicago, Milwaukee & St. Paul Railway provided freight and some passenger service to the fort, but the closest streetcar line to downtown St. Paul on West 7th Street ended abruptly just short of the Ft. Snelling bridge. The closest line to downtown Minneapolis ended at Minnehaha Park. This situation seriously inconvenienced troops stationed at the fort and made it difficult for civilians to get to jobs on the military reservation. It was particularly burdensome for officers and their wives and families living at the fort, who wanted access to civilian amenities. Fort Snelling became a very desirable post immediately after the turn of the century and was considered "the country club of the Army," even though it was only twenty years removed from the frontier and forty years from the Dakota Conflict of 1862.

There were many happy soldiers when the Minnehaha Falls line was extended to the fort in 1905, and even more so when a new bridge was constructed across the Mississippi in 1909 and the West 7th Street line came across, joining with the Minnehaha Falls line. As an accommodation, TCRT built a mile of track from the new bridge into the military reservation. Fort Snelling was a large post, and many of its facilities, including the hospital, barracks, and officers' residences, were a considerable distance from the streetcar line. The army provided the right of way behind the Taylor Avenue row of barracks and officer quarters. In exchange for the rights of way used by the lines from Minneapolis and St. Paul, TCRT had to construct and operate the shuttle free of charge. Schedules called for the shuttle to meet the Minneapolis and St. Paul cars

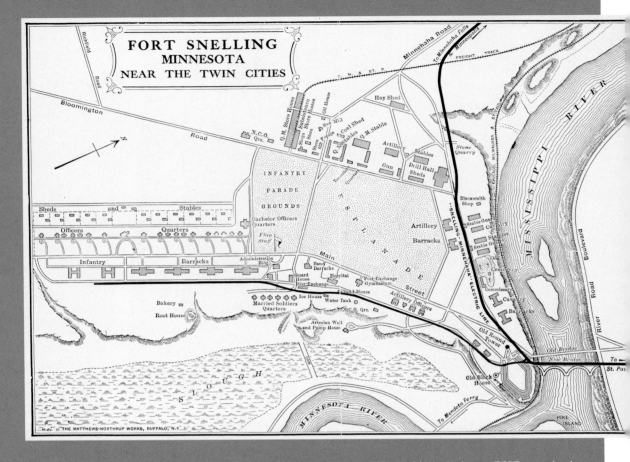

This World War I–vintage TCRT map clearly shows the Minnehaha Falls–Ft. Snelling and West 7th Street lines and the short Ft. Snelling shuttle that served Officers Row.

simultaneously at the wye by the Round Tower. Several times an hour, the three cars lined up nose to tail, exchanged passengers, and went their separate ways.

The Ft. Snelling Shuttle ran until 1952. It was assigned a special double-ended car because there was no wye on the south end of the line. Along with it came the most senior motorman in the system, because it was easy duty with no fares to collect. During

World Wars I and II, Ft. Snelling was an induction center, and the shuttle performed its patriotic duty, moving hundreds of recruits. After World War II, the fort declined and the car became an amusement ride for Nokomis and Highland Park kids who would bike or ride the streetcar to the junction at the 7th Street bridge and then ride the shuttle until the motorman put them off.

The restoration of old Ft. Snelling and the freeway interchange obliterated evidence of the streetcar station and the right of way near the Round Tower. Across Highway 5 to the south, however, the grade can still be seen running parallel to and behind the remaining barracks and administration buildings.

The Ft. Snelling Extension, also referred to as the shuttle or dummy, was one of the few places TCRT used a double-ended streetcar. Regularly assigned car 1230 travels alongside Highway 5. This area is now freeway.

Street to the Minnehaha right of way, bringing streetcar service to the Veterans Administration Hospital at 54th Street and 47th Avenue.

Besides the fort and Minnehaha Park, the line served businesses in the Seven Corners and Cedar–Riverside neighborhoods, Fairview and St. Mary's Hospitals, Augsburg College, and various shops and businesses at 27th Avenue South and Lake Street. Workers from the Minneapolis-Moline farm implement plant just west of 27th and Lake crowded the cars at shift changes. South of Lake Street the line passed through the residential neighborhoods along Minnehaha Avenue, serving them as well as employees of the grain elevators, lumberyards, and light industry that lined Hiawatha Avenue a short distance to the west.

In April 1953, Ft. Snelling cars began turning around at a wye at 54th Street and 47th Avenue South, directly opposite the VA Hospital. Buses had replaced streetcars on the West 7th St. line in St. Paul in 1952. They were extended into Minneapolis, connecting with the Ft. Snelling cars at 47th and 54th. By that date, there was very little passenger traffic to the fort, but the hospital remained an important destination, making it more sensible and convenient to connect the Minneapolis and St. Paul service there.

Cedar–28th Ave. S.– 34th Ave. S.

Years of operation: Cedar–28th Ave. S. (1891–1950), 34th Ave. S. (1926–53)
Cedar–28th Ave. S. paired with:
    Downtown only (1891–94), Emerson (1894–1910), Washington Ave. N. (1910–26), Robbinsdale (1940–48), Downtown only (1948–50)
34th Ave. S. paired with: Washington Ave. N. (1926–50), Downtown only (1950–53)

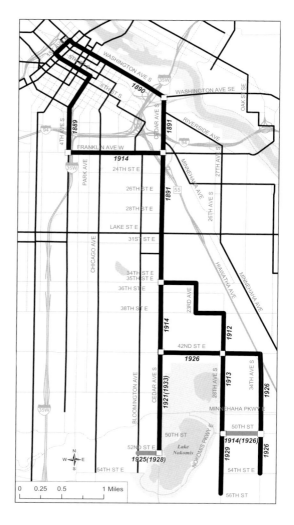

Cedar–28th Ave. S.– 34th Ave. S. line

(At various times between 1914 and until 1933, when the line on Cedar was abandoned south of 42nd, a shuttle car was used on Cedar Avenue. It ran from Lake Street, then 35th Street, then 42nd Street to the south end of the line.)
Service frequency: Fifteen minutes off-peak; extra service provided during rush hours

A 28th Ave. S. car, westbound on 35th Street at 19th Avenue. Photograph from the Minneapolis Star and Tribune News Negative Collection; courtesy of the Minnesota Historical Society.

The junction of Franklin and Cedar Avenues was a contender for the title of "worst intersection in the Twin Cities." The Milwaukee Road's line to downtown passed diagonally through the intersection, tying up traffic and three streetcar lines (one a bus route after 1940). The Minnesota Highway Department diverted Cedar Avenue to the east and grade-separated both streets in 1950. Eventually the railroad was abandoned, to be replaced in 2004 by the Hiawatha Light Rail line. Photograph from Minnesota Highway Department Records; courtesy of the Minnesota Historical Society.

The neighborhoods south of 42nd Street and east of Bloomington Avenue to West River Road did not begin filling in until well after World War I. There were still vacant lots as late as 1960. They were served by streetcars that traveled down Cedar Avenue, then split into three branches that straddled Lake Nokomis along Cedar, 28th Avenue, and 34th Avenue. These were operated in different configurations over the years, but to limit confusion, they are treated as a single streetcar line. When development began in the 1920s, the demand was not for streetcar service but for improved streets, off-street parking, and homes with garages. By the time the last rail was laid on 28th Avenue in 1929, the automobile culture was well estab-

lished. TCRT made multiple reroutings and other service changes to improve operational efficiencies—use of a shuttle car along Cedar Avenue is just one example—but nothing could overcome the low-density, residential character of these neighborhoods and the absence of a strong traffic base. Retrenchment came early.

The Cedar Ave. shuttle waits at 42nd and Cedar. Its short (1.5 mile) trip to 52nd Street and Bloomington Avenue was one of the system's first abandonments in 1933. Photograph courtesy of the Minnesota Historical Society.

The intersection of 42nd Street and 28th Avenue South was unusual because two lines met but did not cross. Instead, each turned. That changed in 1950, when the 28th Ave. line was abandoned south of 42nd Street, and the 34th Ave. line was abandoned north of 42nd. The solution was to connect the rails on 42nd east and west of 28th Avenue, in progress in this photograph.

The Cedar line south of 42nd Street was abandoned in 1933, just twelve years after it opened in 1921. A major railroad grade separation project in 1950 at the junction of Cedar, Franklin, and Minnehaha Avenues forced abandonment of rail operation on Cedar between Franklin Avenue and Lake Street. The 28th Ave. S. line was converted to buses.

From 1942 until 1950, a shuttle bus was provided from the end of the 34th Ave. S. streetcar line at 54th Street to Wold-Chamberlain Field. Airport service was revived in 1952 as an extension of the 28th Avenue bus line.

On the last day of service, April 17, 1953, a 34th Ave. car crosses Minnehaha Parkway.

Streetcar line extensions generally preceded development. In this photograph from 1950, new postwar houses are still being built along the 28th Ave. S. line at 54th Street, even though the track was opened in 1929. Photograph by Norton & Peel; courtesy of the Minnesota Historical Society.

Bloomington

Years of operation: 1891–1953
Paired with: Downtown only (1891–94),
    Plymouth (1894–1919), Central (1919–53)
Service frequency: Ten minutes off-peak; five
    minutes peak

Bloomington Avenue south of 38th Street filled in much later than neighborhoods west of Chicago Avenue. As late as 1920, there was

The last track expansion was 1933, in the depths of the Great Depression, on Bloomington Avenue from 52nd to 54th Streets, serving a newly built, treeless neighborhood just west of Lake Nokomis. Photograph from the Minneapolis Star and Tribune News Negative Collection; courtesy of the Minnesota Historical Society.

Bloomington line

town line. Multiple businesses grew up, including a bank and a large movie theater. In 1922, an experimental electric trolley bus began operating as a shuttle from 38th Street to 48th Street. It ran for a year but was replaced when rails were laid all the way to 48th. The final 1933 extension from 52nd to 54th Street marked the end of streetcar expansion, except for a half mile on Nicollet Avenue in 1948.

Chicago

Years of operation: 1890–1953
Paired with: Downtown only (1890–92),
   Central (1892–1910), Penn–Emerson
   (1910–53)
Service frequency: Five minutes off-peak;
   three minutes (or less) peak

considerable vacant land all the way south to Lake Nokomis. The intersection of Bloomington Avenue and Lake Street became a busy transfer point connecting with the Selby–Lake cross-

Bloomington Avenue looking south toward the crossing of Minnehaha Creek.

Traffic on Chicago Avenue came mainly from residential neighborhoods adjoining the line, with most passenger trips beginning or ending in the downtown business district. Large numbers of passengers transferred at Lake Street to and from the Selby–Lake line. The huge Sears store and warehouse at Chicago and Lake was a major source of business as was Northwestern Hospital at 26th Street and the Minneapolis General, Swedish, and St. Barnabas Hospitals near Chicago Avenue and 6th Street. Neighbor-

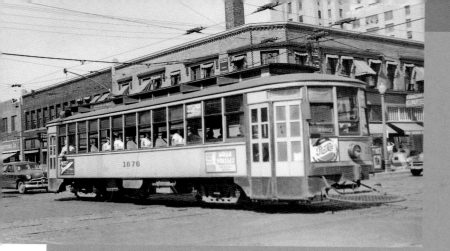

The Sears Roebuck store on Lake Street dominates the background as a southbound Chicago Avenue car crosses Lake.

Chicago Avenue, looking north at 36th Street.

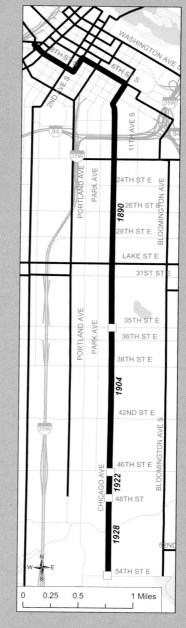

Chicago line

hood stores and shops at Franklin Avenue and Chicago as well as 38th and 48th Streets grew up around the Chicago line. Five-minute service was the norm with bumper-to-bumper cars during rush hour. A schedule was not required to determine when the next car was due as one was always in sight.

A feeder bus connected with the end of the

Chicago Avenue at 41st Street was typical of the great south Minneapolis street grid of single-family homes, interspersed with duplexes, fourplexes, walk-up apartments, and small businesses. Photograph by Norton & Peel.

Passing the Nokomis Theater on Chicago Avenue near 38th Street. The building still stands.

4th Ave. S. line

Chicago car line at 54th Street and Chicago. It operated south on Chicago, to 58th Street, to 10th Avenue, to 57th Street to Longfellow Avenue and Edgewater Boulevard.

4th Ave. S.

Years of operation: 1889–1954
Paired with: Downtown only (1889–92), 6th Ave. N. (1892–1918), Downtown only (1918-1919), Glenwood (Western) (1919–53)
Service frequency: Ten minutes off-peak; five minutes peak

One of the earliest horsecar lines, 4th Ave. S. was the first line in Minneapolis to convert to electric operation, debuting on December 24, 1889. The area was primarily residential south of Lake Street, with occasional shops and small

Incongruously located in the middle of a residential neighborhood at 28th Street, the old Minneapolis Heat Regulator Company became the world headquarters of Honeywell and filled many a 4th Ave. S. street-car with commuters. With the departure of Honeywell, it is now the campus of Wells Fargo Home Mortgage. Severed by Interstate 35W, 4th Avenue has been vacated and reduced to a private driveway.

A 4th Ave. car passes the Hosmer branch library at 36th Street.

businesses near streetcar stops. Over time the neighborhood became the heart of the southside African American community. Minneapolis Vocational High School at 12th Street and Central High School at 35th Street and 4th Avenue generated considerable traffic. North of Lake Street the Minneapolis Heat Regulator plant (later Minneapolis Honeywell headquarters and now occupied by Wells Fargo Home Mortgage) at 28th Street was a large employer that further contributed to the line's prosperity. Two-car trains were used for several years during rush hours, but after 1935 business declined to the point that they were withdrawn. Today, Interstate 35W has obliterated much of 4th Avenue north of 28th Street.

Nicollet cars used Grant Street from Marquette to Nicollet Avenues, passing Wesley United Methodist Church. Photograph by Charles J. Hibbard; courtesy of the Minnesota Historical Society.

Nicollet

Years of operation: 1879–1954 (Motor Line 1879–90)

Paired with: Downtown only (1890–94), Washington Ave. N. (1894–1910), Nicollet from 31st and Hennepin via 31st as "1st Ave. So. & 20th Ave. No." to 32nd & Penn Ave. No. (1900–1905), Central (1910–19), 2nd St. N.E. (1919–54), part of service paired with Northwest Terminal (1920–48), part of service paired with Monroe (1952–54)

Service frequency: Five minutes off-peak; three minutes (or less) peak

Nicollet was so heavily trafficked that it was rarely necessary to consult a schedule. Standing loads were not unknown even during off-peak hours. The neighborhoods and businesses paralleling Nicollet Avenue provided a steady stream of riders. Small shopping districts grew up along the line at 54th Street and 38th Street with a nearly continuous strip of businesses from Lake Street all the way to downtown Minneapolis. Thirty-eighth Street was a busy transfer point for the 38th Street crosstown bus. The intersection of Lake Street and Nicollet Avenue

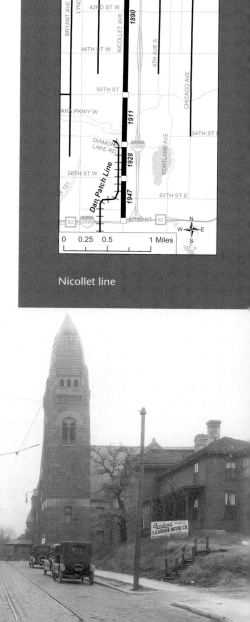

Nicollet line

A southbound Nicollet car rolls over the Minnehaha Creek bridge.

Nicollet Avenue and 26th Street, now the heart of the "Eat Street" restaurant district in south Minneapolis. Photograph courtesy of the Minneapolis Public Library, Special Collections.

Nicollet Avenue, looking north from 17th Street, where Interstate 94 now crosses, and before Oak Grove Street was truncated east of Blaisdell Avenue. Photograph by Norton & Peel; courtesy of the Minnesota Historical Society.

Nicollet Avenue, with a car in the Diamond Lake Road wye. *Minneapolis Journal* photograph; courtesy of the Minnesota Historical Society.

Streetcars directly served the two ballparks in the Twin Cities, Nicollet Park at 31st Street and Nicollet Avenue in south Minneapolis and Lexington Park at University and Lexington Avenues in St. Paul. The Minneapolis Millers and St. Paul Saints were known for their "streetcar" doubleheaders. After the first game in one city, the crowd would pile onto streetcars and travel to the rival ballpark for a second game a couple of hours later. Nicollet Park is letting out as the streetcars from the adjacent Nicollet Station wait. Photograph courtesy of the Minnesota Historical Society.

was one of the busiest transfer points in the system. Nicollet cars passed by Ramsey Junior High and Washburn High School and were well used by students. TCRT's Nicollet Station was located at 31st Street and Nicollet, across the street from the Nicollet Ball Park, itself a big draw for passenger traffic on game days.

Grand

Years of operation: 1907–52
Paired with: Downtown only (via Nicollet 1907–9), via Lyndale (1909–10), returned to Nicollet Avenue in 1910 then paired with Johnson (1918–20), Monroe (1920–52)
Service frequency: Fifteen minutes off-peak; extra service provided during rush hours

The Grand Avenue leg of the Grand–Monroe was a latecomer compared to the rest of the system. Its 1907 construction was an accommodation for residents in the neighborhoods between Nicollet and Lyndale Avenues. They faced a long walk to either the Nicollet or the Bryant lines. The Grand line always competed for riders with the nearby Nicollet line and to some extent Bryant as well. Along Nicollet Avenue, north of Lake Street, Grand cars shared tracks with Nicollet cars and divided the business with them.

There were operational problems. Grand Avenue is narrow, and during the winter streetcars had a difficult time getting by parked automobiles. Company snowplows had it much worse. On encountering a parked car, frustrated

Grand line

The Minneapolis, St. Paul, Rochester & Dubuque Electric Traction Company

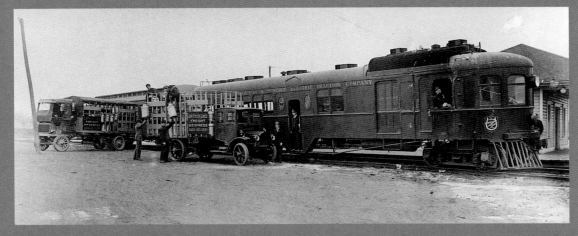

Colonel Marion Savage was a promoter extraordinaire, and he loved horses. In 1902, he bought the famous pacer Dan Patch for $60,000, the highest price ever paid for a horse at that time, and transformed him into a national icon. The colonel owned a 750-acre farm near Hamilton, Minnesota (renamed Savage in 1904). The farm was a showpiece for his International Stock Food Company, which manufactured animal feeds and medicines and sold them by mail order. It boasted a huge heated stable with an onion dome, a one-mile track, and a half-mile covered track. It was nicknamed the Taj Mahal. Savage installed Dan Patch in this palace and used the horse's image and his name to promote his livestock feed. When Dan Patch was not at the farm, he was touring the country in a private railroad car, drawing large crowds at state and county fairs. He set an all-time record, covering a mile in one minute and fifty-five seconds, at the Minnesota State Fair on September 8, 1906. The colonel made a fortune from his feed business and built a large estate, now the site of the Minnesota Masonic Home, on the bluffs of the Minnesota River in Bloomington overlooking the farm.

Sometime during 1905, the colonel conceived the idea that a railroad from his farm to Minneapolis would not only bring visitors to the farm but could be a self-sustaining common carrier if it were built into southeastern Minnesota and northern Iowa. He and other investors incorporated the Minneapolis, St. Paul, Rochester & Dubuque Electric Traction Company in 1907 with the objective of building an interurban electric railway from Minneapolis to Rochester via Northfield, Faribault, and Owatonna. At Rochester it was to connect with a proposed line from Rochester to Dubuque via Decorah, Iowa. Another leg was to be built from St. Paul to a connection with the main line near Lakeville, Minnesota.

Construction on the first phase began in 1908 from 50th Street and Nicollet Avenue, where the line would connect with the TCRT's Nicollet streetcar line and use TCRT's tracks to reach downtown Minneapolis. From 50th and Nicollet, the line would run south through Richfield and Bloomington, cross the Minnesota River at Savage, and continue on through Lakeville to Northfield. Work was completed to Northfield in 1910.

The railroad marketed itself as the Dan Patch Electric Line and adopted as its logo a lightning bolt superimposed on a horseshoe. Unfortunately, the name and the logo were not as effective in attracting investors as they had been at selling livestock feed, and the company was unable to raise enough money to put up

wires and electrify its operations. Instead, it purchased three gas-electric passenger cars from the Strang Gas-Electric Car Company. Although it continued to plan for electrification, the railroad was never able to do so and went on in subsequent years to acquire additional gas-electric equipment from the General Electric-Wason Manufacturing Company. It also purchased a gas-electric freight locomotive from General Electric. It was the first gas-electric freight locomotive used by an American railroad and, today, is in the collection of the Minnesota Transportation Museum.

To promote traffic the company developed a resort and picnic grounds on forty acres adjoining Lake Marion near Lakeville. The elaborate facilities at what was called Antlers Park included picnic kitchens, a baseball park and grandstand, a dancing and orchestra pavilion, a miniature railway, and cabins and cottages that could be rented for longer stays. Boats and canoes were available for rent, and the company operated a steam-powered launch on the lake.

A repair shop was constructed at 60th Street and Nicollet Avenue. In 1912, the company built a passen-

From 1912 until 1928, Nicollet Avenue streetcars terminated at this depot at 54th Street (now Diamond Lake Road). Passengers transferred here to the gasoline-electric powered railcars of the Dan Patch Line for Bloomington, Savage, and Northfield.

ger terminal at 54th Street (now Diamond Lake Road) and Nicollet Avenue, where it exchanged passengers with TCRT's streetcars. TCRT had earlier extended its own line south on Nicollet from 50th to 54th.

To gain a direct entry to Minneapolis for both freight and passenger traffic, the company in 1913 built a new line from what came to be called Auto Club Junction (near the site of the clubhouse of the Minneapolis Automobile Club on the Minnesota River bluffs) through Edina and St. Louis Park to a connection with the Electric Short Line Terminal Company near what is now Glenwood Avenue and Highways 55 and 100. It also obtained trackage rights over the Electric Short Line to its passenger station at 3rd

Avenue North and 7th Street. That same year it began running through passenger trains to Mankato and Randolph on trackage rights over the Chicago Great Western Railway.

This aggressive expansion put severe financial strains on the railroad, and it was nearly insolvent when Colonel Savage passed away unexpectedly on July 13, 1916. His famous horse Dan Patch had died on July 11, and it is thought that the shock of the loss was too much for him. Three days later on July 16, 1916, the Dan Patch Line entered receivership. The receiver ordered curtailment of the through passenger services to Mankato and Randolph and sold most of the passenger equipment. Antlers Park also was sold.

The Minneapolis, Northfield & Southern Railway was incorporated in South Dakota in 1918 and subsequently purchased the Dan Patch Line at a foreclosure action. The new owners resolved to reinvigorate the property and moved to develop its potential as a bypass for freight traffic moving through the Twin Cities. In 1927, an extension was built north through Crystal to a connection with the Soo Line Railway. A trackage rights agreement was negotiated with the Soo Line giving it access to the Soo's Shoreham Yards and the Northtown yards of the Northern Pacific. The Minneapolis, Northfield & Southern now had connections and could interchange traffic with the Rock Island and the Milwaukee Road at Northfield, the Chicago Great Western at Randolph, and the Soo Line, the Northern Pacific, and the Great Northern in Minneapolis, the latter at its Cedar Lake Yards. It also pursued an aggressive plan for industrial development and succeeded in locating several high-volume shippers along its line in Richfield, Bloomington, and Edina. One of its biggest online customers was the Cargill complex in Savage. In later years it developed the Air Lake Industrial Park in Lakeville.

While it turned to freight for most of its revenues, it also attempted to revive the passenger business, reinstating service to Mankato in 1921, a move that proved unsuccessful. There was simply too much automobile competition, and the trains came off in 1931. All passenger service to Northfield ended in 1942. The railroad acquired a number of steam locomotives and used them in freight service until 1948, when it began switching to diesel power.

The Minneapolis, Northfield & Southern was purchased by and merged into the Soo Line in 1982. Its role as a freight belt had declined, and much of its interchange traffic had dried up as a result of railroad mergers and deregulation. However, several important shippers remain in 2006. They are served by Progressive Rail, which operates portions of the line under an agreement with Canadian Pacific Rail, which purchased the Soo Line in the late 1980s.

motormen could only pull on the whistle cord until someone came out to move the offending vehicle or a police officer arrived to tag it and call for a tow truck. Another method was to manually bounce and shove the auto until it was clear. Just as often, the streetcar simply kept going, leaving the creased automobile behind it.

Most lines ended in a wye, rather than a turning loop. Most wyes were located in the middle of intersections, but the Grand Avenue line in south Minneapolis ended just short of 48th Street, at this midblock wye.

Located at North Seventh Street and Holden Street, this is the joint downtown Minneapolis depot of the Minneapolis, Northfield & Southern (Dan Patch Line) to Northfield, the Minnesota Western (Luce Line) to Hutchinson and Gluek, and the Minneapolis, Anoka & Cuyuna Range electric interurban to Anoka. Later it served suburban bus companies. The site is now the 7th Street parking garage over Interstate 394. Photograph courtesy of the Minneapolis Public Library, Special Collections.

Like many streets, Grand Avenue, shown here at 36th Street, was unpaved. The rolled oil-and-dirt surface did not stand up well to the spring thaw. The street was also narrow, creating numerous conflicts with parked cars during the snowy winters. *Minneapolis Star-Journal Tribune* photograph; courtesy of the Minnesota Historical Society.

Bryant line

Bryant

Years of operation: 1890–1953
Paired with: Downtown only (1890–91),
    Monroe (1891–1920), Johnson (1920–53)
Service frequency: Ten minutes off-peak; five
    minutes peak

It took a few years for the Bryant Avenue alignment to sort itself out. From 1884 to 1887, horsecars used Lyndale Avenue as far as 27th Street, then followed 27th to Dupont Avenue South, then along Dupont to 45th Street. The Dupont to 45th segment was abandoned in 1887. The area had not developed, and there was insufficient business. The line was electrified in 1890 and new track put down from Lyndale and 28th Street along 28th to Hennepin Avenue. The track on 28th was short lived and taken up the following year. Electric cars then began running out Lyndale Avenue to 31st Street, to Bryant and then along Bryant to 38th Street. Extensions came along in subsequent years, as the neighborhoods in southwest Minneapolis filled in. A concrete streetcar-only bridge was built across Minnehaha Creek at Bryant and the line extended to 56th Street and Bryant in 1931. Bryant evolved into one of TCRT's more productive lines, serving the prosperous, mainly Scandinavian, middle-class neighborhoods of southwest Minneapolis. There were few businesses along the line except for small

grocery, drug, and hardware stores at major cross streets. Small commercial districts grew up at 36th Street, 46th Street, 50th Street and Bryant Avenue, and at 50th Street and Penn Avenue. Lyndale Avenue and Lake Street became a strong commercial corner because of its proximity to the Bryant and Selby lines.

TCRT built a wye at 54th Street and Penn Avenue, but it selected a rather puzzling location for one of the legs. The intersection of Penn and 54th is on a level grade except for the east side of 54th, which has an abrupt downhill slope. For whatever reason, TCRT chose to place the "tail" of the wye on the east side of 54th rather than on the level grade to the west. That determination had some embarrassing consequences. Periodically, a motorman would have trouble stopping or holding a car on the steep grade, and it would roll off the end of the tracks and keep going

A PCC bangs over the 50th Street and Bryant Avenue wye on its way to 56th Street.

all the way to the bottom of the hill. Then the wrecker would have to be summoned and the errant car winched up the grade until its wheels were on the rails and its trolley pole could reach the overhead wire. Even though this happened with such regularity that it became a neighborhood joke, TCRT never moved its tracks to the other side of the intersection.

Over the years TCRT operated several feeder bus routes in conjunction with the Bryant line. The first, in 1927, met the streetcars at the end of the line at 50th and Bryant. Transferring passengers could ride the bus to 58th and

The single-track extension on Penn Avenue South from 50th Street to 54th Street crossed the scenic valley of Minnehaha Creek on a couple of short, steep grades. Single track was employed as a cost-saving measure on the outer ends of some lines, where a car could make the round trip on the single-track segment before its follower came along.

The Bryant and Oak–Harriet lines met at 50th Street and Penn Avenue South. Photograph by Norton & Peel; courtesy of the Minnesota Historical Society.

St. Louis Park

Years of operation: 1892–1938
Paired with: Connection at Hennepin Avenue (1892–1907), Downtown only (1907–14), Robbinsdale (1914–20), Downtown only (1920–38)
Service frequency: Twenty minutes off-peak; extra service provided during rush hours

An independent company, the Minneapolis Land & Investment Company, originally operated the St. Louis Park line until 1906, when it was purchased by TCRT. Before May 1907, cars ran only as far as Lagoon and Hennepin Avenues, and passengers transferred to one of the Lake Harriet lines. After May 1907, with the line under TCRT ownership, cars began running all the way downtown on Hennepin Avenue.

The bathhouse at Calhoun Beach was a major summertime attraction. That, together with the neighborhoods along Hennepin and the Uptown neighborhood, also served by the Como–Harriet, provided most of the line's business. Settlement was sparse along West Lake Street between Lake Calhoun and the end of

Lyndale. This shuttle ended in 1931 when the Bryant line was extended to 56th Street. The Penn Avenue shuttle bus began in 1947, operating from 54th and Penn to the Minneapolis city limits at 62nd Street and Penn. It was incorporated into the Bryant–Penn bus route that replaced the streetcars in 1953. The Penn–Bryant shuttle ran between 54th and Penn and 56th and Bryant, connecting the two branches of the streetcar line. It operated from 1949 to 1953 and was replaced by the Nicollet–Lyndale branch of the Nicollet Avenue bus.

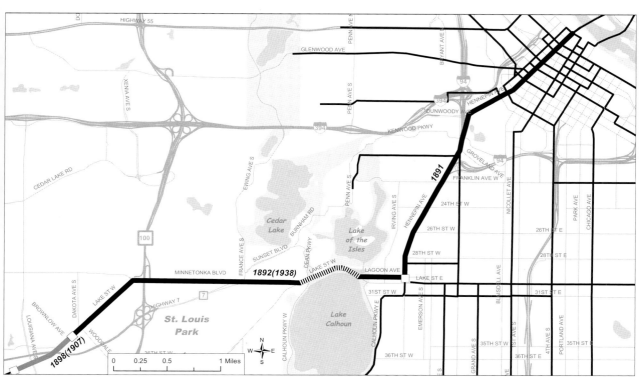

The St. Louis Park line diverged from the Como–Harriet at Lagoon Avenue, by the new movie theater of the same name, since remodeled and renamed the Uptown. Photograph by Norton & Peel; courtesy of the Minnesota Historical Society.

the line at Brownlow Avenue. Thus, in 1938, when plans were announced to widen and improve the highway on the north side of Lake Calhoun, the company decided to switch to buses rather than relocate its tracks. The line became part of the Kenwood–St. Louis Park bus, which was routed via Cedar Lake Avenue and France Avenue to West Lake Street. A separate West Lake Street bus ran between France Avenue and West Lake Street and Hennepin Avenue and Lake Street, providing a connection with Uptown and the Selby–Lake streetcar. In 1947, as St. Louis Park developed after World War II, limited service was extended beyond Brownlow Avenue to Highway 7 and Texas Avenue, future site of the Knollwood Shopping Center.

East- and westbound streetcars on the St. Louis Park line frame the huge Lake Calhoun bathhouse on the lake's north shore. Photograph courtesy of the Library of Congress.

The Minneapolis Land & Investment Company

The Minneapolis Land & Investment Company was the creation of Thomas B. Walker, Calvin Goodrich, Thomas Lowry, Charles Pillsbury, and Louis Menage, among others. It was formed in 1890 to sell land for industrial development in St. Louis Park and proved remarkably successful, attracting the Monitor Manufacturing Company, Jarless Spring Carriage Company, Thompson Wagon Company, and the Minneapolis Esterly Harvester Company.

Incidental to its land business, the company acquired a franchise from St. Louis Park to build a streetcar line from Minneapolis into St. Louis Park to transport workers to the plants. Service opened in December 1892 on a line from 29th Street (Lagoon Avenue) and Hennepin Avenue around the north shore of Lake Calhoun, then out Lake Street in St. Louis Park all the way to Brownlow Avenue.

If the line prospered at all, its prosperity was short lived. The Panic of 1893 shuttered Monitor Manufacturing and Minneapolis Esterly Harvester. Thompson Wagon burned to the ground. In 1897, however, the economy picked up, and the company planned an extension into Hopkins that would proceed south along Monk Avenue in St. Louis Park to Excelsior Boulevard, then turn west on Excelsior Boulevard into Hopkins. Work on the extension was completed in 1899, and the line opened for service.

Three or four cars were rented from the Minneapolis Street Railway Company to open service in 1892. They were used until 1893 when three cars were delivered by the St. Louis Car Company. These cars were double-ended, approximately forty-five feet long, and rode on two trucks. (A double-ended car has two sets of motorman's controls and trolley poles, one at each end of the car. This feature eliminates the need for a turning wye, or loop, at each end of the line. To reverse direction the motorman pulls down one trolley pole, puts up the other, and goes to the other end of the car to resume operation in the opposite direction.) The Hopkins extension required more cars, which were leased from TCRT.

Troubles returned in 1902 and again in 1904. In 1902, the company's carhouse was struck by lightning and burned to the ground, taking with it one of the cars. In 1904, the rebuilt carhouse was badly damaged by a tornado. The same storm blew over a car at the end of the line in St. Louis Park.

TCRT, realizing potential for growth and development in St. Louis Park and Hopkins, determined to make the operation part of its system and purchased the property in November 1906, merging it into the Minneapolis & St. Paul & Suburban Railway. The Hopkins extension was abandoned the following year in favor of TCRT's own line on private right of way from 31st Street and Irving through southwest Minneapolis and Morningside to Hopkins and Lake Minnetonka. Service to St. Louis Park via Lagoon and West Lake Street continued.

The Minneapolis Land & Investment Company opened the St. Louis Park line with these two ornate Pullman Company products. This is the line's carhouse in St. Louis Park.

Kenwood

Years of operation: 1890–1938
Paired with: Downtown only (1890–1902), Oak and Como, some trips routed with 8th St. S.E. (1902–11), Johnson Street (1912–18), E. 25th St. (1918–20), Downtown only (1920–21), E. 25th St. (1921–38)
Service frequency: Twenty minutes off-peak; extra service provided during rush hours

Kenwood was home to Minneapolis's wealthiest and most prominent citizens, including TCRT

In 1937, a year before abandonment, a Kenwood car lays over on Penn Avenue at 21st Street, next to Kenwood School.

Kenwood line

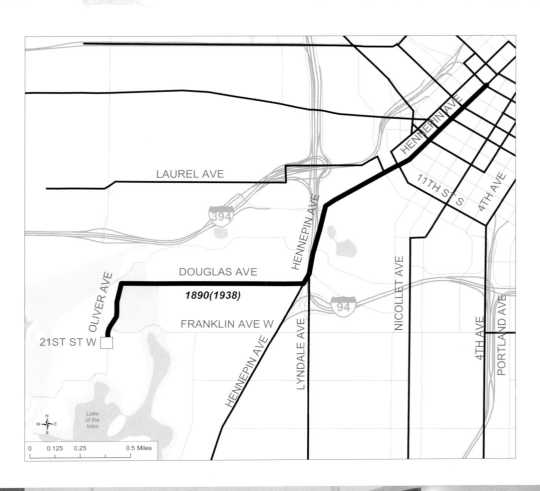

One of the earlier streetcar-to-bus conversions replaced the Kenwood and St. Louis Park lines with a single bus route, shown on its first day of service in 1938. Photograph from the Minneapolis Star and Tribune News Negative Collection; courtesy of the Minnesota Historical Society.

president Thomas Lowry. Few of its nobles rode streetcars, but the maids, cooks, and housekeepers did. Buses took over in 1938, and the line became part of the St. Louis Park route. In 1940, it was extended and routed through downtown Minneapolis as the Kenwood–St. Louis Park–Russell N., taking over the 6th Ave N. streetcar service, which was abandoned because of the construction of Olson Memorial Highway.

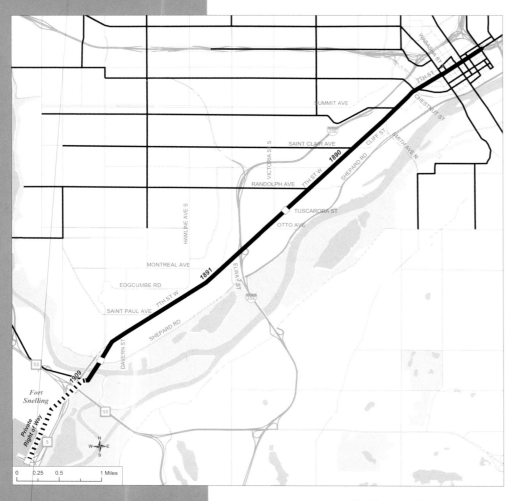

West 7th St. line
Ft. Snelling Shuttle

St. Paul Lines
West 7th St.

Years of operation: 1890–1952
Paired with: Downtown only (1890–93), East
7th St. (1893–1952), Snelling–Minnehaha
(1909–36), Hazel Park (1927–32), Hope
Street (1932–39), Maria (1939–52),
through service to Minneapolis via
Ft. Snelling (1909–36).

An eastbound Maria-Ft. Snelling
car on West 7th Street passes
Davern Street.

Service frequency: Ten minutes off-peak;
extra service provided during rush hours

West 7th Street, also called Fort Road, made
an almost straight line from downtown to Ft.
Snelling, paralleling the Mississippi. Along
the way, it served Anker Hospital, Schmidt
Brewery, and the Randolph Street shops of
the Chicago, St. Paul, Minneapolis & Omaha
Railroad. Several other lines operated over por-
tions of West 7th Street, including Randolph–
Hazel Park, St. Clair–Payne, Dale–Phalen, and
Grand–Mississippi.

At St. Clair Avenue, St. Clair cars diverged
while those of the Randolph and West 7th
St. lines continued on West 7th Street. The
Kessler and Maguire Funeral Home remains
in business today at the same location.
Photograph by Charles P. Gibson; courtesy
of the Minnesota Historical Society.

Randolph

Years of operation: 1891–1900, 1906–52
Paired with: From 1891 to 1900, on Randolph from West 7th Street to Mississippi River Road, abandoned, no service (1900–1906), Downtown only (1906–9), Hope Street (1909–15), East 7th St. (1915–21), Hazel Park (1921–27), Hope Street (1927–32), Mahtomedi (1932–51), Hazel Park (1932–52)
Service frequency: Ten minutes off-peak; five minutes peak

TCRT opened this line in 1891 as the Randolph Extension on Randolph Avenue from West 7th Street to the Mississippi River Road only to abandon it and remove the tracks in 1900. The area did not develop as rapidly as expected, presumably, in part, because of the lingering effects of the financial panic of 1893. Service returned in 1906 as far as Randolph and Pascal Street, but it was extended again, in 1909, to Snelling Avenue. Six years later, in 1915, cars began running north on Snelling Avenue to Como Avenue. Then, in 1916, track was built on Randolph beyond Snelling to Cleveland Avenue with a shuttle car running between Snelling and Cleveland and a connection with the main line to downtown St. Paul. The shuttle was dropped in 1921, and Randolph cars began running from Cleveland and Randolph all the way to downtown St. Paul. The Ford plant was completed in 1924, and another shuttle line opened from Randolph and Cleveland along Cleveland to Ford Parkway and the Ford plant. Through service to the Ford plant began in 1925, and in 1927 the E. 25th St. line was extended across the new Ford Parkway bridge to provide a connection to Minneapolis. Besides the Ford plant, Randolph served a trio of Catholic schools, Cretin High School, Derham Hall High School, and the College of St. Catherine, as well as an important shopping area that grew up at the intersection of Cleveland Avenue and Ford Parkway.

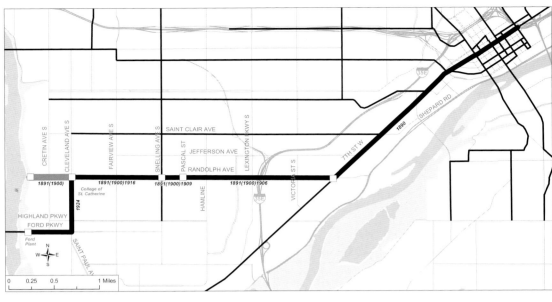

Randolph line

The Highland Park neighborhood filled in after World War II, introducing the strip mall form of retail at Cleveland Avenue and Ford Parkway. Photograph by Norton & Peel; courtesy of the Minnesota Historical Society.

The curving tracks that allowed streetcars to turn from Randolph Avenue to Snelling Avenue were used by cars running Not In Service to and from Snelling Station. This was also a relief point, where the afternoon crew would relieve the morning crew, while the streetcar remained in service. It was not uncommon for a car to see three crews a day. Photograph courtesy of the Minnesota Historical Society.

Streetcars from Minneapolis and St. Paul terminated at the front entrance of the newly constructed Ford assembly plant in Highland Park. Photograph by Norton & Peel; courtesy of the Minnesota Historical Society.

St. Clair

Years of operation: 1915–52
Paired with: Hope Street (1915–27), Payne
(1927–48), Phalen Park (1948–52)
Service frequency: Ten minutes off-peak;
Extra service provided during rush hours

Streetcars came very late to St. Clair Avenue, the first segment opening on St. Clair from West 7th Street to Oxford Street in 1915, with an extension to Cleveland Avenue in 1922. The St. Clair line traversed an area that was entirely residential, notably the southern edge of the Macalester Park Addition, better known as Tangletown. The neighborhoods west of Snelling Avenue to the Mississippi River and south of St. Clair, including all of Highland Park, did not fill in until after World War I. In fact, some undeveloped areas persisted until the late 1940s and early 1950s. The residential character of the area and the absence of schools, businesses, and other sources of traffic made St. Clair one of St. Paul's less heavily traveled lines.

A westbound St. Clair Avenue car pauses at Snelling Avenue in 1952.

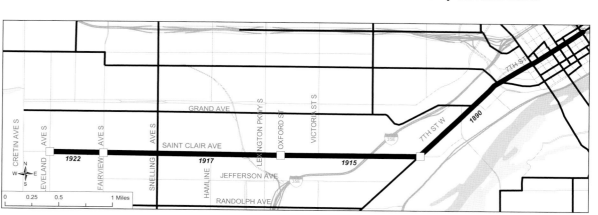

St. Clair line

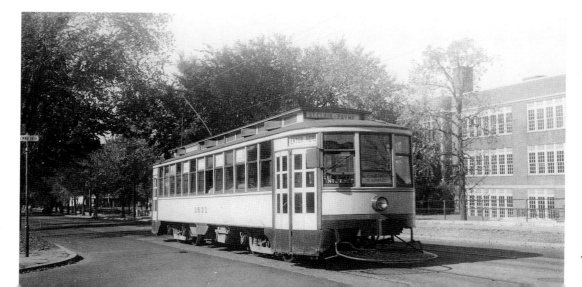

Passing Groveland School, on St. Clair Avenue at Kenneth Street.

Grand line

Grand

Years of operation: 1890–1952
Paired with: Downtown only (1890–1902), Payne (1902–10), Downtown only (1910–20), Payne (1920–27), Downtown only (1927–39), Mississippi (1939–52)
Service frequency: Ten minutes off-peak; five minutes peak

Horsecars appeared on Grand Avenue from Dale Street to Victoria Street in 1883 as part of the St. Anthony Hill line. Four years later, track was laid out of downtown on Ramsey and Oakland Avenues (both now renamed Grand Avenue), creating a separate Grand Avenue line.

Grand Avenue at Dale Street in the 1930s, looking much the same as it does today. The Dale Street line turned at this point.

This Grand Avenue car has just left the end of the line at Cretin Avenue.

Grand Avenue at Oxford Street typifies the tree-lined streets of the Twin Cities before Dutch elm disease took its toll. Photograph courtesy of Forrest Johnson.

The earlier route on Dale Street was discontinued. In 1887 and 1888, the St. Anthony Hill line was abandoned, and Grand Avenue combined with service to the West Side on Winifred and Ohio Streets (via downtown St. Paul) as the Oakland Avenue and West St. Paul.

Grand Avenue was St. Paul's first electric line, commencing operation on February 22, 1890. The neighborhoods on and along Grand subsequently grew into one of St. Paul's finest residential areas, with St. Thomas College, St. Paul Academy, Macalester College, and a concentration of businesses west of Dale Street providing additional traffic.

Rondo

Years of operation: 1891–1948
Paired with: Payne (1891–1902), Maria (1902–39), Stryker (1939–48)
Service frequency: Fifteen minutes off-peak; extra service provided during rush hours

The Rondo line had a long and historic association with St. Paul's African American community. Unfortunately, because of its largely residential character and the absence of a good traffic base, it was always a weak line in terms of overall business. It had no western outlet. The

The Cathedral of St. Paul and the James J. Hill house look down from the ridge at a westbound Grand Avenue car on Ramsey Street (now Grand Avenue) at Smith Avenue. Photograph by Charles P. Gibson; courtesy of the Minnesota Historical Society.

line passed the Catholic Orphan Home on Milton Street and ended abruptly at Griggs Street just short of Concordia College. Moreover, unlike parallel lines on University and Selby

Rondo line

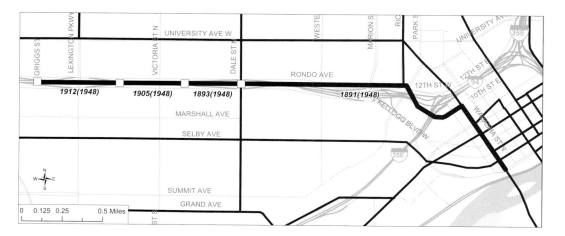

Avenues, it had no crosstown connection with Snelling Avenue. Although it did cross the Dale line, the absence of a western outlet and a Snelling Avenue connection discouraged ridership because westbound passengers had to travel all the way downtown to make connections with other lines rather than transferring at Snelling Avenue. TCRT had plans to convert the line to buses in the late 1930s and would have done so had World War II not intervened. It eventually became a bus route in 1948 and was extended west along St. Anthony Avenue to Pelham Boulevard and Doane Avenue and the Town and Country Golf Club. In the late 1950s, the Minnesota Highway Department made plans for Interstate 94 from downtown St. Paul to Minneapolis. Rondo Avenue and the neighborhoods around it were obliterated once construction got under way in the 1960s.

Everything in this photograph of Rondo Avenue at Arundel Street is gone, replaced by Interstate 94. Photograph courtesy of the Minnesota Historical Society.

The Rondo Avenue line ended at Griggs Street, within sight of the Snelling Shops, yet there was no track connection. Montgomery Ward is in the distance. Photograph courtesy of the Minnesota Historical Society.

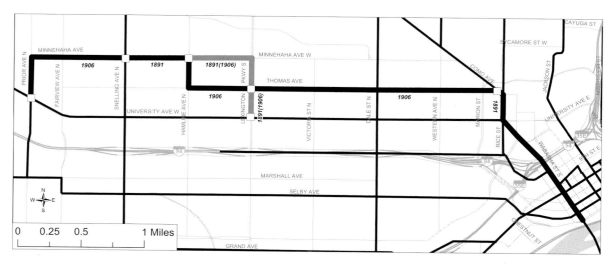

Hamline line

Hamline

Years of operation: 1891–1952
Paired with: Downtown only (1891–1900),
  Jackson (1900–1908), Downtown only
  (1908–20), S. Robert (1920–38), Stryker
  (1938–39), Cherokee Hts. (1939–52)
Service frequency: Ten minutes off-peak;
  five minutes peak

The "Hamline" name seems misplaced because streetcars never used Hamline Avenue for more than a few blocks. When the line opened in 1891, Hamline Avenue was not used at all, although the line always passed near Hamline University. The route, instead, followed University Avenue west to Lexington Avenue, north to Minnehaha Avenue, west to Snelling Avenue, then north along Snelling to Como Avenue.

The Hamline, Como–Harriet, Western, and Rice lines shared Rice Street between Como and University Avenues, where this photo was taken. Photograph courtesy of the Minnesota Historical Society.

An eastbound PCC car on Minnehaha Avenue crosses Snelling Avenue.

In 1906, it was reoriented to serve residential neighborhoods along Thomas and Minnehaha Avenues as well as the Northern Pacific Hospital and the manufacturing and industrial plants served by the Minnesota Transfer Railway near Prior and University Avenues. Most of its traffic was eastbound, directed toward downtown St. Paul. However, its connection with the St. Paul–Minneapolis line at University and Prior

Avenues attracted westbound riders headed for destinations along University Avenue, the Minneapolis campus of the University of Minnesota, or downtown Minneapolis. During World War II, the Sperry plant at Prior and Minnehaha Avenues manufactured the Norden bombsight, employing hundreds of workers, many of whom used the Hamline–Cherokee line to reach the plant.

Snelling

Years of operation: 1905–52
Paired with: Randolph (1909–21)
Service frequency: Fifteen minutes off-peak;
ten minutes peak

By the end of the streetcar era, Snelling Avenue had evolved into an important crosstown line through St. Paul's Midway district connecting the three intercity lines and the Hamline–Cherokee, Grand–Mississippi, St. Clair–Payne, and Randolph–Hazel Park lines. Snelling Avenue cars served Como Park, Bethel College, the Minnesota State Fair, Hamline University, and Macalester College. It was also a regular route for pull-in and pullout cars from the Snelling carhouse and shop complex at Snelling and University Avenues.

Seen from the window of Snelling Station, a Snelling car crosses University Avenue.

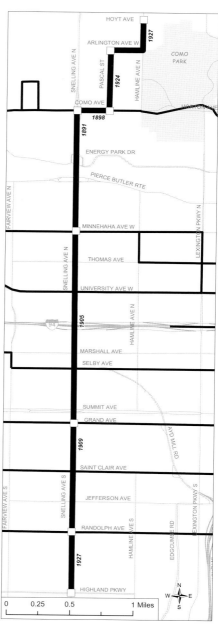

A southbound Snelling car crosses the Hamline line at Minnehaha Avenue.

A shuttle bus began service in 1947. From Snelling and Como Avenues, and a connection with the Como–Harriet and Snelling Avenue car lines, the buses operated north on Snelling to Larpenteur Avenue. The route was extended beyond Larpenteur to Roselawn Avenue in 1947. It was made a part of the Snelling Avenue bus service in 1952.

Northbound Snelling Avenue cars entered from the right, turned right onto Como Avenue and shared the Como–Harriet line tracks for two blocks to Pascal Street, where they turned left and continued to the end of the line at Hamline and Hoyt Avenues. Photograph courtesy of the Minnesota Historical Society.

The Snelling line ended in a wye at Highland Parkway, just down the hill from the landmark Highland water tower. Photograph by C. J. Amos; courtesy of the Minnesota Historical Society.

This view is looking east on Maryland Avenue, with the turning wye in the foreground. Most of the system was double track, but single track was employed as an economy measure at the outer ends of some lines, where service was infrequent and two cars would never have to meet.

Dale

Years of operation: 1914–52
Paired with: Forest (1914–48), Downtown
　only (1948–52)
Service frequency: Fifteen minutes off-peak;
　ten minutes peak

Although it ran all the way to downtown St. Paul on tracks it shared with the Grand Avenue line, Dale was primarily a crosstown link connecting the Grand Avenue line with Selby–Lake, Rondo, St. Paul–Minneapolis, Hamline–Cherokee, and Como–Harriet cars. It also served Como Park from the end of the line at Maryland Avenue and Wheelock Parkway, as well as the Great Northern Railway's large Dale Street shop complex.

The Dale–Hoyt was a bus feeder that connected the end of Dale car line at Dale Street and Maryland with the end of the Snelling line at Hamline and Hoyt Avenues via Hoyt and Maryland.

The Dale Street line ended on Maryland Avenue, across the parkway from the east shore of Lake Como.

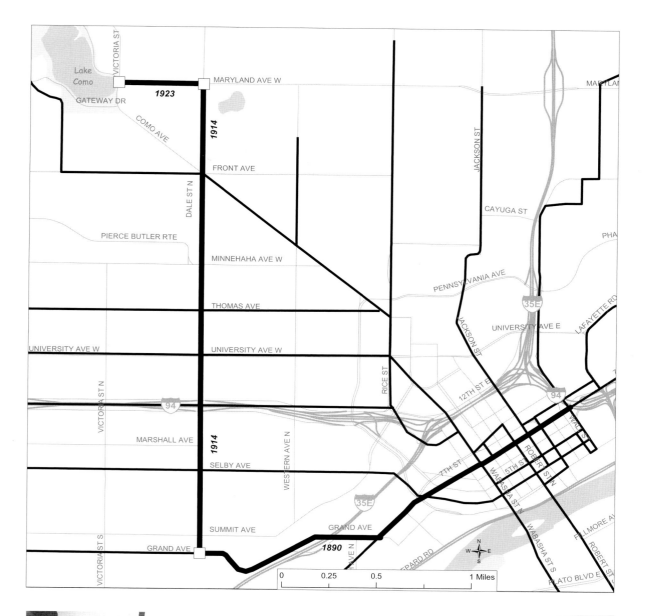

Dale line

Looking north on Dale Street at University Avenue. Photograph by Norton & Peel; courtesy of the Minnesota Historical Society.

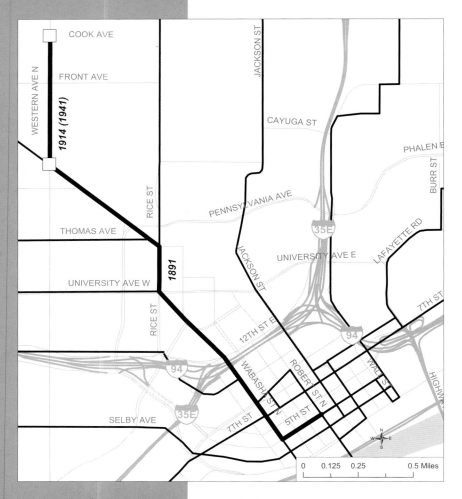

Western line

From 1932 until abandonment in 1941, cars on the Western line no longer went downtown. Instead, a single streetcar shuttled back and forth on less than a mile of track to a connection with the Como–Harriet line at Western and Como Avenues. Surplus following the elimination of the Stillwater local lines in 1932, small, lightweight car 3 was converted to double-end operation and assigned to Western. Here the motorman waits at Como for the connection.

Western

Years of operation: 1914–41
Paired with: S. Robert (1914–20), Jackson (1920–32), shuttle car (1932–41)
Service frequency: Fifteen minutes all day (shuttle car)

TCRT had a few star-crossed lines that never did enough business to fully justify their operation but nonetheless survived for many years because they served isolated neighborhoods or were too politically troublesome to abandon.

Through service was uneconomic, because there were too few passengers to justify running a car all the way downtown. Western is one example; Merriam Park and the Ft. Snelling Shuttle are others.

Western was paired with other lines from 1914 until 1932 but was orphaned thereafter. From 1932 and until 1941, it operated as a shuttle

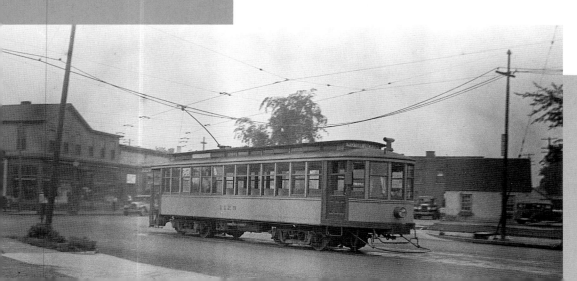

Because of its early abandonment, photos of the Western line are rare. Here it shares the Como–Harriet and Hamline tracks on Como Avenue at Rice Street.

on Western Avenue from Cook Avenue to Como Avenue where it met the Como–Harriet.

Western was unique because it used a double-ended car that did not require a wye or loop to turn around at either end of the line (a double-ended car had controls at both ends). The Western run was so short that it would have taken more time to turn the car around than make a complete trip from one end of the line to the other. It became a bus route in 1941.

Western was made part of the Como–Stryker bus route when the Como–Harriet line was abandoned in 1953.

Rice

Years of operation: 1891–1952
Paired with: S. Robert and South St.
Paul (1891–1914), South St. Paul
(1914–20), Stryker (1920–32), South
St. Paul (1932–52)
Service frequency: Ten minutes off peak;
extra service provided during rush hours

Rice, along with the Como–Harriet–Hopkins, St. Paul–Minneapolis, and Hamline–Cherokee lines, passed the State Capitol and all of the state government buildings on Wabasha Street. The North End neighborhood along Rice Street was lined with small business establishments, which, along with the nearby Dale Street and Jackson Street shops of the Great Northern Railway, provided traffic for the line.

Between 1891 and 1914, Rice was paired with both the South St. Paul and the S. Robert lines. Cars alternated between them.

Beginning in 1948, a bus route connected the outer ends of the Rice and Mississippi lines. That service was discontinued in 1950. During the summers of 1936–38, a bus connected the end of the Rice car line with McCarrons Beach north of Larpenteur Avenue.

Rice line

This car is leaving the wye at the north end of the Rice Street line at Ivy Avenue, just south of the bridge over the Northern Pacific Railway.

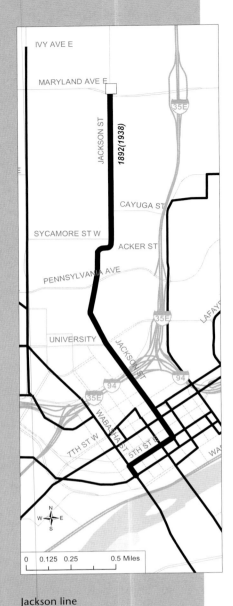

Jackson line

The alignment of Jackson Street is interrupted by this short, one-block jog at Acker Street. Photograph by Kenneth Melvin Wright; courtesy of the Minnesota Historical Society.

Jackson

Years of operation: 1892–1938
Paired with: Downtown only (1892–1900),
  Hamline (1900–1908), Stryker (1908–20),
  Western (1920–32), Stryker (1932–38)
Service frequency: Fifteen minutes off-peak;
  extra service provided during rush hours

Bracketed by railroad yards on the east and Oakland Cemetery on the west, the Jackson Street neighborhood took in a relatively small, lightly populated area. The Great Northern Railway's Jackson Street Shops, partially preserved today by the Minnesota Transportation Museum, provided some ridership, but the Jackson line was never heavily trafficked.

Jackson Street was an early horsecar line that was converted to electric power in 1892. It was a double-tracked, but clearances were unusually tight, and ten streetcars assigned to the line had to have their bodies moved an inch off center to prevent them from rubbing when they passed. These being older cars, the need to replace them combined with the line's low ridership made it an ideal candidate for bus conversion. It was combined with the S. Robert line in 1938, and buses took over. Bus service was extended from Maryland Avenue to Arlington Avenue in 1951.

Mississippi

Years of operation: 1890–1952
Paired with: Cherokee Hts. (1890–1920),
  Merriam Park (1920–32), Cherokee Hts.
  (1932–39), Grand Avenue (1939–52)
Service frequency: Ten minutes off-peak;
  five minutes peak

The Mississippi line passed through an industrial and railroad area north of downtown, separated by the isolated Williams Hill neighborhood that overlooked the Westminster railroad junc-

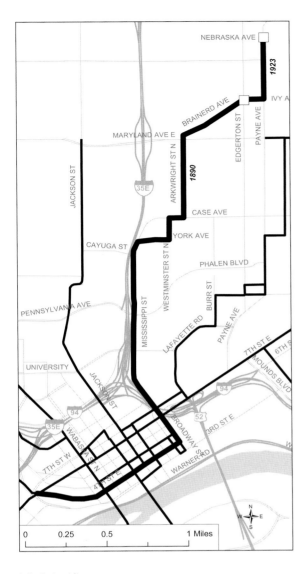

Mississippi line

tion, where the main line from St. Paul Union Depot divided into three routes—the Omaha Road going east to Wisconsin and the Northern Pacific and Great Northern lines going west toward Minneapolis. It then entered an older, working-class residential area. In 1923, the line was extended into a developing, middle-class neighborhood along Payne Avenue north of Maryland Avenue. Most of the line's traffic came from these residential neighborhoods and local industries.

The track on Mississippi Street passed through an area dominated by industry and railroads. To the right is Williams Hill, a long-gone residential neighborhood atop a hill that has since been leveled. The railroad cars are constructing a spur line to the new 8th Street freight terminal. Photograph courtesy of the Minnesota Historical Society.

Two PCC cars meet at the end of the line wye at Payne and Nebraska Avenues. Photograph by George Krambles; courtesy of the Steve Legler Collection.

A southbound Mississippi Street car on Payne Avenue at Wheelock Parkway.

Looking north on Payne Avenue from Minnehaha Avenue East. The Hamm Brewery is a block to the east, out of the photograph. Photograph courtesy of the Minnesota Historical Society.

Payne

Years of operation: 1891–1952
Paired with: Rondo (1891–1902), Grand Avenue (1902–10), Downtown only (1910–20), Grand Avenue (1920–27), St. Clair (1927–52)
Service frequency: Fifteen minutes off-peak; ten minutes peak

The Payne line traversed a rail terminal and industrial area along Lafayette Road. It served the working-class Railroad Island neighborhood, so named because it was surrounded on all sides by tracks, including the roundhouses of the Northern Pacific and Omaha Road. It passed the Hamm Brewery but traveled only a short distance up the Payne Avenue commercial strip, using parallel Greenbrier Street to avoid the steep hill approaching Maryland Avenue. It also served Johnson High School.

In 1927, the Payne Avenue line was extended east on Maryland Avenue from Duluth Street to Kennard Street. On the way it passed under the Northern Pacific's line from St. Paul to Duluth, now a bike trail. This extension was abandoned in 1948.

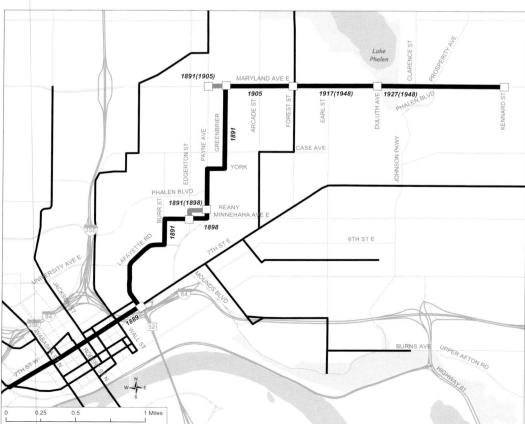

Payne line

At York Avenue, the tracks swung off Payne Avenue a block east to Greenbrier Street. Photograph courtesy of the Minnesota Historical Society.

In 1927, TCRT extended the line on Maryland Avenue to Kennard Street in response to new housing on Maryland east of Lake Phalen. A reorientation and retrenchment occurred in 1948, and track on Maryland Avenue east of Forest Street was abandoned and the line routed on Maryland and Forest to Phalen Park, displacing the former Dale–Phalen through route. Dale cars began turning around in downtown St. Paul.

Forest–Phalen Park

Years of operation: 1913–52
Paired with: Downtown only (1913–14), Dale (1914–48)
Service frequency: Fifteen minutes off-peak; ten minutes peak

Forest–Phalen Park served the Northern Malleable Iron plant (later Whirlpool and 3M) and the Arcade Street commercial strip. Just south of Phalen Park, it served the Minnesota Home for Children, later the Gillette Children's Hospital.

Service to Phalen Park began in 1905 as part of the Payne line from Greenbrier Street and Maryland Avenue via Maryland and Forest

Forest–Phalen Park line

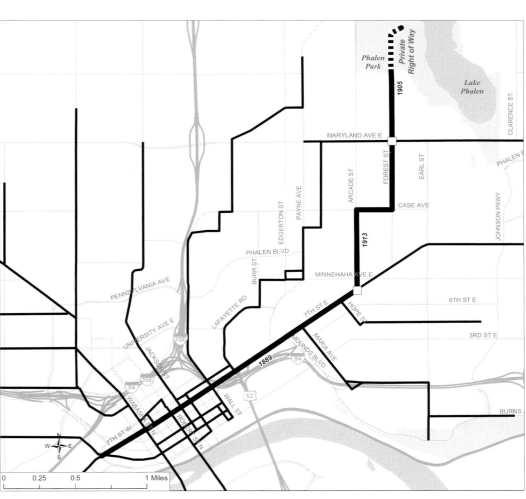

At East 7th and Arcade Streets, Phalen Park cars turned left, while Hazel Park and Mahtomedi cars continued straight on 7th. Photograph courtesy of the Minnesota Historical Society.

Leaving Phalen Park, this downtown-bound car is about to enter Forest Street at Wheelock Parkway.

St. Paul is hillier than Minneapolis: witness Arcade Street looking south from York Avenue. Photograph courtesy of the Ramsey County Historical Society, St. Paul, Minnesota.

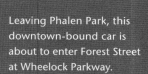

The Phalen Park station was located near the western shore of the lake. To reach it, cars traveled on a private right of way through what is now the golf course.

Street to Phalen Park. Within Phalen Park, the lane operated on a half mile of private right of way to a double track loop adjoining a large brick waiting station near the western shore of Lake Phalen. This was a busy line on summer weekends with extra cars added to accommodate bathers and picnickers.

Hazel Park–Mahtomedi

Years of operation: 1890–1952
Paired with: Downtown only (1899–1917), Randolph–Snelling (1917–21), Randolph (1921–27), Ft. Snelling with through service to Minneapolis (1927–32), Randolph (1932–52).
Service frequency: Ten minutes off-peak; seven minutes peak (to city limits at Hyacinth Avenue)

The line was built and operated by the St. Paul & White Bear Railroad, an independent company, before it was acquired by TCRT in 1899.

Hazel Park–Mahtomedi cars, along with Maria, Hope Street, and Forest–Phalen Park cars, followed East 7th Street out of downtown St. Paul, climbing a long 5 percent grade once surmounted by cable cars of the East 7th Street line. The other lines diverged at Maria, Hope, and Arcade Streets. The Hazel Park line

continued on, passing the TCRT's Duluth Avenue Station and entering private right of way at White Bear Avenue, before turning north to cross the Omaha Railroad tracks on a single-track bridge that remains in use today as a bike trail. Local Hazel Park cars turned on a wye at Hyacinth Avenue, the St. Paul city limits. Mahtomedi cars stayed on the right of way, proceeding through North St. Paul, passing Wildwood Park, and then swinging around the east side of White Bear Lake before terminating at a wye in Mahtomedi. TCRT's branch to White Bear Lake diverged from the Mahtomedi line at Wildwood Park. Its line to Stillwater broke off at Willernie just east of Wildwood.

The lines to White Bear Lake and Stillwater were abandoned in 1932. Wildwood Park closed in 1938. Thereafter, Randolph–Hazel Park cars

The Phalen, Hazel Park, and Hope Street lines shared East 7th Street, which passed over the railroad throat leading north from the St. Paul Union Depot. The bridge was rebuilt under traffic in 1929. St. John's Hospital is at right. Photograph courtesy of the Minnesota Historical Society.

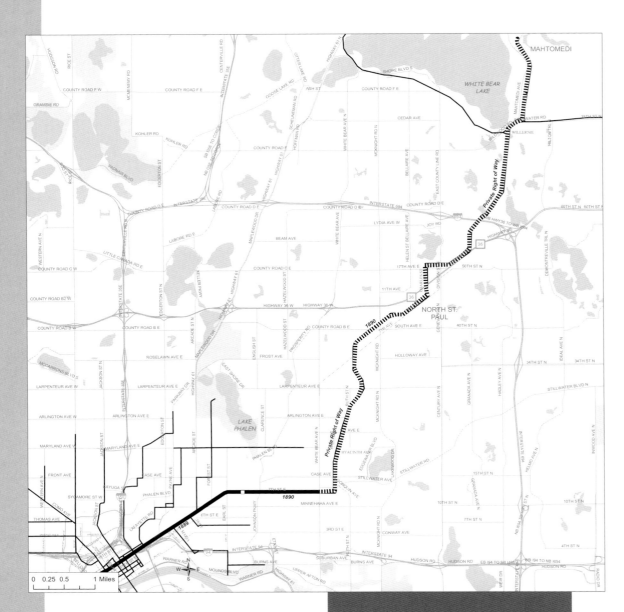

Hazel Park–Mahtomedi line

A northbound Mahtomedi car crosses Larpenteur Avenue and enters Maplewood on the way to North St. Paul.

This is the Hyacinth Avenue wye on Furness Parkway in the Hazel Park neighborhood, where local cars terminated and double track ended. Service beyond this point was handled by Mahtomedi cars.

Trolleys in Your Neighborhood

The Hazel Park–Mahtomedi line crossed the Omaha Railroad on this single-track bridge. Its private right of way aligned with Hazel Street. The bridge survives today and the right of way is a bike and pedestrian trail. Photograph courtesy of the Minnesota Historical Society.

maintained frequent local service at far as the city limits at Hyacinth Avenue. Mahtomedi cars operated hourly from downtown St. Paul with a few cars added to the schedule during morning and evening rush hours. North St. Paul, Mahtomedi, and the area around White Bear Lake were largely undeveloped and rural, so the hourly service was more than adequate. TCRT ended all rail operation beyond Hyacinth Avenue in November 1951. The Arcade–Maryland bus line was extended to North St. Paul with a shuttle bus between there and Mahtomedi. Service to Hyacinth ended in May 1952, when the Randolph–Hazel Park line became a bus route.

Pennsylvania Siding, on the Mahtomedi line in North St. Paul. At this point the track was running behind the commercial buildings fronting the commercial district on 7th Avenue.

This picture captures the country trolley feel of the single-track Mahtomedi line. Motorman Kirt Blewett took the photograph as his car waited for a meet at Colby Siding in North St. Paul.

North of the Soo Line railroad crossing in North St. Paul, the tracks ran along the east edge of Henry Street. At each passing siding was a company phone booth, where the motorman would check in with the dispatcher and receiver clearance to proceed.

A Minnesota Railfans Association fan trip turns on the Willernie wye. The track in the foreground went to Mahtomedi, on the left to Stillwater, and on the right to St. Paul. Photograph courtesy of the Minnesota Historical Society.

A block south of the Mahtomedi wye, a southbound car skirts Hamline Lake.

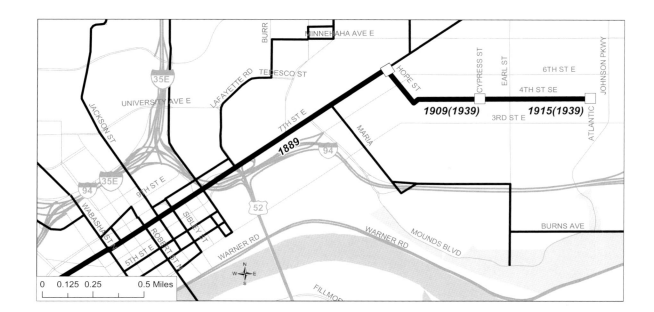

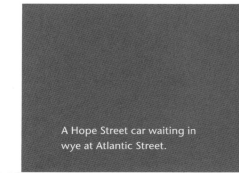

Hope line

A Hope Street car waiting in wye at Atlantic Street.

Hope

Years of operation: 1909–39
Paired with: Randolph (1909–15), St. Clair (1915–27), Randolph (1927–32), Ft. Snelling–Minnehaha (1932–36), Ft. Snelling (1936–39), through service to Minneapolis via Ft. Snelling (1932–36).
Service frequency: Ten minutes off-peak; extra service provided during rush hours

Hope Street served a neighborhood with no major source of traffic other than local residents and a few small businesses. This factor, plus competing bus service on nearby 6th Street, made the line ripe for early abandonment. TCRT discontinued all rail service in 1939, and there was no bus substitution. This was the only line in the system where streetcar service was discontinued without replacement bus service. Presumably, riders switched to the nearby East 6th Street–Stillwater bus.

Maria

Years of operation: 1887–1952
Paired with: Shuttle car (1891–93), Downtown only (1893–1902), Rondo (1902–39), West 7th St.–Ft. Snelling (1939–52)
Service frequency: Fifteen minutes off-peak; extra service provided during rush hours

Following electrification in 1891, a shuttle car operated on Maria Avenue to a connection with the cable line on East 7th Street. When the cable line was converted to electricity in 1893,

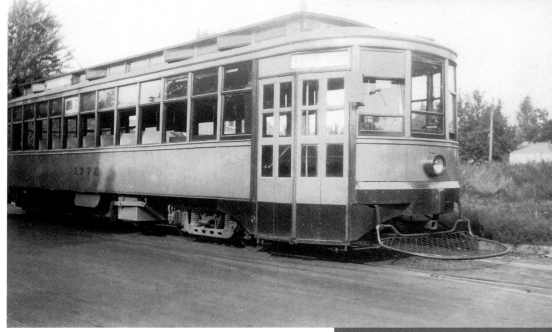

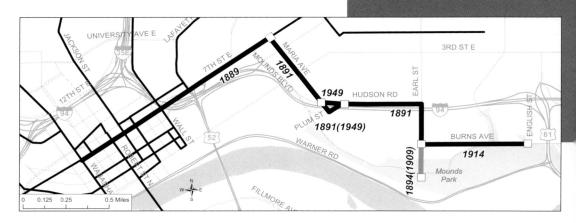

Maria line

The east end of the Maria line on Burns Avenue was single track. This was formerly the free Burns Avenue shuttle.

cars began running from downtown St. Paul via East 7th Street to Maria Avenue, then on to Indian Mounds Park.

TCRT abandoned its track on Earl Street between Burns Avenue and Indian Mounds Park

in 1909. It then became involved in a dispute with the city of St. Paul. The city, prompted by residents, demanded that TCRT extend the line farther east along Burns Avenue. TCRT balked, claiming there was insufficient business, but the city persisted and eventually ordered the company to build the line. TCRT complied, constructing a single track along Burns Avenue between Earl and Clarence Streets. However, rather than providing direct service to downtown St. Paul, it chose to run a shuttle car, forcing people to transfer. Even though it was a free shuttle, most riders thought it a spiteful gesture. TCRT defended its actions by pointing out that there was not enough business to justify through service and that a free shuttle was much cheaper to operate. The combined wages

Looking south on Earl Street at Hudson Road, before the 1949 construction of Highway 12 removed the building on the left. Note how the tracks are spaced farther apart on the curve so that two opposing streetcars could pass without scraping. Photograph by *St. Paul Pioneer Press-Dispatch*; courtesy of the Minnesota Historical Society.

In 1949, Highway 12 was opened through the east side of St. Paul, including this grade separation at Earl Street. Photograph by *St. Paul Pioneer Press-Dispatch*; courtesy of the Minnesota Historical Society.

So. St. Paul

Years of operation: 1891–1952
Paired with: Rice (1891–1920), Downtown only (1920–32), Rice (1932–52)
Service frequency: Ten minutes off-peak; extra service provided during rush hours

of a conductor and motorman were ten dollars a day, and the shuttle only took in three dollars. By eliminating the conductor and running a free car, the company figured it would only lose two dollars a day, not seven. The shuttle lasted until 1931, becoming something of a legend. On summer days neighborhood kids would swarm aboard the car and ride it back and forth all day. TCRT complained about the nuisance but residents thought it was a fair arrangement given the company's obstinacy in not providing better service. Finally, TCRT relented: the shuttle was discontinued, and residents got their one-seat ride downtown.

The Maria line served the Dayton's Bluff neighborhood on St. Paul's East Side along Maria Avenue, Hudson Road, and Earl Street. It was mostly residential, with modest commercial development. The Mounds Park Sanitarium (later Mounds Park Hospital) was located near Burns and Earl and was served by the Maria line. The construction of four-lane Highway 12 through the east side of St. Paul in 1948 replaced the jog via Maria to Plum Street to Hudson Road with a more direct route directly from Maria to Hudson. Buses took over in 1952.

South St. Paul grew up around a large livestock market and meat-processing center. Its Union Stockyards Company and the Swift and Armour packing plants employed hundreds of workers. Those who did not live in South St. Paul took the streetcar to get to jobs there, and those who lived in South St. Paul took the streetcar to St. Paul to do business in the capital city. Besides the city of South St. Paul, the South St. Paul line was well patronized by St. Paul neighborhoods and local businesses along Concord and Robert Streets. It had good traffic in both directions and was a solid contributor to TCRT's bottom line. From 1915 until its abandonment in 1928, cars of the St. Paul Southern Electric Railway,

The So. St. Paul line followed Concord Avenue as it wound along the base of the Mississippi River bluffs.

The Concord Avenue line served the South St. Paul stockyards. From 1914 to 1928, it also hosted the St. Paul–Hastings interurbans of the St. Paul Southern. This rare photo captures northbound TCRT and St. Paul Southern cars meeting a southbound St. Paul Southern car and a TCRT car parked in the Marie Avenue wye. Photograph courtesy of the Library of Congress.

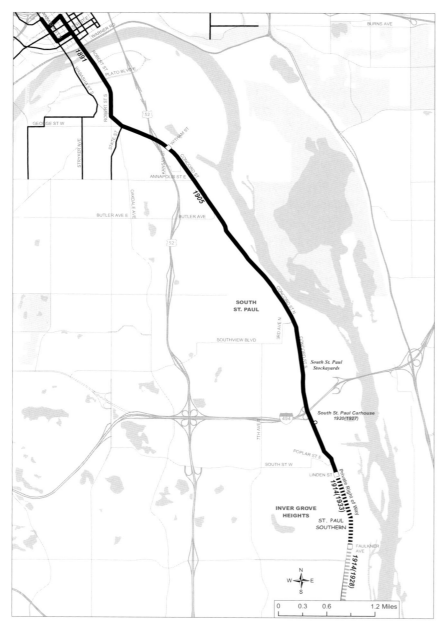

So. St. Paul line

an ill-fated interurban that ran between St. Paul and Hastings, used TCRT's Concord Street tracks to reach downtown St. Paul. When the Southern quit, TCRT briefly extended its South St. Paul service a short distance over the former Southern line from Concord and Linden to Faulkner Avenue and Francis Street in Inver Grove. The extension did not attract enough business and was discontinued five years later in 1933. In 1920, the company constructed a small carhouse and yard on Concord Street between Richmond and Malden Streets to store extra cars for the shift changes at the meat-packing plants. The facility only lasted seven years. Depression layoffs at the packing plants and declining traffic resulted in the closure of the carhouse in 1927.

The Concord Avenue line ended at the Linden Street wye in sleepy Inver Grove. The long-gone St. Paul Southern interurban's tracks to Hastings began just in front of the streetcar. They can be seen curving toward the side of the road.

There are no known photographs of the South St. Paul carhouse on Concord Street, but it survives as a truck parts warehouse. From 1920 to 1927, the building and an adjoining yard were used to store and maintain cars between shift changes at the packing plants.

S. Robert

Years of operation: 1891–1938
Paired with: Rice (1891–1914), Western
(1914–20), Hamline (1920–38)
Service frequency: Fifteen minutes off-peak;
extra service provided during rush hours

S. Robert was originally a horsecar line that began operation in 1887 after completion of the first Robert Street bridge. It was converted to electric power in 1891. The line shared track with cars for South St. Paul as far as State Street. There it diverged, following State Street up the bluff and rejoining Robert Street at the top of the grade. It continued on Robert Street to Annapolis Street and the city limits with West St. Paul.

The neighborhood along State Street and on South Robert Street to the city limits was mainly residential except for a few small businesses catering to local needs. South Robert Street from the bridge to State had a number of small manufacturers, warehouses, and tav-

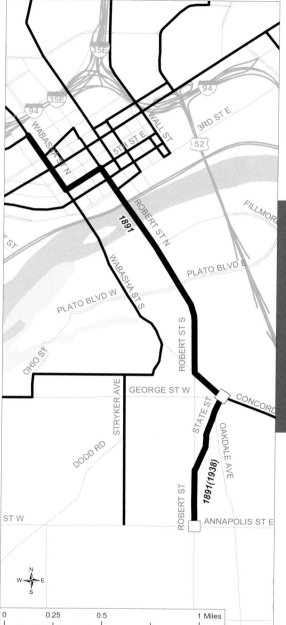

S. Robert line

erns. American Hoist and Derrick built a large plant on South Robert just across the river from downtown St. Paul. For much of the past century, South Robert was home to St. Paul's Mexican American community.

Competition appeared after World War I in the form of an independent company, the South

St. Paul Southern Electric Railway

Promoters boasted that the St. Paul Southern Electric Railway would connect Rochester with St. Paul by way of Hastings, Cannon Falls, Red Wing, and other intermediate points, but it never laid a rail beyond Hastings. Instead ,the Southern, as it came to be known, achieved distinction as one of the least successful interurban electric railways ever built.

The company was incorporated in Delaware in 1913 and immediately issued construction specifications for the building and equipping of an electric railway that would "extend from a point in the City of South St. Paul (where connection will be made with the end of the Inver Grove line of the Twin City Rapid Transit Company) to respective points in the business center of Rochester, Minnesota and of Red Wing, Minnesota, passing through a number of intervening communities, and to such other points as shall be mutually agreed on by the Railway Company and the Construction Company within the one hundred and twenty-five miles (125) miles specified in contract attached hereto."

The line would have a maximum grade of 2.5 percent, use seventy-pound rail set on white oak ties in gravel ballast. Six electric substations along the route would take high-voltage alternating current from the River Falls Power Company and convert it to 600-volt direct current for delivery to the trolley contact wires. There would be a private telephone system for dispatching. Eighteen passenger cars, four express cars, and two electric locomotives were to be acquired. Passenger cars would have a top speed of sixty miles per hour. There were to be three carbarns. Two, one at each end of the line, in Inver Grove and Rochester, were described as terminal carbarns. The third, to be built at an unspecified location, would be a general shop and office building for heavy repairs and use as a crew base. The company would make its headquarters in the Pioneer Building in St. Paul.

This ambitious prospectus was never completely fulfilled. When it opened on November 17, 1914, the St. Paul Southern had completed only 17.54 miles of track from a connection with the Twin City Rapid Transit Company's South St. Paul–Inver Grove line at Concord and Linden Streets to a wye at 2nd and Tyler Streets in downtown Hastings. There were a few scattered farms along the line but little development except near Inver Grove and Hastings. From Inver Grove the single-track line climbed out of the Mississippi River valley roughly paralleling the Chicago Great Western and Rock Island Railroads. Cutting across country through farmland, it met and then ran alongside what became Highway 55. Taking a sharp turn to the east at Pine Bend, it again ran through open country, descending into Hastings on a 2.5 percent grade called Featherstone Hill. Once

in town, the line ran down 5th Street, to Vermillion Street then along 2nd Street to the wye at 2nd and Tyler Streets.

The Niles Car Company of Niles, Ohio, delivered four interurban cars in 1914 at a cost of $8,490.00 each. Two were combination baggage–passenger cars, and two were passenger cars. Interestingly, at a time when most electric railways were buying steel cars or cars with steel underframes (for safety and durability), these four were all wood, a type of construction the TCRT had abandoned in 1905. The cars were fifty-one feet long, weighed 59,000 pounds, and came with four seventy-horsepower motors capable of a top speed of fifty-five miles per hour. The baggage–passenger cars could seat forty-eight persons; the passenger cars, fifty-four. Painted a deep orange, they were classic interurbans with arched windows and clerestory roofs.

Although it eventually obtained a favorable agreement with TCRT to use its tracks to enter St. Paul, the company was not able to start through service until August 22, 1915. Until then, passengers had to transfer at Linden Avenue in Inver Grove, an arrangement that was hardly conducive to building ridership. To complicate matters, the River Falls Power Company was late in hooking up its high-tension line. Once the line was connected, cars still had trouble getting in and out of Hastings because of low voltage. Another substation was needed but never built.

By the end of 1914, promoters had spent $611,000, all of it borrowed money, to build and equip the Southern and would need to raise many thousands more to complete the line. The company was also pressuring its creditors to take stock instead of cash to shore up its shaky treasury, a sure sign of troubles. Still, Hastings put on a huge civic celebration on November 17 to welcome the first car.

When through service began, schedules called for hourly departures from downtown St. Paul and Hastings. The first and last cars from Hastings were at 6:15 a.m. and 10:15 p.m., respectively, and from downtown St. Paul at 5:40 a.m. and 11:10 p.m., with cars taking approximately ninety minutes to cover the 24.85 miles from downtown St. Paul to Hastings at a scheduled speed of eighteen miles per hour, hardly a high-speed performance. Cars could manage upward of thirty-five or forty miles per hour on their own private right of way but were slowed considerably once they entered TCRT tracks at Linden and Concord and fell into line with city cars making local stops on Concord and Robert Streets all the way downtown. Arriving there, they looped through the business district via 8th, Wabasha, and Fifth Streets, then back to Robert Street. The railroad did not have a downtown depot except for a short time, when it leased space

in a building at 109 East 8th Street to handle small items of freight and express carried on the cars. That depot, along with the freight agent's job, was abolished during 1917 as the road's finances deteriorated. At the same time its downtown routing was shortened to provide more recovery time in the schedule. That route was via 3rd, Sibley, and 5th Streets, then back to Robert Street.

At first the line did a modest commuter business between St. Paul and Hastings, and ridership looked encouraging. As the Dakota County seat, Hastings also attracted businesspeople and lawyers from St. Paul and South St. Paul on county government business. Traveling salesmen used it to call on Hastings merchants. It was also a popular and convenient way to go to St. Paul for shopping trips and medical appointments or to visit friends and relatives. For youngsters living on nearby farms, it was the "school bus" that took them to classes in Hastings. Afternoon dismissals occurred just before a car left town, and there are many stories of kids chasing the cars up Vermillion Street after school let out rather than waiting an hour for the next one to leave town. Fishermen from St. Paul used the cars to reach Spring Lake, a popular recreation spot on the Mississippi River.

However, casual riders, commuters, traveling salesmen, students, and fishermen would never provide enough revenue, much less a profit. Nor was there any carload freight traffic. The line had a connection with the Chicago Great Western at Inver Grove, but there were no online shippers. And even if there were, the Southern never owned a locomotive that could haul a train of freight cars. Mail and express business was also light. For any hope of success, the Southern had

A St. Paul Southern interurban trundles down 2nd Street in Hastings, a block from the line's terminus at the Milwaukee Road's depot. Photograph courtesy of the Peter Bonesteel Collection.

St. Paul Bus Service, which followed the streetcar route out of downtown St. Paul to Annapolis Street, crossed the city limits on South Robert Street, and continued on to South St. Paul. TCRT acquired the company in 1925, keeping the parallel streetcar and bus service until 1938, when it abandoned all rail service along State and South Robert and merged the separate streetcar and bus routes into one line.

to reach Rochester and the intermediate towns, but it never did.

The Southern was in trouble. It was heavily mortgaged, and high interest rates on its outstanding debt made it impossible for the road to show a profit. Its first annual report detailing operations from November 17, 1914, to December 31, 1915, showed a gross income after operating expenses of only $1,742. Adding interest on the debt produced a net loss of $8,321. By 1918, the Southern was in receivership, and for a time it appeared the road might pull itself together given improved economic conditions after World War I. Unfortunately, those improved conditions also brought more improved roads and with them more automobiles, trucks, and buses. Things only got worse.

In a last-ditch effort in February 1926, the company petitioned the Minnesota Railroad and Warehouse Commission to restrict or eliminate the bus competition that was taking its business. Every business owner in Hastings signed the petition along with a thousand or more of its citizens. The commission declined any action.

The end came on July 31, 1928. The line had run out of money, and its rolling stock and track were so deteriorated that continuing operation was out of the question. Cars lurched and shuddered as they struggled up the grade out of Hastings. The proposed high-speed electric line of sixteen years before was reduced to a rolling, swaying pile of junk.

When the Southern ceased operations, TCRT extended its South St. Paul line over former Southern tracks from Concord and Linden streets in South St. Paul to Faulkner and Francis Streets in Inver Grove. This extension did not bring in enough business and it was abandoned in 1933.

Portions of the Southern's right of way could be seen into the late 1940s and 1950s until much of it was obliterated by highway construction. Tracks in Hastings streets were removed as part of a World War II scrap metal drive. By 2006, a short walking path at the west end of 5th Street was all that remained of the line in Hastings.

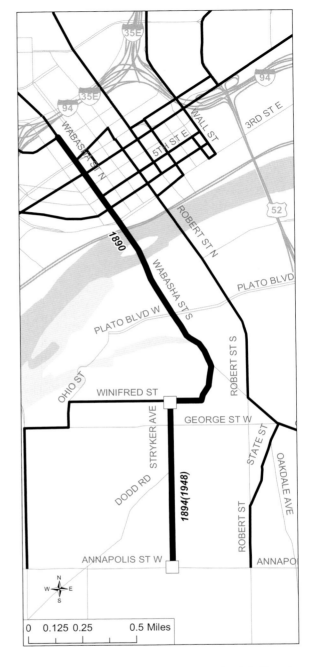

All the St. Paul west side lines, except for Concord Avenue, ended at Annapolis Street, the city limits. This is Robert and Annapolis Streets. Photograph by Kenneth M. Wright Studio; courtesy of the Minnesota Historical Society.

Stryker

Years of operation: 1894–1948
Paired with: Downtown only (1894–1907),
    Jackson (1907–20), Rice (1920–32),
    Jackson (1932–38), Hamline (1938–39),
    Rondo (1939–48)
Service frequency: Fifteen minutes off-peak;
    extra service provided during rush hours

Stryker was one of three lines, the other two being Cherokee Hts. and S. Robert, that climbed the bluff across the river from downtown St. Paul and ended at the city limits at Annapolis Street. Once they climbed off the river flats, all lines served residential neighborhoods, the occasional neighborhood store being the only commercial development. Because of its short length, residential character, and the lack of any substantial development in West St. Paul to lure riders across the city limits, Stryker was never a strong revenue producer for TCRT and, as a result, was paired with two other weak lines, Jackson and Rondo, for most of its existence as a streetcar line. TCRT liked to balance its service frequencies and tended to pair lines requiring similar levels of service on both sides of the downtowns. Stryker, like Rondo and Jackson, was an early bus conversion and was reunited with Rondo as the Rondo–Stryker bus route in 1948.

Cherokee Hts.

Years of operation: 1890–1952
Paired with: Mississippi (1890–1920),
    Downtown only (1920–32), Mississippi
    (1932–39), Hamline (1939–52)
Service frequency: Ten minutes off-peak; five
    minutes peak

The south end of the Rondo–Stryker line, at Stryker Avenue and Annapolis Street, the West St. Paul city limits.

St. Paul's first High Bridge over the Mississippi River was completed in 1889. It was the most direct route into St. Paul's developing west side and its Cherokee Heights neighborhood, and was heavily used by pedestrian, wagon, and, later, automobile traffic. However, the bridge could not handle the weight of streetcars, which took an alternate, modestly graded route out of downtown over the Wabasha Street bridge, then via Wabasha, Winifred, Ohio, and George Streets to Smith Avenue, continuing along Smith to an end of the line at the West St. Paul city limits.

Smith Avenue was named after Robert Smith, the St. Paul mayor who championed the building of the High Bridge. It intersects Dodd Road (today's State Highway 149), an early military route into southern Minnesota. Much of the early wagon and subsequent automobile and truck traffic turned off Dodd Road and followed Smith Avenue across the High Bridge into downtown St. Paul. That pattern of use, along with the Cherokee Hts. streetcar line, turned Smith Avenue into the west side's main commercial corridor. Grocery and drug stores, a movie theater, and other shops spread out along its length from the end of the streetcar line at Annapolis to George Street.

St. Paul's west side was, and remains, a largely residential neighborhood of medium-size homes and small businesses. That mix gave the Cherokee Hts. line an excellent traffic base, and it enjoyed considerable prosperity. In November 1952, Cherokee Hts. was among the last local lines in St. Paul to be converted to buses.

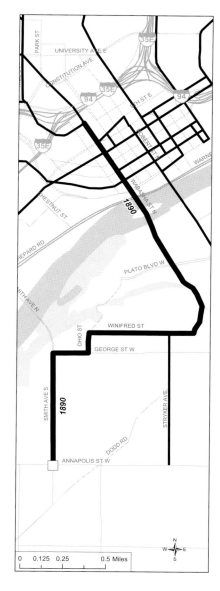

Cherokee Hts. line

Smith Avenue at Wyoming Street, on the Cherokee Hts. line around 1945.

Epilogue: Conspiracy Theories

There is a popular urban myth that General Motors executives, and others from the oil and rubber industries, conspired in a smoke-filled room to snuff out the streetcar; that they intentionally bought up street railway systems through a subsidiary company, National City Lines, with the object of junking them in favor of buses. It is so delicious and complex a tale of corporate skullduggery that Hollywood massaged it into a movie, *Who Framed Roger Rabbit?* Twin Cities' lore, in a variation of the same conspiracy, holds that Charles Green, Fred Ossanna, Isadore Blumenfeld (aka Kid Cann), Tommy Banks, and others were responsible for TCRT's postwar debacle and conspired to dismantle the streetcar system.

There was an investigation and an indictment and trial of GM and National City Lines and its executives for colluding in the sale of buses to transit systems that were owned by National City Lines, but these actions had nothing to do with the disappearance of the streetcar itself. Many of these systems were already bus operated when National City Lines acquired them, and some, like Los Angeles and Philadelphia, continued to use streetcars into the 1960s.

Similarly, Charles Green and Fred Ossanna presided over the scrapping of the Twin Cities streetcar system, but their actions are as much a criticism of the Strouse management, which should have begun conversion to buses immediately after World War II. As for conspiracies, count the number of automobiles sold between 1920 and 1950 and the miles of paved road laid down at public expense and compare them to the declining revenues of the streetcar companies. Then, indict everyone who bought an automobile in those years for conspiring to do away with the streetcar and America's privately owned transit systems. The cause of the streetcar's demise and the problems facing transit systems were much deeper and far more complex, but they all came down to one thing, money.

Like most transit systems in the United States, TCRT's assets were privately owned, but they were publicly managed by several government jurisdictions. Under the terms of franchise agreements with Minneapolis and St. Paul, TCRT was granted a monopoly of the public transportation market within the city limits. It also came under the jurisdiction of the

Minnesota Railroad and Warehouse Commission, an elected political body, on all matters relating to the fares it could charge for its service. In exchange for that monopoly, TCRT agreed to be regulated by, and therefore dependent upon, these elected political bodies. It was an equitable business arrangement for TCRT as long as it held that monopoly and the monopoly itself had value.

As more automobiles appeared after World War I and people became less dependent upon the streetcar, TCRT's hold on the local transportation market weakened, and its monopoly became less valuable because its service was subject to competition. In a few years, its "monopoly" would have little or no value whatsoever. The city governments and the state of Minnesota failed to accept this important change. It was not in their interests, nor was it in the interest of their constituencies, to redefine their regulatory responsibilities. Arguably, after about 1925 there was no longer any good reason for regulation of fares, service, or how that service was to be provided because TCRT was operating in a competitive market. Nationally, deregulation of local transit systems could have been of great help to the industry, much as deregulation revived the nation's railroads in the 1980s. Instead, policy makers refused to abandon the fantasy that these systems needed regulation and that the public needed protection from their business practices, even though the public was expressing its preferences at the automobile dealership. Consequently, transit systems, TCRT among them, were unable to charge fares that covered operating expenses and allowed an adequate return on investment.

In Minnesota, the Brooks Coleman Act gave the Railroad and Warehouse Commission authority to set fares after it had determined the value of the property and established what it believed was an adequate return on the value of the company's assets. The result was a cumbersome, contentious, and ultimately irrelevant process that never achieved a satisfactory resolution. The nickel streetcar fare was in effect from 1875 until 1920. That year the company won an emergency, one-cent increase, which became permanent in 1921. The next increase came in 1929, when the base fare went to a dime. The commission did not grant another adjustment until 1948, when it approved an eleven-cent cash fare. There were several interim changes involving the discounting of token sales, but these never amounted to more than a fraction of a cent. Amazingly, the commission actually reversed itself in 1943, when it rescinded an earlier increase in the token fare, arguing that TCRT was making too much money.

During this same period the nation's economy went through a series of spectacular contortions starting with World War I, and the inflation that accompanied it, followed by the bull market of the 1920s, the Great Depression, and the shortages and price controls of World War II. Employees demanding improved wages and fringe benefits confronted TCRT and organized under the Amalgamated Association of Street, Electric Railway and Motor Coach Employees. TCRT, as a regulated utility fearful of political and economic retaliation, was reluctant to challenge these demands and let employees go on strike. Instead, it agreed to arbitration, effectively turning over its fate to the judgment of third-party arbitrators, who during and after the New Deal were more sympathetic to the interests of workers than they were to transit companies.

Transit systems tightened their belts and hunkered down. As bus technology improved, most systems turned to them as a way to cut costs, but TCRT resisted. It didn't believe the bus could efficiently and economically replace the streetcar in heavy stop-and-go service. It lacked the streetcar's passenger capacity, its amenities, and its speed. At an average rush hour system speed of twelve miles per hour, TCRT ran one of the fastest surface transit systems in the country. Speed meant more efficient use of equipment because fewer vehicles, and fewer employees, could do the same work.

All of these factors offset the additional expense of maintaining track and power infrastructure—up to a point. In 1944, TCRT was spending twenty-eight cents per mile to operate its streetcars, twenty cents for buses. As riders slipped away, TCRT, like other systems, could not earn enough to cover the expense of its streetcar operations. The streetcar remained a superior transit vehicle, especially the PCC cars introduced just before World War II, but after the war it didn't really matter because riders were driving their cars to and from the suburbs, which leads to a rather interesting mystery.

TCRT was taking a careful look at its post-war situation during 1943 and 1944. It ordered a study of its operations by Gilman and Company and was making inquiries about trolley buses to other systems, among them Duluth, which had converted to trolleybuses in 1938. It was also aware of the high-capacity diesel transit buses that GM and Mack would bring out at the end of the war. These new buses came with automatic transmissions and could do the work of streetcars even on the heaviest lines. New York would buy hundreds of them in 1947 to convert all of its Manhattan surface operations.

TCRT management gave every indication that it would begin a changeover to buses. There was no mention of new PCC cars in the Gilman report, which recommended the company convert to buses over a span of ten years. Then, in 1944, the company announced a plan to buy PCC cars and placed an order with the St. Louis Car Company. It also ordered new buses from Mack, but they were smaller models, intended more as replacements for the buses that TCRT already owned.

The only explanation for this about-face is that TCRT's management sincerely believed the streetcar would continue to have an important role in its system, a belief supported by the Gilman report's modestly optimistic ridership projections. The company expected that ridership would decline as the auto industry returned to full production, but it did not foresee the drop in riders that actually occurred, nor, as things turned out, was it able to keep its operating expenses in line with revenues.

The accompanying table shows the effects of the postwar drop in ridership and revenues and the increase in operating expense. TCRT carried more than 201 million passengers in 1946 and earned $1,203,276. Just three years later, 1949, it carried 165 million riders and lost $797,715. It is disturbing that the Strouse management made no efforts to reduce operating expenses (and mileage) in 1947, 1948, and 1949, even though a ridership decline had already set in. Total bus and streetcar mileage actually increased in 1947 and 1948. In fact, the company was operating more miles of service in 1949 with fewer riders than in its peak postwar year, 1946, thereby creating the huge deficit that provided the justification for Charles Green's takeover.

TCRT Postwar Operations and Financial Performance

YEAR	PASSENGERS	MILES OPERATED	REVENUE	EXPENSE	PROFIT (LOSS)
1946	201,527,000	33,056,770	$16,320,684	$14,847,882	$1,203,276
1947	198,921,000	34,278,679	$16,680,822	$16,100,114	$355,309
1948	188,408,000	35,488,268	$18,948,941	$18,403,777	$302.992
1949	165,550,000	34,281,222	$18,558,568	$19,501,283	($797,715)
1950	140,441,000	31,596,658	$18,267,115	$18,205,263	$68,851
1951	127,959,000	29,561,781	$18,087,610	$18,388,865	($301,255)
1952	112,795,000	26,598,853	$16,991,580	$16,933,072	$58,508

Source: Twin City Rapid Transit Company Annual Reports.

TCRT eliminated conductors on the Nicollet Avenue line in 1949, but it was still using them on the Como–Harriet–Hopkins, and the St. Paul–Minneapolis lines and incurring additional expense. It spent almost $1 million for a new boiler at Main Steam Station in 1948. It purchased more PCC cars in 1947 for delivery in 1949 and added four blocks of new track on Nicollet Avenue in Minneapolis from 58th to 62nd Streets. The only bus conversions were the Rondo–Stryker, Northwest Terminal, and Robbinsdale lines in 1948, as well as the eastern end of Maryland Avenue in St. Paul. Meanwhile, the same work was being done with hundreds of employees in the track, power, and maintenance departments as had been done twenty years before.

The system needed new streetcars, and PCC cars would have had an important role in any postwar modernization program. However, had TCRT opted for high-capacity diesel buses and moved to convert the entire St. Paul system, along with the weaker Minneapolis lines, it would have saved hundreds of thousands of dollars, perhaps enough to thwart the staggering losses of 1949. That view was heard in 1949 during Railroad and Warehouse Commission hearings on proposed fare increases. Merrill D. Knox, a consulting engineer retained by the city of St. Paul, argued that the Twin Cities transportation system was obsolete and that all St. Paul operations should be converted to buses. Knox went on to state that more fare increases were inevitable because of maintenance costs and the inflexibility of streetcar service. Commissioner Clifford C. Peterson, opposing the fare increases, agreed, calling the current streetcar system "outmoded" and "costly to maintain." Both men were right.

Converting to buses in 1947 would have permitted closure of the Duluth Avenue carhouse and the separate bus garage in downtown St. Paul, consolidating all St. Paul operations at Snelling. Conversion of the weaker Minneapolis lines would have allowed similar consolidations. Fewer streetcars would have reduced electrical demand, postponing the need to replace aging generating and substation equipment, some of it dating from 1905. Even though there were technical issues, and Northern States Power's postwar rates were noncompetitive, ongoing discussions with NSP as it expanded its generating capacity might have led to a power purchase agreement permitting TCRT to completely dispose of its obsolete power system.

A progressive modernization plan would have rid the system of its expensive and unproductive streetcar infrastructure and services as quickly as possible and freed up cash from the change to upgrade both bus service and those rail lines and services that had potential—and there were several. The St. Paul–Minneapolis, Como–Harriet–Hopkins, Selby–Lake, Nicollet Avenue, and Chicago Avenue lines, with new equipment, might have remained viable streetcar operations and become the core of a future light-rail system.

The Strouse management's stubborn loyalty to the streetcar was tragically wrong. By trying to keep them all and preserve the status quo, it destroyed any possibility of retaining and improving the productive parts of the rail system. By 1950, Charles Green and Fred Ossanna had no options. The streetcar had to go.

Across the country public transit faced an uncertain future in the postwar years. Few big-city systems remained in private hands after 1960. Most sold out or were condemned and taken over by public authorities usually after lengthy and often contentious receiverships. In the Twin Cities, and Minnesota, the attitude was one of disinterest and neglect. The activities of the Green–Ossanna management provoked indignation but little action on the part of public officials. For certain, there was absolutely no support for public ownership and operation. Editorials in Minneapolis and St. Paul newspapers lamented the situation but expressed serious reservations about a metropolitan transit authority. At bottom there was no constituency for transit and would not be for almost twenty years.

TCRT's postwar policies only made things worse. Its management lived in another era, when good service and top-notch equipment could be counted on to attract riders to the system. The words of company president D. J. Strouse, speaking to the press in 1945, say it all: "We are convinced that the streetcar is as necessary to most people as it ever was. The thousands who have to ride streetcars and the other thousands who prefer them, are entitled to good cars and good service, and they are going to have them."

President Strouse had it only partially right. People were entitled to good cars and good service, and TCRT provided them—even though both were becoming more and more irrelevant.

Paradoxically, everyone loved the streetcars, but no one was riding them.

Appendixes

Appendix A

TWIN CITY RAPID TRANSIT
RIDERSHIP TOTALS

YEAR	CASH FARE	TOKEN FARE	MINNEAPOLIS STREETCARS	ST. PAUL STREETCARS	SUBURBAN STREETCARS	TOTAL STREETCARS	TOTAL BUSES	TOTAL BUSES AND STREETCARS
1900	$0.05		31,175,781	22,407,460	2,700,861	56,284,102		56,284,102
1901	$0.05		34,959,790	24,828,123	3,222,044	63,009,957		63,009,957
1902	$0.05		40,441,715	27,770,189	3,619,067	71,830,971		71,830,971
1903	$0.05		45,868,321	31,041,910	3,934,361	80,844,592		80,844,592
1904	$0.05		49,219,657	32,179,821	3,988,686	85,388,164		85,388,164
1905	$0.05		54,630,975	35,073,275	4,962,446	94,666,696		94,666,696
1906	$0.05		62,543,084	40,388,363	6,263,538	109,194,985		109,194,985
1907	$0.05		67,494,352	42,696,966	7,223,329	117,414,647		117,414,647
1908	$0.05		72,093,923	43,840,507	7,573,958	123,508,388		123,508,388
1909	$0.05		80,518,480	49,061,934	6,149,397	135,729,811		135,729,811
1910	$0.05		87,428,903	52,621,104	6,930,546	146,980,553		146,980,553
1911	$0.05		91,176,085	54,754,987	8,449,658	154,380,730		154,380,730
1912	$0.05		95,488,351	57,738,340	9,181,302	162,407,993		162,407,993
1913	$0.05		103,555,709	62,367,504	9,972,598	175,895,811		175,895,811
1914	$0.05		108,494,157	65,544,188	10,314,618	184,352,963		184,352,963
1915	$0.05		110,028,630	67,674,648	7,951,707	185,654,985		185,654,985
1916	$0.05		119,585,274	72,316,026	7,946,796	199,848,096		199,848,096
1917	$0.05		119,236,611	72,793,114	7,591,435	199,621,160		199,621,160
1918	$0.05		111,249,025	69,813,991	7,867,252	188,930,268		188,930,268
1919	$0.05		128,350,204	83,863,697	9,972,922	222,186,823		222,186,823
1920	$0.06		138,632,825	89,020,734	10,735,223	238,388,782		238,388,782
1921	$0.06		132,114,895	84,561,230	11,051,623	227,727,748	4,816	227,732,564
1922	$0.06		135,088,545	81,665,364	9,790,015	226,543,924	41,859	226,585,783
1923	$0.06		132,904,222	79,968,841	8,669,235	221,542,298	44,100	221,586,398
1924	$0.06		126,492,460	75,627,955	7,082,403	209,202,818	50,131	209,252,949
1925	$0.08	$0.06	122,077,903	72,187,755	6,517,448	200,783,106	99,210	200,882,316
1926	$0.08	$0.067	112,816,765	66,887,744	6,007,441	185,711,950	5,114,834	190,826,784
1927	$0.08	$0.067	107,802,005	63,810,891	5,706,128	177,319,024	6,786,716	184,105,740

YEAR	CASH FARE	TOKEN FARE	MINNEAPOLIS STREETCARS	ST. PAUL STREETCARS	SUBURBAN STREETCARS	TOTAL STREETCARS	TOTAL BUSES	TOTAL BUSES AND STREETCARS
1928	$0.08	$0.067	106,117,237	61,114,921	5,384,528	172,616,686	6,877,230	179,493,916
1929	$0.10	$0.075	98,517,171	57,621,959	4,736,675	160,875,805	6,921,797	167,797,602
1930	$0.10	$0.075	89,315,336	51,786,305	3,933,314	145,034,955	6,389,573	151,424,528
1931	$0.10	$0.075	77,232,829	44,593,093	3,098,657	124,924,579	5,966,890	130,891,469
1932	$0.10	$0.075	66,678,141	39,059,412	2,068,164	107,805,717	5,226,842	113,032,559
1933	$0.10	$0.075	59,296,317	35,287,455	1,140,418	95,724,190	4,663,119	100,387,309
1934	$0.10	$0.075	61,930,523	37,471,496	1,154,332	100,556,351	4,914,609	105,470,960
1935	$0.10	$0.075	62,812,773	37,895,383	1,165,142	101,873,298	5,457,344	107,330,642
1936	$0.10	$0.075	67,579,787	40,394,863	1,269,108	109,243,758	5,951,766	115,195,524
1937	$0.10	$0.075	66,576,787	39,162,827	1,279,491	107,019,105	5,750,365	112,769,470
1938	$0.10	$0.075	62,010,066	35,510,409	1,113,556	98,634,031	5,928,112	104,562,143
1939	$0.10	$0.075	61,530,121	34,263,196	1,017,555	96,810,872	7,577,275	104,388,147
1940	$0.10	$0.075	60,739,077	33,473,601	1,041,475	95,254,153	9,059,466	104,313,619
1941	$0.10	$0.083	60,071,370	34,177,495	1,100,067	95,348,932	10,592,936	105,941,868
1942	$0.10	$0.083	72,491,024	41,685,451	1,519,660	115,696,135	13,228,808	128,924,943
1943	$0.10	$0.075	97,351,944	55,398,949	2,179,782	154,930,675	18,349,428	173,280,103
1944	$0.10	$0.075	104,186,431	58,340,999	2,347,353	164,874,783	20,347,764	185,222,547
1945	$0.10	$0.075	108,797,876	60,373,968	2,394,832	171,566,676	22,290,588	193,857,264
1946	$0.10	$0.075	112,807,070	62,013,722	2,450,170	177,270,962	24,256,060	201,527,022
1947	$0.10	$0.090	107,888,541	60,963,800	2,272,590	171,124,931	27,796,264	198,921,195
1948	$0.11	$0.110	97,080,887	53,258,830	1,598,765	151,938,482	36,469,730	188,408,212
1949	$0.12	$0.117	82,630,727	44,049,927	813,904	127,494,558	37,756,366	165,250,924
1950	$0.15	$0.138	70,204,809	37,129,792	908,850	108,243,451	32,197,936	140,441,387
1951	$0.15	$0.138	60,747,033	32,717,904	664,854	94,129,791	33,829,890	127,959,681
1952	$0.15		53,572,070	21,618,283	83,438	75,273,791	37,521,358	112,795,149
1953	$0.20	$0.180	34,091,091	6,534,097	72,497	40,697,685	54,235,705	94,933,390
1954	$0.20	$0.180	4,848,819		30,157	4,878,976	81,714,127	86,593,103

Note: In 1932 the Lake Minnetonka and Stillwater suburban streetcars converted to buses.

Source: TCRT Corporate and Operating Reports.

Appendix B

LAKE MINNETONKA OPERATIONS

YEAR	RAIL PASSENGERS	BOAT PASSENGERS**	PROFIT (LOSS)	OPERATING RATIO (IN %)
1907	1,977,577	309,500	91,950	63
1908	2,293,689	265,220	103,838	62
1909	2,005,603	246,550	81,069	62
1910	2,374,297	235,920	78,160	66
1911	3,720,762	202,950	72,040	63
1912	4,164,506	247,950	85,835	59
1913	4,609,974	246,880	92,236	60
1914	5,020,997	237,300	98,544	58
1915	3,127,801	210,320	71,278	69
1916	2,885,382	235,500	81,624	65
1917	2,678,698	209,320	58,106	74
1918	2,619,352	133,780	36,854	83
1919	3,869,939	181,490	1,716	99
1920*	4,151,346	243,210	11,368	96
1921	5,265,068	220,330	36,368	89
1922	4,824,143	174,540	49,754	84
1923	4,327,782	108,170	31,996	88
1924	3,624,263	68,320	6,038	97
1925*	3,629,280	130,790	(10,671)	105
1926	3,402,788	82,090	(29,639)	114
1927	3,266,808		(13,653)	107
1928	3,083,722		(18,201)	110
1929*	2,778,896		(34,127)	121
1930	2,446,744		(34,407)	124
1931	1,966,966		(50,215)	143

Note: In its twenty-five years of operation, the Lake Minnetonka Division returned $897,862 against its construction costs of $1,272,676. Operating ratio represents expenses as a percentage of revenues (i.e., an operating ratio of 63 percent means that 63 cents of every dollar went to expenses).

*Denotes fare increases.

**Number of boat passengers estimated from fare revenues.

Source: TCRT Corporate and Operating Reports.

Appendix C

STILLWATER RAIL OPERATIONS

YEAR	PASSENGERS	PROFIT (LOSS)	OPERATING RATIO (IN %)
1907	5,245,752	$129,400	51
1908	5,280,269	$119,079	55
1909	4,143,794	$72,427	66
1910	4,556,249	$81,962	65
1911	4,728,896	$82,965	65
1912	5,016,796	$96,332	62
1913	5,362,624	$82,910	69
1914	5,293,621	$90,902	66
1915	4,823,906	$71,126	71
1916	5,061,214	$86,446	66
1917	4,912,737	$67,273	73
1918	5,247,900	$69,075	74
1919	6,102,983	$72,654	76
1920*	6,583,877	$69,675	80
1921	5,786,565	$36,457	90
1922	4,965,872	$39,319	87
1923	4,341,453	$16,995	94
1924	3,458,140	($8,879)	104
1925*	2,888,168	($42,245)	124
1926	2,604,653	($47,209)	129
1927	2,439,320	($34,504)	123
1928	2,300,806	($38,994)	127
1929*	1,957,779	($57,152)	143
1930	1,486,570	($55,031)	154
1931	1,131,691	($64,889)	185

Note: Between 1907 and 1931, the Stillwater Division returned $936,804 against its construction costs of $1,136,391. Operating ratio represents expenses as a percentage of revenues (i.e., an operating ratio of 51 percent means that 51 cents of every dollar went to expenses).

*Denotes fare increases.

Source: TCRT Corporate and Operating Reports.

Appendix D

TWIN CITY RAPID TRANSIT
COMPANY SUBSIDIARIES

Twin City Rapid Transit Company was a holding company with several subcorporations created over the years to accommodate its growing business needs. Not all of these companies were active during its entire corporate life. The two original constituent companies, Minneapolis Street Railway Company and the St. Paul City Railway Company, were merged to form Twin City Rapid Transit. They retained separate identities because of franchise and regulatory agreements with the two cities, but they were in fact one company. TCRT was a New Jersey corporation, until 1939 when it was reincorporated in Minnesota.

Except for text pertaining to the Duluth Connection, which was never part of the TCRT, the following descriptions are taken directly from a corporate brochure issued in 1927, presumably for stockholders.

Minneapolis Street Railway Company

Minneapolis Street Railway Company operates the entire street railway system located within the corporate limits of the City of Minneapolis comprising 241.945 miles of single track. It owns all of this operated property except for the so-called Harriet Right-of-Way owned by the Minneapolis and St. Paul Suburban Railroad Company extending from the easterly line of Hennepin Avenue at 31st Street to the westerly city limits of Minneapolis at South France Avenue, comprising 5.9 miles of single track. The Minneapolis Street Railway Company also owns and operates the so-called Fort Snelling Line, comprising 4.45 miles of single track located in the United States Government Reservation extending from the southerly city limits of Minneapolis to the St. Paul city limits in the middle of the bridge over the Mississippi River. It also operates the Columbia Heights Line owned by the Minneapolis St. Paul and Suburban Railway . . . Minneapolis Street Railway owns seventeen parcels of land on which are situated the car house, office, power station and substation buildings; has about 181 miles of paved track . . . a power distribution system . . . [and] 43 buildings. The rolling stock of the entire Twin City System comprises 1,021 passenger cars and 86 service cars of which the Railroad and Warehouse Commission allocated 62.33% . . . to the Minneapolis Street Railway Company, 35.15% to the St. Paul City Railway Company and 2.52% to the Minneapolis St. Paul and Suburban Railroad Company.

The St. Paul City Railway Company

The St. Paul City Railway Company operates the entire street railway system located within the corporate limits of the City of St. Paul comprising 171.234 miles of single track . . . In addition to the tracks the property principally consists of the Selby Tunnel, seven parcels of land on which are located the general office, car station, substation and shop buildings.

The Minneapolis and St. Paul Suburban Railroad Company

The Minneapolis and St. Paul Suburban Railroad Company comprises a total of 91.352 miles of single track with the necessary overhead lines located largely on private right of way and rendering service to the Lake Minnetonka, White Bear Lake and Stillwater communities and in addition giving service to suburban towns bordering on the Cities of Minneapolis and St. Paul.

The Minnetonka and White Bear Navigation Company

The Minnetonka and White Bear Navigation Company owns certain extensive properties situated on Lake Minnetonka and on White Bear Lake.

The Rapid Transit Real Estate Corporation

The Rapid Transit Real Estate Corporation owns land held for right of way or terminal purposes not at present directly useful for the operation of the railway property although in some instances it has a direct connection therewith. The Real Estate Corporation owns the gravel pit in St. Paul and another one in South St. Paul supplying gravel for construction and maintenance work on the Twin City System.

The Twin City Motor Bus Company

The Twin City Motor Bus Company owns and operates 109 motor passenger buses and 7 service buses. It also owns three modern garages, one of which is located in the City of Minneapolis, one in the City of St. Paul and one in the village of White Bear. It also owns the land on which these garages are located. This Company renders service to and from the cities of Minneapolis and St. Paul and to most of the important suburban towns within the vicinity. The Company has no motor bus competition.

The Company, in addition, owns the majority of the capital stock of Yellow Cab Corporation of Minnesota, the leading taxicab company operating in the two cities. The taxicab company owns over 300 modern cabs, and is consistently adding to the fleet additional cabs of the most improved type.

Transit Supply Company

Transit Supply is the fiscal agent for the Twin City Rapid Transit Company and is responsible for managing its assets, purchasing, and the management of its inventory.

The Duluth Connection

Although never a part of the Twin City Rapid Transit Company, the Duluth system had a connection to the Twin Cities through the investments of Thomas Lowry and some of his associates. Calvin Goodrich served as president of the Duluth Street Railway and Thomas Lowry was on its board of directors. Most of the Duluth rolling stock was built by TCRT in its Snelling shops. TCRT's master mechanic, Walter Smith, held that title in Duluth before joining TCRT. The Duluth system reached its peak in 1919 with thirty-eight million passengers carried. It declined steadily through the 1920s, became bankrupt in 1930, and emerged as the Duluth–Superior Transit Company. All of its rail lines were converted to motor bus or trolley bus operation by 1939.

Appendix E

Twin City Rapid Transit operated a number of bus routes that were never served by streetcars. Some were inherited from other bus companies that it acquired in the 1920s. Most of them were crosstown routes that were connectors or feeders to the downtown-oriented streetcar lines. Three—the Minneapolis downtown loop circulator, the 50th Street crosstown, and the Lexington Avenue crosstown—were experimental and ended when they did not attract sufficient riders. The New Brighton service was wartime only, taking workers from Minneapolis and St. Paul to the Twin Cities Army Ammunition Plant in New Brighton. The rest outlived the streetcars and continue to this day as part of the Metro Transit bus system.

MINNEAPOLIS

Downtown Loop Circulator

Started in 1951, this two-way loop ran every twenty minutes from 9th and LaSalle, 9th, Hennepin, Washington, Nicollet, 10th, Marquette, Washington, Nicollet, 9th, to LaSalle. This was the first attempt at a downtown circulator. It failed to attract ridership and was discontinued in 1952.

50th Street Crosstown

This route opened in 1947 from 56th and Wooddale via Wooddale, 50th, Nicollet, 47th, Cedar, Minnehaha Parkway, 28th Avenue South, 46th Street to 46th Avenue. Discontinued in 1950.

Lowry Avenue Crosstown

Started in 1926 from Xerxes Avenue North to Stinson Boulevard, Lowry Avenue, like 38th Street in south Minneapolis, was a crosstown line serving similar residential neighborhoods on the north side of the city. It was extended to 36th and Washburn in 1931, to 29th Avenue Northeast and McKinley in 1933, and to 33rd and Stinson in 1937. The west end was extended north on Victory Drive to 45th Avenue in 1948.

Twin Cities Army Ammunition Plant

Service to the ammunition plant began in January 1942 via Hennepin, Central, Lowry, and Highway 8, and coincided with shift changes. The line was discontinued after World War II.

Nicollet–Hennepin

This existing route was acquired along with Twin City Motor Bus Company in 1926. From 36th and Hennepin via Hennepin, to 24th Street, to Nicollet Avenue. Nicollet–Hennepin was a busy, prosperous line linking downtown and the commercial district at Hennepin and Lake and the Selby–Lake car line with the densely populated residential neighborhoods along 24th Street between Hennepin and Nicollet Avenues.

North Lyndale Avenue

This line was a rarity, a downtown-oriented radial route that stayed within Minneapolis and was always a bus. It appears to have started in 1919, between downtown and Camden (42nd Avenue) via Lyndale.

38th Street Crosstown

Started in 1926 from Colfax Avenue to 34th Avenue, 38th Street was an important crosstown bus line that tied together south Minneapolis neighborhoods with the major north–south streetcar lines. It was extended to 42nd Avenue in 1929 and to Edmund Boulevard in 1940.

ST. PAUL

Airport

Service from downtown St. Paul to the St. Paul Airport (Holman Field) began in 1942.

East 6th Street–Lake Elmo–Stillwater

This long suburban route traveled from downtown St. Paul to Stillwater via East 6th Street, Earl, Minnehaha, and Highway 5. It was a separate company, acquired by TCRT in the 1920s. It ran express within St. Paul until the Hope Street car line was abandoned in 1939. Then it was rerouted from Earl to Atlantic and opened to local passengers. Branches were added to Tanners Lake/Landfall in 1949, and to Case and Nokomis in 1952.

Highland Park–Cleveland Avenue Crosstown

The Highland route, opened in March 1937, connected to the Randolph car line at Randolph and Edgecumbe and again at Cleveland and Highland Parkway, also feeding the Snelling Avenue line at Snelling and Highland. In July 1937, it was extended north to Prior and University via Cleveland, Marshall and Prior. In 1951, a diversion was added into southern Highland Park via St. Paul Avenue, Montreal, and Fairview.

Lexington Avenue Crosstown

This was an experimental service that began in 1948 and ended in 1950. It ran from West 7th Street on the south to Hoyt Avenue just north of Como Park on the north, crossing all of the east–west streetcar lines.

Twin Cities Army Ammunition Plant

Service to the ammunition plant began in January 1942 via 6th, Summit, Marshall, Snelling, and Highway 10, and coincided with shift changes. The line was discontinued after World War II.

Raymond Avenue

This route opened in 1949 from University Avenue and Raymond Avenue via Raymond Avenue to St. Anthony Park.

Appendix F

BUS CONVERSION DATES

St. Paul Lines

November 3, 1951	E. 7th St.–Mahtomedi
May 3, 1952	Dale Street
May 17, 1952	Randolph–Hazel Park
	Rice Street–St. Paul–Inver Grove
	W. 7th St.–Fort Snelling–Maria
September 6, 1952	St. Clair–Payne Avenue
	Snelling Avenue
November 1, 1952	Hamline–Cherokee
	Grand–Mississippi
July 11, 1953	Como Avenue
	Selby–Lake
October 31, 1953	University Avenue (St. Paul leg of St. Paul–Minneapolis)

Minneapolis Lines

April 16, 1950	Broadway
August 19, 1950	Cedar–28th Ave. So.
August 1, 1952	Ft. Snelling Shuttle
October 18, 1952	Grand Avenue South
February 21, 1953	Bloomington–Columbia Hts.
April 18, 1953	N. Washington Ave.
	34th Avenue
July 11, 1953	Chicago–Penn–Fremont
	Selby–Lake
November 28, 1953	University Avenue (Minneapolis leg of St. Paul–Minneapolis)
	Bryant–Johnson
	Ft. Snelling–Minnehaha
	Plymouth–E. 25th St.
March 6, 1954	Glenwood–4th Ave.S.
March 27, 1954	Nicollet–2nd St. N.E.–Monroe
June 18, 1954	Como–Oak–Harriet
	Inter-Campus

Appendix G

ROSTER OF PASSENGER CARS BUILT
AT 31ST STREET AND SNELLING SHOPS, 1898–1927

31st Street Shops

QUANTITY	CAR NUMBER	DATE OF CONSTRUCTION	NOTES
1	Private car	1898	Lowry's private car
2	737–738	1898	
20	739–758	September to December 1898	
14	759–772	January 1899	
16	773–788	June–September 1899	
1	797	September 1899	
19	798–816	June–August 1900	
15	817-831	July–August 1900	
28	832–859	August–October 1900	
20	833–844, 860–867	April 1901	
32	868–899	February–September 1901	
50	900–949	May–November 1902	
2	950–951	April–May 1903	
40	952–991	May–September 1903	
50	992–1041	April–June 1904	
1	1092	July 1904	Double-deck car
38	1042–1079	November 1904–February 1905	
12	1043, 1080–1090	February–March 1905	
20	1091, 1093–1111	April–June 1905	
12	1112–1123	August 1905	First cars with steel frames
21	1124–1144	September–November 1905	
1	1145	May 1906	Double-deck car
50	1146–1195	May–August 1906	1160 double-deck car
25	1196–1220	September–December 1906	
25	1221–1245	February–April 1907	
20	1246–1265	May–August 1907	

(Total: 535)

Notes: Numbers 789–796 were assigned to cars acquired with the St. Paul and Suburban Railway. Cars 737–738 and Thomas Lowry's private car were the first homebuilt cars constructed by TCRT to a design engineered by W. M. Brown, TCRT's master mechanic. These cars, and cars built through number 1111, were constructed with wood frames. They were also shorter (43–45 feet long) and narrower (8 feet 8½ inches) than the 46-foot length and 9-foot width that was standard on subsequent car orders. All of the early wood cars were either retired during the 1930s or sold to Seattle, Tacoma, Winnipeg, and Duluth.

The double-deck cars were experimental and used briefly on the Lake Minnetonka line. Technical issues and a lack of public acceptance caused their removal.

Cars 1112–1123, 1145–1163, and 1246–1255 were built for Lake Minnetonka and Stillwater service. They were equipped with four GE 73 seventy-five-horsepower motors and C-6-K (Type M control) controllers and geared for high-speed service. A few were used on local lines after 1932. One (1261) became a rail grinder. The rest were scrapped in 1938–41.

Snelling Shops

QUANTITY	CAR NUMBER	DATE OF CONSTRUCTION	NOTES
25	1266–1290	September–November 1907	
19	1291–1309	March–May 1908	
50	1310–1359	November 1908–March 1909	
20	1360–1379	July–September 1909	
25	1380–1404	January–March 1910	
20	1405–1424	April–July 1910	
25	1425–1449	November–December 1910	
1	1450	January 1911	
35	1451–1485	January–February 1911	1482–1485 sold to Duluth
100	1482–1581	February–October 1912	
17	1564–1566	April–May 1913	1564–1566 sold to Duluth
	1582–1595		
40	1596–1635	May–October 1913	
50	1636–1685	December 1913–February 1914	
90	1686–1775	October 1914–February 1915	
17	1776–1792	November–December 1915	
2	1–2	December 1915	See note (1) below.
2	2000–2000A	April 1916	Two-car lightweight train

QUANTITY	CAR NUMBER	DATE OF CONSTRUCTION	NOTES
68	1713, 1716, 1719, 1722, 1724, 1789–1851	November 1916–February 1917	
4	1852–1855	June 1917	
2	2002–2003	November 1921	Two-car lightweight train
4	1–4	April 1925	See note (2) below.
2	2004–2005	July 1926	Two-car lightweight train
25	2006–2030	December 1927–January 1928	Lightweight cars

(Total: 643)

Notes: (1) Two cars were built to TCRT specifications for Minneapolis, Anoka & Cuyuna Range. (2) These four cars were built to TCRT's lightweight design but were shorter (35 feet 10 inches long) and intended for the Stillwater local lines. After Stillwater abandonment, they were used on Broadway in Minneapolis, the Ft. Snelling Shuttle, and the Western Avenue Shuttle in St. Paul.

A number of TCRT cars were sold to Duluth and their numbers subsequently replaced on the roster with newly built equipment. Cars sold and replaced: 1482–1485, 1564–1566,

1789–1792, 1724, 1719, 1716, and 1722. Other cars were sold to Duluth and not replaced. Cars sold to Minneapolis, Anoka & Cuyuna Range and replaced included 1713 and 1855.

Motors on early TCRT cars were GE 67 (thirty-eight horsepower), GE 70 (forty horsepower), GE 57 (fifty horsepower), or GE 87 (sixty horsepower). Standard cars above number 1291 were equipped with GE 203, 213, or 216 motors rated at fifty horsepower per axle.

Motors, trucks, and controllers were frequently shifted among cars as they were reconditioned or rebuilt.

CARS BUILT FOR OTHER COMPANIES

Duluth Street Railway

QUANTITY	CAR NUMBER	DATE OF CONSTRUCTION	NOTES
1	163	1901	Incline railway
15	163–177	1904	
15	183–197	1906	
6	198–203	1908	
11	204–214	1909	
5	215–219	1910	
2	220–221	1911	Incline railway
16	222–237	1911	
10	242–251	1912	
6	257–262	1914	
8	271–278	1917	
1	1 (141)	1911	Wrecker crane
1	1 (146)	1917	Snowplow

(Total: 97)

Minneapolis, Anoka & Cuyuna Range Railway

QUANTITY	CAR NUMBER	DATE OF CONSTRUCTION	NOTES
2	1–2	1915	

Light Weight Noiseless Electric Street Car Company

QUANTITY	CAR NUMBER	DATE OF CONSTRUCTION	NOTES
50	3232–3261, 6219–6238	1924	Chicago Surface Lines
1	375	1925	Grand Rapids Railroad
5	301–305	1925	Duluth St. Railway
4	1-4	1925	TCRT
10	131–140	1926	Tennessee Electric Power, Chattanooga
10	600–609	1926	Tennessee Electric Power, Nashville
13	401–413	1926	Southern Indiana Gas & Electric Company, Evansville, Indiana

(Total: 93)

St. Paul Southern Electric Railway

QUANTITY	CAR NUMBER	DATE OF CONSTRUCTION	NOTE
1	—	1917	Work car rebuilt from passenger car

University of Minnesota

QUANTITY	CAR NUMBER	DATE OF CONSTRUCTION	NOTE
1	—	1914	Work car

CARS SOLD TO OTHER COMPANIES; CAR NUMBERS REPEATED; CARS REPLACED

Duluth Street Railway

QUANTITY	DULUTH NUMBER	TCRT NUMBER	YEAR
12	151-152	1st 833–844	1900
1	178	1st 1043	1905
4	238-241	1st 1482–1485	1911
3	252-254	1st 1564–1566	1912
4	269, 268, 270, 267	1st 1716, 1719, 1722, 1724	1916
4	263-266	1st 1789–1792	1916

(Total: 28)

Minneapolis, Anoka & Cuyuna Range Railway

QUANTITY	ANOKA NUMBER	TCRT NUMBER	YEAR
1	7	1st 1713	1916

CARS SOLD TO OTHER COMPANIES; CARS NOT REPLACED

Duluth Street Railway

QUANTITY	DULUTH NUMBER	TCRT NUMBER	YEAR
1	179	Ex. 1111	1905
3	180–182	Ex. 1108–1110	1906
2	255–256	Ex. 868–869	1912
6	289–294	Ex. 1202, 1204, 1212, 1231, 1232, 1234	1918

(Total: 12)

Minneapolis, Anoka & Cuyuna Range Railway

QUANTITY	ANOKA NUMBER	TCRT NUMBER	YEAR
1	8	Ex. 1855	1917
1	25 (Snowplow)	25	1918

Aurora, Elgin & Chicago Railroad

QUANTITY	AURORA NUMBER	TCRT NUMBER	YEAR
4	208–214 (even)	Ex. 782–785	1913

Tacoma Municipal Belt Line

QUANTITY	TACOMA NUMBER	TCRT NUMBER	YEAR
15	1–15	Ex. 817–831	1918
5	16–20	Ex. 766, 767, 776, 778, 787	1918
(Total: 20)			

Seattle Municipal Railway

QUANTITY	SEATTLE NUMBER	TCRT NUMBER	YEAR
25	300–324	Ex. 763, 765, 768–775, 777 779, 786, 788, 797–799, 803–805, 807, 808, 810–812	1918

Winnipeg Electric Railway

QUANTITY	WINNIPEG NUMBER	TCRT NUMBER	YEAR
20**	800–838	Ex. 832–842, 844–846, 848–853	1920

**All cars sold as bodies; no trucks, motors, or electrical.

Source: Olson, *The Electric Railways of Minnesota*.

Appendix H

TWIN CITY RAPID TRANSIT WORK EQUIPMENT

Over the years TCRT rostered an extensive collection of nonrevenue work equipment that it used, among other things, to repair and construct track, maintain power lines and overhead trolley wires, clear wrecks, and plow snow. In later years, motor vehicles (heavy-duty trucks) replaced rail equipment for some of this work. All work equipment was scrapped. This list shows equipment on the roster and active prior to bus conversion. Unpowered cars are not listed.

NUMBER	TYPE	PURPOSE	NOTES
2, 95, 97	Supply car(s)	Delivering supplies	Rebuilt former passenger cars; delivered supplies from main storehouse at Snelling to carbarns
3–5, 72	Wire car(s)	Overhead wire work	Power department; elevated platform
7–19	Work car(s)	Miscellaneous work	Track and other departments. Flat bed. 14, 16, and 18 later converted to sand cars
19, 46–49			Used for hauling heavy materials
51–56, 62–69			Some used as wreckers
43–45	Sand car(s)	Hauling sand	Track department
20	Locomotive	Switching cars	Used at main power plant to switch coal cars
21, 50, 83	Crane car(s)	Moving disabled cars	Wrecker; used to rerail and move disabled cars damaged in wrecks and derailments
22–24	Snowplow(s)	Clearing snow	Assigned various stations; used throughout the system
36–38	Snowplow(s)		
75–82	Snowplow(s)		
26, 27, 28	Shifter car(s)	Moving cars	Small cars used at Snelling Shops to move cars between shop buildings; former cable cars
96	Rail grinder	Smoothing rail	Track department; former passenger car rebuilt with grinding wheels to remove rail corrugations and other irregularities
58, 61	Cupola car	Track welding	Track department
59	Sprinkler car	Street sprinkling	Track department; car had large tank for water/ oil storage

Sources: Olson, *Electric Railways of Minnesota;* Swett, *Interurbans Special,* No. 14

Appendix I

TWIN CITY RAPID TRANSIT SHOPS AND CARHOUSES, 1872–1954

Horsecar Barns (Minneapolis)

NAME	LOCATION	YEAR BUILT	DISPOSITION
Washington	Washington and 3rd Avenue N.	1875	Sold
University	4th Street S.E. and 14th Avenue S.E.	1875	Sold
Franklin	16th Avenue S. and Franklin Avenue	1878	Sold
4th Avenue	4th Avenue S. and 24th Street	1878	Sold
Riverside	24th Avenue S. and Riverside Avenue	1880	Sold
Broadway	2nd Street N.E. and Broadway Street	1881	Sold
8th Avenue	8th Avenue S. and Franklin Avenue	1881	Sold
Monroe	Monroe and Broadway Street N.E.	1882	Sold
19th Avenue N.	19th Avenue N. and Washington Avenue	1882	Electric cars
Lyndale	28th Street and Dupont Avenue S.	1883	Electric cars
Minnehaha	27th Avenue S. and 26th Street	1884	Electric cars
3rd Avenue N.	3rd Avenue and 2nd Street N.	1885	Electric cars

Note: Except for the building at 3rd Avenue and 2nd Street North, none of the structures on these sites still exists. Exact dates and eventual disposition of the buildings and properties are unknown. The Lyndale barn burned in 1906. Of those converted to electric carhouses between 1890 and 1892, only the Minnehaha carhouse remained in service in 1897. The others, made obsolete by East Side and an improved and enlarged 31st Street, were being used to store out-of-service electric cars.

Horsecar Barns (St. Paul)

NAME	LOCATION	YEAR BUILT	DISPOSITION
4th Street	On 4th Street between Wabasha and St. Peter (stable only)	1875	Sold
Kent Street	University Avenue and Kent Street	1881	Fire, 1895
Laurel Avenue	Laurel Avenue, Dale to Kent Street	1882	Sold
Exchange	Exchange between 3rd and 4th Streets	1872	Sold
St. Peter	4th and 5th streets–Wabasha	1879	Converted to department store in 1884
West 7th	7th Street–Lee Street to Tuscarora Avenue	1882	Fire, 1891
Smith Avenue	Ramsey Street–Smith to Thompson	1884	(See note)
Rice Street	Rice Street and Front Avenue	1884	(See note)
Greenbrier	Maryland Avenue and Greenbrier Street	1888	Sold

Note: Kent Street (converted to an electric carhouse) stored out-of-service equipment until it burned. Smith Avenue and Rice Street became electric carhouses. Smith was severely damaged by fires in 1892 and 1899, and became a storage facility after 1907; the building was demolished in 1911. Rice Street stored out-of-service cars until 1911. The St. Peter facility was demolished in 1911, and the site was used for the Lowry Building.

Streetcar Carhouses (Minneapolis)

NAME	LOCATION	YEAR BUILT	DISPOSITION
31st Street	31st Street and Nicollet Avenue	1890–91	(see note)
Bloomington	31st Street and Bloomington Avenue	1891	Closed 1911
East Side	1st Avenue N.E.–University and 4th Street S.E.	1891	Closed 1954
North Side	26th Street and Washington Avenue N.	1914	Bus, 1953
Lake Street	E. Lake Street, 21st–22nd Avenue	1910	Closed 1953

Note: Renamed Nicollet after 1912, 31st Street opened as a repair shop for the Minneapolis, Lyndale & Minnetonka Railway (Motor Line) in 1884. It was rebuilt and renovated several times: first as a streetcar repair facility and carhouse in 1890–91, again in 1898, and finally in 1912. It became a bus garage in 1953. The site is still in use by Metro Transit. East Side was closed in 1954 and the building sold to Superior Plating; it still stands as of 2007. North Side became a bus garage in 1953. It was sold by Metro Transit in the mid-1980s and is now a business center with multiple tenants. Lake Street was demolished, and the site was developed as the Hi-Lake Shopping Center.

Streetcar Carhouses (St. Paul and Suburbs)

NAME	LOCATION	YEAR BUILT	DISPOSITION
Duluth Avenue	Duluth Avenue and East 7th Street	1889	Closed 1952
Selby Avenue	Selby Avenue and Dale Street	1888	Closed 1907
Grand Avenue	Grand Avenue and Victoria Street		
Midway	University Avenue–LaSalle and Carlton	1891	Closed 1907
Owen Street	Stillwater	1899	Closed 1932
Snelling	Snelling and University Avenues	1907	Bus, 1952–54
South St. Paul	Concord and Malden Streets	1920	Closed 1927

Note: Duluth and Selby were originally built as cable car houses. Midway was replaced by Snelling and closed in 1907. The building was sold but remains in use as an office building. The carhouse at Grand and Victoria was used for the first electric line; its dates are unknown. All rail and special work, including the connecting leads to Concord Street, were removed from the South St. Paul carhouse on April 12–15, 1927. The building was sold in 1938 and remains in use today as a truck parts warehouse. A large carhouse and multiple shop buildings occupied the Snelling site until bus conversion in 1954; then the carhouse and all but three of the original shop buildings were demolished and half the property was sold for development as Midway Center. What remained became a bus maintenance facility and was used by Metro Transit until 2002, when it was closed and all of the buildings razed. At the time of publication in 2007, the site awaits redevelopment.

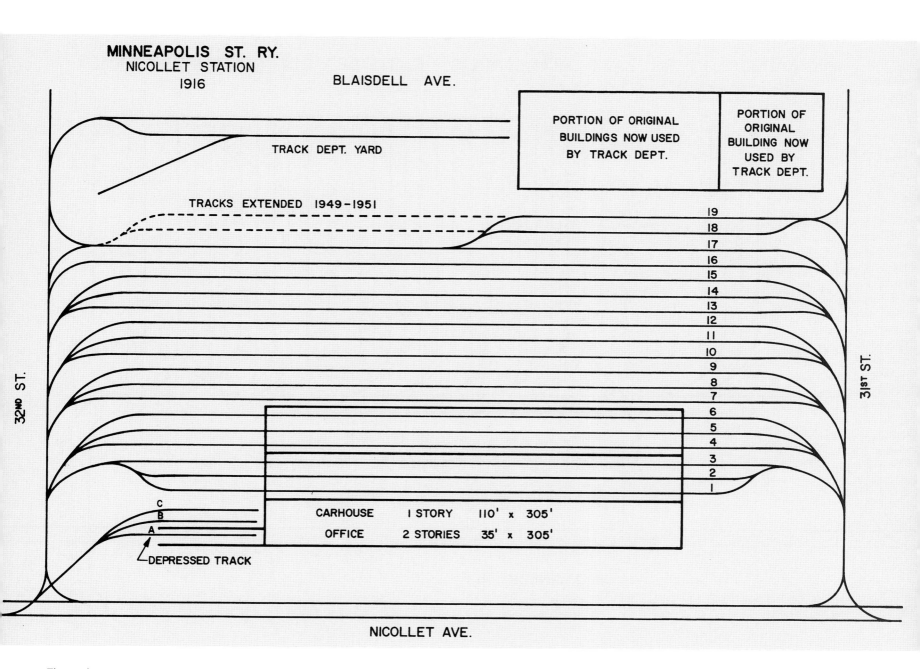

MINNEAPOLIS ST. RY.
NICOLLET STATION
1916   BLAISDELL AVE.

PORTION OF ORIGINAL BUILDINGS NOW USED BY TRACK DEPT.

PORTION OF ORIGINAL BUILDING NOW USED BY TRACK DEPT.

TRACK DEPT. YARD

TRACKS EXTENDED 1949-1951

32ND ST.

31ST ST.

19
18
17
16
15
14
13
12
11
10
9
8
7
6
5
4
3
2
1

C
B
A

CARHOUSE   1 STORY   110' x 305'
OFFICE   2 STORIES   35' x 305'

DEPRESSED TRACK

NICOLLET AVE.

The track arrangement at Nicollet Station would change very little from this 1916 view until it was closed and remodeled as a bus garage in 1953. The two-story carhouse building fronting on Nicollet Avenue had mechanical and dispatcher's offices and a trainmen's room on the ground floor. The second floor had a medical department office and sleeping and recreation rooms for off-duty conductors and motormen. The underground electrical department was headquartered in the basement. Work cars used depressed track A to bring reels of electrical cable in and out of the basement. Over the years Nicollet supplied cars for the Bryant–Johnson, Nicollet–2nd St. N.E., Glenwood–4th Ave. S., and Grand–Monroe lines. The combined capacity of the carhouse and yard was 158 cars. Tracks 4, 5, and 6 and portions of the yard and the track department buildings were used for buses after World War II. The Nicollet site continues in use as a bus garage for Metro Transit. Illustrations by Kent Dorholt are reprinted from *The Electric Railways of Minnesota*; courtesy of Russell L. Olson.

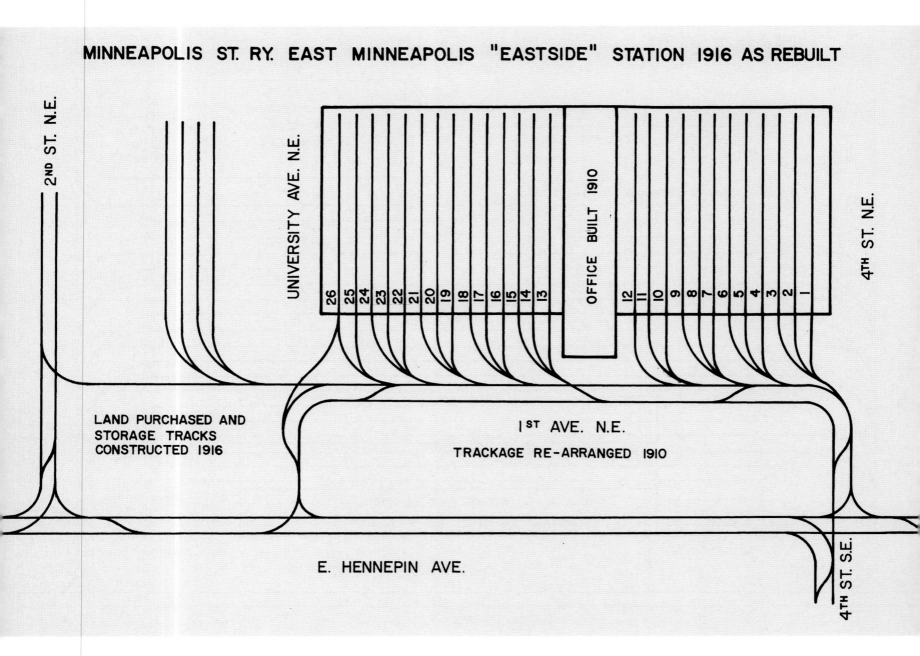

MINNEAPOLIS ST. RY. EAST MINNEAPOLIS "EASTSIDE" STATION 1916 AS REBUILT

East Side Station opened in 1891. A 1910 remodeling provided additional space for dispatch and mechanical offices and trainmen's quarters. Except for outside storage tracks that were added in 1916, and then subsequently abandoned, all East Side cars were stored indoors. East Side's proximity to downtown Minneapolis minimized deadhead pullout and pull-in mileage, which made it very attractive operationally. As a result, more lines were assigned to it over the years than any other carhouse in the system. East Side provided cars for the Como–Harriet, Como–Hopkins, Oak–Harriet, Bryant–Johnson, Grand–Monroe, Nicollet–2nd St. N.E., Bloomington–Columbia Hts., Plymouth–E. 25th St., Inter-Campus, Lake Minnetonka, and St. Paul–Minneapolis lines. It held 178 cars. East Side was the last carhouse to operate in the system, closing on June 19, 1954. The building survives in 2007.

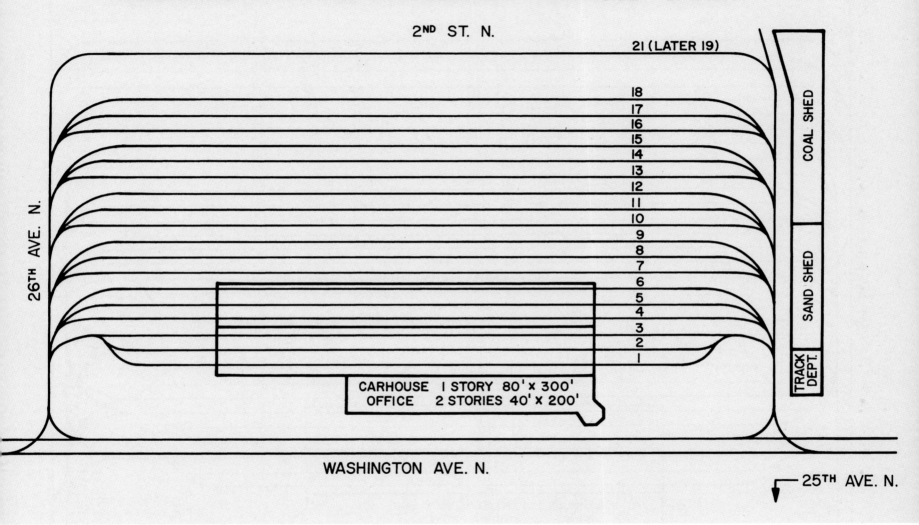

MINNEAPOLIS ST. RY. NORTH MINNEAPOLIS "NORTHSIDE" STATION

2ND ST. N.

21 (LATER 19)

18
17
16
15
14
13
12
11
10
9
8
7
6
5
4
3
2
1

26TH AVE. N.

COAL SHED

SAND SHED

TRACK DEPT.

CARHOUSE 1 STORY 80' x 300'
OFFICE 2 STORIES 40' x 200'

WASHINGTON AVE. N.

25TH AVE. N.

TCRT built North Side Station in 1914 to relieve overcrowding at its other Minneapolis facilities. Except for a slightly smaller footprint, the overall design of the carhouse building was a copy of Lake Street Station. North Side housed 148 cars and was home to the Chicago–Penn-Fremont, Broadway, 28th Ave. S.–Robbinsdale, and 34th Ave. S.–N. Bryant lines. Shortly after World War I, TCRT began using a portion of the carhouse building and yard to store and maintain the buses it used on its early Camden, Humboldt, and Lowry shuttle lines. North Side was rebuilt as a bus garage in 1953. The building is extant in 2007, although it is no longer used for transit purposes.

MINNEAPOLIS ST. RY. LAKE ST. STATION 1916

CARHOUSE   1 STORY   130' x 300'
OFFICE   2 STORIES 50' x 300'

E. LAKE ST.

22ND AVE. S.

21ST AVE. S.

Lake Street Station was placed in service in 1910. As with other TCRT car stations, mechanical, dispatch offices, and the trainmen's room were on the ground floor of the carhouse building. A lounge and sleeping rooms occupied the second floor. Cars assigned to Lake Street worked the Selby–Lake, Minnehaha–Ft. Snelling, Ft. Snelling Shuttle, 28th Ave. S.–Robbinsdale, 34th Ave. S.–N. Bryant, and Plymouth–E. 25th St. lines. Lake Street could accommodate 180 cars. Buses were assigned to Lake Street in its later years. Lake Street closed in December 1953. The building was razed, and the property became the Hi-Lake Shopping Center.

ST. PAUL CITY RY. DULUTH AVE. STATION AS REBUILT

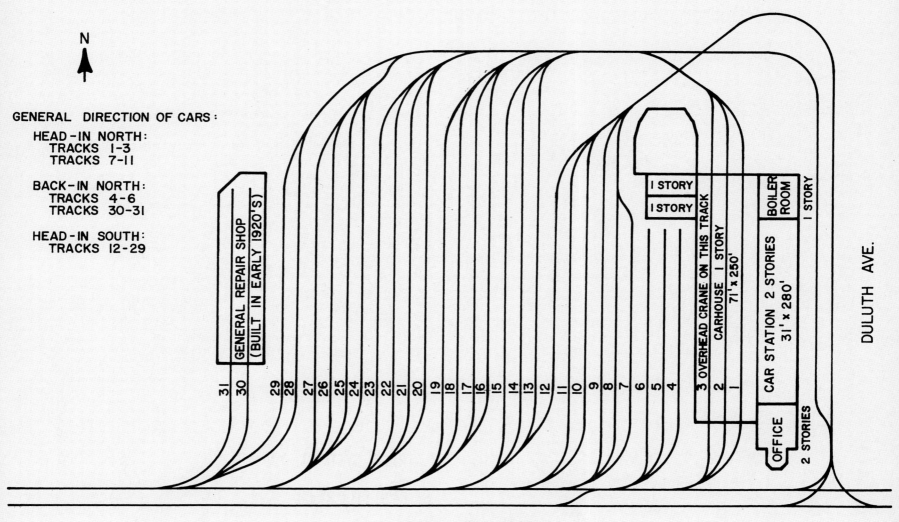

GENERAL DIRECTION OF CARS:

HEAD-IN NORTH:
TRACKS 1-3
TRACKS 7-11

BACK-IN NORTH:
TRACKS 4-6
TRACKS 30-31

HEAD-IN SOUTH:
TRACKS 12-29

N

GENERAL REPAIR SHOP (BUILT IN EARLY 1920'S)

I STORY

I STORY

3 OVERHEAD CRANE ON THIS TRACK

CARHOUSE I STORY 71' x 250'

CAR STATION 2 STORIES 31' x 280'

BOILER ROOM

I STORY

OFFICE

2 STORIES

DULUTH AVE.

EAST 7TH STREET

(REBUILDING OCCURRED SOMETIME DURING THE 1902–1912 PERIOD)

Duluth Avenue Station, originally East 7th Street Station when it was home to the East 7th Street Cable car line, was rebuilt in stages from 1906 through 1914. It was renamed Duluth Avenue Station in 1918. A separate repair shop building was added in 1920. This, later, became a bus garage. Duluth Avenue Station accommodated 134 cars assigned variously to the Stillwater, Grand–Mississippi, Hamline–Cherokee Hts., St. Clair–Payne, Dale–Phalen, Randolph–Hazel Park–Mahtomedi, Rice–So. St. Paul, Rondo–Stryker, and Maria–Ft. Snelling lines. Duluth Avenue Station was closed in 1952 following conversion of the St. Paul lines to bus operation. The buildings were demolished and the property sold.

Appendix J

MAPS OF THE TRACK SYSTEMS OF THE MINNEAPOLIS
STREET RAILWAY COMPANY AND THE ST. PAUL CITY RAILWAY COMPANY

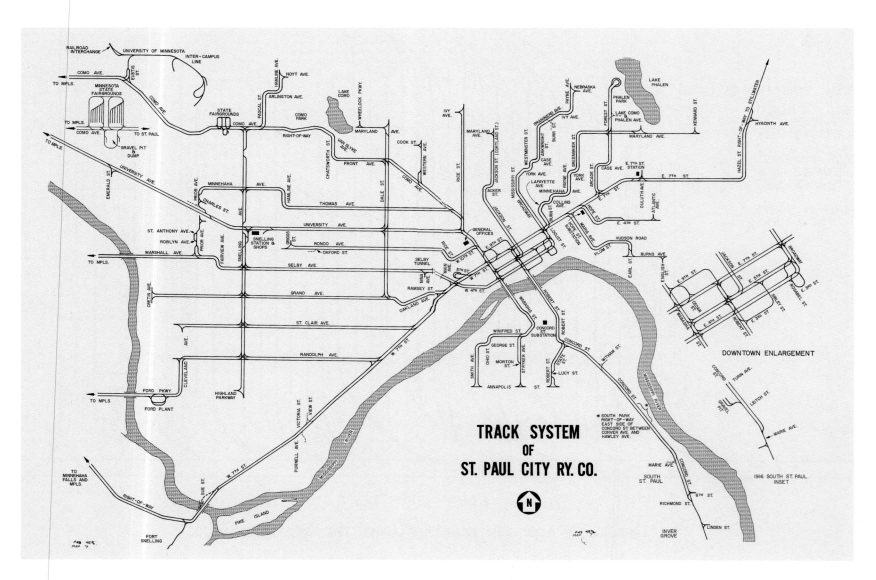

These track maps of the Minneapolis Street Railway Company and the St. Paul City Railway Company appeared in *The Electric Railways of Minnesota,* published in 1976. All single- and double-track mileage is shown together with the location of turning wyes or loops and junctions (switches) where tracks and routes combined or diverged. This is the system as it was at its greatest extent, including track segments that were subsequently abandoned because of bus conversion, street or highway construction, or line realignment. Maps by Kent Dorholt; reprinted courtesy of Russell L. Olson.

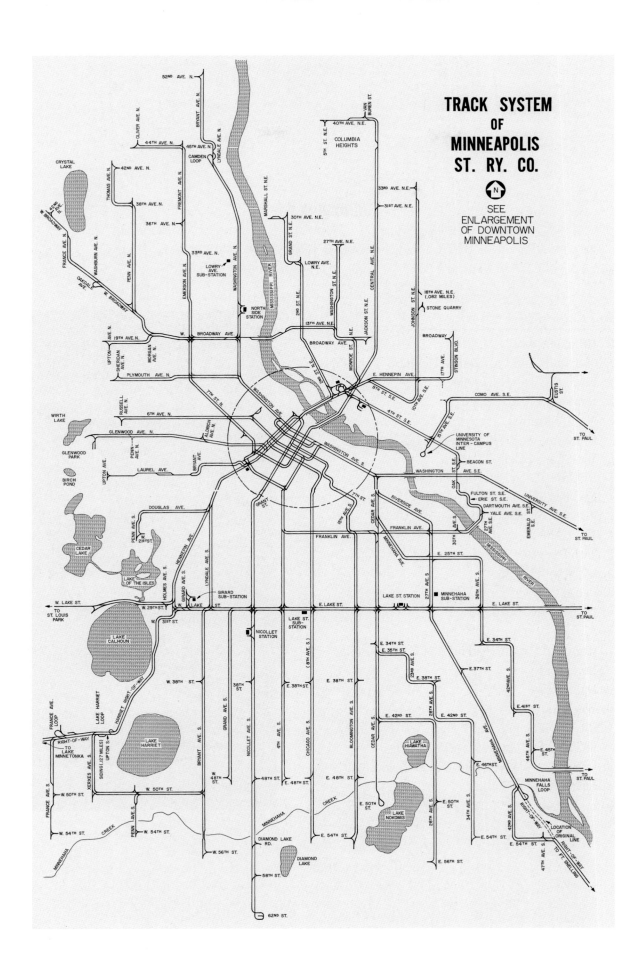

TRACK SYSTEM
OF
MINNEAPOLIS
ST. RY. CO.

SEE
ENLARGEMENT
OF DOWNTOWN
MINNEAPOLIS

Appendix K

MAPS OF THE TWIN CITY RAPID TRANSIT COMPANY BUS LINES

Key to the Lines

1. Humboldt Ave.
2. 30th and Grand–Columbia Heights
3. Franklin Ave.–N. Lyndale
4. Lowry Ave.
5. N. W. Terminal
6. Kenwood–St. Louis Park–Russell N.
7. West Lake Street
8. Hopkins–Glen Lake–Excelsior
9. Nicollet–Hennepin
10. Minneapolis–St. Paul Express
11. West 39th St.
12. 38th Street
13. 46th–50th Street
14. Penn Ave. S.
15. Chicago Ave.–57th Street
16. Airport
17. Highland Park–Cleveland
18. Rondo–Stryker
19. Dale–Hoyt
20. Western Ave.
21. Rice St.–Payne Ave.
22. Jackson–S. Robert–S. St. Paul
23. White Bear–White Bear Beach–Bald Eagle
24. East 6th St.–Stillwater
25. St. Paul Airport

The entire TCRT system was converted to bus operation between 1952 and 1954. Before then, buses were relegated to service on lightly traveled crosstown routes or as feeders to the streetcar lines. To guard its transportation monopoly, TCRT purchased and took over a few bus routes from independent operators during the 1920s, but company management remained both a strong believer in the superiority of the streetcar and a supporter of streetcar technology. That view would change somewhat as ridership declined during the Depression, and the company turned to buses to replace streetcars on unprofitable lines or on those where highway construction would have required extensive and expensive track renewal. The suburban lines to Lake Minnetonka and Stillwater were the first to disappear in 1932, followed by a handful of local lines in Minneapolis and St. Paul. In 1948, the year of this map, buses accounted for 9,232,591 revenue miles out of a system total of 35,488,288 revenue miles of operation. The relationship between the various streetcar lines and bus routes can be seen by comparing this map with the streetcar system map in chapter 7.

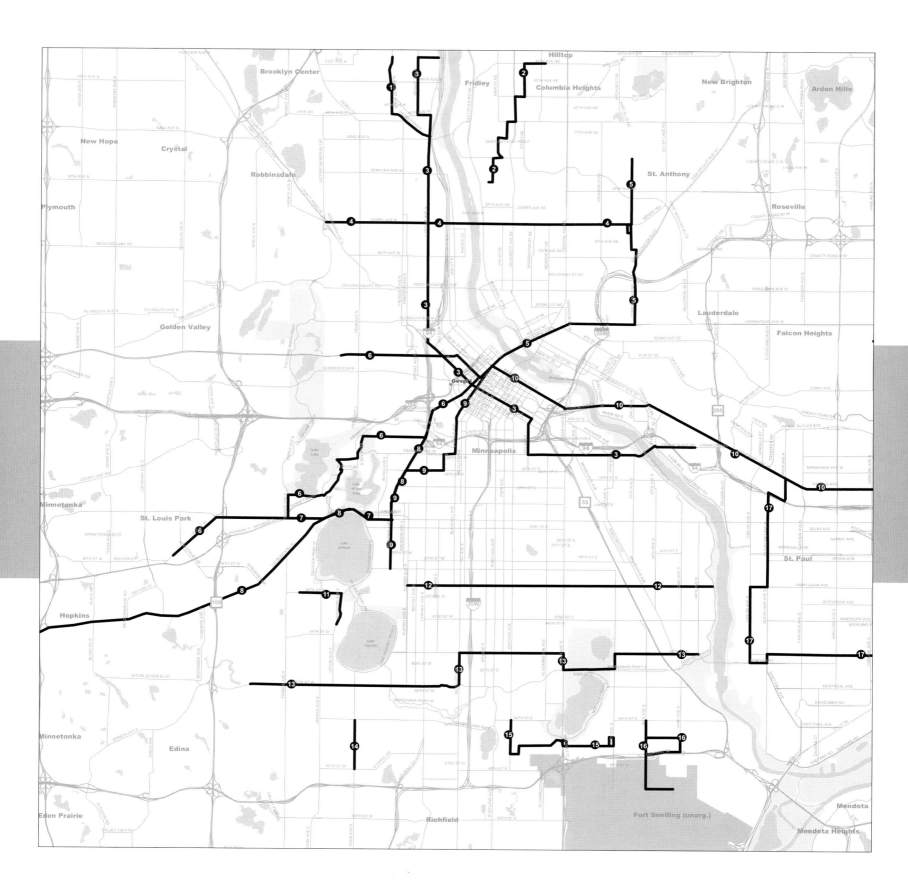

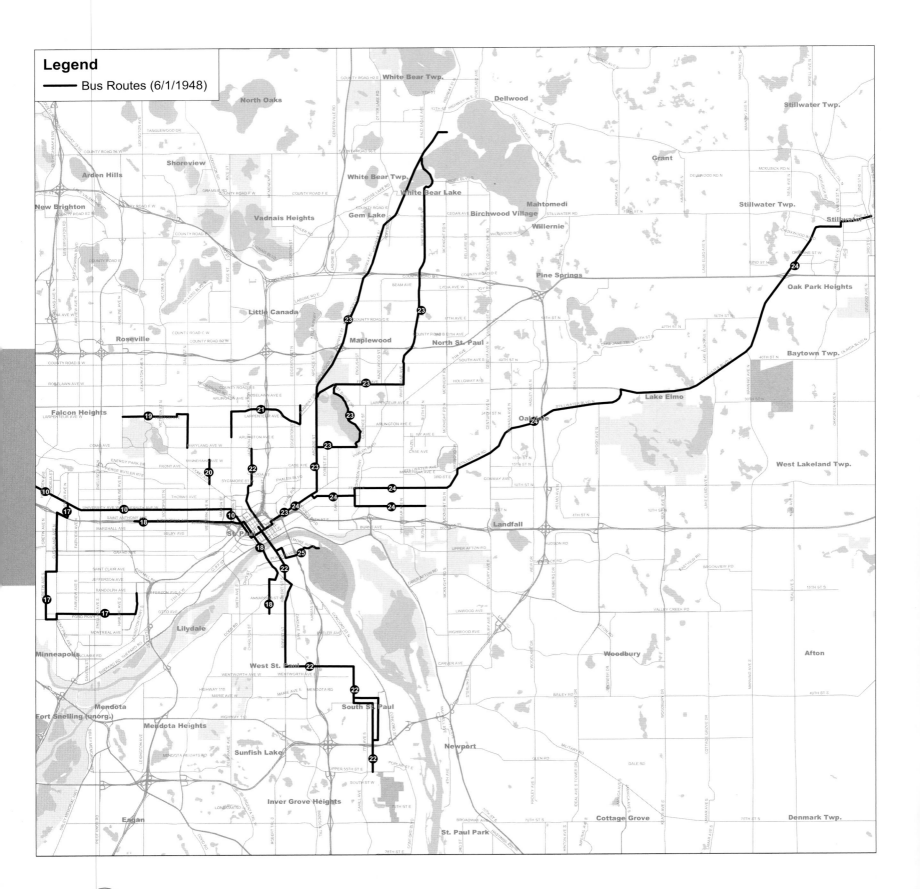

Legend

— Bus Routes (6/1/1948)

Appendix L

TWIN CITY RAPID TRANSIT PRESENT PLAN OF ORGANIZATION, JANUARY 1950

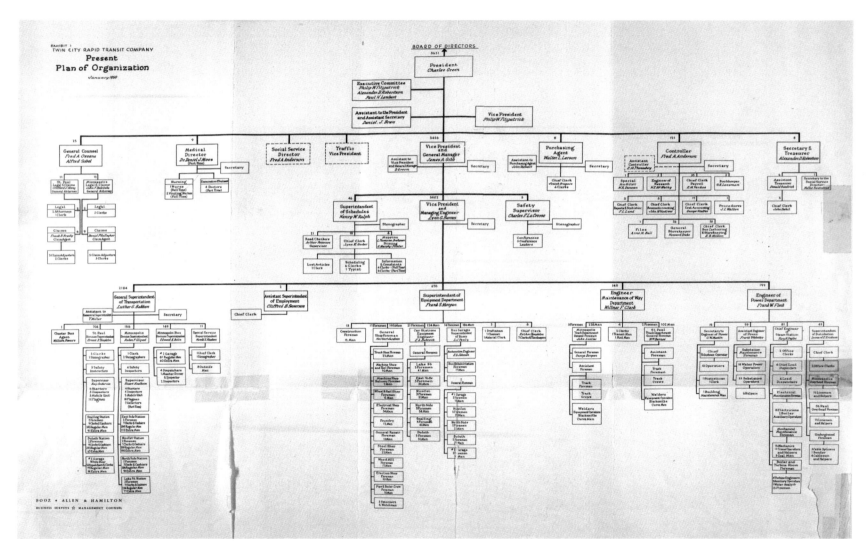

Dwindling patronage and increased operating expenses combined to create a loss of more than $750,000 on TCRT's operations in 1949, and this organizational chart explains why. The company was a warren of departments and some 3,631 employees, half of them supporting a rail operation that was no longer sustainable. President Charles Green retained the consulting firm of Booz, Allen & Hamilton to make recommendations for departmental reorganizations and force reductions. Their report recommended eliminating seventy-one positions, which, along with other changes, would produce a savings of $211,500, hardly enough to return the company to profitability—or, more urgently, avert bankruptcy. It would take 525 new buses and the conversion of the entire system to do that. Source: Booz, Allen & Hamilton Study, January 1950; reproduced courtesy of the Minnesota Historical Society.

Bibliographic Resources

More than fifty years separate this book from the big yellow streetcars of the Twin City Rapid Transit Company. Still, interest in the streetcar and TCRT persists, even though the automobile has mostly won the battle for urban mobility. As a measure, one need only look to the thousands of people who come out every summer to watch and ride the restored Twin City Rapid Transit streetcars operated by the Minnesota Streetcar Museum at its Lake Harriet and Excelsior sites. That enthusiasm, together with the absence of a popular history of the Twin City Rapid Transit Company, is the reason for this book.

Published histories of the Twin City street railway system and the Twin City Rapid Transit Company are extremely rare. Three were used as sources for this book. Although none of them is currently in print, copies may still be available in libraries or private collections.

The Electric Railways of Minneapolis and St. Paul, by Ira Swett, was published in 1953 in the midst of the changeover from rail to bus and was written primarily for electric railway enthusiasts. It presents a detailed, though relatively brief, study of the company, including its corporate history, a complete list and history of each car line, and a complete roster of all passenger and work equipment. Swett had access to original company documents and knew many people who worked for TCRT at the time of the conversion to buses.

Transit and the Twins, by Stephen Kieffer, was originally written as an honors thesis at the University of Minnesota. The Twin City Rapid Transit Company published it as a corporate history in 1958, just as the Ossanna scandals were breaking. Although the book presents scant detail on streetcar operations or services, it is a good general history of the company, if a bit too enthusiastic about the merits of the conversion to buses spearheaded by Fred Ossanna. It includes an excellent brief discussion of how the streetcar influenced the growth and development of the Twin Cities.

The Electric Railways of Minnesota, by Russell L. Olson, published in 1976 by the Minnesota Transportation Museum, is the gold standard for TCRT historians and is a superb resource for information on the company. The book's approach is very technical, and it is therefore more a reference work than a popular history. Available copies are extremely rare and generally command a high price. Olson worked briefly for TCRT in the early 1950s and had access to original documents from that era; he was instrumental in saving many of them from destruction. His research and the materials he collected over the years are now in the collections of the Minnesota Historical Society. He prepared a supplement to *The Electric Railways of Minnesota* and published it privately in 1990.

Other books on TCRT, not used as sources here but of possible supplementary interest to readers, include the following:

Twin City Rapid Transit Pictorial, by Alan R. Lind (1984), gives a good overview of the Twin City system. The text is limited and relies on secondary sources. Copies are rare.

Twin City Lines, the 1940s, by Aaron Isaacs and Bill Graham, is a magazine-format booklet for general readers, mainly a nostalgia piece for those seeking memories of the streetcar era in the Twin Cities during World War II. It is not a complete history of the company and the streetcar in the Twin Cities and has been out of print since 2002.

The Como-Harriet Streetcar Line, by Aaron Isaacs, Bill Graham, and Byron Olsen, is a study of the Twin Cities' most scenic and best-remembered streetcar line. It was published as a remembrance for visitors to the Como–Harriet site of the Minnesota Streetcar Museum near Lake Harriet in south Minneapolis.

Primary Sources

Surviving corporate records of the Twin City Rapid Transit Company and its subsidiaries have been archived and are on file in the manuscript collections of the Minnesota Historical Society. Among them are financial, engineering, mechanical, and construction records, along with operating department records and valuation studies. Additional materials are available among the Russell L. Olson papers. These documents were used extensively in researching this book.

In the 1950s and 1960s, Mr. Olson and others were able to collect and preserve much of the TCRT corporate material under the auspices of the Minnesota Railfans Association and the Minnesota Transportation Museum, and arrange for its subsequent donation to the Minnesota Historical Society. The Metropolitan Transit Commission also donated material from its files following its acquisition of Twin City Lines, Inc.

Sadly, considerable material has been lost. In the late 1950s, TCRT closed and sold its corporate headquarters building at 11th Street and Hennepin Avenue and moved its offices to the second floor of the Nicollet Garage. At the time of the move, many records and documents from the streetcar era, long in storage and of no immediate use, were discarded. Company records and photographs used in the Ossanna trials documenting the conversion to buses and the activities of company officials were placed in storage by the federal court at the conclusion of the trials. The authors were unable to locate them, and those documents, too, are presumed lost. In the mid-1960s, a large number of TCRT records stored in the basement of the Nicollet Garage were destroyed when the basement flooded in a torrential rainstorm.

The authors worked for the Metropolitan Transit Commission for many years and became good friends with many senior employees who worked for TCRT during the streetcar era. Over the years, many of those employees saved documents about to be thrown out and kept them as private mementoes. Aware of the authors' interest, they generously passed the documents along, knowing that they would be treasured and preserved. The authors similarly found many long-forgotten documents and photographs stored in obscure places and set them aside before they could be damaged or discarded. Among these artifacts are maps, track diagrams, building and equipment blueprints, equipment specifications, photographs, advertising brochures, schedules, annual reports, consultant studies, labor contracts, rulebooks, company bulletins, and books of newspaper clippings from the 1940s and 1950s.

One of the most significant finds that came into the authors' possession is a series of hardbound ledger books maintained by TCRT's schedule department that document every route and schedule change, special operation, or extra service operated by the company from the turn of the century to the end of the streetcar era. This is a day-by-day journal of the company's street operations and an important source for this book, especially for chapter 7, "Trolleys in Your Neighborhood."

General Works

One book that deserves special recognition and was recently brought back into print in a paperback edition is *The Electric Interurban Railways in America,* by George W. Hilton and John F. Due, published by Stanford University Press in 1960. Hilton remains one of America's foremost scholars of the railroad industry. This book is the most in-depth study of the electric railway industry ever written and is an absolute must for anyone studying the rise and fall of streetcar and interurban transportation.

For those interested in Thomas Lowry, *Streetcar Man,* by Goodrich Lowry, Thomas Lowry's grandson, is an excellent biography with insights into Lowry's personality that only a family member could have.

A Union against Unions: The Minneapolis Citizen Alliance and Its Fight against Organized Labor, 1903–1947, by William Millikan, is an outstanding source on the labor movement in the Twin Cities during the first half of the twentieth century. There is extensive material on the streetcar strike of 1917 and Horace Lowry's role in the Citizen Alliance, a pro-business organization formed to oppose the activities of labor unions.

BOOKS

Borchert, John. *America's Northern Heartland.* Minneapolis: University of Minnesota Press, 1987.

Carlson, Stephen P., and Fred Schneider III. *PCC—The Car That Fought Back.* Glendale, Calif.: Interurban Press, 1980.

Goddard, Stephen B. *Getting There: The Epic Struggle between Road and Rail in the American Century.* New York: Basic Books, 1994.

Goodrich, C. G. *A History of the Minneapolis Street Railway Company: Covering Thirty-five Years, 1873–1908.* Minneapolis: Minneapolis Street Railway Co., 1909.

Hilton, George W., and John F. Due. *The Electric Interurban Railways in America.* Stanford, Calif.: Stanford University Press, 1960.

International Correspondence Schools. *Electric-railway Systems: Line and Track, Line Calculations, Motors and Controllers, Electric-car Equipment, Multiple-unit Systems, Single-phase Railway System, Efficiency Tests, Mercury-vapor Converters, Voltage Regulation.* Scranton, Pa.: International Textbook Company, 1905.

Isaacs, Aaron, and Bill Graham. *The Como–Harriet Streetcar Line: A Memory Trip through the Twin Cities.* Virginia Beach: Donning Company Publishers, 2002.

Isaacs, Aaron, Bill Graham, and Byron Olsen. *Twin City Lines, the 1940s.* St. Paul: Minnesota Transportation Museum, 1995.

Kieffer, Stephen A. *Transit and the Twins: A Survey of the History of the Transportation Company in Minneapolis and Saint Paul: An Analysis of the Role of Public Transportation in the Growth of the Twin Cities.* Minneapolis: Twin City Rapid Transit Company, 1958.

Lind, Alan R. *Chicago Surface Lines: An Illustrated History.* Park Forest, Ill.: Transport History Press, 1986.

———. *Twin City Rapid Transit Pictorial, Thirtieth Anniversary Edition.* Park Forest, Ill.: Transport History Press, 1984.

Lowry, Goodrich. *Streetcar Man: Tom Lowry and the Twin City Rapid Transit Company.* Minneapolis: Lerner Publications Company, 1979.

Luke, William A. *Bus Industry Chronicle: U.S. and Canadian Experiences.* Spokane, Wash.: William A. Luke, 2000.

Martin, Albro. *James J. Hill and the Opening of the Northwest.* New York: Oxford University Press, 1976.

Middleton, William D. *The Time of the Trolley.* Milwaukee, Wis.: Kalmbach Publishing Company, 1967.

Millett, Larry. *Lost Twin Cities.* St. Paul: Minnesota Historical Society Press, 1992.

Millikan, William. *A Union against Unions: The Minneapolis Citizen Alliance and Its Fight against Organized Labor, 1903–1947.* St. Paul: Minnesota Historical Society Press, 2001.

Olson, Russell L. *The Electric Railways of Minnesota.* Hopkins, Minn.: Minnesota Transportation Museum, 1976.

———. *Electric Railways of Minnesota: Supplement.* St. Paul: Minnesota Transportation Museum, 1990.

Richey, Albert S. *Electric Railway Handbook: A Reference Book of Practice Data, Formulas, and Tables for the Use of Operators, Engineers, and Students.* New York: McGraw-Hill, 1924.

Swett, Ira. *The Electric Railways of Minneapolis and St. Paul.* Los Angeles: Interurbans Press, 1953.

Wingerd, Mary Lethert. *Claiming the City: Politics, Faith, and the Power of Place in St. Paul.* Ithaca, N.Y.: Cornell University Press, 2001.

ARTICLES, TECHNICAL STUDIES, AND REPORTS

Booz, Allen, & Hamilton. *Report and Review of Organizational Structure of Twin City Rapid Transit Company.* Commissioned by Twin City Rapid Transit Company, 1950. Twin City Rapid Transit Company Records, Minnesota Historical Society.

A. L. Drum and Company. *Report on the Value of the Property of the Minneapolis Street*

Railway Company as of January 1, 1925; Minneapolis St. Paul and Suburban Railway Company as of January 1, 1926; St. Paul City Railway as of January 1, 1925. Chicago: A. L. Drum and Company, 1925. Twin City Rapid Transit Company Records, Minnesota Historical Society, St. Paul.

W. C. Gilman and Company. *Report on Twin City Rapid Transit Company.* New York: W. C. Gilman and Company, 1944.

Minnesota Department of Highways. *Origin and Destination Traffic Survey of St. Paul, Minnesota, and Minneapolis, Minnesota.* St. Paul: Minnesota Department of Highways, 1950.

Robertson, A. M. *Statement by A. M. Robertson, Secretary of the Company, Covering History and Summary of Events in the Growth of the Street Railway System before the Railroad and Warehouse Commission of the State of Minnesota.* St. Paul: Twin City Rapid Transit Company, 1923.

Schendel, Gordon. "How Mobsters Grabbed a City's Transit Line." *Colliers,* 29 September 1951.

Slater, Cliff. "General Motors and the Demise of Streetcars." *Transportation Quarterly* 51, no. 3 (Summer 1997): 45–66.

Snell, Bradford. *American Ground Transport: A Proposal for Restructuring the Automobile, Truck, Bus, and Rail Industries.* Washington, D.C.: U.S. Government Printing Office, 1974.

Stone and Webster Engineering Corporation. *Report on Operations and Management of the Twin City Rapid Transit Company and Subsidiary Companies.* New York: The Hamilton Press, 1934.

TCRT DOCUMENTS

Twin City Rapid Transit Company. *Annual Reports to Shareholders.* 1899, 1903, 1916, 1920, 1924, 1925, 1927, 1928, 1931–48, 1950–54. Twin City Rapid Transit Company Records, Minnesota Historical Society, St. Paul.

———. *Annual Reports of Employees Mutual Benefit Association.* 1916–34.

———. *Operating Rules for the Government of Trainmen.* November 1921.

———. *Organization and Rules. General Rules.* January 1918.

———. *Organization and Rules Operating Department.* January 1918.

———. *An Overview and History of the Company.* 1927.

———. *Rules and Instructions Power and Equipment Department.* June 1911.

———. *Rules and Regulations for the Government of the Operating Department.* December 1904.

———. *Rules and Regulations of the Twin City Lines Bus and Trainmen's Guide.* 1950.

Minnesota Streetcar Museum

The memory of the great Twin City Rapid Transit Company and the streetcar era in the Twin Cities has been preserved by the Minnesota Streetcar Museum, a not-for-profit, all-volunteer organization. The museum's collection includes four TCRT streetcars, which it operates on a portion of the former Como–Harriet line at Lake Harriet in south Minneapolis and in Excelsior near Lake Minnetonka. One car, number 1300, is a TCRT standard one man–two man car that ran on the Como–Harriet line until the last day of service on June 19, 1954. Other cars in the collection include a TCRT gate car, a TCRT PCC, and car number 265, a TCRT car that was sold to the Duluth Street Railway in 1916 and operated in Duluth until 1939. A fifth car, number 78, built in 1893 by LaClede for the Duluth Street Railway, is one of the oldest operating electric streetcars in the United States.

Besides these operational cars, the museum owns several from other Minnesota cities that are awaiting restoration and eventual operation. It also maintains an extensive archive of photographs and documents from the streetcar era, many of which were used in this book.

The museum offers rides to visitors during its regular operating season from May through October, as well as special holiday trolleys operated at Halloween and between Thanksgiving and Christmas. More information can be found at its Web site, www.trolleyride.org.

Index

John W. Diers has worked in management in the transit industry for thirty-five years, including twenty-five years at the Twin Cities Metropolitan Transit Commission, where he started as a bus driver–dispatcher, then moved on to administrative assistant to the general manager, division superintendent, chief of radio communications, and manager of maintenance administration. He also worked with ATE Management and Services as general manager of the Racine, Wisconsin, transit system. He is now an independent consultant on transit operations and a writer and researcher on transportation history; he has written for *Trains* magazine and various transit publications. He has been active in historic preservation and has served on the board of the Minnesota Transportation Museum and on the editorial board of the Ramsey County Historical Society. He is a member of the Minnesota Streetcar Museum.

Aaron Isaacs has had a lifelong interest in public transportation. During his thirty-three years with the Twin Cities Metropolitan Transit Commission, he has been a route and schedule planner, operations analyst, productivity analyst, and facilities planner. He has been active in the Minnesota Streetcar Museum for more than thirty years, serving as its magazine editor and photograph archivist since 1990. He authored the publications *Twin City Lines—The 1940s, The Como-Harriet Story,* and *The Como-Harriet Streetcar Line.* Since 1996, he has edited *Railway Museum Quarterly,* a journal on rail preservation.

EMP[...]
Lake S[...]
1[...]